Architecture of Life

In memory of my father,
Genrikh Vronsky

CONTENTS

Note on Transliteration from Russian — ix

INTRODUCTION
Life An Ideology for Modernity — xi

ONE
Space Formalist Architectural Pedagogy at the VKhUTEMAS — 1

TWO
Orientation El Lissitzky's Evolutionist Urbanism — 31

THREE
Fitness Nikolay Ladovsky's Architectural Psychotechnics — 71

FOUR
Process Organicist Aesthetics of Soviet Standardization — 107

FIVE
Energy Soviet Wall-Painting and the Economy of Perception — 141

SIX
Personality Gorky Park as a Factory of Dealienation — 163

CONCLUSION
History From the Monistic to the Terrestrial — 197

Acknowledgments — 209
Notes — 213
Index — 263

NOTE ON TRANSLITERATION FROM RUSSIAN

Slavic studies and Russian history publications commonly use the Library of Congress (LoC) system of the romanization of Russian. This is the most precise system, which, unlike the older ones, ensures that every Cyrillic letter has a Latin letter equivalent. However, it often leads to an unnecessary complicating of Russian names and contradicts many established spellings (for example, *Lissitzky* would be spelled *Lisitskii*). To combine the advantages of both, throughout the book I use the LoC system when citing sources and providing original Russian word spellings, and the old spelling system elsewhere.

INTRODUCTION

Life

An Ideology for Modernity

Beyond Form and Function

The hyperrationalization, utilitarianism, and technocratic aspirations of European interwar modernism are commonly described as functionalism. This much-used concept, which often appears as synonymous with European interwar modernism, is, however, misleading. To the architectural historian and theorist Stanford Anderson, it seemed "weak" and "inadequate for the characterization or analysis of . . . architecture."[1] "The fiction of function," Anderson argued, was fabricated on American soil in 1932, when Henry-Russell Hitchcock and Philip Johnson, grappling with how to describe their project of the International Style for the seminal MoMA exhibition, distinguished between architecture that exhibited style, or form, and architecture that did not—that was instead built for some functional purpose.[2] The roots of the opposition of form and function, in fact, go even deeper, and so does the history of its criticism.[3] As a rhetorical device, this opposition was borrowed from morphology, a subfield of evolutionary theory that deals with the formal structure of organisms.[4] In *Form and Function* (1916), the Scottish evolutionist Edward Stuart Russell presented the history of morphology as that of rivalry between two methodological approaches: formalism, which focused on the structure and form of animals, and functionalism, which explored the role of function in shaping form. Russell considered the dichotomy to be false, explaining it as a difference in focus.[5] Similarly, the present book suggests not only that function and form were equally important for modernist architecture, but that inspired by contemporary science, it often juxtaposed form and function only to deliberately reject this opposition, turning, instead, to more organic and monistic models. It focuses on Russia, a country that in the aftermath of the revolution of 1917 became the focus of international progressivists' attention. Playing an outstanding role in the formation of international modernism (here considered not as a style but as an attempt at formulating a radically new theory of art and architecture), Russia became a site of the development of principles and ideas that acquired international significance later in the twentieth century. These principles, as the book will detail, were premised on life sciences, above all on the sciences of the human.

During the interwar period, biology, including the work of Jacob von Uexküll, Ernst Haeckel, Raoul Francé, and D'Arcy Thompson (to name just a few most influential authors), captivated the imagination of artists and architects.[6] In the 1920s, the German architectural critic Adolf Behne could contend in *The Modern Functional Building (Der moderne Zweckbau)* that modern architecture is dominated by two rival approaches, functionalism and rationalism. Influenced by von Uexküll, who was a prominent critic of mechanicism, Behne described the polemics as an organicist dialectics of the whole and its part. By beginning with the part (an organ within the body, which Behne likened to a room in a building), the functionalists, such as Hans Scharoun, neglected the whole. Represented by Le Corbusier, rationalism, on the other hand, began with the whole (the organism): preoccupied with a general idea, it was at risk of congealing into formalism.[7] Just as the whole and the part were inseparable in nature, so form and function too, Behne believed, were to be harmonized in modern architecture. In 1925, before Behne's book came out in its original German edition, his friend El Lissitzky, the Soviet architect, artist, and graphic designer, had already embarked on the Russian translation of the manuscript, convinced of the importance of the work for the Russian architectural scene.[8] Some important deviations notwithstanding, Behne's scheme, indeed, described the architectural dynamics of postrevolutionary Russia, where the two major modernist architectural groups, the Association of New Architects (Assotsiatsiia novykh arkhitektorov, ASNOVA) and the Organization of Contemporary Architecture (Ob'edinenie sovremennykh arkhitektorov, OSA), were known respectively as the rationalists (whom their opponents also labeled as the formalists) and the functionalists (or the constructivists). Led by Nikolay Ladovsky and counting Lissitzky and Nikolay Dokuchaev among its members, ASNOVA prioritized the exterior and the form of the building, whereas OSA, headed by Moisei Ginzburg and Alexander Vesnin, focused its attention on the building's plan and the distribution of functions. Although the history of Soviet postrevolutionary architecture is often seen as a polemical confrontation between these two factions, Behne's argument elucidates their similarity, which enabled figures such as Lissitzky to navigate comfortably within both. In this light, the architectural debate between ASNOVA and OSA can be seen as that between two versions of organicism: a preeminently psychological one, focused on form, and a biological one, focused on process.

Figure I.1. El Lissitzky's *Wolkenbügel* on the cover of Adolf Behne, *Der moderne Zweckbau* (Munich: Drei masken Verlag, 1926).

Soviet architecture indeed relied not on a binary but rather on a unifying epistemological model. This model, popular among scientific-minded philosophers, was commonly known as *monism*. Originally, the term referred to a synthetic philosophy that aimed to overcome the body-mind dichotomy. Rooted in the philosophy of Baruch Spinoza, monism postulated that the opposites of the modern dualistic worldview—form and function, the mind and the body, idealism and materialism, freedom and necessity—were integrated within the natural world, whose ultimate epistemological subject was life itself. In its expanded sense, monism was used as an umbrella term for a host of heterogeneous methodological, philosophic, and scientific approaches associated with life sciences. By the end of the nineteenth century, members of the social-democratic movement in different parts of the world had embraced monism enthusiastically, seeing it not only as a philosophical movement but as the worldview based on life sciences and thus as the universal ideology of scientific modernization. Its rising role was marked by the founding of one of America's most influential philosophic journals, *The Monist,* in 1890. Publishing articles by both physiologists and positivist philosophers including John Dewey, Gottlob Frege, Hans-Georg Gadamer, Ernst Mach, Charles Sanders Peirce, and Bertrand Russell, the journal was conceived as a platform for forging a modern notion of subjectivity.

This book presents Soviet architectural modernism as a part of this monistic tradition. It views architectural formalism and functionalism as two sides of the same coin—a vision of architecture, society, and the human inspired by burgeoning human sciences, which were employed to define the subject of architecture and, consequently, to postulate its goals and principles. Psychophysics, physiology, scientific management, psychotechnics, psychoanalysis, ergography, eugenics, and personality theory were just a few among the approaches explored by Soviet interwar architects, who translated them into a system of architectural concepts, analytical strategies, and theoretical postulates. While assessing the engagement of Soviet interwar architecture with human sciences, this book approaches it from the perspective of intellectual history. It is less interested in tracing the mechanisms and networks of borrowing particular concepts than in reconstructing the discourse that enabled the rhetorical and actual engagement of Soviet architects with modern biological and psychological thought. Indeed, although the formal and material legacy of Soviet interwar architecture and its institutional dynamics have been relatively well studied, the theories and ideas behind this legacy are less known. The chapters that follow thus focus not on buildings but on projects and schemes, theories and debates, pedagogical strategies, architectural research, and experimental work conducted at such pedagogical institutions as the Moscow Higher Art and Technical Studios (Vysshie khudozhestvenno-tekhnicheskie masterskie, VKhUTEMAS) and at such architectural "think tanks" as the Construction Commission (Stroykom), the State Trust for Wall-Painting Works (Malyarstroy), and the Central Park of Culture and Leisure in Moscow. What the chapters examine is how the discursive preeminence of human sciences affected the methods and principles of architecture, the understanding of its economic role and social mission, and the construction of human subjectivity by architectural means.

Tragedies and Challenges of Soviet Modernization

As an approach that was seen as progressive and "Western," the monistic worldview was firmly inscribed in the quest for economic modernization that guided the social and economic changes in Soviet Russia, unfolding at a breathtaking pace between the revolution of 1917 and the beginning of the Second World War. Announcing a turn to industrialization, the centralization of economy, and eventually toward the rise of Stalin's terror, the system of five-year economic plans (which would persist in the Soviet Union until its demise) replaced the earlier liberal New Economic Policy, which had allowed for elements of market economy and private economic initiative. The First Five-Year Plan of Economic Development, scheduled to span 1928/29 to 1933 and completed ahead of schedule at the end of 1932, was intended to be a crucial step in turning Russia into a modern industrial state.[9] It focused on the creation of heavy industry—the means of production—with the help of Western engineers and technologies. The forced industrialization came at a hefty price. The GULAG (Main Directorate of Camps) was established in 1930 and grew exponentially throughout the decade, supplying construction sites with incarcerated labor: even according to conservative estimates, the brutal living and working conditions led to the death of 1.6 million prisoners. Moreover, the First Five-Year Plan relied on the "collectivization" of agriculture, a ban on individual farming and the creation of collective farms. This program aimed at appropriating agricultural products from peasants and selling them on the international market to procure foreign currency necessary for the needs of industrialization. Collectivization caused the devastating famine in 1932–33, particularly in the agricultural regions of Ukraine, southern Russia, and the Volga River. At a somewhat more moderate tempo, the Second Five-Year Plan, which followed from 1933 to 1937, continued to focus on the development of heavy industry, hardly valuing the life and needs of an individual and doing little to alleviate material scarcity. The purges, intensifying during this time to culminate in 1937, further contributed to devaluing individual life and creating the atmosphere of fear. Among many others, they claimed the lives of several prominent figures in the world of architecture, including architect Solomon Lisagor, sociologist Mikhail Okhitovich, and nearly the entire leadership of the Soviet Academy of Architecture.[10]

How ethical is it then, to paraphrase Theodor Adorno's famous saying that writing poetry after Auschwitz is "barbaric," to write an intellectual history of Soviet interwar architecture? Betty Glan, who had played an important role (which will be examined in chapter 6) in shaping Soviet culture until subjected to repression in 1937 (she was to spend eighteen years in the GULAG system while her husband, Yugoslav communist Milan Gorkić, was executed), had an opinion. When in the wake of glasnost in the late 1980s, a journalist asked her about her GULAG experience, she declined to respond, explaining: "One cannot reduce life, and not only ours but the life of the entire generation, to one, even if deeply tragic, year. As if we were interesting only insofar that we survived 1937, only in how we lived precisely after the arrest." "It is clear today that bright and strong people were destroyed. Write about what made them such, about our youth, happy and joyful," she instead asked—"Otherwise . . . otherwise it appears that my life . . . and the big and difficult work of Milan was not the most important in our lives."[11] As if echoing the then-nascent subaltern studies, Glan argued that the conditions of subjectivity and objectification are necessarily intertwined, and that by focusing on repression alone, presenting those who went through repression solely as passive objects of torture, historians deprive them of agency, reenacting, as it were, the act of violence on the epistemic level.

Indeed, even during the darkest years of Stalinism, Soviet intellectual and architectural life did not fully stop. Until the early 1930s, Soviet orthodox dialectical materialism was still in the process of formation, and Russia was open to a wide variety of ideas that would soon be considered unorthodox.[12] In architecture, the principles of "socialist realism" took even longer to formulate. In fact, as Danilo Udovički-Selb painstakingly documents, it was not until 1936 that the party for the first time directly prescribed a course of action to Soviet architecture, while modernism did not fully disappear in the Soviet Union until the beginning of the Second World War.[13] As Udovički-Selb explains, the purges were primarily directed against the members of the Communist Party, which none of the major Soviet avant-garde architects had joined.[14] The former leaders of the architectural avant-garde thus retained prominent positions: in the 1930s, Nikolay Ladovsky, Moisei Ginzburg, the Vesnin brothers, Konstantin Melnikov, and Ilya Golosov each headed one of the twelve architecture and planning workshops of the city of Moscow, while Viktor Vesnin became the head of the Union of Soviet Architects. Throughout the decade, these architects were able to retain at least some opportunities for creative thinking, in particular, in what concerned the ways of modernization.

Aiming to address this complexity of Soviet interwar architectural and intellectual life, the present book thus questions not only the opposition of form and function as a framework for the analysis of modernism, but also a host of other binary categories that have been traditionally applied to Soviet history and culture: left and right, oppression and freedom, the official and the underground, the avant-garde and totalitarianism, to name just a few.[15] By doing so, it aims to disrupt the two mutually supporting received historiographic narratives: the first, based on the notion of utopia and focusing on the early 1920s avant-garde, is condescending even if sympathetic to the revolution (a utopia is, after all, essentially naïve and unrealistic); the second, which deals with the totalitarianism of the 1930s, reduces culture to a function of the repressive apparatus.[16] Both of these narratives treat the existence of the Soviet Union as an aberration of history, disregarding connections between Russian and international intellectual culture. Rather than romanticizing the Russian revolution as a radical overturn of social hierarchies or enumerating the crimes committed by the Soviet state (which should not be taken as a denial of these crimes), this book thus surveys the entire interwar period, paying a special attention to the mid- to late 1920s, a period equally distant from the two benchmarks of Soviet political history, the revolution of 1917 and the peak of the purges in 1937. It scrutinizes the dialog between Soviet and foreign architectural and intellectual traditions, viewing Soviet architectural culture as an integral, even if radical, part of modernity, not merely informed by Western ideals but actively participating in their formation. By examining theoretical and creative production that often led to undeniably dehumanizing results, it identifies well-intended—in fact, proclaimed humanist—aspirations behind Soviet cultural production, which delineated a zone in which modern ethical categories were conflated but not canceled.[17] Like its international counterparts, the ideology of Soviet architectural modernization relied on a set of closely knit concepts: neo-Lamarckian evolutionism and energeticism as its scientific methodology; unconscious perception as its preferred epistemological mechanism; imperial domination over nature as its moral and political program; and efficiency, organization, and planning as its economic priorities. Employed by architects as well as by artists, philosophers, and sociologists, such bioeconomic perspective merged a managerial objectification of the human with holistic romanticism, leading to the ethical and political paradoxes that permeated Soviet interwar architecture.

This constellation of ideas was related to the set of international cultural and ideological transformations unleashed by the second industrial revolution. According to James Kloppenberg, beginning in the 1870s, a transatlantic and transdisciplinary community of social democrats and progressive philosophers discarded "accepted distinctions between idealism and empiricism in epistemology, between intuitionism and utilitarianism in ethics, and between revolutionary socialism and laissez-faire liberalism in politics," seeking instead a via media between these extremes. Their sources included socialism, Christian social criticism, as well as German and English economic theory, classical liberalism, positivism, and Darwinism.[18] Another historian, Cathy Gere, argued that the intellectual crisis generated by the second industrial revolution resulted in a general "rejection of the liberal tradition that privileged the rational, autonomous subject as the main unit of political and moral reasoning—modernism setting its face against modernity, so to speak."[19] The two viewpoints are not contradictory, as liberal values were gradually sidelined alongside the polarization of society during the late nineteenth century, and monistic ideology was shifting toward political authoritarianism as the only path toward a true liberalism. In Russia, such monistic, antiliberal concept of subjectivity became most influential before and during the First Five-Year Plan, providing the philosophical platform for industrialization.

In his *Homo Sacer: Sovereign Power and Bare Life* (1995), Giorgio Agamben distinguished between *zoē*, or biological life, and *bios,* "which indicated the form or way of living proper to an individual or a group," which thus included political life. "The entry of *zoē* into the sphere of the polis—the politicization of bare life as such," according to Agamben, constituted "the decisive event of modernity."[20] Agamben described the new modern subjectivity through the figure of *homo sacer,* an outcast person of Roman law: devoid of *bios,* his life could be described as pure *zoē*. Biopolitics and politics were thus not opposed but intricately interrelated, and accordingly, democracy and totalitarianism— the ultimate manifestation of biopolitics—were linked by a regime of "inner solidarity."[21] The emergence of this model of governmentality was indistinguishable from the rise and proliferation of human sciences. As this book will delineate, turning to the latter, Soviet interwar architectural theory sought to not only employ this biological model of subjectivity, but to understand and overcome its ethical and political limitations.

The University of Minnesota Press gratefully acknowledges financial support for the publication of this book from the University of Kassel: Papers of the Department of Architecture, Urban Planning, and Landscape Architecture of the University of Kassel, No. 5.

Chapter 1 was previously published in a different version as "Composing Form, Constructing the Unconscious: Empiriocriticism and Nikolai Ladovskii's 'Psychoanalytical Method' of Architecture at VKhUTEMAS," in *Architecture and the Unconscious,* ed. John Hendrix and Lorens Holm (London: Ashgate, 2016), 77–96; reprinted with permission of INFORMA UK LIMITED (Taylor and Francis) through PLSClear. Portions of chapter 5 were previously published in *Narkomfin,* ed. Wilfied Wang and Danilo Udovicki-Selb, O'Neil Ford Monograph Series 6 (Austin: University of Texas at Austin, 2015), 97–102.

Copyright 2022 by the Regents of the University of Minnesota

All rights reserved. No part of this publication may be reproduced, stored in a retrieval system, or transmitted, in any form or by any means, electronic, mechanical, photocopying, recording, or otherwise, without the prior written permission of the publisher.

Published by the University of Minnesota Press
111 Third Avenue South, Suite 290
Minneapolis, MN 55401-2520
http://www.upress.umn.edu

ISBN 978-1-5179-1226-0 (hc)
ISBN 978-1-5179-1227-7 (pb)

A Cataloging-in-Publication record for this book is available from the Library of Congress.

Printed in the United States of America on acid-free paper

The University of Minnesota is an equal-opportunity educator and employer.

28 27 26 25 24 23 22   10 9 8 7 6 5 4 3 2 1

Architecture of Life

Soviet Modernism and the Human Sciences

ALLA VRONSKAYA

University of Minnesota Press
Minneapolis
London

Life

"What are the aims before humanism?" wondered Julian Huxley, a well-known supporter of both the Soviet Union and modernist architecture (and soon the first director-general of UNESCO), British evolutionary biologist, eugenicist, and internationalist, in 1943.[22] He concluded, "One phrase, to my mind, really contains them all: to have life and to have it more abundantly."[23] His use of "life" integrated such predicates as vitality and dynamism with a Darwinist vision of the struggle for survival, in which the disappearance of the weak was a fundamental natural law. The category of life was elaborated in the course of the polemics between vitalists, whose defenders counted philosophers and psychologists including Wilhelm Wundt and later Henri Bergson, and mechanicists, mostly represented by zoologists and evolutionary biologists.[24] Peaking around 1930, the polemics mirrored the architectural debate between formalism and functionalism. It resulted in a synthesis that asserted life as a unifying principle of nature at all levels, from inorganic rocks to plants, animals, and, ultimately, humans, and at all scales, from molecules to planetary systems (Plate 1). In the words of philosopher Alfred North Whitehead, the dualism that had dominated Western philosophy since the seventeenth century was now subverted by "the concepts of life, organism, function, instantaneous reality, interaction, order of nature."[25]

As a scientific alternative to the metaphysical notion of being, the concept of life proved to be central for the monistic discourse. Nineteenth-century monism originated in Germany, where zoologist Ernst Haeckel (whose scientific work was as popular in Russia as elsewhere) developed it as a worldview and even a religion. Haeckel's monism was propagated through his widely read book *The Riddle of the Universe (Die Welträtsel)*, first published in 1899 (its Russian translation appeared in 1920 and was reprinted until 1937), and the formation of the German Monist League (Deutscher Monistenbund) in 1906.[26] According to Haeckel, "the riddle" was solved by the recognition of the fact that the unity of knowledge paralleled the unity of mind and matter: evolutionism was the method shared by both natural and social sciences. Haeckel drew upon the "synthetic philosophy" of Herbert Spencer, which aspired to synthesize biology, economics, sociology, and political theory.[27] Spencer's *Principles of Biology* (1864, Russian translation 1870) enriched Darwinism with a Lamarckian idea of the inheritance of adaptational transformations, suggesting the vitality of the species as its ultimate ethical value—and, consequently, laid the ground for postulating eugenics as the ultimate ethical system. Spencer, furthermore, applied evolutionary theory to society, interpreting culture as a form of adaptation developed by *Homo sapiens*.

Spencerianism permeated late nineteenth-century culture, inspiring, among numerous other concepts, the formula of architectural modernism (often misleadingly simplified to "form follows function"), which was originally articulated by Louis Sullivan in 1896: "Whether it be the sweeping eagle in his flight, or the open apple-blossom, the toiling work-horse, the blithe swan, the branching oak, the winding stream at its base, the drifting clouds, over all the coursing sun, form ever follows function, and this is the law. Where function does not change, form does not change."[28]

In the Spencerian worldview, the transformation of the environment—a complex notion that involved the natural, social, and human-made milieus— necessitated changes in the morphology of a species, and consequently one could engineer a species by manipulating its environment. "On the one hand there is the Environment in its action upon the organism; and on the other the Organism in its reaction to and action upon the environment; the dynamic relation, in its twofold aspect, is called Function," had explained Huxley's student, biologist and town planner Patrick Geddes and his coauthor Arthur Thomson.[29] Even though, due to its racist implications, Mendelian eugenics (the design of a species through controlled breeding) never acquired the same prominence in Soviet Russia as it did elsewhere, as the design of the species through the control of the environment, neo-Lamarckian evolutionism became an important part of Russian progressive culture.[30]

After the initial injection of Haeckel's evolutionism, the Monist League was reoriented toward "energeticism" by Wilhelm Ostwald, who assumed its presidency in 1911.[31] By the end of the nineteenth century, the concept of energy had come to be viewed as an alternative to mechanism. As a broader worldview based on the primacy of energy over matter, energeticism at the turn of the century was supported by prominent scientists, philosophers, and sociologists, including Ernst Mach, Richard Avenarius, Henri Poincaré, and Pierre Duhem. Accordingly, monistic ethics now shifted away from the ideal of a species' health and toward Ostwald's "energetic imperative": "Do not squander energy—utilize it!" Ostwald's other related concern was organizational theory, which he promoted through Die Brücke (The Bridge), an "institute" that aimed "to organize intellectual work" by activities such as cataloging information and standardizing paper formats; good organization, he believed, allowed economizing productive and perceptual energy.[32]

Although neither Haeckel nor Ostwald considered themselves Marxists, monism and Marxism were not incompatible. While later critics, such as Hannah Arendt, saw Marxism's compatibility with life sciences as a flaw leading to the bestialization of the human, many welcomed the possibility of the synthesis.[33] For Karl Marx, labor was "first of all, a process between man and nature, a process by which man, through his own actions, mediates, regulates and controls the metabolism between himself and nature." As such, labor was none other than the worker's "life-activity, the manifestation of his own life."[34] According to German social democrat Heinrich Pëus, "social democracy strives for a specific form of life, monism for a specific method of thinking and living. Both, however, will always remain friends."[35] In 1913, the Monist League officially entered into cooperation with social democracy. To Marxists, monistic Spencerianism offered a promise of directing social evolution by the willful organization of the environment. In turn, enriched by Marxism, monism gained practical orientation and fascination with dialectics.

Human Ecology

In 1913, German biologist Hermann Reinheimer could claim that "the central problem of Life, and, *a fortiori,* of Organic Evolution, is production—production of the necessaries and utilities of life first, and the requirements of progress after."[36] The synthesis of biological and economic contexts that informed the notion of life became the subject of a modern new discipline, ecology. Sharing its Greek root, *oikos* (household or living place), with *economics,* the term *ecology* had been coined in 1866 by Haeckel, who defined it as "the science of economy, of ways of life, of exterior life-relationships of organisms with each other."[37] In the words of the environmental historian Donald Worster, the term referred specifically to "an economy of nature," a science of rational management and care of resources that developed alongside industrial capitalism.[38] The colonial dimension of this productivist ecological discourse should not be overlooked. As early as 1761, Count de Buffon wrote in his *Natural History* that

> the first mark of man's civilization is the empire he assumes over the animals; and this first mark of his intelligence becomes afterwards the greatest evidence of his power over Nature: For it is only after he subjugates and tames animals, that he is enabled, by their assistance, to change the face of the earth, to convert deserts into fertile ground, and heath into corn.[39]

Nature was seen as the repository of natural resources, whereas mining these resources, which would otherwise lie idle in the earth's depths, became a moral rather a merely economic imperative: as Huxley's collaborator, writer H. G.

Figure I.2. The cover of the 1919 edition of Alexander Bogdanov's *Engineer Menni* (1913) illustrates the modernist imperative of the rational reorganization and management of the world by man.

Wells, would put it during the interwar period, "the conquest of substances," or "the subjugation of matter to human needs," was synonymous with civilization.[40] Employing such terms as "energy," "resource," "expansion," "frontier," "colonization," "rationalization," and "efficiency," colonial administrations claimed the development of colonized territories as their priority.

Although Russia did not possess overseas colonies, its vast territories, some of which had been acquired fairly recently, were described and governed in similar ways.[41] Even Russia's core, Slavic-populated territory, one could argue, was conceived as both a colony and the metropole: with its agricultural export-based economy and a population that had remained in serfdom until 1861 and was still largely illiterate by the time of the revolution, it was economically dependent on Europe, whose culture and even language were embraced by Russian elites. As elsewhere in the colonial world, development was seen as the key to modernization, and the revolution aimed at liberating Russia by assuming the control of development. This rhetoric intensified during the industrialization, when the exploration and economic exploitation of northern and Siberian resources, presented as "the conquest of the North," became a trope in Soviet media. Architecture, which now focused on the creation of factories and new cities in these areas, became an important instrument of colonization. Although at first sight the theories discussed in this book might seem unrelated to it, based on the ethos of development, they provided the theoretical context for colonization.

In the second and third decades of the twentieth century, a new ecological model emerged. It was based on interdependence and cooperation, which replaced the nineteenth-century ideal of free enterprise on the one hand, and efficiency and productivity on the other.[42] As Michael Osman recently argued when tracing the architectural history of this model in the United States, the term "regulation" came to inform thinking about nature, domesticity, and production.[43] This confluence determined the rise of planning during the first decades of the twentieth century, influencing the activity of organizations such as Huxley and Wells's Political and Economic Planning (PEP) organization, a socialist think-tank whose aim was to stop "laissez-faire individualism, for that is not organic."[44] Because of Wells's pro-Soviet politics, PEP was often critical of bourgeois democracy: while Wells advocated for "a regime of authoritarian enlightenment," Huxley's political manifesto, unequivocally titled *If I Were a Dictator,* delineated a vision of "scientific humanism"—a technocratic society governed by scientists who use rational planning to bring order to social chaos.[45]

A key natural resource that according to the logic of development, had to be regulated was the human. This vision formed the core of human ecology, an eclectic multidisciplinary intellectual endeavor, which attracted sociologists, anthropologists, biologists, psychologists, and public intellectuals from Wells and Geddes, to Whitehead and Kurt Lewin.[46] As Wells, his son the zoologist G. P. Wells, and Huxley argued in their best-seller *The Science of Life* (1927):

> The science of economics—at first it was called Political Economy— is a whole century older than ecology. It was and is the science of social subsistence, of needs and their satisfactions, of work and wealth. It tries to elucidate the relations of producer, dealer, and consumer in the human community and show how the whole system carries on. Ecology broadens out this inquiry into a general

Figure I.3. El Lissitzky's model of the Soviet pavilion at the *Pelz* (Fur) exhibition in Leipzig (1930; likely exhibited within the pavilion) presents nature as conquered by humans. The photograph shows the skin of a Siberian tiger, a species that symbolizes both the beauty and the danger of nature, topped with the architectural model. Courtesy of the Getty Research Institute, Los Angeles (950076).

study of the give and take, the effort, accumulation and consumption in every province of life. Economics, therefore, is merely Human Ecology, it is the narrow and special study of the ecology of the very extraordinary community in which we live.[47]

The economic focus of human ecology linked monism with the imperial managerial approach, giving rise to a discourse that was simultaneously organicist and productivist.

In Russia, this ethos of scientific management of territorial and human resources was elaborated within the framework of "the scientific organization of labor"—*nauchnaia organizatsiia truda,* abbreviated as NOT. Its concerns encompassed labor management, psychotechnics, standardization, engineering, rationalization, advertisement, economic planning, psychology, pedagogy, statistics, and typography, among other fields. NOT was explored by such organizations as the Central Institute of Labor (1921–40), headed by the revolutionary poet Alexey Gastev, and the Time League (1923–25), a powerful organization with branches in many Soviet cites. Among the latter's members were politicians, scientists, and cultural figures, such as Leon Trotsky, constructivist artist Gustav Klutsis, poet Vladimir Mayakovsky, reflexologist Vladimir Bekhterev, psychoanalyst Aron Zalkind, psychotechnician Isaak Spielrein, pedologist Pavel Blonsky, economist Stanislav Strumilin, and Vladimir Lenin's wife, Nadezhda Krupskaya.[48] NOT theorists inscribed labor into a network of practical organizational sciences, and some of them (such as Strumilin) later participated in the development of the system of five-year economic plans, the economic basis of Soviet industrialization. With its practical orientation, the NOT movement came to be viewed as the applied science of modernity, whose subfield architecture was to become.

Meanwhile, in Britain, Huxley and Wells developed their interest in architecture and their social ties with architects and designers, particularly left-leaning emigrants from Nazi-controlled Germany, including László Moholy-Nagy, Walter Gropius, Marcel Breuer, and Herbert Bayer. The other members of their circle included the Irish communist and biologist John Bernal, architects Serge Chermayeff, Aladar Olgyay, and Victor Olgyay, and architectural engineer Ove Arup.[49] As the secretary of the London Zoological Society, Huxley secured for the Russian émigré Berthold Lubetkin the commission to design the now-famous penguin pavilion in the London Zoo in 1934. Both Huxley and Wells visited Soviet Russia and, although there is no evidence of their immediate contacts with Soviet architects, would be instrumental in transmitting the Russian experience, including ideas about architecture, to their British fellow-thinkers. The ideas elaborated by Soviet "monistic" architects were thus not forgotten—exported from the Soviet Union by the socialist biologists, they informed the development of modernism under the British welfare state and its later retransplantation on American soil.

Monism, the Ideology of the Russian Revolution

With its strong intellectual traditions of Spinozism and radical scientism, Russia became particularly receptive to the politicization of monism, which appeared as the revolutionary ideology of modernity.[50] In 1895, the recognized "father" of Russian Marxism, Georgy Plekhanov, published *The Development of the Monist View of History (K voprosu o razvitii monisticheskogo vzgliada na istoriiu)*, which, as Lenin acknowledged, was a book "on which an entire generation of Russian Marxists was educated."[51] Furthermore, Lenin endorsed Haeckel's *Riddle of the Universe*, claiming that his dialectical materialism was none other than "real" monism.[52] The most celebrated of revolutionary writers, Maxim Gorky, likewise confessed, "For me, the value of Bolshevism resides in its being the creation of monists."[53]

In 1895, Gorky's future long-term friend and collaborator Anatoly Lunacharsky, then a radically minded Kyiv gymnasium student preoccupied with an attempt "to create an emulsion of Spencer and Marx," moved to Zurich to study with Avenarius, the author of the energeticist theory of "the least measure of force" and a leader of the subjectivist philosophy of empiriocriticism.[54] Lunacharsky's self-designed program of study included seminars with biologists—anatomy with Rudolf Martin, physiology with Justus Gaule, and physiology of perception with Rudolf Wlassak—and economists and political theorists—political economy with Fritz Platten and Marxism with Russian Menshevik emigrant Pavel Akselrod. But for Lunacharsky, "all this faded into the background . . . compared to the work with Avenarius."[55] Adapting Avenarius's program to his own aesthetic interests and his revolutionary activity, Lunacharsky merged it with Nietzschean vitalism: beauty was, for him, the "mighty and free life" itself.[56] This life was manifested as "activity, courage, the joy of combat."[57] The biological category of life, for Lunacharsky, dialectically sublated the opposition of collectivity and individuality:

> The growth of species *self-consciousness* is a great process of a return of reason to biological subconscious truth. Of course, here we are dealing not with a self-rejection of individuality, not with its return to the slavery of species instincts, but with a harmonic union, with high vitalist aesthetics, which will teach individuality

to appreciate the development of might, beauty and happiness of species as a whole above all else, and which will at the same time teach the truth that precisely this mighty, beautiful and happy species, which develops in constant struggle for a new might, is expressed in its most beautiful individuals.[58]

Lunacharsky's brother-in-law and collaborator, Alexander Bogdanov, created his own idiosyncratic blend of Spencerian monism, empiriocriticism, Ludwig Noiré's energeticist "monistic epistemology," experimental psychology, and Marxism, which he called empiriomonism: "Instead of this [Avenarius's] theory I presented another one, the origins of which I trace to Spinoza, and the main material for which was provided, in my opinion, by the views of Meynert and, partially, by the James-Lange theory of emotion," he explained.[59] In 1904, Bogdanov, Lunacharsky, Gorky, alongside several other social-democratic thinkers, published a programmatic volume *The Foundations of Realist Worldview (Osnovy realisticheskogo mirovozzreniia)*. Opening the volume, Sergey Suvorov's article "The Foundations of the Philosophy of Life" called for an ontological and epistemological unity (nature, it argued, is the connection of events in time and space, life is a phenomenon of nature, and psyche is a phenomenon of life) and for psychophysical parallelism as the foundational principle of the philosophy of life.[60]

Bogdanov, Lunacharsky, and Gorky, all influential within the radical Bolshevik faction (to which Lenin also belonged) of the Russian Social-Democratic Party, rivaled Lenin's leadership from a radically left standpoint. They enjoyed a reputation as Bolshevik intellectuals, and in response, Lenin, in his only philosophical work, *Materialism and Empirio-Criticism: Critical Notes on One Reactionary Philosophy (Materializm i empiriokrititsizm: Kriticheskie zametki ob odnoi reaktsionnoi filosofii*, 1908), attempted to annihilate "the Bogdanovites" on their own—philosophical—territory to break the radical intelligentsia's fascination with empiriocriticism. In 1909, Bogdanov was expelled from the Bolshevik faction. After the revolution, however, he and Lenin reconciled, and the former Bogdanovites assumed the leadership of a nascent Soviet culture, in which Lenin, preoccupied with political concerns, demonstrated little interest.[61] During the early 1920s, Bogdanov headed the powerful Proletarian Culture (Proletkult) movement, which was instrumental in promoting NOT; Gorky was celebrated as the most distinguished revolutionary writer; and Lunacharsky, who became the head of the Narkompros (the Soviet Ministry of Culture and Education, or, literally, the Ministry of "Enlightenment") in 1919, remained in this position until 1929.[62] His programmatic *Foundations of Positive Aesthetics (Osnovy pozitivnoi estetiki)* of 1903, reprinted without revision in 1923, contributed to the further dissemination of monistic aesthetics and became a frequent point of reference for artists and architects.[63] The leading roles played by Gorky, Bogdanov, and especially Lunacharsky and the respect and influence that they enjoyed among writers, artists, and architects made their empiriocriticist version of monism the aesthetic foundation of Soviet modernism.

During the 1920s and early 1930s the monistic worldview in the Soviet Union was sustained due to the connections of the Soviet regime with Western scientists and progressivists, which was institutionalized through a network of international and internationalist movements.[64] The founding members of the German Society of Friends of New Russia included Behne, Bruno Taut, theater director Erwin Piscator, writers Thomas and Heinrich Mann, neuroscientist Oskar Vogt, as well as Albert Einstein.[65] Other Friends of New Russia societies in the UK and the United States attracted liberals, academics, and social reformers, among them Wells, Huxley, John Dewey, Jane Addams, Upton Sinclair, Ernest Hemingway, George Bernard Shaw, Jack London, J. B. S. Haldane, and John Maynard Keynes.[66] Meanwhile, in the sphere of art, internationalism was exemplified by the Berlin-based "international constructivist" movement, which historian Oliver Botar termed "biocentric avant-gardism." It included Behne, Lissitzky, Moholy-Nagy, Hans Richter, Hannah Höch, Raoul Hausmann, Theo Van Doesburg, Ludwig Mies van der Rohe, Ludwig Hilberseimer, and Walter Benjamin. This movement developed monistic ideas about life, nature, and the human, which Botar identifies at an intersection of neovitalism, monism, neo-Lamarckism, holism, biologism, the German reform movement, anarchism, and *Lebensphilosophie*.[67]

The popularity of monism in the Soviet Union peaked around 1925, the year when *The Monism of the Universe (Monizm vselennoi),* by philosopher and space engineer Konstantin Tsiolkovsky, and "Psychoanalysis as Monistic Psychology," by psychologist Alexander Luria, were published, and when constructivist theoretician Boris Arvatov formulated the theory of "the monism of things." Three years later, Bogdanov died following a blood transfusion experiment that he conducted on his own body—based on a neo-Lamarckian assumption that blood transmitted an organism's acquired characteristics and inspired by the desire to increase vitality through "physiological collectivism," this experiment was his final monistic project.[68] It ended his life but not the influence of his ideas: supported by Stalin, the agronomist Trofim Lysenko continued to develop the now-notorious Lamarckian theory of environmentally acquired inheritance throughout the 1930s.[69]

The importance of monism for Soviet aesthetic thought was documented by Soviet artist Alexander Toporkov, whose book *The Technical Everyday and*

Contemporary Art (1928) delineated an aesthetic theory that identified art with life:

> We should acknowledge that the beautiful and art are manifestations of life. But life itself should be understood not only in terms of simple description and analysis, but first of all dialectically. Using certain categories, we can talk about the necessity and freedom of life. The man lives and acts under certain conditions, which determine him, and to which he, in this or another way, has to adapt. At the same time he, through his energy, can "teach his teacher," i.e., modify his environment. The man participates in creating the conditions under which he lives, which mostly becomes the most important subject of technical activity. A passive subordination to the surroundings, a simple experience of the given cannot form the basis of art and does not lead to the creation of the beautiful.
>
> The realm of pure necessity does not know art, beauty, or culture in general. The activity of man interprets the surrounding conditions and through an immediate praxis leads to the creation of new reality. In this positive activity lies freedom, which is closely connected to necessity because purposeful praxis is possible only on the basis of understanding the environment. Our practical activity puts in front of us certain tasks, whose achievement changes the conditions of our existence.[70]

Although hardly an original theoretician (and hence little-known today), Toporkov was a brilliant synthesizer, whose theory integrated the ideas of thinkers such as Lissitzky and Lunacharsky, a codifier, as it were, of the state of Soviet aesthetic theory at the end of the 1920s. For Toporkov, art was an active and conscious transformation of the environment based on the understanding of natural necessity. The theory of Soviet interwar architecture was grounded in this very belief: Soviet architects aspired to design not merely buildings but the spatial environments that facilitated humanity's survival and directed its evolutionary progress. To put it differently, by designing its environment, Soviet architects aspired to redesign *Homo sapiens*.

Soviet Monistic Modernism and Its Echoes

In the chapters that follow, I examine how Soviet modernist architecture was motivated by human sciences and their monistic notion of the human as the agent of life. I analyze the architectural production of both ASNOVA and OSA, focusing on the work of their major theorists (Ladovsky, Lissitzky, and Ginzburg) as well as the work that was created outside of these groups. Different architectural groups and individual architects foregrounded different parts of the monistic discourse, such as psychophysiological, organizational, economic, managerial, or evolutionary theories. Offering different responses to the same set of problems and guided by shared values, these diverse approaches were—their polemical confrontations notwithstanding—fundamentally reconcilable, complementing rather than contradicting each other.

Each of the book's six chapters pairs a key principle of the monistic discourse with one of the disciplinary concerns of interwar modernist architecture (form-making, urbanism, pedagogy, standardization, interior design, and landscape architecture), examining how the former was mobilized for responding to the latter. The chapters are arranged in a roughly chronological way, moving from the early 1920s to the mid-1930s. This structure highlights major transformations in the way of thinking about architecture, from the early interest in the perception of form to a managerial concern with use of this perception for increasing productivity and, ultimately, to the exploration of how architecture could direct social evolution. Yet, the book does not have an ambition to construct a neat chronological narrative or to make causal connections between these case studies. Rather, it aims to unpack a heterogeneous discourse, which was represented by distinct actors who often disagreed with each other.

The first chapter, "Space," addresses an attempt to devise a methodological foundation for architectural theory in the early 1920s. It focuses on Ladovsky's "psychoanalytical method," which desexualized Freud's psychoanalysis and merged it with empiriocriticism, redefining architecture as an activation of unconscious perceptual mechanisms. The views of Lissitzky on urbanism, formulated in the mid-1920s, form the subject of chapter 2, "Orientation": fascinated with perceptual transformations generated by urban modernity, Lissitzky argued for an architecture that could organize and order metropolitan chaos without succumbing to anthropocentrism. Chapter 3, "Fitness," addresses the status of architecture as a profession. It focuses on the activity of the Psychotechnical Laboratory, opened by Ladovsky in 1927 to test the physiological and psychological abilities of architecture students; with the aim of optimizing the division of labor in architecture, the laboratory construed the architect as a perceiving machine. Chapter 4, "Process," examines the first Soviet programs of standardization: architect Alexander Rozenberg's theory of normalization and Lissitzky's and Ginzburg's typification efforts around 1929; both programs, it argues, departed from a naturalistic understanding of function as process. Continuing the discussion of Ginzburg's theory, chapter 5, "Energy," examines the architect's collaboration with the Bauhaus designer Hinnerk Scheper between 1929 and 1931. With wall-painting, which the two developed as an emerging modern subfield of architecture, they aspired to use unconscious perception to transform everyday processes into a meaningful activity by improving the energetic functionality of the subject. Finally, chapter 6, "Personality," is focused on landscape architecture, scrutinizing the program of the Central Park of Culture and Leisure (commonly known as Gorky Park) in Moscow, the model Soviet urban public space developed under the influence of Lunacharsky between 1928 and 1934. It defines the park as a humanist (and yet productivist) heterotopia intended to remedy the detrimental effects of divided factory labor.

These stories not only record encounters between architecture and the human sciences in the interwar Soviet Union but also contribute to an understanding of the transnational monistic culture—a culture that produced social democracy and the welfare state, but also inadvertently sustained twentieth-century totalitarian regimes. Indeed, Spinozian ethics sublated the opposition of freedom and necessity—the projection of the form/function dichotomy on the ethical plane—by postulating necessity not as the opposite but as the very foundation of freedom. Nature, says Spinoza, was governed by purposefulness and logic and could not be described in the categories of good and evil.[71] In his neo-Spinozian article "The Freedom of Necessity" (1942), Bernal likewise argued that although freedom is usually juxtaposed to cooperation, and individuality to the state, these oppositions are false: "The answer lies not in trying to decide the issue between anarchy and order, but in revising our organization of the state and our education of the individual."[72] Once introduced to the political discussion, the ecological concept of life transformed its agent from a passive and powerless *homo sacer* to *Homo sapiens,* who acted through the knowledge of natural necessity.

By animalizing the human, monism laid the ground for exploitation and extermination as well as for socialization, collectivity, and personal development. Although the atrocities of the Second World War made obvious the evilness of monism's eugenic aspirations and the naivety of its heroic humanism, elements of its doctrine of humanness have persisted until this day. Agamben, in his own words, threw "a sinister light on the models by which social sciences, sociology, urban studies, and architecture today are trying to conceive and organize the public space of the world's cities without any clear awareness that at their very center lies the same bare life (even if it has been transformed and rendered apparently more human) that defined the biopolitics of the great totalitarian states of the twentieth century."[73] Yet, the legacy of monism encompasses not only the minimalist logic of modernist public housing (the immediate target of Agamben's criticism), but also the movements that resisted it, such as the postwar turn of architecture and planning toward image and perception, the epistemological privileging of the unconscious that underlined architectural phenomenology, and, more recently, neuroaesthetics and the studies of sensorium and affect. Contemporary concerns about climate change and the role of humanity in shaping our planetary environment as well as the emerging interest in the intersection of biology, computation, and architectural design likewise evoke the logic of monism. As humans cannot avoid their bodies, architecture is unable to evade *zoē*. Prompted by the climate crisis, contemporary architecture theorists again turn to life sciences in search for models of designing architecture not only for particular clients—or even, as the modernists did, for particular social ends—but for the planet. Although architects no longer approach nature as a resource, the similarities between contemporary and modernist organic approaches to architecture are evident. For contemporary architecture, then, the story of Soviet interwar modernism appears as more than an episode from a distant historical and political context. It is, rather, a material for reflection—simultaneously a precedent and a warning.

ONE

Space

Formalist Architectural Pedagogy at the VKhUTEMAS

The story of Soviet modernist architecture began on a cold evening in the spring of 1920, in a poorly lit room in the Second Independent State Artistic Studios (Svobodnye gosudarstvennye khudozhestvennye masterskie, SGKhM) in Moscow, the center of artistic avant-garde in postrevolutionary Russia. Unlike the departments of painting and sculpture, the architecture department was still run by traditionalists. Attracted by the announcement of a new, modernist, architectural studio, students filled the room. They were addressed by a little-known architect, Nikolay Ladovsky, who began by condemning the old academic approach, which, he declared, obstructed true architectural creativity. Rather than studying classical orders and proportions, his new studio promised that the aspiring architects would focus on the human who perceived them.[1] Of everything Ladovsky professed, his maxim "Space, not stone, is the material of architecture" made the greatest impression on the audience.[2] The Collective Studio of Architecture, which Ladovsky would proceed to teach at the SGKhM (shortly after to be reorganized as VKhUTEMAS, Vysshie khudozhestvenno-technicheskie masterskie, Higher Art and Technical Studios), was grounded in this maxim. To unpack its meaning, this chapter examines the origins of Ladovsky's theory, known as rationalism, in formalist aesthetics and the philosophy of science. Viewed from this perspective, the rationalist architectural space emerges as the site where psychological and emotional perception was mobilized for economic goals, making humanist vitalism collide with Taylorist mechanicism, and therapeutic concerns with emotional manipulation.

Proletarian Formalism

Ladovsky's appearance at SGKhM was a result of recent political upheavals. Although immediately after the revolution of 1917, the Bolshevik Commissariat of Culture and Education (Narkompros) hoped to gain the support of university professors by endowing universities with the autonomy for which they had fought during tsarist times, the commissar (minister) Anatoly Lunacharsky soon realized that the professoriate nevertheless remained disloyal to the new political power.[3] In response, he reoriented Narkompros toward radical-left, proletarian students. Casting himself as the representative of the latter, Ladovsky used the moment to obtain a faculty position at SGKhM. The manifesto of Ladovsky's Collective Studio was posted on the walls of SGKhM by three working-class students (Viktor Balikhin, Sergey Mochalov, and Nikolay Krasilnikov), who called for a shift of power from professors to students. It was illustrated with a suprematism-styled hierarchical organizational scheme, which presented the studio as an assembly of three main groups and the laboratory of technology and art. Under the motto "Down with Individualism, Long Live Individuality!" which evoked Lunacharsky and Alexander Bogdanov's collectivist philosophy, the studio promised "ample opportunities for developing independent initiative and building a solid comradely discipline." The role of the professor was redefined as that of "the collective's elder."[4] Ladovsky's signature method of design using clay models was another outcome of this proletarian identity: his students were easily recognizable in their dirty working smocks, contrasting with the clean "bourgeois" attire of others.[5] Aligned with the Narkompros politics and relying on Lunacharsky's collectivist philosophy and his empiriocriticism, Ladovsky's architectural pedagogy aimed to intertwine politics, aesthetics, and science.

Ladovsky's theory had been elaborated within the expressionist group Zhivskulptarkh ([Synthesis of] Painting, Sculpture, and Architecture), in which he and his associates Vladimir Krinsky, Nikolay Dokuchaev, and Georgy Mapu participated in 1919 and 1920, along with artist Alexander Rodchenko and cubist sculptor Boris Korolev, among others.[6] The discussions were continued within the Moscow Institute of Artistic Culture (Institut khudozestvennoi kul'tury, INKhUK), under the umbrella of the Narkompros. The head of INKhUK, Wassily Kandinsky, created a program that aspired to define the "foundational elements" of arts from a psychological standpoint. Kandinsky's psychological approach was criticized by Rodchenko, who was instrumental in creating the autonomous Working Group of Objective Analysis within the institute. For Rodchenko and his contemporaries, the term "analysis" (as, for example, in Picasso's "analytical cubism") was associated with a modern and scientific approach to art.[7] Although critical of Kandinsky's subjectivism, the group, among whose members were Varvara Stepanova, Vladimir and Georgy Stenberg, and Lyubov Popova, as well as Ladovsky and Krinsky, nevertheless inherited his formalist aesthetic program.

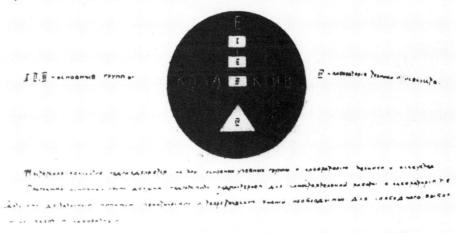

Figure 1.1. The proclamation of the Collective Studio of Architecture, posted on the walls of SGKhM by Viktor Balikhin, Sergey Mochalov, and Nikolai Krasilnikov in 1920, was illustrated by a suprematism-styled hierarchical organizational scheme. The collective consists of three main groups (I, II, III) and the laboratory of technology and art (IV). Published in V. Petrov, "ASNOVA za 8 let," *Sovetskaia arkhitektura* 1–2 (1931).

As an outcome of the struggle with liberal professorship, in the fall of 1920, the Narkompros abolished university autonomy, and "independent studios" (SGKhM) were reorganized as "higher art and technical studios" (VKhUTEMAS). Ladovsky, Krinsky, and Dokuchaev each became the head of a studio in the newly reorganized institution. The three studios immediately formed Obmas (Ob'edinennye levye masterskie, United Left Studios), which, having gained autonomy within VKhUTEMAS, effectively became a new center of architectural education, successfully counterbalancing academic studios. Although Obmas was in turn disbanded in 1923, Ladovsky and his circle continued using its pedagogical methods well into the 1930s. Their

Figure 1.2. Continued by Ladovsky's former students, the "Space" course inevitably relied on modeling in clay and other materials. *Above:* Exhibition of student works on revealing and expressing mass and weight in 1927–28. Courtesy of the Museum of the Moscow Institute of Architecture. *Below:* "Space" course students work on the assignment on revealing mass and weight in 1925. Courtesy of the A. V. Shchusev State Museum of Architecture, Moscow (KPnvf 915/72).

most important pedagogical endeavor, the course "Space," served as a general introduction to architecture. Its program was based on "a discrete and consecutive (according to complexity) study of formal regularities of artistic forms, their elements and qualities on the basis of the physiology of perception."[8] "Space" was one among several "analytical" (so-called propaedeutic, or introductory) courses offered, like the Bauhaus *Vorkurs,* to incoming students of all specializations.[9] Unlike traditional, or "synthetic," courses, these courses segregated art into formal elements: space, color, volume, and line. Most of them were taught by the members of the Group of Objective Analysis: in addition to "Space," the cycle included "Color" (an introduction to painting), with Popova and Alexander Vesnin; "Volume" (an introduction to sculpture), with Korolev; and "Drawing" (an introduction to graphic design), with Rodchenko.[10]

In 1921, the Working Group of Objective Analysis organized a four-month-long theoretical debate about the definitions and the mutual relationship between the notions of construction and composition.[11] The disagreements that emerged during the debate divided the group along the disciplinary axis: artists versus architects. These two factions would later identify as the constructivists and the rationalists. Whereas most artists dismissed composition as arbitrary formal arrangement, the architects defended it, evoking the approach of literary formalism (which, according to Mikhail Bakhtin's sarcastic remark, replaced the question of architectonics with the compositional "question of laying bricks").[12] For the architects, construction and composition possessed equal value but represented two different organizational approaches. Ladovsky defined construction as the absence of superfluous materials and elements, illustrating his vision with a cube whose proportions were made apprehensible by the articulation of surfaces. Composition was characterized as the hierarchy and subordination of elements. Ladovsky depicted it as a cube, in whose sides he inscribed squares accentuating a small dark opening at the bottom of one side ("the door") as the center to which the entire arrangement was subordinated "according to the principle of similarity and movement."[13] Whereas construction, he believed, illustrated the principle of technical rationality, composition exemplified architectural rationality. Both, however, were indispensable for architecture: while construction was essential for building, composition guided the process of design. In both, the goal was a balance between expended resources and obtained result, the principle known as energy-economic.

In March 1921, in response to the debate, Ladovsky and Krinsky founded the Working Group of Architects within INKhUK. The group continued meeting for a year, elaborating an epistemological foundation for architectural theory. Ladovsky hoped to publish their findings as an illustrated dictionary

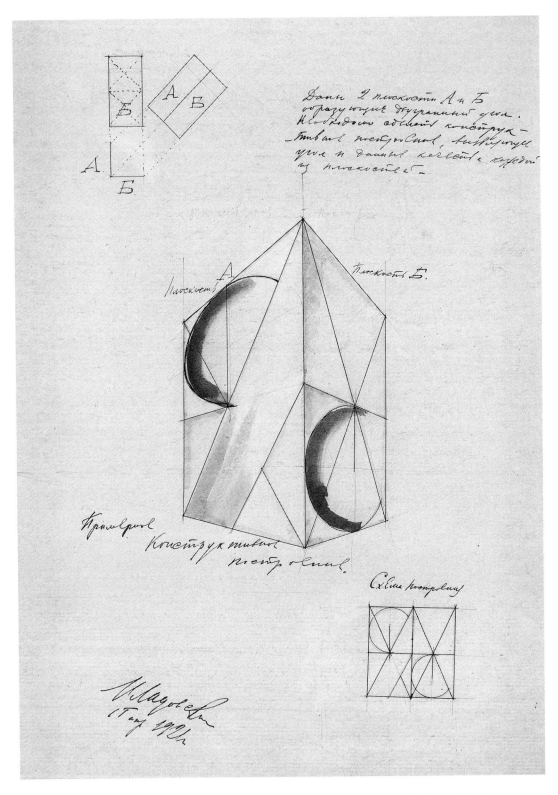

Figure 1.3. Nikolay Ladovsky, "An example of constructive arrangement," 1921. The explication reads: "Given are two planes, A and B, forming a dihedral angle. [The task is] to make constructive arrangements that reveal the angle and the given qualities of each plane." Courtesy of the Costakis Collection, Museum of Modern Art, Thessaloniki.

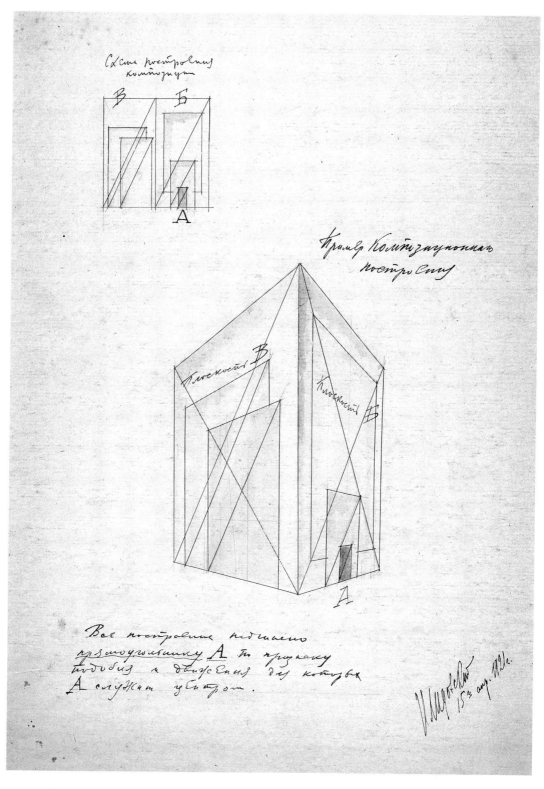

Figure 1.4. Nikolay Ladovsky, "An example of compositional arrangement," 1921. The explication reads: "The entire arrangement is subordinated to the rectangle A according to the attribute of semblance and movement, for which A is the center." Courtesy of the Costakis Collection, Museum of Modern Art, Thessaloniki.

of architecture, which would codify "the terminology and definitions of architecture as a form of art, architecture's separate properties, qualities, and so forth, and the relationships between architecture and other arts."[14] For him, architecture was a science, whose universalized objects were subordinated to a set of objective laws. With his knowledge of Yiddish, a language closely related to German, which was used by eastern and central European Jews (he was born into a Jewish family in Volyn, in the west of Ukraine), Ladovsky would have had easy access to German-language philosophy of science and aesthetic theory.[15] The Working Group of Architects discussed the writings of Wilhelm Worringer, Hermann Muthesius, and Heinrich Wölfflin, along with those of Ernst Mach and the British mathematician and eugenicist Karl Pearson (whose books had been translated into Russian by biologist Kliment Timiryazev and "Bogdanovite" economist Vladimir Bazarov).[16] The program of study followed by the working group was later solidified and disseminated through the Association of New Architects (Assotsiatsiia novykh arkhitektorov, ASNOVA), founded in 1923, whose members Ladovsky recruited among his VKhUTEMAS students.[17]

Ladovsky's efforts to align architectural theory with the politics of the Narkompros legitimized his claims to representing proletarian architecture. Although Lunacharsky's influence exposed him to the philosophy of empirio-criticism and related scientific perspectives on the world and the human, unlike his rationalist followers, Ladovsky remained unsusceptible to Lunacharsky's vitalism, clinging to the scientific ethos of "the analytical method" as pioneered at INKhUK. The conflict between Ladovsky's more formalist interpretation of energy and his colleagues' more vitalist one would later plague rationalist theory, eventually leading to a split between Ladovsky and the first generation of his followers.

(Psycho)Analysis and the Economy of Energy

Ladovsky's pedagogical method was known as analytical or, in the second half of the 1920s, as psychoanalytical. Although the first term referred to the method of objective analysis, the use of the Freudian term "psychoanalysis" might seem surprising. Yet it was more than a coincidence. Sigmund Freud's name and ideas would have been well known to Soviet architects. "In our country the interest in Freud has developed into a real psychosis. . . . Freudianism and Freudianism, again and again, for or against Freudianism, and with each new day . . . we have fewer and fewer healthy Marxists," critic Vladimir Friche bemoaned in 1925.[18] Psychoanalysis was particularly influential among literary and art critics, who eagerly applied it to biographical studies. In the 1920s, a number of authors—most notably the psychologist Alexander Luria—attempted to reconcile Freud and Karl Marx by downplaying the sexual component of psychoanalysis and identifying it, instead, as a scientific study of the unconscious.[19] Introduced by Johann Friedrich Herbart in the 1820s, the notion of the unconscious was elevated to a major philosophical principle by Eduard von Hartmann, whose *Philosophy of the Unconscious* (*Philosophie des Unbewussten*, 1869) linked the unconscious to animal instinct. Translated in the early 1870s, Hartmann's treatise remained popular in Russia well into the 1920s. In 1923, young philosopher Bernard Bykhovsky, initiating the Soviet discussion of psychoanalysis, suggested that the value of the notion of the unconscious lay in its inherent antisubjectivism:

> Psychoanalysis [is] a study of the unconscious, of something that happens beyond the subjective "I." The unconscious has an actual effect on human reactions, frequently orchestrating them. The unconscious cannot be studied through cognition, subjectively. This is why Freud studies objective manifestations of the unconscious (symptom, mistake, etc.), seeking for the conditions of minimal participation of reason (dream, childhood).[20]

In the article "Psychoanalysis as a System of Monist Psychology" (1925), Luria echoed Bykhovsky, arguing that psychoanalysis not only dispenses with idealism and metaphysics but lays, alongside reflexology, "a solid foundation for a psychology of materialist monism."[21]

The notion of libido (sexual energy) related Freud's approach to other energeticist theories, opening the door for economic interpretations of psychoanalysis. In *Psychoanalytical Psychotechnics* (*Psychoanalytische Psychotechnik*, 1924, Russian translation 1926), the German psychologist Fritz Giese aspired to integrate psychoanalysis with psychotechnics, or applied psychology. Libido, he professed, could be converted to an economically productive activity.[22] Giese argued for the importance of psychoanalysis for all three constituent parts of psychotechnics: differential psychology (psychological testing assessing fitness for a profession), studies of work productivity and fatigue, and the psychology of advertisement.[23] Ladovsky, who, as will be discussed in chapter 3, was an ardent champion of psychotechnics, shared this vision, approaching spatial perception as an energetic process that architecture could optimize and regulate.

The energy-economic principle had been formulated in 1876 by Richard Avenarius in *Philosophy as Thinking about the World according to the Principle of the Smallest Measure of Force* (*Philosophie als Denken der Welt gemass dem Prinzip des kleinsten Kraftmasses,* Russian translation 1913): "The soul invests in an apperception no more energy than necessary, and when presented with several possible apperceptions, prefers the one that achieves the same result with the least expenditure of energy or the best result with the same expenditure of energy."[24] Thinking, or inventing new notions, was, according to Avenarius, energetically wasteful, and whenever possible the soul tended to save energy by displacing thought into the domain of the unconscious. Lunacharsky, Avenarius's student at Zurich University, participated in the two seminars offered by the philosopher, one on philosophy and another on "bio-psychology," which discussed Avenarius's book *The Critique of Pure Experience* (*Kritik der reinen Erfahrung,* 1890), a Russian-language account of which he published in 1905.[25] In his own major aesthetic treatise, *Foundations of Positive Aesthetics* (*Osnovy pozitivnoi estetiki,* 1903, republished in 1923), Lunacharsky called aesthetics "a subfield of biology," defining art as a form of higher nervous activity that helped the organism to adapt to its biological environment.[26] The means of this adaptation were energetic: the aesthetic was that which replenished the organism's repository of energy.[27] Lunacharsky, however, viewed Avenarius's scientific energeticism through a vitalist lens: he identified the energy of perception with life energy, manifested emotionally as enthusiasm and excitement, and behaviorally as artistic creativity, political struggle, and life-creating, constructive activity.

Among the readers of Avenarius was the predecessor of literary formalists Alexander Potebnya, who saw the study of unconscious cogitative processes as the clue to understanding poetic language. Potebnya's follower Dmitry Ovsyaniko-Kulikovsky considered attention a waste of psychic energy; he believed that unlike attention, automatism, or the unconscious, allowed for achieving results without expending energy: "This means that all the work was gratuitous for us, and a great economizing of intellectual power is obvious."[28] The idea of the productive unconscious later found support among other theoreticians of nascent Soviet culture, such as Lunacharsky's protégé, the proletarian literary critic Fedor Kalinin, who described in Bogdanov's journal *Proletarskaya Kultura* (*Proletarian Culture*) how Henri Poincaré once made a mathematical discovery while sitting in a car and thinking about unrelated matters. "Our psyche is more than consciousness," Kalinin concluded:

> [the latter] forms only its bright, immediately given area. Behind it lurks a vaster, darker side of the psyche—the unconscious, the richest repository of experience. . . . When consciousness finishes the job of accumulating and organizing material, then, if the discovery is ripe, the unconscious comes to help, connects it with

the conscious area, storming into it as a mighty fruitful stream, and from its hidden treasures adds that which was needed for the solution for the task.[29]

The principle of the economy of energy provided the context for the term "rational architecture," or "ratio-architecture" (*ratsional'naia arkhitektura* or *ratsio-arkhitektura*)—shortened to "rationalism" in subsequent historiography—which Ladovsky in the second half of the 1920s also used to refer to his method.[30] Evoking his earlier definitions of construction and composition, he explained:

> Like technical rationality, architectural rationality is based on the principle of economy. The difference lies in the fact that technical rationality is the economy of labor and material expended in the creation of an expedient building, whereas architectural rationality is the economy of psychic energy expended in the perception of spatial and functional qualities of a building. Rationalist architecture is the synthesis of these two rationalities.[31]

German authors equated rationalization with scientific management or, sometimes, with the energetic principle in general. Summarizing earlier heterogeneous definitions, Giese concluded that rationalization (*Rationalisierung*) dealt with "rational [*vernunftgemäß*] (practically regulated by scientific knowledge) intensive optimal design of energetic relationships." Rationalization, he argued, was "not an 'art' or a trick, but a theory, a phenomenon that was to be scientifically explored and therefore striving for application." It was none other than "practical design," whose goal was "an optimum" rather than "a maximum."[32] In the 1920s, Osip Ermansky, a former revolutionary and now a professor of economics, identified rationalization with the scientific organization of labor (NOT), elaborating its principle as "physiological optimum" $m=R/E$, in which m is "the coefficient of rationality," R the result of the work, and E the energy expended in the working process.[33] Ermansky contended that his formula offered a more humane and holistic way of organizing industrial production than Western approaches. "What is the criterion of the rationality of work?" he asked, concluding that whereas Western luminaries of scientific management prioritized modes of being (Frederick Winslow Taylor was interested in time, while Frank Gilbreth favored space), Soviet rationalization had to be guided by "the essence of life phenomena"—the balance or "the collaboration" of forces.[34] Relying on the psychotechnics of Giese and Ermansky, Ladovsky, who would proceed to open the Psychotechnical Laboratory of Architecture in 1927, embraced its energy-economic humanism.

The Analysis of Sensations

As Avenarius wanted to rationalize philosophical thinking by introducing general notions, Ladovsky proposed to start with determining and defining the general notions in architecture and with "freeing it from atrophying forms."[35] The first assignment that Ladovsky gave in his newly organized course at VKhUTEMAS in October 1920 asked the students to design the simplest of three-dimensional figures, a parallelepiped (or rather, a rectangular prism). It was, for Ladovsky, the primitive hut of modernist architecture—a statement about the minimal conditions of the discipline.[36] The rectangle had been described as the basic geometrical "enclosure" "enframing" all animals, including humans, by Johannes Bochenek in his treatise on the normalization of human representation (1875).[37] Ladovsky sympathized with such geometrical abstraction of organic form. In 1921, during a discussion within the Working Group of Architects, he opposed fellow rationalist A. Petrov who, following literary formalist Roman Jacobson, argued that the poetic method of personification could be applied to urbanism (such as, for example, in Vladimir Mayakovsky's line "one-eyed [city] square sneaked nearby").[38] Evoking Worringer's distinction between abstraction and empathy, Ladovsky warned against identifying the object and the human (a method that was, he argued, more appropriate for poetry than for architecture), and instead argued for architecture that would evoke not the humans but their organization. The act of perceiving architectural form, he contended, would let the beholders "see, feel, and understand" their own organization, of which they had previously been unaware.[39]

Architecture thus turned into an epistemological mechanism that revealed hidden organizational principles of the form. As a result, revealing, or explaining, the form became the first task of architecture. Dokuchaev explained:

> To *reveal* [*vyiavit'*] a form means to make its structural properties—all the basic characteristics of form—visually clear and sharply perceived. In other words, an artist, an architect, wishing to endow his architectural form with certain qualities and properties, has to make these properties correctly perceived (according to his vision) by considering all possible impediments, such as: changing conditions of light, the distance and viewpoint from which the form is viewed, the impact and influence of the surroundings on the form, etc. Here, the artist has to approach the task as a *composer*.[40]

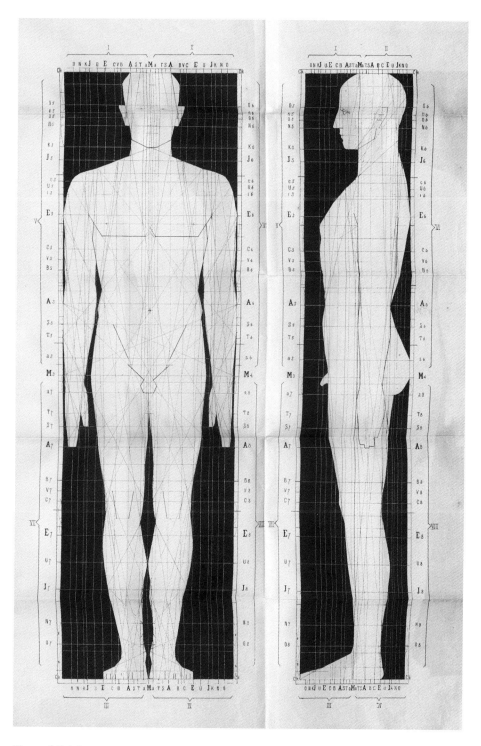

Figure 1.5. Johannes Bochenek considered the rectangle the basic geometrical "enclosure" enframing all animals. This corresponded to Ladovsky's argument that architecture should evoke not the form but its organization. Image from Johannes Bochenek, *Die männliche und weibliche Normal-Gestalt nach einem neuen System* (Berlin: A. Haak, 1875).

The Russian word for revealing, *vyiavlenie,* comprises the prefix *vy-* (signifying the movement outward) and the root *iav'* ("reality"), meaning to reveal the inner truth through phenomena. Introducing it as a concept to architectural theory and pedagogy, Ladovsky relied on *The Problem of Form in the Fine Arts (Das Problem der Form in der bildenden Kunst,* 1893, Russian translation 1914) by the German sculptor and aesthetic thinker Adolf von Hildebrand.[41] Attention, for Hildebrand, was an expenditure of perceptive energy, and accordingly, a good work of art was the one whose formal idea was immediately clear.[42] Following Hermann von Helmholtz, the sculptor distinguished between "effective form" *(Wirkungsform),* or the phenomenal representation of an object ("a joint product of the object, on the one hand, and of its lighting, surroundings, and our changing vantage point, on the other"), and the ontological inherent form *(Daseinsform).*[43] In Hildebrand's terms, Ladovsky's method of revealing exposed the *Daseinsform* through the *Wirkungsform.*

"What does it mean to *reveal a geometrical image*?" wondered Ladovsky, explaining the assignment on the parallelepiped. "Would we see in a mathematically correct parallelepiped some other form—a sphere, a cone, a cylinder, etc.? No, we will see neither a sphere nor a cylinder, but neither will we see a parallelepiped of the geometrical qualities specified in the assignment."[44] He supplemented the assignment with a set of data related to geometrical properties and the appearance of the object: its dimensions (20 × 20 × 30 meters), conditions of light (sunny), the spectator's viewpoint (moving, but no farther than thirty meters away from the object), and the speed of movement (no more than fifteen meters per second). The students had to reveal spatial orientation, the equality of the figure's sides, the relationship between its width and height, and the fact that all angles were 90 degrees. The task could be accomplished with the use of chiaroscuro, vertical and horizontal articulations of surfaces, or by engaging the texture *(faktura)* of the object. Describing a successful solution by one student, Petrov, which recalls and predates his own sketches of construction and composition, Ladovsky praised it for exposing the identity of the figure's sides through the articulation of surfaces, most notably through inscribing circumferences into its sides.[45] Additional half circumferences helped to comprehend the ½:1 relationship between the base and the sides of the parallelepiped; they were reinforced by the tripartite horizontal division of the figure: each half circumference was inscribed into one of the resultant identical rectangles. The vertical proportions of the parallelepiped were emphasized with the help of vertical divisions, which visually and, as it were, structurally tied together its three rectangular constituents.

Figure 1.6. Nikolay Ladovsky highly praised the solution of his student V. Petrov to the assignment "Parallelepiped: Abstract Assignment on Revealing Form" (1920). The image was published in *Izvestia ASNOVA*, no. 1 (1926): 5.

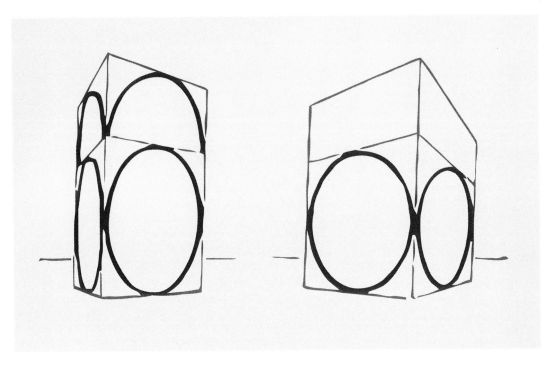

Figure 1.7. Nikolay Ladovsky's geometrical analysis of Petrov's project explains that inscribing circles within the sides of the parallelepiped makes its proportions intuitively apprehensible. Image published in *Izvestia ASNOVA*, no. 1 (1926): 4.

Instead of departing from architectural details and gradually moving toward larger forms as was common within the academic tradition, the rationalist pedagogy began with a study of elements of perception, subsequently progressing to their combinations, and finishing by mastering space as the complex psychological projection of external reality. Beginning with geometrical form, the students moved on to explore such properties as surface, volume, mass, weight, and construction. A typical rationalist plan of student work explored and categorized these properties:

Geometric qualities of form in space.
1. Types of surfaces: (a) plane; (b) curved surfaces (cylindrical, conical, etc., convex and concave); (c) angles formed by polyline surfaces or by intersection of planes—internal and external.
2. Volume as a form, comprising a closed system of surface. Typical volumetric forms: cylinder, parallelepiped, cone, sphere, etc., and their combinations. . . .

Physical-mechanical properties of form.

1. Mass (of volume)—enclosed space infilled with matter. Systems of elements, which expose mass, have to evoke a visual penetration inside the volume and the sensation of the degree of density of its infill with mass.
2. Weight (of volume)—the movement of mass downward under the force of gravitation.
3. Construction—a balancing system of couplings of interacting forms under the effect of the gravitation force.[46]

The rationalist approach departed from *Contributions to the Analysis of Sensations* (*Beiträge zur Analyse der Empfindungen*, 1886), the philosophical opus magnum of Austrian physicist and philosopher Ernst Mach, which, alongside Avenarius's work, solidified the theory of empiriocriticism as based on the economic principle. Mach suggested an epistemological reduction of the material world to color, sound, temperature, and other elements of perception. Since every physical quality (or element, in Mach's terminology) exists in the mind as sensation, the dualism of spirit and matter was explained away as a linguistic misunderstanding. The mosaic of elements or sensations that the world presents, so Mach, is not chaotic but is rather organized as complexes, which, although never absolutely stable, demonstrate a certain permanency. For the sake of our orientation in the world, relatively stable complexes of sensations are called bodies. As a result, concluded Mach, it is not bodies that produce sensations but, on the contrary, complexes of sensations (or elements) that comprise bodies.[47] No single body is absolutely stable: "My friend may put on a different coat. . . . His complexion, under the effects of light or emotion, may change." Nevertheless, we recognize a complex of sensations as our friend based on permanent qualities, which outnumber transitory ones. Even the self, for Mach, was only a relatively permanent combination of qualities, a "complex of memories, moods, and feelings, joined to a particular body (the human body)."[48] This postulation of the ultimate instability of the ego allowed Mach to argue that the "I" and the world are inseparable, most vividly illustrated by his self-portrait showing how closing one eye forcefully merges the body with its environment.[49] Similarly, Adolf Behne, in a passage from *The Modern Functional Building* that El Lissitzky marked as crucial for understanding the book, argued that form is a result of interaction between at least two people, a prerequisite of any social association.[50]

Subverting the familiar distinction between subject and object was, for Ladovsky, the key lesson of Mach's epistemology. "Perceiving material form,

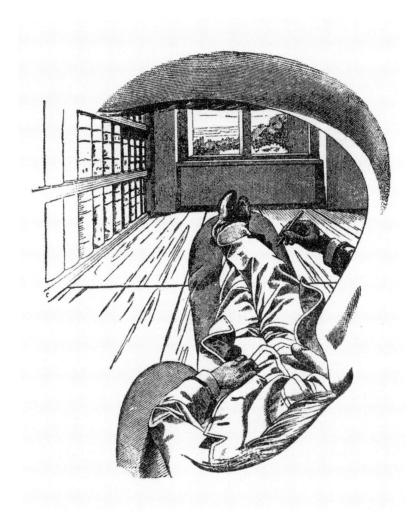

Figure 1.8. Ernst Mach's illustration to *Contributions to the Analysis of Sensations* demonstrates how closing one eye makes one's own body visually dissipate within the environment. From Ernst Mach, *Beiträge zur Analyse der Empfindungen* (Jena: G. Fischer, 1886), 14.

we see in it not only a 'thing-in-itself,' but a mirror-like reflection of the entire world," stated a draft of his programmatic article on the principles of rationalist aesthetics.[51] This monistic lesson, the architect believed, equally undermined the constructivists' absolutization of matter and Kantian idealism. During a discussion of the laws of mechanics in architecture within the Working Group of Architects in May 1921, Ladovsky argued for the importance of empiriocriticism for architecture, presenting it as a theory that replaced the Kantian distinction between organisms and mechanical objects with a vision of a more or less loosely connected complex of elements:

I will introduce you to the opinion of Mach, to his argumentation. You have drawn a construction and you argue that this is architecture. Let us take a watch: it too has a construction, but this does not make it architecture. We have, therefore, to start with establishing scientific terms.

Mach says: "Objects do not exist in the world." Earlier, some theoreticians and philosophers told us that an object exists, while others claimed that only our perceptions are real. Both arguments, as it seemed, were correct, and no one could recognize a mistake in the assumptions. There is no difference between you and a thing . . . "I" can be infinitely extended. Existent are your body, mind, watch. A body is connected to a thing—through the eye and the brain. I say about the eye "this is me." But I can also say "the watch is also me." There is no boundary between myself and the external world. I can connect myself to the globe. There is no boundary, but there is a link that is convenient to confine oneself to.

What is an object? Earlier [one] thought about the object itself and its properties as an object. This led philosophers to mistakes. Think only of Kant's useless attempts to give corresponding notions. Mach is attempting to remove this strange error. He determines that "only complexes of elements exist." They are changeable, but connected in time. And those whose connection is more stable—these are the ones we talk about. Here is a dress. We could have said now that it is a complex of certain forces. But this would be inconvenient, because there are more stable and more temporal values; the latter do not give it a definite character. Thus Mach says: only changeable complexes of qualities temporally exist, while there are no things in themselves.[52]

In the absence of objects that previously served as basic structural units of architectural language ("a wall, a roof, a column, a beam, a plinth, a pediment, etc."), the new architectural theory was to comprise perceivable spatial qualities in the same way that Mach's epistemology imagined the internalized universe as a set of elements of perception.[53] Just as Mach suggested going from sensations to bodies rather than from bodies to sensations, Ladovsky insisted on defining architectural elements first, and only then, based on these definitions, developing a new notion of architecture: "from a study of separate properties and qualities of a phenomenon—to building on these foundations conclusions and definitions of the phenomenon itself."[54]

These qualities—formal, subjective properties of spatial perception—in turn formed the object of architectural creativity: space, not stone, was the material of architecture. Whereas construction was the method of object creation, the elusive psychological space was to be designed by compositional means.

Synthesis

Having dissected the spatial environment into a set of elements of perception, Ladovsky's psychoanalytical method culminated with their reassembly as space—the architectural work par excellence. Such an understanding of space was an outcome of modern psychology. In the 1870s, the German psychologist Carl Stumpf argued that "what we perceive originally and directly is the visual field, the whole visual field. . . . If this continually changes through movement, we retain the disappearing parts in our minds and unite them with the newly perceived spaces into a whole. Thus, out of many spaces arises one space."[55] At the end of the nineteenth century, Stumpf's theory (along with related discussions by Wilhelm Wundt, Robert Vischer, and Theodor Lipps) was applied to architecture by August Schmarsow, who defined space as a concatenation of images, and, via Schmarsow, informed the thought of Auguste Choisy, Sigfried Giedion, and Le Corbusier. Like these theorists, Ladovsky saw space as a function of movement—a *dispositif* linking and ordering visual sensations that unfolded as the subject progressed along a linear path.

This approach redirected Ladovsky's attention from the architectural to the urban dimension. In 1928 he founded another architectural organization, ARU (Ob'edinenie arkhitektorov-urbanistov, Association of Architects–Urbanists), recruiting its members from the most recent generation of his graduates. Ladovsky reportedly liked to walk along Moscow streets early in the morning, before the flows of traffic and people could prevent him from observing contrasts and changes of spatial perspectives, to understand urban landscape as a spatial whole.[56] His concept of the embodied, peripatetic viewer evoked the "picturesque" urbanism of Choisy, whose *Histoire de l'architecture* (1899, Russian translation 1935) would be famously employed by Sergei Eisenstein a decade later in his theory of architectural montage.[57] When during the academic year 1929/30 Ladovsky's student Viktor Kalmykov created a clay model of Avtostroy, a socialist town to be built near Nizhniy Novgorod, he suggested filming the model and montaging the film to make it appear as if perceived by a moving viewer.[58] Yet this cinematic approach to architecture

Figure 1.9. To convey the perception of a moving subject, Viktor Kalmykov filmed his model of the Avtostroy town in 1929–30. Image published in *Sovetskaia arkhitektura* 1–2 (1931): 22–23.

was different from the spatial approach of Eisenstein to film: unlike the latter, Ladovsky was interested not in the emotional but in the perceptual effect of montage.

As Ladovsky's interests moved toward urban planning, the development of the theory of architectural composition was left to his former ASNOVA colleagues who remained at VKhUTEMAS as the teachers of "Space": Dokuchaev, Krinsky, and former students Mikhail Korzhev, Balikhin, Mikhail Turkus, V. Petrov, Yury Spassky, and Ivan Lamtsov.[59] The group rejected Ladovsky's scientism, embracing a more vitalist perspective. The goal of rationalism, for them, was not a formalist "aestheticization" but a "healthy aesthetics."[60] As Dokuchaev had earlier articulated:

> Contemporary aesthetics . . . lies in the economy of psychophysical energy within a person. The main task of aesthetics is not to teach and [not to] contribute to the development of capacities for the passive contemplation and admiration of architectural

objects. Rather, it is to solve problems through the expression and organization of form and space, which would enable it to raise up, awaken energy, and enrich people's emotions.[61]

The results of their work were published by Krinsky, Turkus, and Lamtsov as *Elements of Architectural-Spatial Composition* (*Elementy arkhitekturno-prostranstvennoi kompozitsii*, 1934).[62] Instead of the technique of revealing, which was favored by Ladovsky, the new rationalist compositional theory prioritized expressivity as the method of making form recognizable. The term expressivity (Russian *vyrazitel'nost'*) referred to hyperbolizing and otherwise accentuating properties of form to augment the viewer's emotional response. In his antiformalist pamphlet "Formalism in the Science of Art" (1924), Lunacharsky had hailed it as the quality that endowed the artist with a social function, allowing for the "deepest psychological effect of the artwork."[63]

The book recommended that the key expressive compositional qualities, dynamism and the intensity of psychological effect, could be achieved though division, a hierarchical ordering of elements, and the creation of a compositional center.[64] Korzhev had already explored these qualities in an "industrial" assignment he had submitted at Ladovsky's studio as a student. While conceptual, or abstract, assignments such as the parallelepiped served to flesh out the student's formal idea and were submitted in clay, paper, wire, wood, and other sculptural media, the purpose of rather traditional-looking industrial assignments, which were presented as architectural plans and drawings, was to prepare students for practical work. In 1921 and 1922, the parallelepiped was paired with the "grain elevator" as "an industrial assignment on revealing and expressing architectural form."[65] Korzhev organized the structure as four equal cylinders arranged in a row. A contrast of rectangles and circles created a tension of dynamism and statics. The articulations of cylindrical sections made the facade of the elevator appear as a grid of horizontal rectangles, while the diagonals of the pedestal and the loft neutralized each other, conveying a feeling of dynamic monumentality, accentuated by a slight narrowing of the cylinders toward the top. Meanwhile, the circles (curves of the cylinders, wheels, and quadrants) emphasized the rotation that lay at the heart of the elevator's functional program, making the beholder visually trace the movement of the grain: starting at bottom left, up the conveyor belt to the highest point of the structure, then moving downward following the diagonal traversing the wheels, abruptly falling down into the elevator and slowly running toward the starting point, where the process, as it were, began anew.

Hierarchical order and an accentuated centrality, the rationalists explained, endowed composition with direction, translating aesthetic experi-

Figure 1.10. "Grain elevator" was the "industrial" (applied) correlate of "the parallelepiped" as the assignment on revealing and expressing architectural form. Mikhail Korzhev's solution (1922) is exploring the interplay of circles and rectangles while highlighting the dynamics of the elevator's movement. Courtesy of the A. V. Shchusev State Museum of Architecture, Moscow (Pla 14552).

ence to bodily reaction and stimulating physical movement.[66] This order resulted from a repetition of elements, or their arrangement in compositional rows (Plate 2). Rationalist compositional theory distinguished between two types of such rows: rhythmical, based on increasing or decreasing intervals, or metric, whose intervals were equal. Like musical bars, metric rows formed the spatial skeleton of composition; their combinations expressed force, serenity, monumentality, and scale. Conveying lightness and dynamism, rhythm, meanwhile, was defined as the law of the connection of spatial forms and elements. During the interwar period, the notion of rhythm became essential for fields as diverse as psychology, musicology, eugenics, labor theory, pedagogy, aesthetics, and political propaganda.[67] Physiologists studied the rhythms of heartbeat and breath, and labor theorists explored the rhythms of the machine and the worker. Biological definitions prevailed, while mechanistic rhythms were subjected to criticism. "Lines, rails or chains" in Ford's plants "move without interruptions," Giese observed, making the worker follow the rhythm of the machine, "hour after hour, week after week."[68] In response, economists such as Karl Bücher (whose widely read *Work and Rhythm* [*Arbeit und Rhythmus,* 1896] was translated into Russian twice, in 1899 and 1923), as well as artistic, aesthetic, and esoteric thinkers, including Kandinsky, Rudolf Steiner, and Émile Jaques-Dalcroze, explored the humanizing potential of rhythm.[69]

Rhythm had been a key category of Lunacharsky's *Foundations of Positive Aesthetics*, which identified it as the principle of the pupil's physiological movement and therefore the source of pleasing aesthetic sensation.[70] Citing Gustav Fechner and the theoretician of the golden section Adolf Zeising, Lunacharsky associated rhythm with simplicity, order, and regularity. His account of the aesthetic effect of the Gothic cathedral relied on emotional contrast rather than on linear narrativity:

> Gradually, the pleasing and mighty excitement of visual organs . . . penetrates all of your nervous system: a new rhythm, the rhythm of this stone prayer, the rhythm of these glaring patterned windows seems to be flowing into you; it washes away, wins over tremblings and spasms . . . expressed in anxiety, bad memories, sickness; it strives, at the very least, to replace the disharmony of your regular spiritual life with one chord. And then, at the moment when the feeling of mighty and quiet harmony begins to capture you, a shadow of sorrow that falls over your soul becomes ever more obvious. . . . Here, one perceives, as it were, the contrast between those parts of the psyche (or, physically, the nervous-brain system) that are captured by the aesthetic rhythm, and other [parts]—unreconciled, aching, ulcerated by life. . . . And if the thirst for beauty is still alive in you, it will turn into anger with reality, and when the fever of anger recedes—into a desire to again retire into the corners of beauty—or into the desire to make reality more beautiful, to harmonize it, to create.[71]

Plunging the human into a sublime "sweet, semi-hypnotic state," rhythm, to Lunacharsky, captured the soul, transgressed the boundaries of the aesthetic, and awakened the desire to strive for an active transformation of life. The future theoretician of architectural constructivism Moisei Ginzburg was likewise fascinated with the potential of rhythm for a (hypnotic) stimulation of constructive activity. His early book *Rhythm in Architecture* (1922), which was indebted to Lunacharsky's aesthetics, opened with an epigraph taken from

Friedrich Nietzsche's study of classical music: "Rhythm is a compulsion. It produces an irresistible desire for imitating, conforming; not only feet but the soul itself (including the souls of gods) follows the musical bar."[72] The book romantically observed the rhythms of planetary systems, of the pulsation of the human heart and the circulation of blood, detecting rhythm at the essence of every architectural creation.[73] Rhythm, for Ginzburg as well as for ASNOVA theorists of composition, was the principle that united architecture with nature, the exemplification of the organic and synthetic notion of life.

The boundary between expressionist vitalism and consumerist or totalitarian compulsion turned out to be elusive. A hypnotizing technique, rhythmical movement was mobilized by both Western and Soviet consumer and political propaganda, becoming an "ideal ideological cipher" (a similar role, one could note, was assigned to psychoanalysis).[74] Giese discovered that rhythmically repeated objects exerted upon the psyche of the consumer a stronger emotional effect than single objects (an array of electric bulbs, for example, was more impressive than one bulb).[75] Accordingly, in Soviet Russia and elsewhere, rhythm became a principle of design for settings of parades and rallies.[76] Transforming the disinterested monadic visitor into an emotionally engaged member of the collective organism, the theory of spatial rhythm relied on the concept of mass celebration as the site of forging collective subjectivity, which had been developed by Lunacharsky in the immediate aftermath of the revolution.[77] By the time ASNOVA began the work on the theory of composition, the concept was revived on a new, mass, scale as the political rally, an organized and aestheticized form of mass action tasked with providing ideological support for industrialization.

In the 1930s, when Kalmykov (who had earlier followed Ladovsky to ARU) began to devise the principles for planning stadiums, parks, and rally grounds, he rejected metric rows in favor of rhythmical ones.[78] Although, like Ladovsky, he departed from the figure of the peripatetic viewer, unlike his teacher, he relied on emotional rather than on physiological perception. Kalmykov advocated thoroughfares leading from the main entrance to the park's center, which he suggested designing as rhythmical rows proportionally intensifying toward the endpoint (monotonous repetition of metric rows, he explained, would have provoked boredom). Rhythmical accents were to be created with the help of vegetation, sculpture, and small architectural forms, which orchestrated perspectives and viewpoints, inconspicuously regulating the visitors' movement.

In the rationalist theory of composition, Lunacharsky's aesthetics, which had been interpreted by Ladovsky from a positivist, psychotechnic, and energeticist perspective, was returned to its vitalist expressionist humanism.

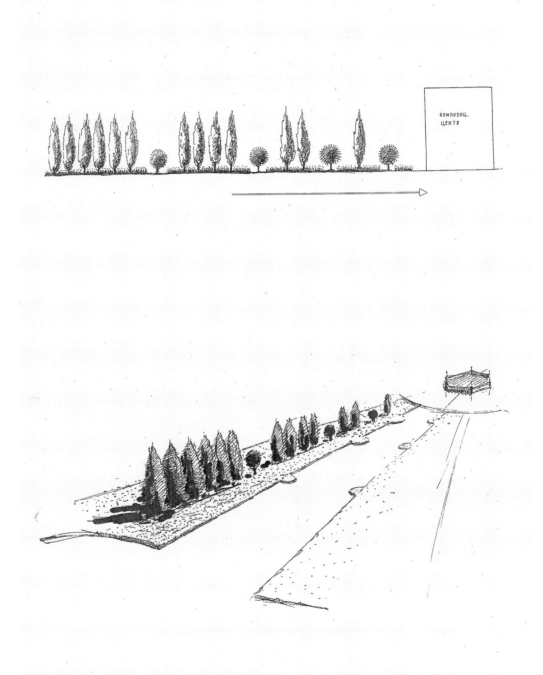

Figure 1.11. Viktor Kalmykov applied the rationalist compositional theory to landscape architecture in his 1936 lecture "Architectural problems of parks (Report on the first stage of work on the subject)." The manuscript is in the collection of the Russian State Archive in Samara (F. P-147, D. 20). These schemes provide examples of "simplest rhythmical groupings of vegetation." Courtesy of the Russian State Archive in Samara.

This rift between Ladovsky and his former students reflected the problem of the monistic via media approach, which left too much room for interpretation. Aspiring for a compromise between or, rather, a dialectical sublation of the oppositions of individuality and collectivity, specificity and universality, mechanicism and vitalism, Soviet rationalism vacillated between the presumed objectivity of scientific management and the politics of affect. What it ultimately struggled to achieve was a solution for the key problem that modernization posed in front of the country: how its ethos of productivism could be reconciled with humanism.

The rationalist theory of space found two—at first sight, unlikely—counterparts in the Western intellectual tradition. Both Gaston Bachelard and Henri Lefebvre elaborated their concepts of space during the 1920s, relying on a related entanglement of ideas and interests: the monistic concept of life, epistemology and philosophy of science, and psychoanalysis. Both, moreover, would proceed to elaborate their own notions of space: Bachelard's phenomenological *The Poetics of Space* (*La poétique de l'espace,* 1957) was followed by Lefebvre's sociological and Marxist *The Production of Space* (*La production de l'espace,* 1974). Both books presented space as subjective, individual reality that resisted Carthusian abstraction. In his dissatisfaction with philosophical rationalism, Bachelard turned to psychoanalysis and, subsequently, to surrealism: while the latter, he argued, expanded the meaning of "reality," demonstrating its fluidity and variety, his own "surrationalism" revealed the elusive character of reason.[79] Bachelard's special interest was the sphere of the psychological, suspended between consciousness and the unconscious: it was in this sphere, which he called reverie, where poetic imagery emerged. As early as 1936, he suggested that "in exactly the same way that we refer to psychoanalysis, so there is a place for rhythmanalysis in psychology. A sick soul—especially one that suffers the pain of time and of despair—has to be cured by living and thinking rhythmically."[80] Lefebvre's final book, *Elements of Rhythmanalysis: Space, Time and Everyday Life* (*Éléments de rythmanalyse: Introduction à la connaissance des rythmes,* 1992), builds upon Bachelard's ideas, suggesting a study of rhythms as a tool for grasping the multiplicity and complexity of life as a unity of the biological and the social. Rhythm, for Lefebvre, emerged at the intersection of space, time, and energy, revealing "that which is not thought: the game and the risk, love, art, violence, in a word, the world, or more precisely the diverse relations between human being and the universe."[81] However, Lefebvre acknowledged that rhythm was just as much a part of discipline and normalization, or dressage, as he called it.[82] It was the latter that Ladovsky, who turned away from rhythm at the moment when others were discovering it, successfully avoided. Whereas Bachelard and Lefebvre, like ASNOVA theorists of composition, explored rhythm as the Freudian unconscious of place—the hidden structure that enabled its uniqueness—Ladovsky was rather interested in unconscious perception as a strategy of universalization. Yet his energetic rationalization too was a humanist strategy, which, even while mechanicist, rigid, and depersonalized, proved to be less susceptible to appropriation by state and corporate ideologies than its more expressive Soviet counterparts, which salvaged individuality only to subordinate it to the order of the transindividual.

TWO

Orientation

El Lissitzky's Evolutionist Urbanism

In 1925, after four years spent in Germany and Switzerland, El Lissitzky returned to Russia. A foreign representative of ASNOVA since the association's foundation in 1923, upon his return he began participating in its activities, most notably coediting, together with Nikolay Ladovsky, the first and, as it turned out to be, the only issue of *Izvestia ASNOVA (ASNOVA Newsletter)* (1926).[1] Betraying ASNOVA's fascination with technologized modernity— "Americanism," as it was then called—the issue was devoted to skyscraper construction.[2] For Lissitzky, the work offered an opportunity not only to publish his *Wolkenbügels* (a series of eight unrealized "horizontal skyscrapers"— literally, "cloud-hangers"—that he had designed for Moscow between 1923 and 1925) but to elaborate a theory of modern, metropolitan urbanism. This theory was summarized, in metaphorical form, in the photo collage that appeared on the last page of the newsletter. The accompanying text proclaimed:

> MAN IS THE MEASURE OF ALL TAILORS
> [Our] great-grandmothers believed that the Earth is the center of the
>   world,
> And man is the measure of all things.
> [They] said about these objects: "What a mighty giant!"
> And this even now is compared with nothing else but a fossilized animal
> Compare this neither with bones, nor with meat,
> Learn to see that which is in front of your eyes,
> Directions for use: Throw [your] head back, lift the paper, and then you
>   will see
> Here is the person, the measure of the tailor,
> But measure architecture with architecture.[3]

The message puzzled subsequent readers. In the 1930s, following the return of classicism, and with it of anthropocentrism, to Soviet architecture, opponents

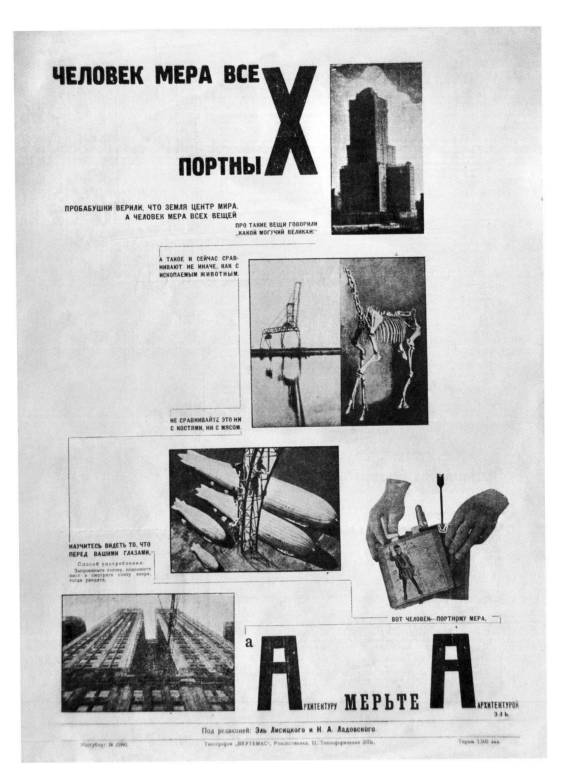

Figure 2.1. El Lissitzky's photo collage "Man Is the Measure of All Tailors" metaphorically summarizes the ASNOVA theory of urbanism. Published in *Izvestiia ASNOVA*, no. 1 (1926): 1.

used it to accuse Lissitzky of calling for *l'art pour l'art*.[4] Later scholars were more sympathetic. Selim Khan-Magomedov argued that the photo collage called for an architecture expressive of an image *(obraz)*; according to Margarete Vöhringer, it pointed to the smallness and pettiness of the human in comparison with the modern city.[5] Neither of these interpretations, however, explains Lissitzky's antianthropocentrism, exemplified in the call for "measuring architecture with architecture." This chapter aims to unpack this message by focusing on Lissitzky's theory of urbanism. Beginning with its theoretical formulation as the photo collage and ending with its application in the *Wolkenbügels*, it relates his vision for the city to the evolutionist discussions of modernity and the new modes of adaptation that it necessitated.

The Eye of an Architect

Lissitzky's iconic 1924 photomontage, the self-portrait known as *The Constructor* among scholars, could provide a point of entry to this discussion. The graph-paper background, the geometrical axes that delineate the space of the image, and a compass held by a hand that seems to emerge directly from the artist's eye, all suggest a reading of *The Constructor* as a celebration of engineering and technology. Indeed, for a long time scholars had interpreted it this way.[6] More recently, historians have begun to doubt this interpretation, pointing to intentional disruptions of clarity, such as areas of darkness and the slight tilt of the axes, which, they suggest, could refer to irrationality.[7] Lissitzky, after all, worked on the portrait from a sanatorium near the Swiss Locarno, where he underwent a surgical treatment of tuberculosis while simultaneously collaborating with Zurich Dadaists. As Leah Dickerman convincingly demonstrated, the self-portrait expressed an embodied, binocular model of vision.[8] Employed to criticize perspectival representation, this model related the self-portrait to his earlier Proun paintings (or, as he called them, "interchange station[s] between painting and architecture").[9] But what is more, as this chapter argues, the self-portrait can be read as a statement about the goals, methods, and principles of modern architecture—a self-portrait of an architect. Trained as an architect-engineer at Riga and Darmstadt polytechnic institutes, Lissitzky did indeed consider architecture his main profession, to which he returned in Locarno as he assumed the work on the *Wolkenbügels* while simultaneously exploring photography.[10]

Why is the constructor-architect's eye eclipsed by his (transparent) hand, holding a compass? And what does the triangular relationship between eye, hand, and compass reveal about architecture? In the early twentieth century,

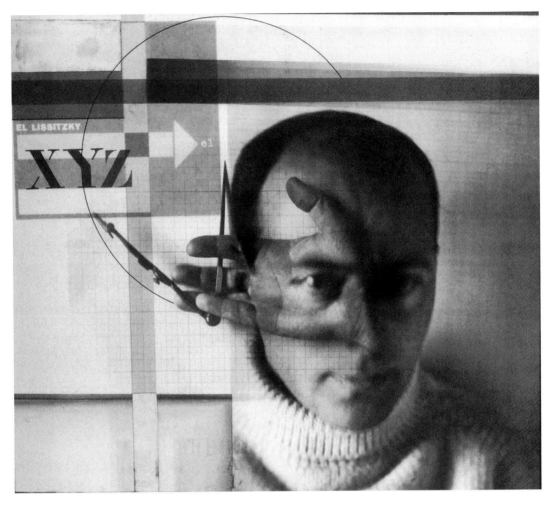

Figure 2.2. El Lissitzky, self-portrait (1924), photomontage. Often referred to as *The Constructor*, El Lissitzky's photomontage can be read as a self-portrait of an architect: a statement about the methods, goals, and principles of modern architecture.

the compass, a counterpart of the T-square, often appeared as the symbol of architecture: in 1919, it was considered, for example, as the emblem of Moscow Architectural Artel, of which Ladovsky was a member.[11] The roots of this symbolism go back to the Renaissance. Discussing Raphael's *School of Athens,* Giorgio Vasari identified the bending figure holding a pair of compasses with the architect Donato Bramante. Furthermore, Vasari reported that Michelangelo believed that "it [was] necessary to have a good eye for measurement rather than a steady hand, because the hands work while the eyes make judgments: he also held to this same method in architecture."[12] Lissitzky insisted that measurement is not merely formal but productive

Figure 2.3. Raphael, *The School of Athens* (1509–11), fresco, Palatium Apostolicum, the Vatican, fragment. The compass was used as a symbol of architecture by Raphael; the bending figure with a pair of compasses has been identified with Donato Bramante.

work: "Construction is an intention to create an independent and concrete object. Unlike composition, which merely discusses various formal possibilities, construction asserts. Compass is the chisel of construction—the brush is an instrument of composition," he responded to the INKhUK debate about the relationship between construction and composition.[13] His own description of the portrait, in a letter to his wife Sophie Küppers, as "my monkey-hand" evokes Friedrich Engels's well-known account of the role of labor in "transition from ape to man": the hand, according to Engels, was the first organ shaped by labor (or purposeful work performed with the help of a tool), stimulating the evolution of the rest of the organism, including higher nervous functions.[14] Ernst Kapp, whose "evolutionary history" of culture appeared nearly simultaneously with Engels's study, similarly saw the hand as the first human tool—"the tool of tools," contained, in an embryonic form, in all instruments that were or would be subsequently developed by humanity, including optical devices, language, and the state.[15] Making a statement about architecture's productive role, the hand holding the compass appears on the Lissitzky-designed cover of the booklet *Architecture VKhUTEMAS* (1927), which publicized the work of the Architecture Department. Insisting that the school prepared students for the practical tasks of socialist construction, the image was deployed to defend the reputation of VKhUTEMAS against accusations of utopianism that followed the notorious thesis defense of Georgy Krutikov (to be discussed later in this chapter).[16]

And yet, as *The Constructor* testifies, the eye was an equally important tool of the architect. Its presence in the photomontage alongside coordinate axes dematerialized architectural labor, presenting it as the work of seeing. "Seeing, of course, is also an A.," stated Lissitzky's epigraph to his 1925 article "A. and Pangeometry" ("K. und Pangeometrie").[17] Here, Lissitzky famously replaced the word "art" with its first letter, reducing it to a geometrical notation—a measuring point in the coordinate system. His technologized eye consisted of "lenses and eye-pieces, precision instruments and reflex cameras, cinematographs which magnify or hold split seconds, Roentgen and X, Y, Z rays," which "have all combined to place in my forehead 20, 2,000, 200,000 very sharp, polished searching eyes."[18] Appearing on the photomontage, the letters X, Y, Z refer to both geometric notations and technologized seeing—to new geometries that modernity brought. Later, reviewing Erich Mendelsohn's popular photo album *America: The Album of an Architect (Amerika: Bilderbuch eines Architekten)*, Lissitzky praised the unusual perspectives that technology opened for architecture: "The modern architect equips himself with the most modern instrument—a small photo camera. He only has to observe well. To be able to see—that is his whole art."[19]

Lissitzky's later lecture on furniture design brought the eye, the hand, and the compass together.[20] It associated the hand with industrial production, arguing that aesthetically good objects "are designed by the hand of the human with the help of the processing part of a modern machine." The eye referred to the precision of seeing: "The eye takes it [a piece of furniture], in its entirety, as true, without wandering around in confusion and getting stuck in it." Finally, the compass represented geometrical regularity: "Its form as a whole and in its details can be constructed with a ruler and a compass."[21] *The Constructor* too could be read as a statement that brings together production, geometry, and perception: new tools of building and seeing resulted in new, disorienting geometries, and modern architecture was tasked with helping the user adapt to them. In what follows, I will unpack this constellation to highlight its effects for Lissitzky's concept of urbanism.

Figure 2.4. Appearing on the cover of the booklet *Architecture VKhUTEMAS* (1927), designed by El Lissitzky, the hand with the compass intended to present the work within the Architecture Department as practical rather than utopian.

Return to Nature

Although asserting seeing as the crucial work of an architect, Lissitzky was quick to distance himself from Renaissance humanism. By the 1920s, the idea that the Renaissance was the defining period in the history of modern culture as articulated by historian Jacob Burckhardt had been subjected to criticism, most prominently by Burckhardt's younger colleague at Basel University, Friedrich Nietzsche, who argued that the human is not "a sure measure of all things" (an everlasting, unchangeable being) but a constantly evolving Hegelian becoming. The philosopher saw his task as "translating man back into nature" by stripping humanity of the deceptive layer of culture.[22] For Burckhardt, Renaissance humanism was a secular worldview that elevated the human to an unprecedented role of master of the universe. This worldview brought to life a set of new orientational mechanisms—artistic techniques of representing and analyzing reality. The most important of those, linear perspective, invented by Filippo Brunelleschi in the fifteenth century, was a mode of pictorial representation that positioned the beholder in the center of the constructed world. It was supported by explorations of the "Vitruvian man"—studies of an idealized human body as the standard of proportionality.[23] Finally, the human body–derived measurement system, which existed since times immemorial, was inscribed into the Renaissance anthropocentric mode of orientation. Declaring that man is the measure of all tailors, Lissitzky assumed a Nietzschean perspective to oppose this anthropocentrism, which was for him associated with bourgeois, rationalist philosophy of the subject, made obsolete by modern science and technology.[24] After all, in Russia, bodily standards of measurement were replaced with the metric system, based on the size of the globe, in 1918, while the burgeoning Gestalt psychology exposed perspective as a visual illusion: according to Soviet psychologist Alexander Luria, this illusion was pertinent to abstract, theoretical culture and was allegedly unknown to practical "primitive" peoples, such as Uzbek peasants.[25] "This is the perspective representation of a pyramid. Where does the tip lie? In depth, or in front?" questioned Lissitzky, exposing, in the manner of psychological illustration, the illusionistic quality of perspective.[26]

Lissitzky's other photographic self-portrait, created simultaneously with *The Constructor*, eloquently illustrates this antianthropocentrism. An ironic postcard, the so-called *Self-Portrait with Wrapped Head and Compass* depicts the artist's head, covered with a hospital patient's cap, in the measurable distance between the compass's legs. Produced as a photogram, the image inverts the appearance of an X-ray, presenting the compass as negative, in the same way that Roentgen technology (which was used in Lissitzky's own

Figure 2.5. "The man in the distance appears to be larger than the boy, though both are of the same height. The illusion is due to the perspective effect." Illustration to David Katz, *Psychological Atlas* (New York: Philosophical Library, 1948), 55, defines perspective as a visual illusion. Courtesy Philosophical Library, New York.

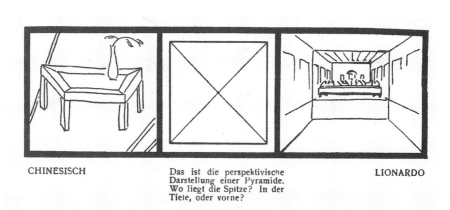

Figure 2.6. "This is the perspective representation of a pyramid. Where does the tip lie? In depth, or in front?" asked El Lissitzky, highlighting the illusionistic quality of the perspectival space. The pyramid appears between representations of reverse ("Chinese") and Renaissance perspective. El Lissitzky, illustration to "A. and Pangeometry" (1925). First published in *Europa-Almanach,* ed. Carl Einstein and Paul Westheim (Potsdam: Kiepenheuer Verlag, 1925), 103–13.

Figure 2.7. El Lissitzky, self-portrait (1924). In contrast to the nearly simultaneous *Constructor*, El Lissitzky's *Self-Portrait with Wrapped Head and Compass* presents its author not as the measurer but as the measured object. Courtesy bpk-Bildagenur.

medical case management) represents internal organs. Meanwhile, similarly reproduced letters that say, in Russian, "eto vam" ("this is for you"), appear within a rectangular field at the bottom, reminiscent of the way information is stamped on medical X rays. In dramatic contrast to *The Constructor*, *The Self-Portrait with Wrapped Head and Compass* presents its creator not as an active explorer of reality but as an object of medical investigation and practice—not as the measurer but as the measured object, not as the divine creator but as a sick, imperfect, and weak body.

In his essay "The Measure of All Things," Lissitzky's collaborator, the Dadaist Jean Arp, accused humankind of attempting to order the universe according to its own standards, which resulted in chaos and madness:

> Man behaves as if he had created the world and could play with it. Pretty much at the beginning of his glorious development he

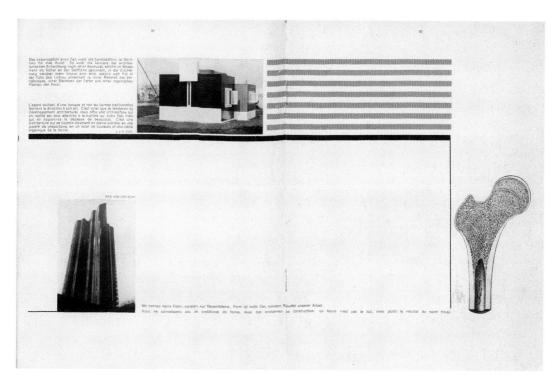

Figure 2.8. The 1924 issue of *Merz*, coedited by El Lissitzky and Kurt Schwitters, compared Mies van der Rohe's "glass skyscraper" project (1922) with "Crane Head and Femur," a drawing from surgeon Julius Wolff's *The Law of Bone Remodeling* (*Das Gesetz der Transformation der Knochen*, 1892), which relied on the analysis of mathematician Karl Culmann.

coined the saying that man was the measure of all things. Then he quickly went to work and turned as much of the world as he could upside down. The Venus de Milo lies shattered on the ground. Man has measured with the measure of all things, himself, measured and presumed. . . . Confusion, unrest, nonsense, insanity and frenzy dominate the world."[27]

Far from simply rejecting reason, Arp went on, Dada called for a better rationality than the limited anthropocentrism fabricated by the Renaissance, which, according to Arp, signified the mind's assault on nature and life. Rather than reducing the world to his own measure, man had to let "all things and man . . . be like nature, measureless."[28]

Quoting the Brokhaus encyclopedia in an editorial for the issue of Dadaist journal *Merz* that he coauthored with Kurt Schwitters, Lissitzky identified such measureless nature with becoming and evolution, as "everything that develops, forms, and moves in and of itself, through its own energy."[29] This

41

processualism was indebted to biologist Raoul Francé, according to whom plants were perfect constructions and as such could provide models for technology.[30] The issue compared Ludwig Mies van der Rohe's curvilinear "glass skyscraper" project (1922) not with a plant, but with a section of the upper end of the human femur. This bone had earlier attracted the attention of scholars and aesthetic thinkers, who observed that its arrangement follows the laws of graphical statics. Zurich mathematician Karl Culmann demonstrated that a mechanical crane given a similar shape exhibited the same tensile and compressive lines as the femur.[31] In other words, adapting to its environment, a good work of architecture led to the same result as the work of nature.

In slightly different terms, the transition from rational anthropomorphic to natural system of measuring was described by Kapp as that from metric (German *Maßstab*) to measure (German *Maß*): "Measure is at work in the sphere of the organic; metric is inserted ready-made into the mechanism. Measure is the reflection of a relation among orders of magnitude, while metric is the expression of a number. In measure, life processes are in motion, while metric is enforced from without."[32] Whereas mechanical objects were numerically measurable, an organism was assessed as ratios between its structural elements. Inasmuch as these ratios were often inexpressible in rational numbers, modern artists became interested in the mathematical concept of irrationality.

Among others, Lissitzky embarked on an exploration of such mathematical concepts as Carl Friedrich Gauss's imaginary numbers and Georg Cantor's irrational numbers and uncountable sets.[33] The title "A. and Pangeometry" betrays his fascination with the 1855 book *Pangeometry* by mathematician Nikolay Lobachevsky, which offered an early theoretical account of a non-Euclidian geometry. For the modernists, who associated Euclidian geometry with perspectival representation, the emergence of new geometries testified to the urgent need of transcending perspective. Urbanism, according to Lissitzky, had already transitioned from the centralized Renaissance city to the geometric regularity of the modern American grid: scrutinizing the plan of Manhattan, he had earlier noted that whereas the planning of earlier European cities was subordinated to local topography, the grid remained uninterrupted by it, becoming, as it were, a model of non-Euclidian geometry on a curved surface.[34]

In "A. and Pangeometry" (which was first conceived as a chapter in a book titled *1 = 1,* an equation discussed by Francé as describing a perfect state of natural harmony), Lissitzky delineated an evolutionist vision, according to which every epoch in the history of science generated its own concept of

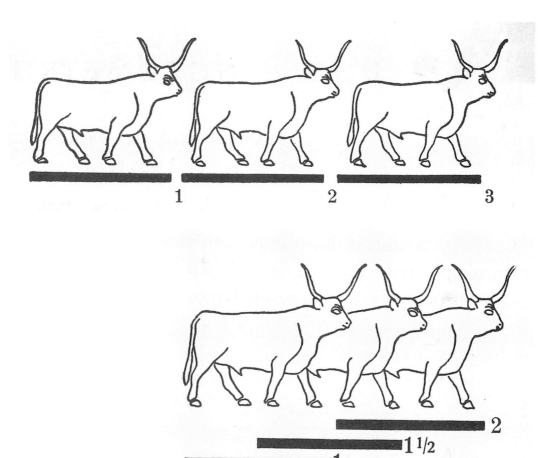

Figure 2.9. Lissitzky's argument in "A. and Pangeometry" relied on Oswald Spengler's *Decline of the West* (*Der Untergang des Abendlandes,* first volume, 1918), which paired mathematical systems of different civilizations with their artistic achievements. "Planimetric space" (represented here), which informed ancient Near Eastern art, was, for Lissitzky, a product of calculus. He traced its evolutionary development from the simple, flat numerical progression "1, 2, 3,…" *(above),* in which all objects are fully visible, to a more complex, relief-like progression "1, 1 ½, 2, 2 ½,…" in which parts of the objects are obscured, resulting in the emergence of relief *(below).* El Lissitzky, [Planimetric space], illustrations to "A. and Pangeometry."

space and its way of representing space. His classification, as Peter Nisbet suggested, relied on Oswald Spengler's popular *The Decline of the West* (*Der Untergang des Abendlandes,* first volume published in 1918).[35] Spengler's "reactionary modernist," "morphological" approach saw all human artefacts, including architecture, as externalizations of "life" (sometimes equated with *Gestalt,* design), which was juxtaposed to abstract law played out in technology and epitomized by the modern city.[36] Whereas the organic epistemology of life was based on the notion of fact, lifeless science was looking for abstract "truths." However, Spengler was far from simply denouncing technology and the city. Technology, he believed, possessed a spirit *(Geist)* of its own that was expressed in the Faustian struggle against nature and understood by the engineer, "the erudite priest of the machine."[37] This animation of technology allowed Spengler to claim that he avoided the reductive opposition of idealism (which had simply dismissed technology) and materialism (which had remained blind to technology's cultural significance).

Departing from Spengler's approach, Lissitzky paired mathematical systems of different civilizations with their artistic achievements. A product of calculus, planimetric space, "A. and Pangeometry" argued, had informed ancient Near Eastern art. The invention of Euclidian geometry led to its replacement by three-dimensional perspectival space, which was subsequently destroyed by Lobachevsky, Gauss, and Riemann. These mathematical discoveries were developed by artistic movements: impressionism, cubism, and, ultimately, suprematism. Having rejected the Renaissance anthropocentric order, twentieth-century art and architecture arrived at an Einsteinian fragmentation of the world. Lissitzky's epistemological program challenged the status of bourgeois, rational culture with its anthropocentric system of orientation based on perspective, the golden section, and the anthropometric standard. To measure architecture with architecture, the modern architect had to reject this obsolete rationalism with its claims of truthfulness and completeness and, as will be discussed below, to partake instead in the unrationalizable urban and technological environment, in order to understand its *Geist* and to establish a new system of orientation in it.

The Riemann Space

Lissitzky had first used the motif of the eye and the compass in 1922, when his collage *Tatlin at Work on the Monument to the Third International* presented the eye as the compass measuring a universe of suprematist and Proun-like geometrical figures and planes (Plate 3).[38] *Tatlin at Work* can also be read as Lissitzky's symbolic self-portrait: Vladimir Tatlin, after all, had little to do with suprematism, and his famous Monument to the Third International does not appear on the image. Lissitzky, moreover, had related his Prouns to the mathematical discussions of infinity and irrationality, which are referenced by the formulas on the collage. Finally, the horizontally tilted female face, whose mouth and half of an eye are sealed with suprematist rectangles, and—tellingly—whose only visible eyeball is encircled with a line in pencil, provides a further clue: perspective, the collage affirmed, was a product of the Renaissance, monocular model of vision.

Indeed, perspective presumed the existence of an immobile, abstract outside viewer. In the words of Lissitzky's friend Adolf Behne, perspective was a "naturalistic construction of spatial or temporal kind, a construction that presupposed for the artist a fixed, static position outside of the body and the story."[39] As demonstrated by Jonathan Crary, the dissolution of perspective arrived with the rejection of monocularity: this rejection led to the disorientation and fragmentation of the worldview inasmuch as it eliminated the presumption of truthfulness (the visual image was a psychological effect fabricated in the brain of the beholder).[40] If the static monocular space was the space of painting, the binocular space was that of sculptural relief. Relief (and thus depth) was perceived, according to common psychological knowledge, in the process of the kinetic movement of the eyeballs. "The relief is given by the play of the optic axes in uniting, in rapid *succession,* similar points of the two pictures," explained the inventor of lenticular stereoscope David Brewster in 1856.[41] Some forty years later, Adolf von Hildebrand distinguished between two types of vision: seeing (*schauen*) and scanning (*abtasten*).[42] Seeing occurred when an object was observed from a distance, visible in its entirety; it resulted in a two-dimensional image (*Gesichtsvorstellung*). Scanning, meanwhile, occurred when the distance between the subject and the object was minimal: proximity necessitated movements of eyeballs and resulted in obtaining several fragmented "kinesthetic images" (*Bewegungsvorstellungen),* which allowed an evaluation of depth. Whereas sculpture, according to Hildebrand, operated with kinesthetic ideas and painting expressed a visual idea on a plane, two other arts—relief and architecture—engaged both.[43]

Discussing the consequences of the planar (relief-like) organization of space, Crary observed that this model entailed a fundamental ambiguity about the distance between planes and thus expressed a worldview marked by a lack of order.[44] Gilles Deleuze and Félix Guattari called this model the "Riemann space," observing that "each vicinity in a Riemann space is like a shred of Euclidian space but the linkage between one vicinity and the next is not defined."[45] This model referred to topology—a modern field of mathematics that disregards the geometric form of the figure and instead analyzes connections between its different parts. Topology and architecture have been historically connected: the earliest formulation of a topological problem is said to be a 1741 article by Leonhard Euler in the journal of the St. Petersburg Academy of Sciences, which proved that it was mathematically impossible to pass through all the seven bridges of Königsberg without going through the same bridge twice.[46] In the nineteenth century, topology was developed, among others, by Bernhard Riemann as "qualitative geometry," distinct from traditional geometry, which focuses on quantitative relations. This model was explored in the early 1920s within the Berlin international constructivist movement, in which Lissitzky participated, in particular, by Theo van Doesburg and Mies van der Rohe, who defined space as a series of planes the distances between which remained indistinct.[47] Speaking of suprematist painting, Lissitzky likewise explained that the distances between depicted figures "are measured only by the intensity and the position of the strictly defined color-areas. These distances cannot be measured by any finite measure."[48]

Infinity, Lissitzky believed, was best expressed by axonometry, a mode of architectural representation that he had employed in the Prouns. Pioneered in the late nineteenth century by architectural historian Auguste Choisy and enthusiastically used at the Bauhaus, axonometry presented three-dimensional objects without perspective foreshortening: parallel lines remained parallel, which allowed for a consistency of scale.[49] Lissitzky likened the objective, nonillusionistic character of axonometry to mathematical representations of four-dimensional and other physically impossible spaces. Advancing "the ultimate tip of the visual pyramid . . . into infinity," axonometry, he claimed, created "the ultimate illusion of irrational space, with its infinite extensibility into the background and foreground."[50]

The importance of mathematical and esoteric theories of irrational (mathematically conceivable but physically impossible) spaces for modernist art has been well documented.[51] The founder of suprematism Kazimir Malevich, Lissitzky's senior colleague and interlocutor since 1919, opposed "logic, natural order, and philistine meaning and prejudice" from the standpoint of the esoteric thought of P. D. Ouspensky. A "different form of reason," Malevich argued, arose within him, making him reject traditional forms of rationality, replacing them with the "transrational"—not an absence of order, but a new order that "has its own law and construction and also meaning."[52] As early as 1880, British mathematician and science fiction writer Charles Howard Hinton suggested that three-dimensional figures might be imagined as cross-sections of four-dimensional forms passing through a three-dimensional plane; later scholars compared architect and theosophist Claude Bragdon's 1913 visualizations of Hinton's ideas to suprematist art.

Emphasizing the role of spatial localization (rotation) of figures, Bragdon's illustrations evoke the Prouns of Lissitzky, according to whom, "Rotating, we screw into space."[53] A similar spatial concept was later employed by Georgy Krutikov in the psychotechnical tests on spatial combination that he developed at VKhUTEIN under Ladovsky's and possibly Lissitzky's supervision.[54]

Figure 2.10. El Lissitzky's "Proun on the theme of the horizontal skyscraper" (early 1920s) is an example of a Proun (from Russian "Project of the Affirmation of the New"), a novel art system invented by the artist in 1919. Defined as "interchange station[s] between painting and architecture," the Prouns are axonometric representations of abstract geometric volumes. Courtesy of the State Tretyakov Gallery, Moscow.

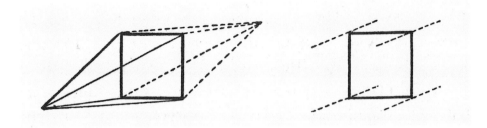

Figure 2.11. This diagram illustrated Lissitzky's concept of irrational space in "A. and Pangeometry." Advancing "the ultimate tip of the visual pyramid ... into infinity," axonometry, Lissitzky argued, created "the ultimate illusion of irrational space, with its infinite extensibility into the background and foreground." First published in *Europa-Almanach*, ed. Carl Einstein and Paul Westheim (Potsdam: Kiepenheuer Verlag, 1925), 103–13.

Such tests, which asked students to arrange flat and volumetric forms in space, were commonly used by psychologists.[55] However, Krutikov's approach differed in its reliance on the methods of mathematical combinatorics, a subfield of set theory that studied combinations within sets. Combinatorics had been a field of special interest for Wilhelm Ostwald, whose *Atlas of Forms* (1922–23) began with three basic forms—the triangle, the square, and the hexagon— that were subjected to three basic operations: translation, rotation, and reflection.[56] Having turned to combinatorics at Ladovsky's suggestion, Krutikov soon realized that he had to supplement it with additional formulas, which, in the spirit of Bragdon, considered the spatial localization of objects. He established correlations between the number of possible spatial combinations, the quantity and shape of figures, and the number of axes along which they were rotated. A circle, a square, and a rectangle rotated along four axes, for instance, would produce 192 possible combinations. Against Ladovsky's initial expectation that the number of possible combinations would be finite—and that they could thus be rationalized—Krutikov concluded that the number was infinite.[57] Spatial disorientation was a law of modern mathematics.

In the modern city, the effect of disorientation resulted from the change of viewpoint. In the 1870s, architect Hermann Maertens had determined that a building was best observed from a position that formed an angle of 27 degrees between the eye and the highest point of the cornice because a broader (45 degree) angle made the eye dissolve the details, whereas a narrower (18 degree) angle caused the image to dissipate within the environment.[58] Distant seeing disappeared in the modern city, where the angle of viewing, as Lissitzky noted, approached 90 degrees. Reviewing Mendelsohn's *America*, Lissitzky pointed out that it offered not photographs but "a dramatic film": "Quite unusual scenes unfold in front of our eyes. One must lift the book above the head

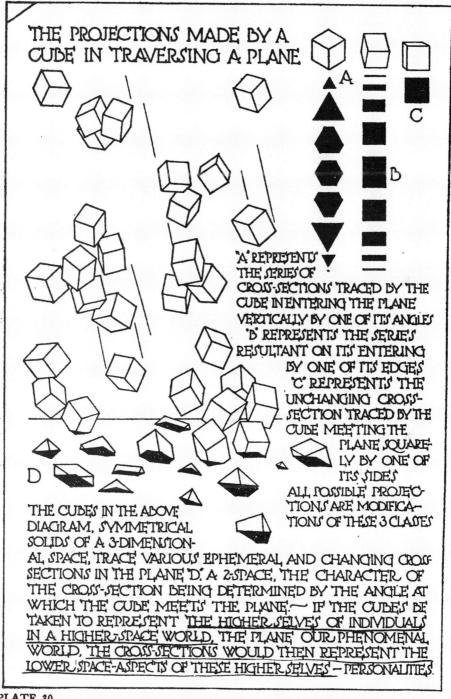

Figure 2.12. This image from architect and theosophist Claude Bragdon's book *A Primer of Higher Space (The Fourth Dimension)* (1913) visualized nineteenth-century mathematician Charles Howard Hinton's idea that three-dimensional figures might be imagined as cross-sections of four-dimensional forms passing through a three-dimensional plane. Claude Bragdon, *A Primer of Higher Space (The Fourth Dimension)* (Rochester, NY: Manas Press, 1913).

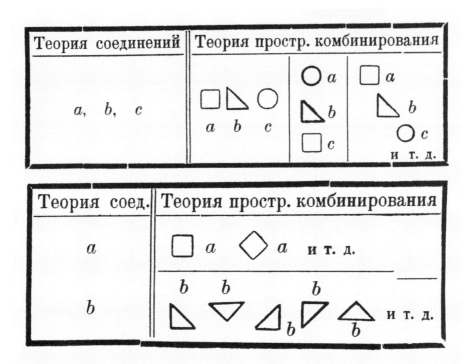

Figure 2.13. Ladovsky's student Georgy Krutikov researched the potential for applying mathematical combinatorics in architecture, establishing correlations between the number of possible spatial combinations, the quantity and shape of figures, and the number of axes along which they were rotated. This image illustrates his article "The application of the theory of combinatorics to research and measurement of the capacity for spatial combination," *Arkhitektura i VKhUTEIN*, no. 1 (1929): 5.

and rotate it to understand some of the photographs. The architect shows us America not from a distance, but from inside, leading us through the street canyons."[59] The modern (photo) eye of the architect was a doppelganger of Dziga Vertov's cine-eye, which equally dispensed with the immobility of the monocular beholder, affirming, instead, constant motion and defamiliarizing viewpoints.[60] The modern architect had to notice and appreciate this change: "Learn to see that which is in front of your eyes. Directions for use: Throw [your] head back, lift the paper, and then you will see." Resulting from this approach would be an architecture that "is not only viewed from a distance, by the eye (painting), and not only touched by the hand (sculpture) but is that in which one lives and moves—an architecture of space and time."[61]

Lissitzky's *Izvestia ASNOVA* collage compared the Shelton Hotel in New York, by Arthur Loomis Harmon (1922), with the statue of the Russian emperor Alexander III (the image was removed from the published version), and

Figure 2.14. Fritz Giese's geometric thinking test from his *Handbuch psychotechnischer Eignungsprüfungen* (Halle: Carl Marhold, 1925), 76, provided Krutikov with a model for testing spatial imagination.

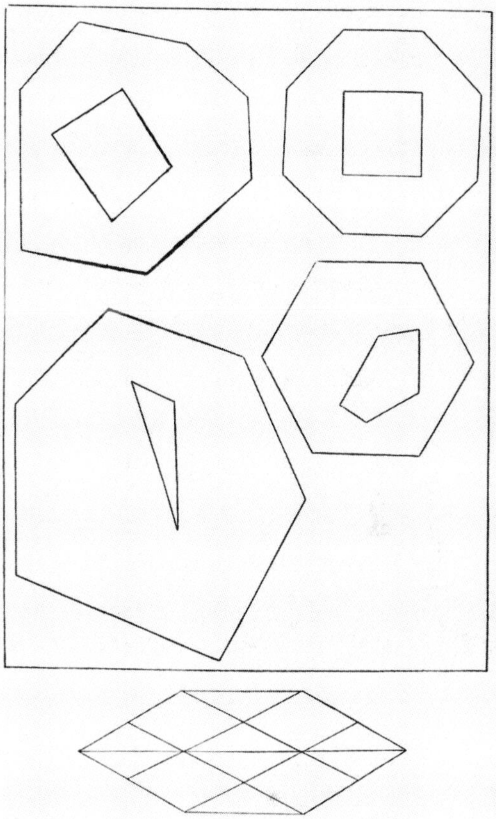

Abb. 12. Geometrische Teilfiguren.

a port crane with a fossil skeleton. The effect of distance, the comparisons confirmed, deformed even the most modern buildings, casting them as regressive relics of old historic and even paleontological epochs. Close-up views from below, on the other hand, distorted and defamiliarized the city. Seen abruptly from above, a dirigible mast appeared to curve.[62] Meanwhile, the building masses and profile of the 1923 Equity Trust Building in New York, when captured directly from below, "narrowed ... toward the top (a new law of perception)."[63] The kinetic, binocular city lost its painterly qualities, perceived solely as relief—a series of *Bewegungsvorstellungen*. Without the perspectival viewpoint, the humans could no longer compare buildings with their bodies—in the modern world, only commercial sewing patterns, an instrument of the standardization of clothing that appeared at the end of the nineteenth century, were measured according to the size of the body.[64]

For Lissitzky, disorientation was not only an artistic technique intended, like Viktor Shklovsky's notion of estrangement, to destabilize the habitual

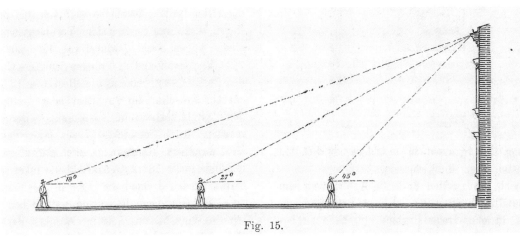

Figure 2.15. In the 1870s, architect Hermann Maertens determined that a building was best observed from a position that formed an angle of 27 degrees between the eye and the highest point of the cornice because a broader (45 degree) angle made the eye dissolve the details, whereas a narrower (18 degree) angle caused the image to dissipate within the environment. Illustration to Hermann Maertens, *Der Optische Maßstab, oder, Die Theorie und Praxis des ästhetischen Sehens in den bildenden Künsten: Auf Grund der Lehre der physiologischen Optik* (Bonn: Max Cohen & Sohn, 1877), 49–50.

viewpoint and thus bring attention to what otherwise remains unregistered by consciousness: it was the everyday predicament of modernity. In his Hannover and Dresden "demonstration spaces" that he designed for art exhibitions in 1926–28, Lissitzky not only represented but intentionally provoked this condition.[65] Yet, it was the disorientating character of modernity that provided new opportunities for orientation. As he had declared as early as 1920, "emptiness, chaos, the unnatural, become space, that is: order, certainty, plastic form."[66]

From Pangeometry to Panarchitecture

Irrational space was superseded, Lissitzky maintained, by imaginary space, which not only represented movement but was generated by it, such as when rotation transformed rods into disks and planes into cylinders. "Time now becomes a factor of prime consideration as a new constituent of plastic F[orm]," he explained, identifying the illusion of space caused by our perception of motion:

> Our visual faculty is limited when it comes to the conception of movement and indeed of the whole state of the object: ex.,

Figure 2.16. El Lissitzky, "Man Is the Measure of All Tailors," photomontage, unpublished draft version. El Lissitzky's photomontage from *Izvestia ASNOVA* compared an American skyscraper, the Shelton Hotel in New York (Arthur Loomis Harmon, 1922), with the statue of the Russian emperor Alexander III (the image was subsequently removed), and a port crane with a fossil skeleton. The comparisons served to demonstrate that distance deformed even the most modern buildings, while close-up views from below (the new modern metropolitan viewpoint) distorted and defamiliarized the city. Having lost the perspectival viewpoint, humans could no longer rely on their bodies as the standard of measuring the city. Courtesy of the Russian State Archive for Literature and the Arts, fond 2361, op.1, ed. khr. 59, l. 51.

> disconnected movements separated by periods shorter than 1/30
> of a second create the impression of a continuous movement. . . .
> It generates an entirely new object, that is to say, a new expres-
> sion of space, which is there for as long as the movement lasts
> and is therefore imaginary.[67]

"Space is a reality of sensory experience," Lissitzky's fellow constructivist László Moholy-Nagy likewise declared.[68] Evoking Moholy-Nagy's attempts at dematerializing reality through photography and kinetic and light sculpture, Lissitzky claimed that he "arrived at an a-material materiality." He strove for a similar effect in his demonstration spaces: in both of them, a forest of vertical laths, white on one side and black on the other, transformed a wall, making the room seem white, grey, or black depending on the position of the spectator. According to Sigfried Giedion, who reviewed Lissitzky's *Abstract Cabinet* (the demonstration space in Hannover), the effect of the strips was to "throw vertical clefts of shadow and dematerialize the wall to the point where it seems to dissolve completely."[69]

In 1925–26, Lissitzky explored the dematerializing effect of movement in his photo collage *Record* (possibly a maquette for a photographic mural intended to decorate ASNOVA's Red Stadium in Moscow[70]), which reused one of the photographs published in Mendelsohn's *America—Broadway at Night* by the Danish architect and photographer Knud Lönberg-Holm. "Uncanny," wrote Mendelsohn about the effect produced by the nocturnal metropolis: "The contours of houses are wiped out. But in the mind they nevertheless rise, run into each other, collide with each other." The modern city, which Mendelsohn classified as grotesque, was "unordered in its excessiveness," yet "still full of fantastic beauty."[71] Overlaying Lönberg-Holm's photograph with an image of a jumping hurdler, Lissitzky's photo collage introduces the concept of motion to the visual account of the modern city: the distorting photographic effect of motion produced by long exposure was similar, it confirmed, to the effect received when sources of light were photographed at nighttime.

The concept of imaginary space as a product of movement informed the diploma project that Krutikov defended in 1929.[72] Scandalizing critics with its "utopianism," the diploma drew from the experience of Krutikov's earlier collaborations with Lissitzky on the "architectural design of [Konstantin] Tsiolkovsky's dirigible" within the ASNOVA Section of Transportation Architecture (1926), on the design of the All-Union Printing Trades Exhibition in Moscow (1927), where Lissitzky's *Record* appeared among the exhibits, and on the Soviet pavilion in the Pressa exhibition in Cologne (1928), whose centerpiece, a giant red star, was decorated with neon lights.[73] Modernity, Krutikov

Figure 2.17. El Lissitzky, *Record* (1926), photomontage. Lissitzky reused Knud Lönberg-Holm's photograph *Broadway at Night,* reproduced in Mendelsohn's *America.* Introducing the image of the jumping hurdler, Lissitzky compared the photographic effects of fast motion and urban light.

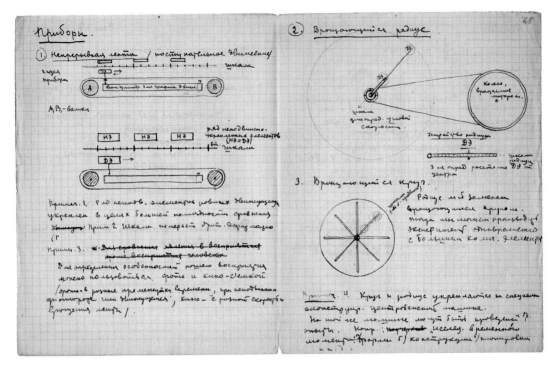

Figure 2.18. At the Psychotechnical Laboratory Georgy Krutikov studied the perception of moving form with the help of specially invented apparatuses. His notebook sketches illustrate their principles. The first device, a moving band attached to a "dynamic element" that ran in front of a fixed scale with two "static elements" of the same size, was to evaluate the perceived change of size caused by movement. The second, a rotating wheel, was to demonstrate changes in the perceived distance between an element and the center, which depended on the speed of the wheel's rotation. Courtesy of the A. V. Shchusev State Museum of Architecture, Moscow ("Panarchitecture" sketchbook from Georgy Krutikov collection at the Archive of the Museum, KPof 5291/131).

declared, led to a dramatic expansion of the very notion of architecture: "That which is today understood as architecture, in fact, is only a case of architecture in general, or, as I call it, panarchitecture." "Panarchitecture is a system of spatial relationships in a four-dimensional continuum. The conditions of space, time, and gravitation determine architectural systems, which, combined, comprise panarchitecture."[74] To explore the laws of this four-dimensional architecture, which was to be brought to life by technologies of movement, Krutikov conducted research at the Psychotechnical Laboratory, inventing machines that measured the perception of moving form. The purpose of one, a moving band attached to a "dynamic element" that ran in front of a fixed scale with two "static elements" of the same size, was to evaluate the perceived change of size caused by movement; another, a rotating wheel, demonstrated changes in the perceived distance between an element and the center, which depended on the speed of the wheel's rotation.

An outcome of this research, Krutikov's diploma consisted of two parts, the theoretical and the visual. The theoretical part included sixteen illustrated tables that paired the formal evolution of human dwellings with the evolution of transportation. The first three of them, "The Visual Deformation of a Dynamic Form," "The Composition of Dynamic Structures," and "The Form-Making of Dynamic Element," articulated the main theoretical problems posed by the introduction of a temporal dimension for architecture (Plate 4).[75] The remaining thirteen tables delineated the evolution of architecture from the cave to "the house in the air" as a consequence of the conquest of "new spaces and novel viewpoints"—an idea that had earlier been espoused by Lissitzky in the essay "Wheel, Propeller, and What Follows" ("Rad, Propeller und das Folgende," 1923), which postulated that the evolution of architectural form followed the development of transportation from foot (architecturally reflected in the pyramid) to wheel (reflected by trains, ocean liners, and cars) to propeller (reflected by airplanes).

These theoretical discoveries assumed a visual shape as "The City of the Future," a project that responded to such contemporaneous international projects as the suspended houses of Heinz and Bodo Rasch (1927–28) and Buckminster Fuller's Lightful Towers from the same period. While the Rasch brothers acquired a reputation among modernist architects due to their work at the Weißenhofsiedlung and publications, Fuller's work would have been accessible to Lissitzky through Lönberg-Holm, who moved to the United States, where he became the American representative of ASNOVA, shortly after meeting him in 1922.[76] Radicalizing these projects, Krutikov's city consisted of two parts. The vertical, which served as housing, was suspended in the air, appearing as a paraboloid formed by hovering individual residential complexes located in tiers one above the other. The horizontal part, devoted to production, was located beneath the vertical, sprawled over the surface of the earth. The connection between the two was provided by a universal "individual moving cell" (similarly to Fuller's 4D Transport, it functioned on land, on water, and in air)—both a vehicle and a minimal dwelling unit. However, unlike Fuller, who identified the fourth dimension with longevity and duration, Lissitzky and Krutikov saw it as a phenomenon of perception. In Krutikov's drawing, whose stylistic effects evoke night photography, the rings of hovering residential complexes became a gleaming thimble, which appeared as if perceived from an individual moving cell taking off from the earth to its harbor in the residential section. The architecturalization of imaginary space, illusionary and fluctuating panarchitecture was as "grotesque" as the modern city (Plate 5). What it first needed was an orientational system. Designed slightly earlier, Lissitzky's *Wolkenbügels* intended to provide just that.

Figure 2.19. Krutikov's analytical Table 14, "Conquering new spaces and novel viewpoints," demonstrates how technologies of movement determine the perspective from which the human sees the world. Georgy Krutikov, "The City of the Future," diploma project, VKhUTEIN (1929). Courtesy of the A. V. Shchusev State Museum of Architecture, Moscow (PIa 11200/14).

Hängehäuser von Brüder Rasch. Schnitt. Am Mast verläuft die gesamte Installation

Zwölf Wohnetagen von 15 m Durchmesser sind an Masten aus genietetem Stahlrohr aufgehängt. Die Masten sind zickzack aufgestellt und fortlaufend miteinander verspannt. Der Zugang zu den Etagen ge-

Hängehäuser von Brüder Rasch. System

156

schieht über Zugangsstraßen von 4 m Breite. Die Zugangsstraßen regulieren durch das Gewicht die Ausdehnungsdifferenz der Kabelverspannung. Alle zwölf Masten befindet sich ein Wohnhausaggregat mit Treppen, Aufzügen usw. Die Montage geschieht von oben nach unten. Aus diesem Grunde ergibt sich ein mehr oder weniger großer notwendiger Spielraum über der Bodenfläche. Dadurch ist die gesamte Bodenfläche für Verkehr und Anlagen frei. Die Straßenführung ist unabhängig von der Bebauung.

1. Mast für 12 Wohnetagen, 49 m Höhe.
Der Mast ist aus einzelnen Schalen zusammengenietet, bildet ein Rohr mit Fischleib, das an der weitesten Stelle einen Durchmesser von 1,50 m besitzt und endigt in Kugelflächen von 32 cm Durchmesser. Der Mast ist genügend sicher gegen Winddruck, Knickung und jede Belastung, die sich aus den aufgehängten Etagen ergibt. Die auf dem Boden aufsitzende Kugelfläche von 32,5 cm Durchmesser besteht aus Stahl. Sie liegt in einem entsprechenden Stahllager, das auf einem runden Betonfundament von 9,50 m Durchmesser befestigt ist.

2. Verspannung.
Die Masten sind mit gut isolierten Drahtseilen in einem Neigungswinkel von etwa 45 Grad verspannt, und zwar so, daß bei der Verspannung lauter Dreiecke entstehen. Die Drahtseile müssen eine Tragkraft von 104 Tonnen besitzen. Sie sind mit Betongewichten von etwa 100 cbm im Boden verankert. Der Durchhang der Seile beträgt nur 24,5 cm maximal. Die größtmögliche Schwankung der Masten durch Winddruck beträgt an der Spitze 3 cm, also so gut wie null.

3. Aufhängung der Etagen.
An der Spitze des Mastes sind an Flacheisen die einzelnen Etagen aufgehängt. Die Flacheisen werden durch einen Druckring, der über der obersten Etage liegt, auf die Entfernung von 5 m vom Mast abgedrückt. Jede Etage ist an einem eigenen Flacheisen befestigt, so daß durch die obere Etage ein Bündel von 12 Flacheisen hindurchgeht.

157

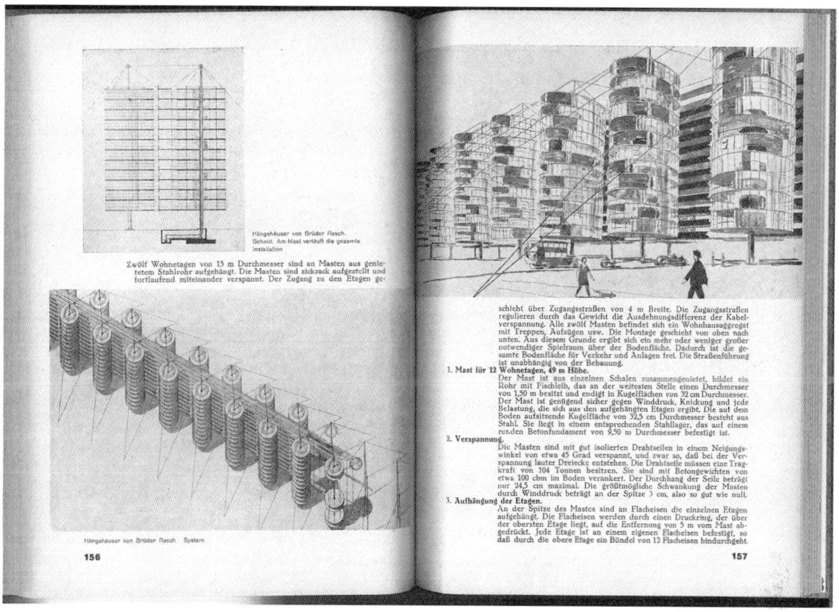

Figure 2.20. Brothers Heinz and Bodo Rasch developed the structural system of "suspended houses" in 1927–28. They published it in their book *Wie bauen? Materialien und Konstruktionen für industrielle Produktion* (Stuttgart: Wedekind, 1928), 156–57. A page earlier, the same book features a work by Mikhail Korzhev from Ladovsky's studio.

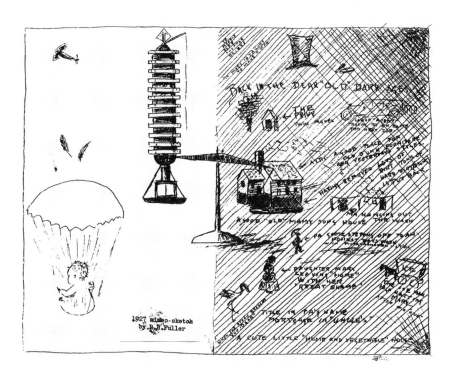

Figure 2.21. Buckminster Fuller's 4D Lightful Tower project (1927–28) explored the possibilities of lightweight construction. Pioneering the use of plastic in architecture, the project consisted of a central service core and plastic envelope. As this sketch illustrates, the resultant building would be so light that it could soar into the air. In Fuller's project, this soaring remains a metaphor. Courtesy of the Estate of R. Buckminster Fuller.

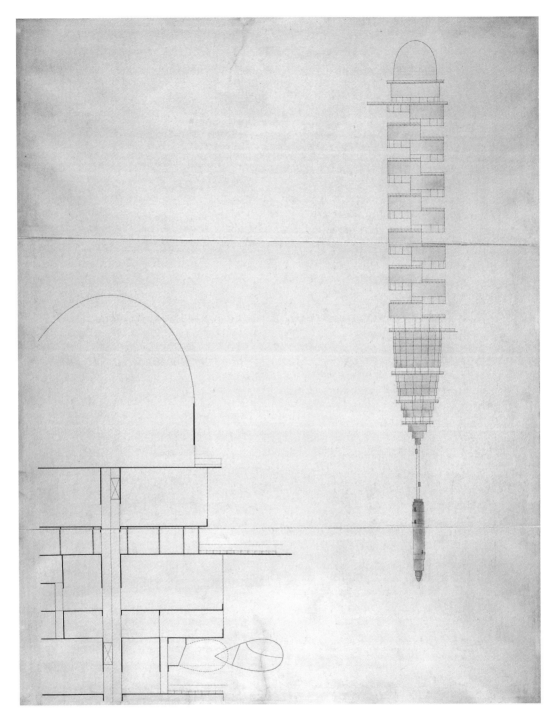

Figure 2.22. Georgy Krutikov, "Hotel-Type Dwelling," part of "The City of the Future," VKhUTEIN diploma project (1929). Dubbed "The Flying City," the visual part of Georgy Krutikov's diploma project was a speculation on the formal problems that the evolution of the dwelling would pose for architecture. The "Hotel-type dwelling" (here, in facade and section) can be seen as Fuller's Lightful Tower that tore the umbilical cord of infrastructure and literally soared into the air. The lowest part of the hotel was a structural matrix for plugging in individual flying cells, which functioned as minimal dwelling units; the middle part provided more developed housing units for longer stays; the upper part served as communal space. Courtesy of the A. V. Shchusev State Museum of Architecture, Moscow (PIa 11201/1).

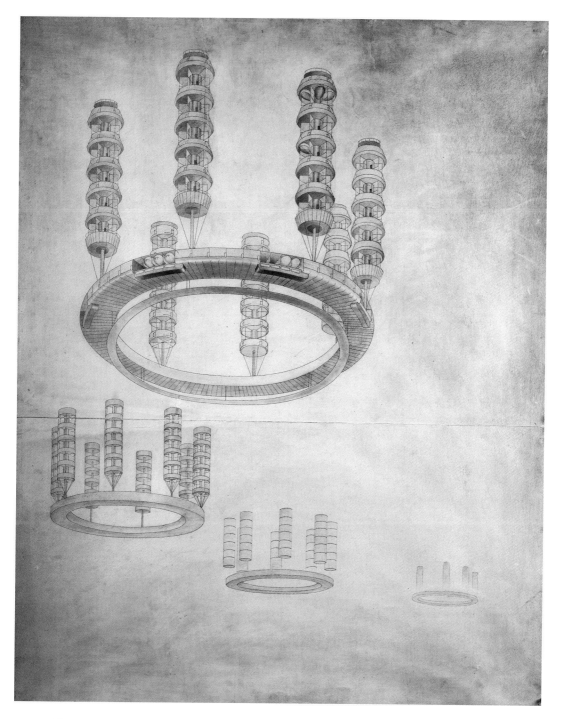

Figure 2.23. Georgy Krutikov, "The Labor Commune," part of "The City of the Future," VKhUTEIN diploma project (1929). The Labor Commune was a complex of eight housing blocks anchored in the ring that served as the communal block. Each individual unit had a slot for berthing the individual flying cell; additional berthing slots for guests were located in the communal block. Courtesy of the A. V. Shchusev State Museum of Architecture, Moscow (PIa 11116/1).

Scale

Mendelsohn's *America* spoke to a circulating set of beliefs about Americanism, as if illustrating the urban environment that Georg Simmel in 1903 famously diagnosed as provoking the loss of mental energy.[77] Fast movement, the flickering of neon lights, the noise of traffic, the unprecedented and sometimes illogical scale of buildings ("an isolated building growing without restraint, almost like tropical vegetation"), all disoriented and confused the urban dweller, requiring new modes of reasoning.[78] The disorientation was further augmented by the absence of the compositional center in the modern grid. Architectural historian Michael K. Hays interpreted Dadaism and the early work of Mies van der Rohe as such attempts at demonstrating "the futility of conventional modes of reasoning in the face of the chaotic city." Both the *Merz* column by Schwitters and the "glass skyscraper" by Mies, according to Hays, "attest to the fact that the humanist conceptions of formal rationality and self-creating subjectivity cannot cope with the irrationality of actual experience. In the modern city such constructs of rationality fail to function, and the mind, the subject, is consequently unable to perceive a pattern in the chaos."[79] Instead, Schwitters and Mies, Hays argues, suggested reflecting upon the causes of crisis and resisting it by asserting radically different, subversive objects within the critically perceived environment. The position of Lissitzky, who in the early 1920s was close to both, simultaneously supports and complicates this assessment.

"The conditions out of which old cities developed have long since disappeared, but we continue to live in their petrified shells," Lissitzky pronounced. In the modern city, "Traffic has become a major problem. It is increasingly becoming a question of time rather than space." Modern urbanism, according to Lissitzky, faced the choice between "geometry" and "the organic": whereas the capitalist city opted for geometry (the grid) as a system of order and control, in a socialist city, "a community organizes itself into a living organism, with each individual playing his inseparable part, incapable of separate existence."[80] The city, in other words, was the field of an ongoing battle between the receding irrational and the emerging imaginary space.

Looking for an organic way of making the city "as clear and logical as a beehive," Lissitzky turned to the scale of buildings.[81] This very cause of disorientation in the capitalist city, he had realized early on, could became a new orientational mechanism:

> There is one element to which special importance attaches—
> scale. Scale gives life to relationships in space. It is that which de-

termines whether every organism remains whole or is destroyed—it holds all the parts together. The index for the growth of modern man is the ability to see and appreciate the relative scales of everything that has been made.[82]

At the beginning of the century, scale was discovered as a tool for ordering the city by articulating its hierarchy and structure, in particular, in the work of Hildebrand and art historian Albert Erich Brinckmann.[83] Relying on their work, Soviet rationalists differentiated between the two varieties of scale, actual and perceived: if the former was accurately conveyed by axonometry and technical drawing, the latter became the task of architecture. Nikolay Dokuchaev suggested aligning the size of a building's segments with human height to give a building the measure with which its height can be evaluated by the human.[84] With a renewed importance, the question of the size of the module was posed by standardization: Le Corbusier and Ernst Neufert would later reintroduce their versions of the Vitruvian man as the module of standardized architecture. The editors of *Izvestia ASNOVA,* however, argued against any possibility of reviving anthropomorphism. Asserting scale as the central architectural problem of skyscraper construction, Ladovsky's article in the newspaper called for a compromise between excessively emotional German (expressionist) and too mechanist American (technological) approaches, while for Lissitzky, any anthropocentric scale appeared as a deep anachronism predicated upon a perspectival model of seeing: a 90-degree angle of view, after all, makes any scale unrecognizable.[85] In the modern world, the photomontage confirmed, repeating the statement made by the *Self-Portrait with Wrapped Head and Compass,* the human body was measured and standardized, becoming a model for ready-made sewing patterns.

Lissitzky's *Wolkenbügels* were conceived as orientational devices that mobilized scale without anthropomorphizing it. Acupuncturally marking strategic positions on the confluence of a city's major circle and radial thoroughfares, they articulated its structure, giving the city "a new scale, which responds to the situation when man measures not with his elbow but with hundreds of meters."[86] Each painted in contrasting colors, they would be easy to distinguish and visible from afar, providing convenient orientation points.[87] A model for such architecture Lissitzky discovered in another project by Mies—a rectangular, bulky, and massive concrete-skeleton office block, whose character was dramatically different from the elegant zoomorphic transparency of the glass skyscraper. "Enough weaving intricate compositional ornaments—contemporary man, travelling by tram, automobile, train, does not notice details. What is needed are clear, unequivocal, big masses, like semaphores for

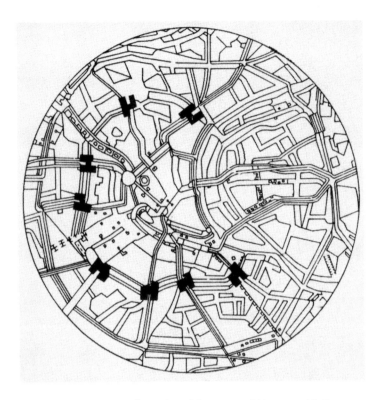

Figure 2.24. El Lissitzky, "The plan of the center of Moscow with the skyscrapers along the A circle" (1926). The *Wolkenbügels* were to occupy strategic positions on the confluence of Moscow's major circle and radial thoroughfares. The Circle A, also known as the Boulevard Circle, was a nineteenth-century "green ring" encircling the center of the city, which also served as the core part of Moscow's streetcar network. Published in *Izvestiia ASNOVA*, no. 1 (1926): 2.

orientation in the space of the city," he explained examining the office block in "Americanism in European Architecture" (1925).[88] His disciple Alexander Toporkov elaborated the psychological rationale behind such architecture: "To ensure his safety, in the surrounding chaos the man creates a secure zone, which could be correlated with what the man is and with what is the subject of his thought. The man needs markers that lead his way, as well as fortified spaces inside which he feels secure."[89]

With one of their three pylons extending underground to the subway, and two others sheltering ground-level tramway stops, the *Wolkenbügels* opened not to the street but to public transit, to be observed and experienced by passengers rather than by pedestrians. "The man, speeding in the miles-devouring automobile, is immobile and most comfortably reclines in a deep and soft seat," Toporkov explained the cinema-hall effect of fast movement,

Figure 2.25. Ludwig Mies van der Rohe, Concrete Office Building, drawing (1923). The rectangular, bulky, and massive Concrete Office Building provided a model for Lissitzky's concept of building as the semaphore "for orientation in the space of the city." Original at the Museum of Modern Art, New York. Image courtesy of and copyright VG Bild-Kunst (Bonn, 2020).

during which the driver "sits all tense, attentive, almost turned into a statue, watchfully looking ahead."[90] Addressing this immobile and yet rapidly moving subject, the long and low identical office blocks of the *Wolkenbügels* evoked Mies's project in their accentuated horizontality. Freed from their load-carrying function, the walls of Mies's building turned into horizontal strips, which Lissitzky saw as "unbroken stretches of filing cabinets on the inside, alternating with unbroken stretches of windows above."[91] However, unlike Mies's office block with its giant footprint, his *Wolkenbügels* hover above the urban fabric, visually framing without physically intervening: the *pilotis* of Mies's project are here turned into massive concrete pylons housing elevator shafts. The buildings were to grow organically at the busiest intersections without slowing the movement of traffic, without necessitating demolitions, and (inasmuch as they could be erected without scaffolding) without closing the square for traffic during the construction period.[92]

As reference points, the *Wolkenbügels* allowed for economizing the energy of perception, automatizing navigation through the city in the same way as the Proun Room, which Lissitzky had designed in 1923, was "so organized that of itself it provides an inducement to walk around in it."[93] Already Eduard von Hartmann viewed the unconscious as the mechanism allowing organisms to orientate themselves in the environment. Yet, it was precisely the

Figure 2.26. Lissitzky's drawing simultaneously illustrating plan and construction of the *Wolkenbügel* was published in *Izvestia ASNOVA*, no. 1 (1926): 2. It shows the "horizontal skyscraper" hovering above the intersection, framing the boulevards in the manner of a triumphal arch.

Figure 2.27. This scheme illustrates the changes of the perceived form of the *Wolkenbügel* depending on the position of the viewer: (1) from above; (2) from below; (3) toward the Kremlin; (4) from the Kremlin; (5) along the boulevard; (6) to the opposite. Published in *Izvestiia ASNOVA*, no. 1 (1926): 3.

unconscious character of orientation that allowed activating the humans, awakening them from the state of passivity in which they were plunged by the overstimulating medley of the metropolis. In the demonstration spaces, Lissitzky elucidated, this activation was achieved by the perceived change of color from white to black.[94] Maria Gough defined the character of this activation as the interruption of "the cacophonous simultaneity" of the overstimulating metropolis.[95] Similarly interrupting the city, Lissitzky's skyscrapers activated the modern human by encouraging new ways of experiencing it. He carefully considered how the location of the beholder determined the perceived shape of *Wolkenbügels.* Some of his sketches employ a surprising mode of representation—perspective, which allowed for relating the psychological experience of the beholder. A view from the west presents both the front and the bottom sides of the skyscraper at Nikitsky Gates Square, implying rapid movement toward and under it.[96] Destroying "the one axis of the picture which stood at right angles to the horizontal," the *Wolkenbügels* completed the movement from painting to architecture announced by the Prouns, which, in the words of Lissitzky, had ceased to be a picture and turned, instead, "into a structure round which we must circle, looking at it from all sides, peering down from above, investigating from below."[97] For Lissitzky, the conscious and the automatic did not contradict but rather supported each other. Rationalizing the expenditure of attention and mental energy, the *Wolkenbügels* redirected them away from orientation toward the more rewarding and thus humane epistemological task of understanding the environment.

Lissitzky's organicist urbanist theory critiqued bourgeois anthropocentrism by arguing that monocular perspective, which exemplified it, was an obsolete adaptational mechanism, incapable of helping the human to orientate within the modern metropolis. New mechanisms of analyzing and ordering the environment were thus needed. Lissitzky searched for these mechanisms in the mathematical studies of non-Euclidian geometry and in the experimental psychological investigations of the perception of moving form. In a paradoxical, dialectical manner, his theory asserted visual illusion and disorientation as the conditions for the emergence of new orientational systems. The parallel evolution of geometric and urban space was none other than the process of returning to the organic: the very dizzying speed and superhuman scale of the modern metropolitan environment were to provide opportunities for new adaptational—orientational—solutions, which his *Wolkenbügels* were intended to offer.

The 1930 competition for the complex of the newspaper *Pravda*—a program that was seen as the Soviet response to the *Chicago Tribune* competition—

Figure 2.28. El Lissitzky's drawing presents both the front and the bottom sides of the *Wolkenbügel* at Nikitsky Gates Square, implying rapid movement toward and under it. Courtesy of the State Tretyakov Gallery, Moscow.

Figure 2.29. The competition for the complex of the newspaper *Pravda* allowed El Lissitzky to find a more pragmatic application (which also remained unrealized) for his vision of a building as semaphore for orientation. Competition model photograph, 1930. Courtesy of State Tretyakov Gallery, Moscow.

gave Lissitzky an opportunity for a more pragmatic application of his vision. With its complex spatial arrangement, hanging and projecting volumes and bridges, accentuated horizontality, and more-than-human length, Lissitzky's project was intended to be observed from an automobile, evoking the bulky aesthetics of Mies's office block. It comes closest to what Hays described as the aesthetics and ideology of posthumanism—a response "to the dissolution of the psychological autonomy and individualism" that he detected in the work of Ludwig Hilberseimer (also a member of the Berlin international constructivist circle) and Hannes Meyer.[98] Today mostly known through the work of N. Katherine Hayles and Donna Haraway, the concept of posthumanism describes the dissolution of the liberal notion of the human in contemporary society. Although the term "post-Human" was first used by the esotericist Helena Blavatsky in 1888, the historian Bryan Moore traced the roots of posthumanism to Spinoza, who urged humans to understand their biological relationship with nature. This tradition, Moore demonstrated, was developed by Nietzsche and approached from the evolutionary perspective by H. G. Wells, who remained its most widely read proponent.[99] Whereas for Hays post-humanism was a predecessor of postmodernism (which similarly negated the autonomous subject), Moore sees it as a precursor of contemporary "green" theory, which replaces anthropocentrism with ecocentrism. In contrast to the interpretations of Haraway, Hayles, and Hays, Lissitzky's vision preserved the integrity and the agency of the human subject while introducing technology into the naturalistic Spinozian model. To achieve this, Lissitzky redefined the *anthropos* as a biotechnological complex, an amalgamation of the body and its means of transportation. Lissitzky's antihumanism did not negate or demote the human vis-à-vis other species; rather, having rejected Cartesian rationalism as an ineffective adaptational strategy, the modern human was to draw a new system of coordinates that would enable building a new environment. As Lissitzky had declared as early as 1920, "THE ARTIST BUILDS A NEW SIGN. THIS SIGN IS NOT A FORM OF KNOWLEDGE ABOUT SOMETHING ALREADY FINISHED, ALREADY BUILT, [ABOUT SOMETHING] THAT ALREADY EXISTS IN THE WORLD—IT IS A SIGN OF THE NEW WORLD, WHICH IS TO BE BUILT FURTHER AND WHICH EXISTS THROUGH THE HUMAN."[100]

THREE

Fitness

Nikolay Ladovsky's Architectural Psychotechnics

In 1928, when Le Corbusier visited Moscow to examine the site for his future Union of Cooperatives (Tsentrosoyuz) building, he became interested in the activity of the new research laboratory of the Architecture Department at VKhUTEIN (Higher Art and Technical Institute, the recently renamed VKhUTEMAS), commonly known as the Psychotechnical Laboratory. The purpose of the laboratory, opened by Nikolay Ladovsky in February 1927, was to support his pedagogical and theoretical activity by investigating the perception of architectural form. To researchers of spatial perception, it offered equipment for conducting experiments, and for pedagogues, it replaced the arbitrariness of studio reviews with the presumed objectivity of laboratory testing. Le Corbusier asked for permission to visit the laboratory and be tested on Ladovsky's psychotechnic devices—but, so the story goes, with a disappointing result. The test on the so-called space-meter, which measured the optical perception of depth, proved that the Swiss master was physiologically incapable of architectural work.[1] The result confirmed a medical condition from which he indeed suffered: a defect of stereoscopic vision—in fact, by that time, the architect had almost lost sight in his left eye.[2] This chapter scrutinizes this test and the psychotechnical approach to architecture that informed it. It explores how in the work of Soviet architects, depth became a cypher for modernity, and how in the first half of the twentieth century the discipline of architecture—and with it, the body and the eye of the architect—was reconfigured and subjected to psychological and physiological mechanisms of control.

Americanism and Its Discontents

During the second half of the 1920s, "avant-garde" artistic and architectural practices in the Soviet Union and elsewhere were reformulated as scientifically organized disciplines endowed with an economic function. In 1925,

Walter Gropius gave the Bauhaus its new motto, "Art into Industry," while in the Soviet Union, the constructivists redefined their program as productivism. In 1926, the rebranding of VKhUTEMAS as VKhUTEIN (changing "studios" to "institute") followed the same logic. Eventually, in 1928, the economic and political terms of this trend toward productivism were defined by the inauguration of the First Five-Year Plan, which subordinated the entire life of the country to the goal of economic modernization.

In the language of the time, the pursuit of efficiency, industry, and organization was known as "Americanism." In the late 1920s, Americanism fascinated and excited, even if sometimes repelled, Europeans.[3] The German sociologist Siegfried Kracauer could scarcely subdue his enthusiasm when describing a visit to a modern American factory, where work was "rationalized down to the last detail":

> [The commercial director] points to diagrams whose colorful networks of lines illustrate the whole operation. The plans hang in frames on the walls of his room. On the other wall, there are two peculiar cases that look a bit like children's abacuses. Within them brightly colored balls, arranged on vertical cords, rise in close formation to varying heights. One glance at them and the director at once knows all about the firm's current situation. Every couple of days the little balls are repositioned by a statistics clerk.[4]

Calling this method of regulation "brainwork" (after Frederick Winslow Taylor), Michael Osman aptly compared the image of the factory as a system that constantly fluctuates in response to market demands to the ecologist's vision of nature as a dynamic system.[5] The mechanisms of its regulation became a matter of debate, in the Soviet Union no less than elsewhere.

In architecture, American rationalization was exemplified by the work of Albert Kahn's Detroit office, renowned for its numerous large-scale industrial projects, most notably those for the Henry Ford automobile plants. Kahn's inexpensive, robust, standardized, flexible open-plan structures could be designed and built, all by the same office, within a record time of several months. This is why, in February 1930, the Soviet government signed a contract with Kahn, and over the next two years his team would design over five hundred factories in different parts of the country, effectively making Kahn the architect of the First Five-Year Plan. Entire factories, such as the tractor plants in Stalingrad, Kharkiv, and Chelyabinsk, were prefabricated in New York, delivered to the Soviet Union by water and land, and assembled on site by over five

Figure 3.1. The "Western" factory organization chart was promoted in the Soviet Union as a tool of the rationalization of management. The accompanying text reads: "Abroad, such stands with diagrams illustrating factory work are displayed in a prominent place and in the office of the factory director. These diagrams enable an easy orientation in the work of the factory, [easy] decision-making and giving appropriate directions." Published in *Vremiia,* no. 4 (1924): 51.

hundred American engineers and builders, assisted by the Russian workers they oversaw and trained.[6]

Although at first sight, these commissions seem to be driven by considerations of economy alone, Kahn's mission was more ambitious. The size and complex organization of Kahn's office, where architectural work was structured according to an industrial model, mirrored the scale and organization of labor in the buildings it produced. In other words, while designing Ford's factories, Kahn introduced to architecture the principles of Fordism—a system of optimizing mass production by rationalizing the division of labor, which at Ford's factories was famously achieved by the assembly line.[7] It was this industrialized design method that the Soviet government hoped to import, in addition to industrial infrastructure.[8] Anticipating Hannes Meyer's functionalist maxim, "Building is just an organization," Kahn's system undermined both academic and avant-garde visions of architecture as art driven by inspiration and genius. Henry-Russell Hitchcock, the American architectural historian and the champion of modernism, argued that the "strength of a firm such as Kahn . . . depends not on the architectural genius of one man (there is sufficient evidence that Kahn was a mediocre architect considered as an individual), but in the organizational genius which can establish a foolproof system of rapid and complete plan production."[9] Kahn's factory-style organization of work was very different from that to which Soviet architects were accustomed. The architect Nikolay Ilyinsky described the habitual scene in a Soviet architectural office, which included "a common hall, which hosts a small number of workers of different specializations. Architect-constructor, draftsman, quantity surveyor often sit next to each other and are united in the same group." Unlike their Soviet counterparts, American offices such as Kahn's, Ilyinsky explained, "follow strict separation and intentionally place architects, constructors, and specialized departments on different floors."[10]

Forty-five of Kahn's architects and engineers were employed by Gosproektstroy (the State Trust of Design and Construction of the Supreme Council of the People's Economy), a central design office that had been created in Moscow in 1930 with the arrival of the Americans in mind. The mission of Gosproektstroy—the fulfillment of the goals of the Five-Year Plan—was to be achieved by industrializing architecture with the help of American expertise. Replacing the previous system of independent design workshops as "one powerful organization," Gosproektstroy, indeed, acted on an American scale: the arriving specialists had to train over two thousand Soviet ones.[11] But Gosproektstroy was more than a centralized design office: it was "an educational-industry organization, which, receiving American experience in the process of its industrial activity," was to "transmit this experience to the utmost possible number of construction organizations and young Soviet specialists."[12] The economic promise of standardization and rationalization of labor outweighed ideological differences. Kahn believed that (American) standardization and (Soviet) centralized planning complemented each other— centralization enabled greater standardization, which meant a dramatic reduction of costs. Meanwhile, communist bureaucrats, economists, and even artists enthusiastically welcomed American "ideologically neutral" techniques of efficiency, including Fordism and Taylorism. In the words of Mary McLeod, the advocates of industrial management believed social justice to be "a product of technical rationalization, not of material equality."[13] Among others, Soviet revolutionaries welcomed it as an instrument of revolutionizing society by modernizing the subject—something akin to artist Vladimir Tatlin's *Letatlin,* a flying device that provided the human subject with prosthetic wings.

At the beginning of the twentieth century, American pioneers of indus-

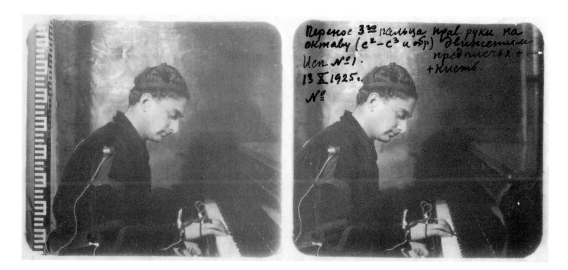

Figure 3.2. Working under the umbrella of Alexey Gastev's Central Institute of Labor, physiologists Nikolay Bernstein and T. Popova studied physical trajectories of the corporeal joints of a wired pianist. The employment of stereoscopy not only added accuracy to the representation of movement by introducing the third dimension but also cast this representation as modern and objective. N. Bernstein and T. Popova, stereocards, 1925. Courtesy of Andrey Smirnov.

trial management Frank and Lillian Gilbreth suggested using chronocyclegraphs (photographs that captured movement) to rationalize the movement of workers and their work environment. Along with the theories of Taylor and Ford, their methods inspired the activity of Alexey Gastev's Central Institute of Labor, in which he collaborated with physiologist Nikolay Bernstein.[14] Describing his approach to the physiology of movement, Bernstein coined the term "biomechanics," which was soon picked up by another eminent admirer of motion studies, the avant-garde theater director Vsevolod Meyerhold.[15] Gastev and Bernstein modified the Gilbreths' method by bringing together physiology and motion studies with the help of cyclogramometry (using cyclograms for measuring movement) and stereoscopic photography.[16] The employment of stereoscopy in the Institute of Labor's analysis of the movements of a piano player, which redefined musical talent as correctly performed labor, not only added accuracy to the representation of movement by introducing the third dimension, but also cast this representation as modern and objective.[17]

Contemporaries accused motion studies of mechanicism, which eclipsed life's holistic dimension, and both Taylor and Gastev became common targets of criticism and satire in the United States as well as in the Soviet Union. Although as the head of the Proletarian Culture movement, Alexander

Bogdanov provided Gastev with a platform for the research and publication of his ideas, he was one of the most vocal critics of Gastev's Taylorism. Social life and culture, Bogdanov contended, could not be reduced to technology, and even economic processes were dependent on human creativity no less than on mechanic efficiency.[18] Lenin likewise called Taylorism "a 'scientific' system of squeezing sweat," which turned the human into a slave of the machine.[19] The mechanicism of Kahn's architectural production was criticized along the same lines. When in 1930 the young constructivist architect Andrey Burov, an admirer of Le Corbusier, whom he had met in Moscow two years earlier, visited Kahn's American office, he condemned what he saw. Kahn's industrialism, for him, was antagonistic to the nature of architecture:

> As for architecture, it is absolutely dull. Instead of architects they have a giant office. . . . The first impression is that one is designing a sketch, another—a plan, the third—a facade, the fourth— interiors, the fifth, the sixth, the seventh, the -teenth—electricity, constructions, plumbing, sewage, ventilation, refrigeration, etc. All this is signed by the owner of the firm, who has nothing to do with all this. The result is an American work of art.[20]

Burov's skepticism echoed debates that had earlier raged around Narkompros's attempts to humanize secondary and adult education in the Soviet Union. Anatoly Lunacharsky opposed industrialized specialist education, instead promoting a "polytechnic" educational system inspired by Renaissance universalism. Like liberal arts education, this model focused not on one narrowly defined professional skill but on a broad understanding of scientific, political, economic, cultural, and social contexts of work. While polytechnic education remained an aspirational ideal resulting from the original humanist agenda of the revolution of 1917, the new practicalities of the country's economy required specialists, and Lunacharsky was soon forced to seek a compromise. Modern economy and social life, he had to agree, were based on the division of labor, which allowed humanity to accumulate knowledge—even though human culture would have disintegrated without an understanding of the work of others.[21]

Lunacharsky's nearly failed attempt at introducing polytechnic education revealed the victory of state capitalism in the USSR—and with it, of the division of labor and of the organizational ethos. According to German modernist Bruno Taut, who worked in Moscow in 1932–33 (returning in disappointment to Berlin):

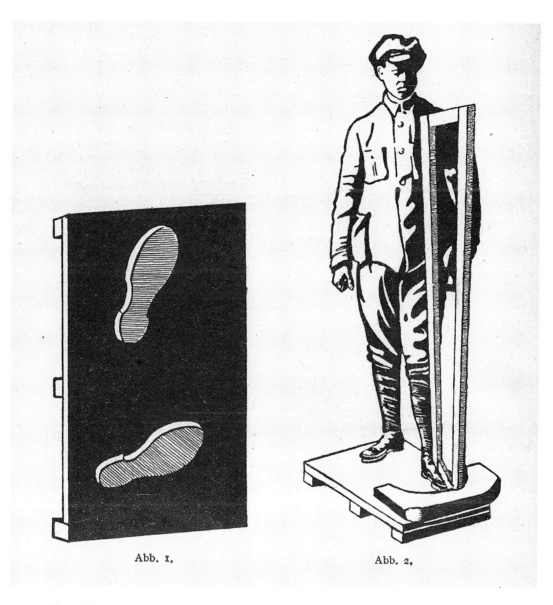

Figure 3.3. The Central Institute of Labor's templates for correct positioning of feet and for posture (the 1920s) illustrate Gastev's much-criticized mechanicism. Illustrated in Franziska Baumgarten, *Arbeitswissenschaft und Psychotechnik in Russland* (Munich: R. Oldenbourg, 1924), 20.

It is characteristic that the construction university in Moscow (VASI) divides its department according to different types of construction, thereby from early on sacrificing students to fatal professional narrowness. Introduced in hyper-American form, such a misunderstanding of the calling of the architect can inflict

Figure 3.4. Kukryniksy [artist collective], "The Worker and the Machine: Gastev's Setup" (1930). The image satirically represents Gastev turning workers into screws and machine belts in accordance with the technical drawing visible behind his back. Published in *Smena,* no. 16–17 (1930): 28.

utmost harm on construction in the economic and technical as well as in the artistic sense.[22]

And yet the victory of industrial management did not equal an unmitigated acceptance of mechanism. Within this discourse, room for discussion and debate emerged as architects and theorists sought, in the manner of Lunacharsky, opportunities for compromise. In what follows, I will examine one such compromising program, psychotechnics, which aspired to reconcile industrial management with individuality.

From Motion to Talent

The Soviet debate about the American approach to architecture was informed by a related discussion in industrial management—the debate between two forms of the Fordist organization of labor, motion studies (represented by the work of Taylor and the Gilbreths) and psychotechnics. Unlike motion studies, which focused on physiological aspects of work, psychotechnics was concerned with individual psychological differences. Rejecting the Taylorist conception of the body and the society as machine, psychotechnics substituted it with an organicist vision of society as ecosystem. In this model, individuals were grouped according to their "psychological profiles," which assigned everyone to a particular social niche in accordance with their innate physiological, psychological, and intellectual abilities. Coining the term "psychotechnics" in 1900, psychologist William Stern suggested that this goal could be achieved through the study of individual differences, while psychotechnics's most notable proponent, American-based Hugo Münsterberg, believed that a study of differences offered a middle ground between "reckless capitalism" (industrial efficiency) and "feeble sentimentality" (social reformism).[23] Yet the roots of this program could also be discerned in the psychometrics of Francis Galton and his followers, such as Rudolf Schulze and James McKeen Cattell, whose laboratory instruments, tests, and devices were actively used by psychotechnics's proponents.[24]

Its origins in capitalist Germany and the United States notwithstanding, during the 1920s, psychotechnics quickly gained popularity in Soviet Russia, becoming particularly vibrant after the announcement of the First Five-Year Plan, whose goals it promised to support. Münsterberg's *Foundations of Psychotechnics* (*Grundzüge der Psychotechnik*, 1914) appeared in Russian translation in 1924, followed by other translations of foreign authors.[25] The first Soviet psychotechnical laboratory was opened in 1922 by Isaak Spielrein under the umbrella of Gastev's Institute of Labor. The All-Russian Psychotechnic Society, founded in 1927, published two journals and had branches in Moscow, Leningrad, Kazan, and Sverdlovsk. By 1930, more than one hundred psychotechnical institutions, including large laboratories, departments within institutes, and regional offices, existed throughout the country.[26] A related field, testology (the science of psychological testing), which had experienced a rise in Russia during the first years of the twentieth century, was incorporated into the framework of psychotechnics; the Moscow Testological Association was also founded in 1927.[27]

In the aftermath of the revolutionary education reforms, psychological testing seemed to offer a viable alternative to the traditional grading system, and psychotechnics was embraced by education theorists, in particular those adhering to the equally popular experimental pedagogy, a science based on child psychology and physiology.[28] It proved to be compatible with the humanist, Lunacharsky-inspired pedagogical model, which favored multisidedness and erudition. According to education theorist and psychologist Avgusta Dernova-Ermolenko, the pedagogue of the future

> will have to learn not less but more than the builder of edifices, bridges, roads, and machines. He will have to know anatomy, physiology, and partially pathology as a doctor; physics and chemistry as a scientist; mathematics and mechanics as an engineer. Like a skillful strategist, military commander, politician, and activist-organizer, he will have to manage complex manifestations of the developing nervous system of a children collective; like an astronomer, he will have to operate with complex mathematical calculations.[29]

The debate between Taylorism and psychotechnics continued on the cultural front. On one side was Meyerhold's Taylorist "biomechanic" theater, for which constructivist artists Alexander Vesnin (soon to become a leading figure in constructivist architecture) and Lyubov Popova produced stage-set designs in the early 1920s, treating the body of the actor as a mechanical automaton whose movements they aspired to optimize. "With the invention of a new theater," writes Tijana Vujošević, "came the invention of both a new kind of space and a new kind of man, one who inhabits and traverses the new space and who understands movement of his own body in a way that corresponds to the demands of the modern age of technology and progress."[30] On the other side were the likes of theater director Konstantin Stanislavsky, who critiqued

Meyerhold for failing to make actors perform as live human beings, arguing that "though important, Meyerhold's theatre—without human, alive people on stage—was dead."[31] Instead, Stanislavsky subscribed to the James-Lange theory of emotion, which postulated that emotions result from physiological changes in the body rather than vice versa, as well as to Indian yoga tradition. He elaborated a method of acting that he called psychotechnics—a system by which the actors identified with their stage roles through the full physical experience of emotions rather than merely represented them. According to Stanislavsky, these (unconscious) emotions had to be released by conscious means. In this model, consciousness and the unconscious were not opposed but rather supported each other:

> Psychotechnics must help organize unconscious material because only organized unconscious material can assume artistic form. The sorceress organic nature can create it. It owns and manages the most important centers of our creative apparatus. Human consciousness does not know them, our sensations do not orientate there, but a true creativity is impossible without them.[32]

It was this compromise approach that Ladovsky chose to follow in his quest for individuality without individualism.[33] Quoting from Münsterberg, whose laboratory at Harvard University he took as the model, he later explained, "Psychotechnics cannot create artists . . . , but it can provide all of them with a basis for achieving in the most reliable way those particular goals to which they aspire and, above all, for avoiding certain pitfalls."[34] For the rationalists, psychotechnics presented an opportunity to establish a relationship between the formal aspects of architectural composition and "socioemotional needs."[35]

In April 1930, the journal *Stroitelstvo Moskvy (Moscow Construction)* published an article by Ladovsky's former student, the architect Alexander Karra, titled "For a Socialist Reorganization of Design Offices." Although generally sympathetic to Americanism, Karra suggested revising it to make it more humane, reconciling its ethos of efficiency with socialist values of collectivity and mutual support.[36] The differentiation and specialization of labor, Karra argued, necessitated a synthesis. If it were to unify separate tasks into a single organized and organic process, this synthesis required a new institutional structure, which Karra elaborated as "the brigade method." "The brigade method" was a popular term in both industrial and educational contexts in Russia and beyond. In education, the brigade method emerged as a modification of the Dalton Plan, a project-based pedagogical technique developed in the United States by Helen Parkhurst and advocated by John Dewey. During the 1920s, it was embraced by Narkompros as a teaching strategy for elementary and middle schools. Unlike the Dalton Plan, which advocated individual work on projects, the brigade-laboratory method organized students in groups.[37] Hannes Meyer used it as a pedagogical principle of the Bauhaus, where he united students of different academic standing (from first year to last year) into brigades, enabling them, so he hoped, to learn from each other. In 1930, Meyer moved to the USSR as the head of the Rot-Front (die Rote Front) Brigade, which included several of his former Bauhaus students. According to one of them, Philipp Tolziner, for German architects, the "brigade" meant "a group of co-thinkers who share views, behavior, perception, and education."[38] In Soviet industry, the brigade method structured labor as work units (brigades), which shared responsibility and benefits in the cause of "comradely competition."[39] The brigades were organized both vertically and horizontally—hierarchically structured and differing by specialization (there could be, for example, brigades of bricklayers or woodworkers). While solidifying the division of labor, the brigades also mitigated its dehumanizing effects, creating small, family-like teams, whose members, at least in theory, were tied by bonds of comradeship.

Introducing the brigade method to architectural work, Karra defined it as based on "strict organization, on freeing designers from any additional work, on maximal differentiation of their labor and its surveying, on selection and training of employees according to their inclinations and abilities for this or that kind of work based on scientific methods."[40] He juxtaposed the brigade method not only to "craft-universal [kustarno-universal'nyi]" but also to "office" and "group" methods, which were based on consecutive elaboration of the project by different specialist teams. Unlike the latter, the brigade method presupposed simultaneous work on the project by several brigades to increase efficiency and coordination. The actions of different workers would provide "the chain of the same operation, the same general, organically united process," which would eliminate "the gaps between the initial project (idea, concept) and subsequent surprises of constructional, technological, or other order." The method simplified and rationalized the structure of a design office, replacing its complex hierarchy (typically consisting of the chief architect, the head architect, constructors, engineers, technicians, draftsmen, and so on) with a quadripartite structure: the leadership brigade (mirroring the modern American factory's planning department), the design ("idea") brigade, the specialist brigade, and the draftsman brigade.[41] This, Karra believed, could reduce the number of work operations (communications between different units) necessary for a design of the building from more than forty to ten.

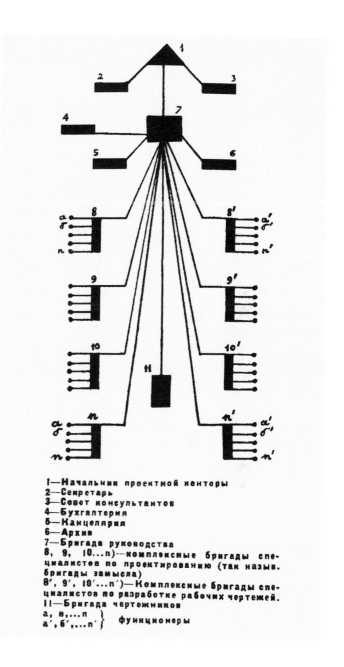

Figure 3.5. Alexander Karra, "Approximate scheme of the organization of a design office" (1930). The diagram illustrates his brigade method of architectural design organization. At the top (1) is the head of the design office, who is connected to the secretary (2), the consulting board (3), and the governing brigade (7), which forms the center of the scheme. The latter is connected to the finance department (4), the chancellery (5), the archive (6), as well as a number of specialist brigades. Among the latter are "complex brigades of design specialists (so-called idea brigades)" (on the left) and "complex brigades of specialists on the development of working drawings" (on the right); the brigade of draftsmen (11) is in the middle. Published in *Stroitel'stvo Moskvy*, no. 4 (1930): 4.

Reminiscent of Fritz Kahn's contemporaneous popular anatomic illustrations that presented the body as factory, in Karra's anthropomorphic scheme, the "leadership brigade" functioned as the nervous system: it received commands from the brain (the office head), organized the work of body organs (complex brigades of designers and specialists), and coordinated the output mechanism (the draftsmen brigade). Whereas Fritz Kahn's homunculus industrialized the human, Karra's scheme aspired to humanize the modern production place. In Karra's vision, each employee became an organic cell fulfilling its natural purpose. Such a biologization promised not only to mitigate the dehumanizing effects of the modern division of labor but also to forge a balance between the interests of the individual and those of the collective. In doing so, it reflected the aspirations of his teacher Ladovsky, who had in 1919 defined the goal of the Moscow Architectural Artel as strengthening "the ties between separate architectural-artistic forces into a single creative organism (the collective), which will allow separate individualities [to influence each] other in a wholesome way due to their constant communication and creative interaction and [to] create forms of collective creativity through personal experience."[42] In 1927, speaking about secondary education, Lunacharsky similarly argued that it "cannot oppress individuality, but it equally cannot allow apostasy. Its goal is a creation of socialist individuality, of that which can be called a collectivistically educated originality."[43] What consequences did this dialectic entail for the individual worker, and how was it to regulate the division of labor?

Discussing the division of labor, Karl Marx had distinguished between skilled and unskilled labor (a division that he explained as based on education), while Hannah Arendt was to juxtapose labor and work (as based on their cultural significance and the durability of their results). In his turn, Karra, who grounded his scheme in the presumed innate and acquired abilities of workers, explained the divide as a difference between creative and technical labor. Karra specified that "Cultivation *[kul'turnost']* [and] a talent for combination of spatial forms is the central quality of the architect-designer, who conducts complex design work (in the conceptual sphere)."[44] Meanwhile, "brigades of working drawings" would include "lesser qualified and talented comrades." This hierarchical division nevertheless remained porous and could be overcome as the architects improved their skills. In this picture, psychotechnics emerged as a mechanism of the assessment, evaluation, and development of these abilities. The Psychotechnical Laboratory at the VKhUTEIN was to play a key role in both fostering this new organic professionalism and promoting a new vision of the architect as a worker whose labor, although divided, was natural and thus not subjected to alienation.

From Harvard to Moscow

The Psychotechnical Laboratory (or, officially, the Architectural Research Laboratory) at VKhUTEIN, in fact, had a broader mission, extending its activity in several directions: vocational selection and pedagogy ("the psychotechnics

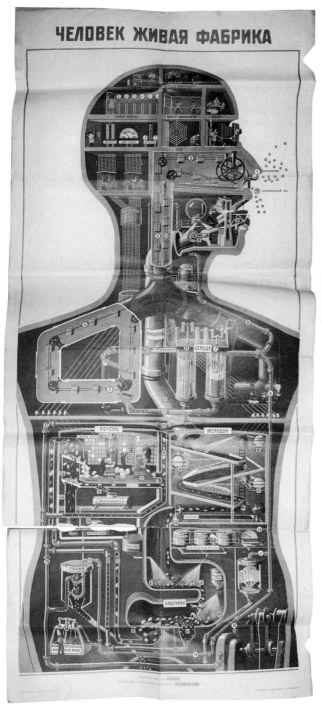

Figure 3.6. A famous representation of modern mechanicism, Fritz Kahn's *Der Mensch als Industriepalast* (*Man as an Industrial Palace,* 1926) was published, with a supplementary brochure by surgeon Professor Vladimir Oppel, in the Soviet Union by the journal *Iskry nauki (Sparkles of Science)* in 1928. Whereas Fritz Kahn's homunculus presented the man as a factory, Karra's scheme presented the factory as a living organism, thereby aspiring to rehumanize the modern production space.

of the architect"), social reform ("the education of the consumers of architecture and the development of workers' housing"), devising a new theory of architecture ("the fundamentals of architecture"), furthering architectural psychology ("the experimental testing of spatial disciplines"), and finally, the development of the methodology for landscape architecture.[45] Student Arkady Grudzinsky, for example, was responsible for the rationalization of drafting and the reform of the drafting table.[46] Ladovsky, with the help of his former student Georgy Krutikov, oversaw the psychotechnical section, which remained the laboratory's flagship. It is unknown whether Ladovsky was familiar with Münsterberg's vision of an architect as a technical specialist elevated above his peers by the love of art and the knowledge of foreign languages and art history. Although Ladovsky would have agreed with Münsterberg that architecture was a polytechnic discipline (which, according to Münsterberg, "demands more than a mere specialistic training" and "is to take its energy from all sides of human life"), his understanding of what constituted architectural work was a far cry from Münsterberg's ideal of aesthetic feeling cultivated by drawing from casts and "decorative figure-design."[47] Instead, Ladovsky and Krutikov identified architectural talent as the ability to see, or "spatial dexterity," a faculty they found to be "as vital for an architect as the sense of equilibrium is for a pilot."[48] It was this ability that the psychotechnical section aspired to test and analyze.

Ladovsky recorded the results of his tests in each student's personal profile form, which he borrowed from existing psychotechnical literature and which, he hoped, would eventually supplement academic transcripts. Resembling the forms developed by Russian "testologists" as early as the 1910s and later developed by such advocates of psychotechnics as Fritz Giese in Germany and Petr Rudik in the Soviet Union, Ladovsky's form consisted of three columns (Index, Rank, and Category), a grid for a graphic of architectural giftedness, and a space for a general conclusion.[49] According to the cumulative result of the tests, students were divided into five categories, so that even before meeting a student in person the pedagogue was aware of the weak sides of his or her talent. Later on, as adequate pedagogy was to foster the development of the student's talent, the profile would allow the monitoring of improvement, thus illustrating the success of architectural education.

Like Rudik, whose work targeted students of science and technology, Ladovsky began his tests by examining attention and memory before proceeding to evaluate a student's capacity for processing perceptual data. For Rudik, the key among these second-order properties was intellectual giftedness—the acuity of understanding and remembering material. The psychologist defined intellectual giftedness not as a cognitive but rather as a psychological,

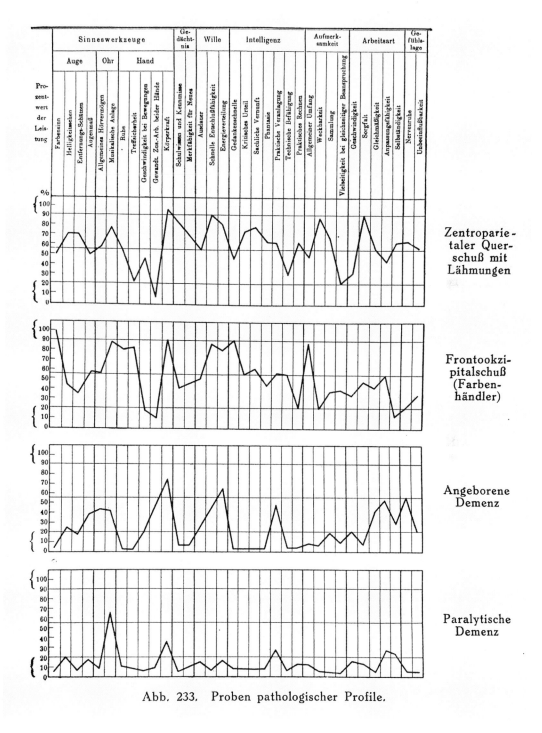

Figure 3.7. The psychotechnical profile with "pathological" graphs by German psychotechnician Fritz Giese provided a model for Ladovsky's student profile forms. This graph is from Giese's *Handbuch psychotechnischer Eignungsprüfungen* (Halle: Carl Marhold, 1925), 674.

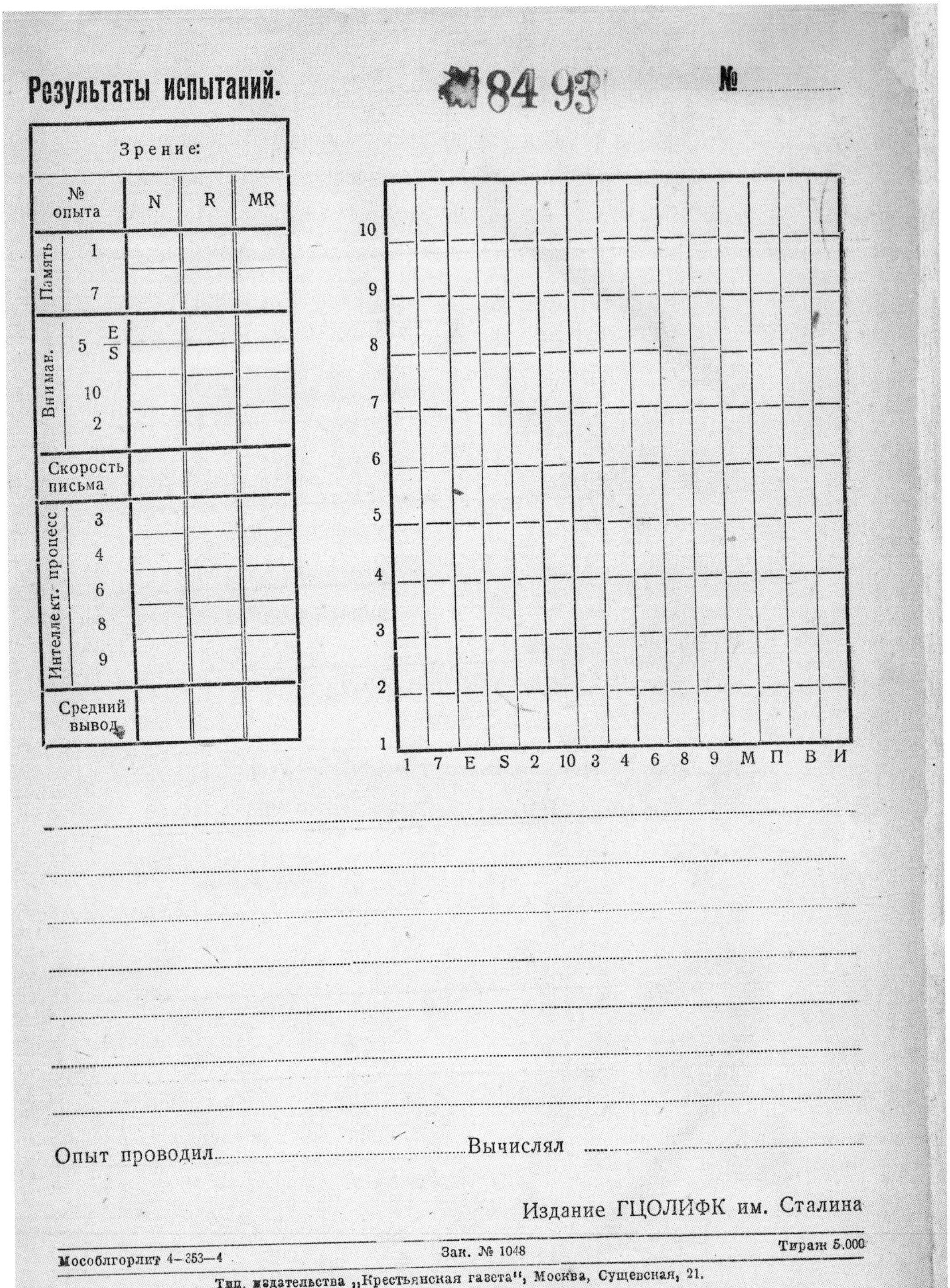

Результаты испытаний. 84 93 № ....

Зрение:				
№ опыта		N	R	MR
Память	1			
	7			
Вниман.	5 E/S			
	10			
	2			
Скорость письма				
Интеллект. процесс	3			
	4			
	6			
	8			
	9			
Средний вывод				

Опыт проводил.......................... Вычислял ....

Издание ГЦОЛИФК им. Сталина

Мособлгорлит 4—353—4 Зак. № 1048 Тираж 5.000

Тип. издательства „Крестьянская газета", Москва, Сущевская, 21.

Figure 3.8. The psychological profile of general giftedness (Series A2) by industrial psychologist Petr Rudik, who specialized in testing students of science and technology, provided another, easily accessible model for Ladovsky. Published in P[etr] A. Rudik, *Umstvennaia odarennost' i ee izmerenie* (Moscow: Izdatel'stvo Kommunisticheskogo universiteta, 1927).

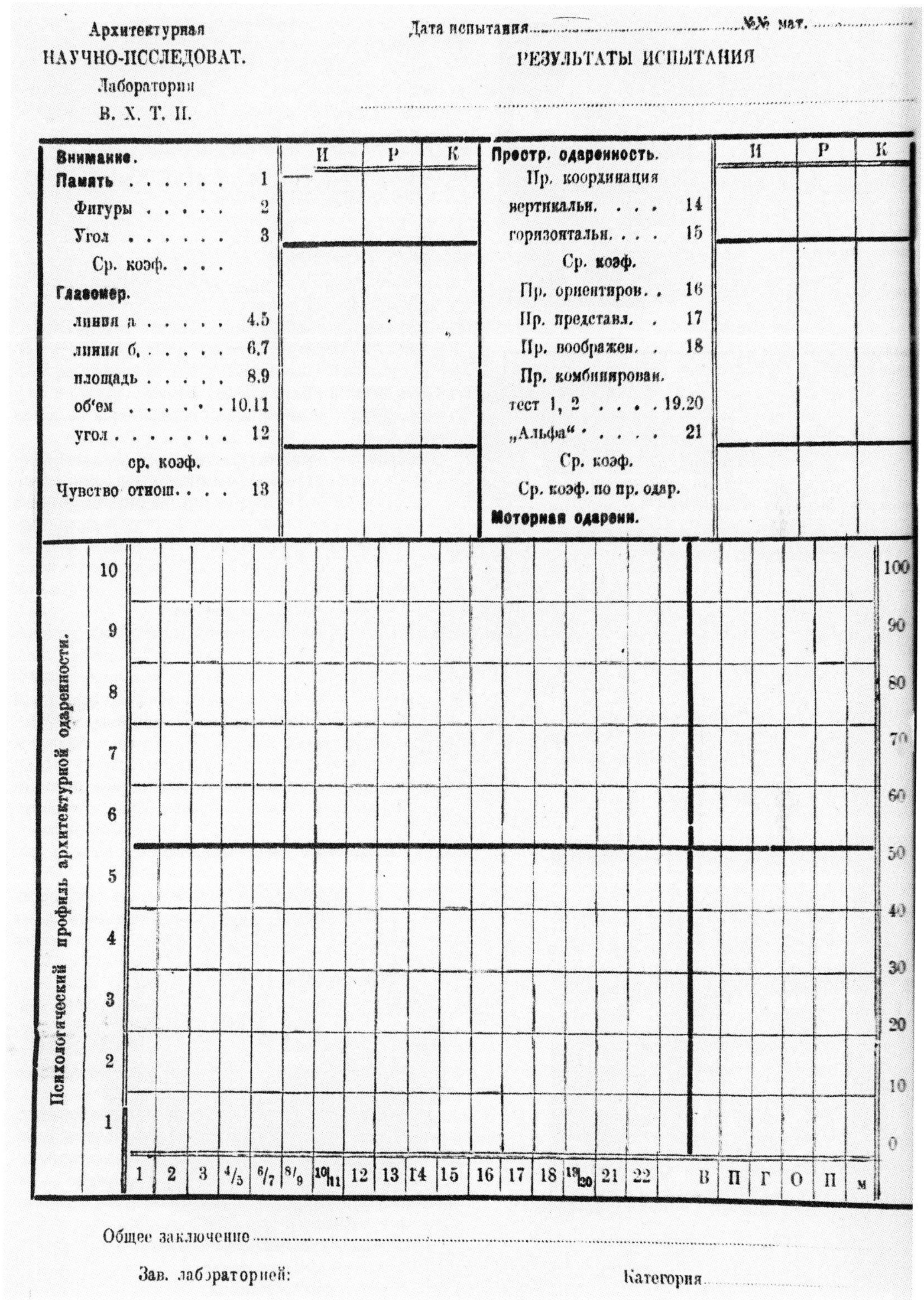

Архитектурная
НАУЧНО-ИССЛЕДОВАТ.
Лаборатория
В. Х. Т. И.

Дата испытания........... №№ мат. ....

РЕЗУЛЬТАТЫ ИСПЫТАНИЯ

Внимание.	И	Р	К	Простр. одаренность.		И	Р	К
Память 1				Пр. координация				
Фигуры 2				вертикальн. . . . 14				
Угол 3				горизонтальн. . . . 15				
Ср. коэф. . . .				Ср. коэф.				
Глазомер.				Пр. ориентиров. . 16				
линия а 4.5				Пр. представл. . 17				
линия б. 6.7				Пр. воображен. . 18				
площадь 8.9				Пр. комбинирован.				
об'ем 10.11				тест 1, 2 . . . . 19.20				
угол 12				„Альфа" 21				
ср. коэф.				Ср. коэф.				
Чувство отнош. . . . 13				Ср. коэф. по пр. одар.				
				Моторная одарен.				

Психологический профиль архитектурной одаренности.

10 — 100
9 — 90
8 — 80
7 — 70
6 — 60
5 — 50
4 — 40
3 — 30
2 — 20
1 — 10
0

1 2 3 4/5 6/7 8/9 10/11 12 13 14 15 16 17 18 19/20 21 22 В П Г О П М

Общее заключение ....

Зав. лабораторией: Категория...........

Figure 3.9. Nikolay Ladovsky's Student Profile Form, developed for VKhUTEIN, tailored psychotechnical profile forms for students of architecture. Published in *Arkhitektura i VKhUTEIN*, no. 1 (1929): 3.

unconscious property. He referred to the work of the British psychologist Charles Edward Spearman, who saw giftedness as a general function of the central nervous system, and who thus treated humans not as autonomous agents but as biological organisms interacting with their environment. "The task of education," stated the Soviet psychologist Solomon Gellerstein, espousing a similar opinion, "is to create a balance between an organism and the environment that surrounds it."[50] Tailoring Rudik's scheme to students of architecture, Ladovsky replaced intellectual giftedness with such abilities as visual estimation and spatial giftedness (which included spatial coordination, spatial orientation, spatial visualization, spatial imagination, and spatial combination). His interest in seeing emerged against a rich background of discussions of this notion in psychology, physiology, aesthetics, and art history, initiated by Hermann von Helmholtz's psychological studies of vision.[51] Helmholtz, arguing against the nativism of Ewald Hering, postulated an empiricist theory, according to which stereoscopic vision was not an innate but a learned ability, which depended on memory and attention. The idea that seeing could be learned inspired the rising discipline of art history. Heinrich Wölfflin interpreted seeing *(das Sehen)* as the driving force of stylistic change. Similarly, the epistemological concept of *das Anschauung,* "the looking at an object in its immediate presence" (which had been used already by Immanuel Kant), was developed by Albert Brinckmann, who called for *die Anschauungstheorie,* a general system of ways of looking.[52] The work of both authors was translated to Russian and read by ASNOVA members.[53] In 1926 Nikolay Dokuchaev had distinguished the physiological function of looking *(smotrenie)* from the analytical process of seeing *(videnie),* the latter leading to an understanding of that which is "the most characteristic of an object—what it consists of and how its elements are united in a coherent architectural whole."[54] Unconscious visual perception thus provided a key to conscious spatial analysis. To explore it, Ladovsky recommended to Soviet architects the studies conducted in Münsterberg's Harvard laboratory, whose research on the perception of forms possessed, he argued, immediate relevance for architecture.[55]

Already the first modern philosophers such as John Locke had postulated a hierarchical structure of the human interpretation of the world. The lowest level comprised sensation, purely physiological and pertinent to both animals and humans; sensory data was then transmitted for interpretation to the brain in a process known as perception. These two basic processes, nineteenth-century philosophers added, were subsequently continued by the work of spatial imagination, association, and memory, which belonged to the domain of higher (and uniquely human, as it was then believed) psychic processes. If the founder of experimental psychology, Wilhelm Wundt, was preoccupied with sensation, during the twentieth century scientific interest shifted toward perception and, ultimately, imagination. Ladovsky's psychotechnics, and particularly the notion of visual estimation (*glazomer* in Russian, or *Augenmaß* in German—both words literally translate as "measuring by the eye"), which came to be seen as the elementary unit of spatial interpretation, reflected this shift. Münsterberg and Wundt defined *Augenmaß* as a physiological sensation of eye muscles; Wundt believed that eyeballs required different amounts of energy for different types of movement: vertical lines, for example, seemed longer because a vertical movement was more energy-consuming than horizontal. Ladovsky, instead, aligned himself with the psychological and empiricist approach of Helmholtz and Theodor Lipps, who treated *Augenmaß* as an apperception (a comparison with present and past experience based on the principle of contrast, during which the subject became aware of the act of perception).[56] Taking place in the mind and yet relying on sensation, visual estimation, for Ladovsky, was suspended between the physiological and the cognitive: the conscious idea emerged as a product of the psychological process of comparison. The ambiguity of visual estimation as apperception betrayed the limits of psychotechnics's rehumanizing ambitions; although reintroduced, the conscious remained restrained and subordinated to the unconscious and the physiological.

To test the faculty of visual estimation, Ladovsky acquired a special room in the VKhUTEIN building. Following the example of Münsterberg's Harvard laboratory, this room was entirely painted in black, from floor to ceiling, to avoid distractions and possible spatial reference points.[57] According to the anecdote, the workmen who were hired to paint it were so appalled by the unusual idea that they refused to perform their job, leaving Ladovsky and his students to do it on their own. A contemporary remembered that "the black room produced a whimsical impression, all filled with various devices with stretched threads and bright color spots for experiments with color. It looked as if after a fire."[58]

Ladovsky could have modeled such laboratory devices as color wheels and threads after those described in psychotechnical textbooks and catalogs, but one group of apparatuses remained idiosyncratic.[59] These devices, which Ladovsky considered his own contribution to psychotechnics, were designed to test just one group of subjects—architects.[60] Almost all of them had the Russian word for visual estimation (*glazomer*) in their title. Some of these devices were adaptations of existing psychological testing machines, while others had no immediate analogs. Quite similar to a device for testing the visual estimation of tramway and bus drivers developed by the Central Institute of

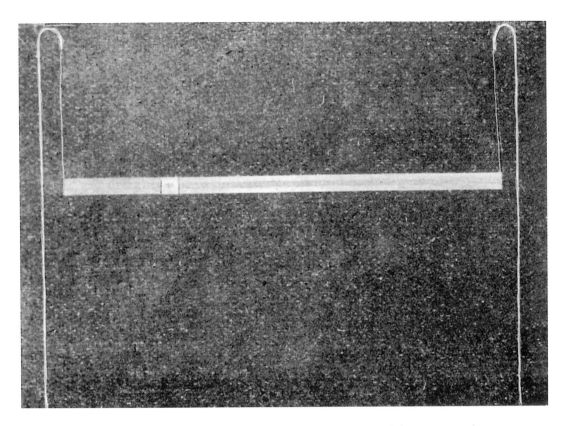

Figure 3.10. Nikolay Ladovsky's *liglazomer* was the simplest of Ladovsky's apparatuses. It consisted of a freely hanging ruler turned with its back toward the subject, who was asked to mark the required length with the help of a slide. Published in *Stroitel'naia promyshlennost',* no. 5 (1928): 372.

Labor psychologist Nikolay Levitov, the simplest of Ladovsky's apparatuses, the *liglazomer* (from Russian *linia*, line), consisted of a freely hanging ruler turned with its back toward the subject. The subject was asked to mark the required length with the help of a slide; the deviation could be then measured by the scale on the ruler's back side.[61] The subject tested by the *ploglazomer* (from *ploskost'*, surface), derived from Münsterberg's *Augenmassapparat*, was asked to cut a certain part of a flat figure using a sliding glass plane. Based on Walther Moede's device that Gellerstein described as an *uglomer* (from *ugol,* "angle," and root *-mer,* "measure"), Ladovsky's *uglazomer* consisted of a rotating circle with a line for marking an angle of required magnitude; the fixed vertical hand and the measuring scale on the back allowed checking the precision of estimation. The *oglazomer* (from *ob'em,* "volume") was a set of vessels of various geometrical shapes that the subject had to fill with the requested volume of liquid that came from graded glass cylinders via a system of rub-

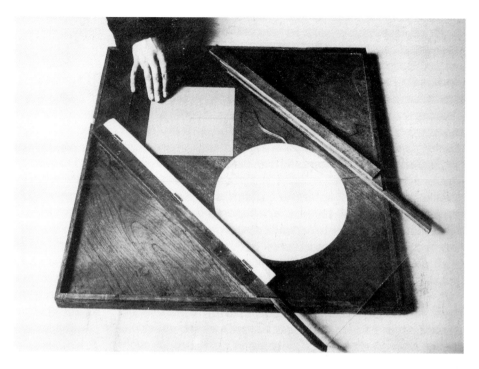

Figure 3.11. The subject tested on Nikolay Ladovsky's *ploglazomer* was asked to cut a certain part of a flat figure using a sliding glass plane. Published in *Stroitel'naia promyshlennost',* no. 5 (1928): 372.

ber pipes and faucets (no analogs of this device have been found). Finally, the *prostrometr* (from *prostranstvo,* "space," and *izmeriat',* "to measure") featured two pairs of surfaces that served as supports for objects and tested the capacity for spatial perception.

Visual estimation, the first-order psychological quality, was the prerequisite for more complex functions, such as spatial combination. According to the rationalists, the ability to combine spaces was key for architectural composition—a crucial second-order component of architectural talent. Ladovsky evaluated this quality with the help of psychotechnical paper tests, whose development he delegated to Krutikov, his advisee and subsequently doctoral student.[62] As discussed and illustrated in the previous chapter, Krutikov's exploration of combinatorics (a branch of set theory) resulted in new formulas that described the spatial location (rotation) of the object. Krutikov wanted to create a system of classification for the potentially infinite variety of possible spatial combinations. Combinatorics allowed him to rationalize and accommodate individuality, subordinating it to an organizing idea in the same way as psychotechnics, transforming individuality to difference, as he attempted

Figure 3.12. Hugo Münsterberg's *Augenmassapparat* (instrument for investigating the power of the eye to compare lengths) provided a model for Ladovsky's *ploglazomer*. Image cropped from a photograph of Harvard Psychological Laboratory published in *Psychological Laboratory of Harvard University* (Cambridge, Mass.: Harvard University Press, 1893). Courtesy Harvard University Archives (HUF 715.93.72).

to study and systematize it for the benefit of the collective corporate whole. While Krutikov's figures performed a spatial dance to contribute to the unity of architectural composition, in psychotechnics, composition became a model for social organization, in which each element, albeit different, had a particular place and function, defined not only by what it was but also by what it was not.

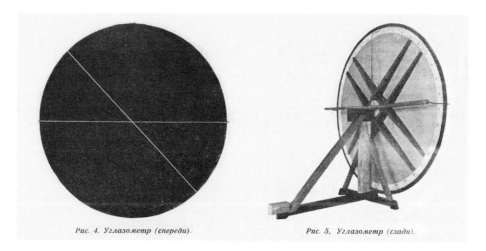

Figure 3.13. Nikolay Ladovsky's *uglazomer* consisted of a circle on which an angle of a certain magnitude had to be marked. Published in *Stroitel'naia promyshlennost',* no. 5 (1928): 374.

Figure 3.14. Walther Moede's angle-measuring device provided a model for Ladovsky's *uglazomer.* From Solomon Gellerstein, *Psikhotekhnika* (Moscow: Novaia Moskva, 1926), 145.

Figure 3.15. Nikolay Ladovsky's *oglazomer* (volume-visual-estimation[-meter]) consisted of a set of vessels of varied geometrical shape into which the subject had to pour the requested volume of liquid. Reproduced in *Stroitel'naia promyshlennost'*, no. 5 (1928): 373.

The Space-Meter

Of all the aspects of visual estimation, the estimation of depth—and thus space—was singled out by Ladovsky as the core of the architect's talent. By that time, the identification of space with stereopsis was a well-known psychological postulate. In the 1830s, Charles Wheatstone demonstrated that binocular parallax—the disparity of planar images received by the two eyes—enabled the emergence of a three-dimensional image in the human mind. Spatial perception later became the subject of the most heated debate in the history of nineteenth-century psychology, known as the Helmholtz–Hering controversy. Whereas Helmholtz argued, from an empiricist position, that humans learn to perceive space by visual experimentation in the course of the early months of life, Ewald Hering (supported, among others, by Ernst Mach) contended that spatial perception is innate.[63] Meanwhile, ensuing aesthetic

Figure 3.16. This photograph from 1927 shows the space-meter. Photograph from unidentified collection, photographer unknown. Published in S. O. Khan-Magomedov, *Ratsionalizm (ratsio-arkhitektura) "Formalizm"* (Moscow: Arkhitektura-S, 2007), 369.

theories, such as that of August Schmarsow, proceeded to pair architecture, as a three-dimensional genre of fine arts, with spatiality. "Space, not stone, is the material of architecture," Ladovsky likewise believed.[64] In the context of the psychotechnics of the architect, the Helmholtz–Hering debate acquired a new significance: the question was not only about the mechanisms of perception, but whether architectural talent is innate or acquired.

The space-meter *(prostrometr)* was an instrument that could help answer that question. For the rationalists, it was thus more than a psychotechnical testing device. Indeed, although Soviet psychologists used an apparatus named *glazomer* ("[the meter of] visual estimation") to study the precision of eye-measuring, Ladovsky preferred a different name.[65] Singled out by Krutikov as a device whose prime purpose was not psychotechnics but an experimental study of space, the space-meter was, in fact, the only one of Ladovsky's devices that did not have the part *-glazomer* in its title.[66] Moreover,

Ladovsky chose not to use Rudik's version of *glazomer,* which rejected the compact laboratory device in favor of a system that was as close to real-life perceptual conditions as possible (in Rudik's system, the subject, standing by a wall of the room, was estimating the distance between two points on the opposite wall seven meters away), even despite its simplicity and inexpensiveness in comparison to laboratory apparatuses.[67] What was missing in Rudik's *glazomer* was the aspect of binocularity. Unlike it, Ladovsky's space-meter consisted of two identical pairs of intersecting transverse surfaces, which could change their angle of incidence, with additional suspending devices.[68] This construction enabled diverse spatial placement of testing objects, while a system of scales allowed for measuring magnitudes. The subject was to occupy a fixed position in front of the rectangular binocular frame, which isolated and, when necessary, enlarged the analyzed space.[69] The frame was located exactly on the axis of the boundary between the two horizontals, making the subjects unable to estimate the degree of the surfaces' incidence, while a system of scales measured the precision of their judgments (Plate 7).

The space-meter was derived from Hering's apparatus for measuring depth perception *(Tiefenwahrnehmungsapparat).* First described by its creator in 1879, it had since then become a standard instrument for studies of strabismus.[70] Most importantly, the space-meter was related to a modification of the *Tiefenwahrnehmungsapparat* devised by Giese and used in professional fitness testing.[71] Hering invented the instrument to conduct the "fall test," which proved his hypothesis that depth is perceived retinally rather than kinetically (in other words, that it was independent from movement). The apparatus fixed the subject's head, directing her or his eyesight with the help of a cardboard cylinder that pointed to a small object (such as a bead) suspended within a two-meter-long rectangular frame that ended with a black screen. The experimenter dropped small balls through the opening in the lid of the apparatus. Unlike a person suffering from strabismus or another defect of stereoscopic vision, a visually healthy subject would inevitably be able to tell whether the ball fell ahead of or behind the bead. Hering's followers, including the psychotechnician Giese, made the subject look at the ball not through a cardboard cylinder but through a diaphragm, which limited the viewing period to fractions of a second to exclude possible movements of eyeballs. Giese, moreover, suggested a test in which the subject was positioned perpendicularly to the device, at two or three meters' distance, and was asked to estimate the distance between the main rod and the side threads suspended from the top. Significantly, both Hering and his followers believed that depth perception, although innate, could nevertheless be developed and improved with experience, and that the *Tiefenwahrnehmungsapparat* could be used to train it.[72]

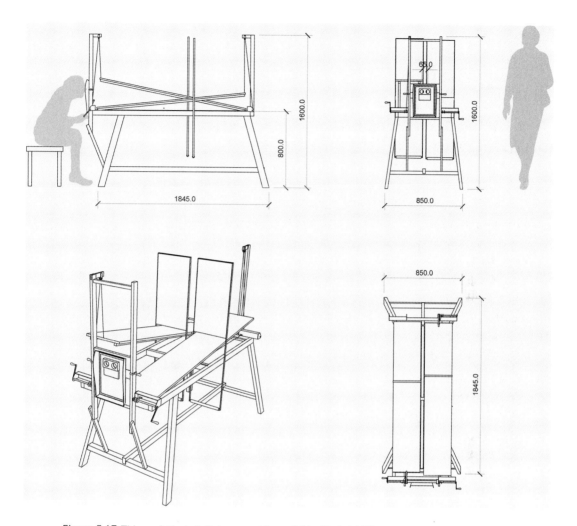

Figure 3.17. This analytical digital parametric model by Pierluigi D'Acunto and Juan Jose Castellon Gonzalez illustrates the mechanics of the space-meter's work. Courtesy of the authors.

Sharing this belief, Ladovsky adapted the psychologists' apparatus to his own concept of spatial perception in architecture. He replaced the diaphragm with a lens, asking the subject to focus not on falling, but on static objects. Thus eliminating the pressure of time, he let the subject move his or her eyeballs and practice binocular comparison, which he considered crucial for an architect. At the same time, he made the two horizontal boards movable, placing objects not only in front of or behind but also above or below each other, thus complicating their spatial relationships.

The novel, optical part of Ladovsky's space-meter consisted of a lens providing a slight magnification, which directed vision to the objects in front

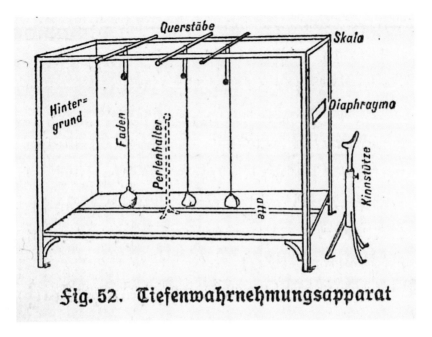

Figure 3.18. The space-meter was based on the modifications of Ewald Hering's *Tiefenwahrnehmungsapparat*. This diagram by Fritz Giese illustrates the principles of its work. The main elements of the apparatus are diaphragm, scale, perpendicular rods on top, a slat at the bottom, the vertical beads container, suspended threads, and the back screen. To the right of the instrument is the chin support. Illustration from Fritz Giese, *Psÿchologisches Wörterbuch*, vol. 7 (Wiesbaden: Springer Fachmedien, 1928), 162.

of the eyes and eliminated everything else from view.[73] This part was based on the stereoscope, an instrument for testing binocular vision invented by Wheatstone in 1838. The stereoscope separated the fields of vision of the two eyes, presenting each with a view taken from a slightly different standpoint: the disparity of these images (imprinted on the so-called stereocards) mimicked binocular parallax. Like the space-meter later, most stereoscopes (for instance, the widely produced Brewster's stereoscope) included lenses that divided the eyes' fields of vision while simultaneously compensating for the shortness of the distance between the eyes and the images. It is difficult to overestimate the importance of the stereoscope, which quickly became a popular entertainment device, for nineteenth- and early twentieth-century culture.[74] Among others, Vladimir Lenin acquired a stereoscope as a part of the Gorki manor, and enthusiastically used it after moving there in 1921.[75]

Examining the history of the stereoscope, Jonathan Crary linked spectatorship with social discipline while identifying a shift from one model of perception to another in the first half of the nineteenth century. Each of these

Figure 3.19. Hering's *Tiefenwahrnehmungsapparat* belonged to a set of instruments indispensable for an experimental psychology laboratory. This period photograph (photographer unknown) is from David Katz, *Psychological Atlas* (New York: Philosophical Library, 1948), illustration 56. Courtesy of the Philosophical Library, New York.

models was represented by its own optical device. The monocular model, a product of sixteenth-century optics, was embodied by the *camera obscura*, whose mechanics repeated the physiology of the eye. The stereoscope, instead, was based upon a binocular model of vision, presenting the eyes with two disparate planar images, while a third one, the "true" three-dimensional picture, different from the other two images, emerged in the mind of the beholder. This model, Crary argued, reflected not only modern optics but also the modern economic system: the stereoscope transformed the eye into a mechanical element that complemented the technology of the device. Both

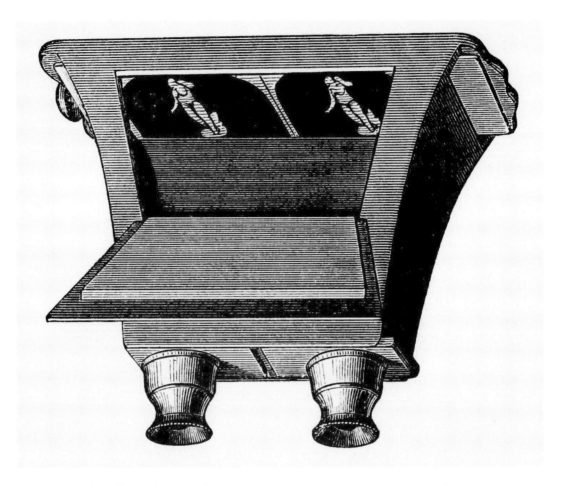

Figure 3.20. The optical part of the space-meter was based on the stereoscope. Like the space-meter later, David Brewster's lenticular stereoscope (1849, pictured here) included lenses that divided the eyes' fields of vision while simultaneously compensating for the shortness of the distance between the eyes and the images. Reproduced in *Popular Science Monthly* 21 (May–October 1882): 47.

the eye and the device thus became elements of the physiological-mechanical complex and could function only as a support for each other; the coordination of the two followed the economic principle of the division of labor.[76] The invention of the stereoscope coincided with another major technological innovation of the century, photography. Wheatstone's stereoscope preceded the invention of the daguerreotype by just one year. The two technologies were soon synthesized in the invention of the stereograph, a pair of photographic images to be used in the stereoscope.[77] Stereography was claimed by science when Ernst Mach suggested applying it to Roentgen technology to create three-dimensional images of internal organs, and when Gastev and

Bernstein used it to analyze working movement.[78] The use of stereography within the Institute of Labor proved, as it were, the scientific status of biomechanics. And what is more, inasmuch as stereography became a tool of the industrial manager, the act of seeing emerged as not only a psychological but also a socially valuable and productive activity—the work of the organizer. Tellingly, the 1932 book by the psychologist Sergey Kravkov, who had taught a course on visual perception at VKhUTEMAS, was titled *The Eye and Its Work (Glaz i ego rabota).*[79]

Psychologists explained this work of vision as the labor of comparison, performed by the brain during the process of synthesizing the nonidentical data of two planar images in a three-dimensional picture. It was the process of comparison—that of two objects in space or of a current sensation with the memory of a past one—that defined visual estimation.[80] According to Kravkov, visual estimation was "a faculty of the eye to compare spatial magnitudes," while Levitov explained that the processes of comparison, differentiation, and evaluation "possessed a special importance" for the ability to visually assess space.[81] The concept of comparison was soon applied to psychological aesthetics, particularly to the aesthetic perception of space. In 1886, Eduard von Hartmann, the author of the first theory of the unconscious, had argued that visual estimation was no less important for architects than the musical ear for composers: while music was perceived directly, as a pleasing or displeasing sensation, architecture was perceived as an understanding of relationships between objects.[82] Likewise, Adolf von Hildebrand believed that comparison allowed the mind to unite discrete spatial objects into a coherent picture.[83] The idea was subsequently developed by Wölfflin, whose binary pairs, as well as the double slide projection method of art history lectures that he pioneered, asserted contrast and comparison as a principle of both art and its history.[84] Ladovsky responded to these arguments by inventing a "device for testing spatiality *[prostranstvennost']*, ponderability *[vesomost']* and balance [that] enables the visual comparison of architectural projects in regard to the above-mentioned qualities."[85] Comparing the data received by the two eyes rather than that of two different experiences, his space-meter likewise relied on the principle of comparison.

As Zeynep Çelik Alexander observed, stereoscopic vision provided proof that "the ability to synthesize form was precisely that which distinguished the human eye from that of the machine."[86] The organizational work of comparison, emerged as productive activity that was simultaneously modern and humanist. Here, the division of labor was not rejected but sublated in the process of synthesis, which relied on prior analytical work. Having transcended the mechanism of the physiological, modern subjectivity—and the modern architect as its epitome—thus emerged within the zone of psychological indeterminacy between consciousness and the unconscious. "One-eyed reason, deficient in its vision of depth" was Alfred North Whitehead's criticism of eighteenth-century philosophic mechanicism.[87] By 1925, when these words were written, stereoscopic vision, or the capacity for the psychological production of space, was firmly established as a synonym for humanness.

For Ladovsky and other rationalists, the organizational work of the architect consisted in enabling the adaptation of the humans to their three-dimensionality through synthesizing reality fragmented by the division of vision and labor. The product of this architecture was space as a legible psychological interface that structured and regulated the world and the human. Accordingly, the architect had to possess superb physiological and psychological abilities for the analysis of space. These abilities were innate but improvable and could be measured by the space-meter—simultaneously a psychotechnical testing device, a pedagogical instrument, and a laboratory apparatus for spatial research. Merging productivist and aesthetic concerns, Ladovsky's rationalism turned architecture into an activity in which the economy of perception became indistinguishable from the economy of work.

Seeking a middle ground between collectivity and individuality, nativism and empiricism, humanism and Taylorist efficiency, the organism and the machine, psychotechnics remained both ethically and politically ambiguous. Its answer to the problem of alienation was to naturalize the division of labor—making it appear as if stemming from the biological and psychological abilities of workers. It aspired to perform this naturalization by prioritizing the psychological as the middle ground between the physiological and the conscious. Salvaging psychological individuality from Taylorist mechanization, it subjected this individuality to technocratic control. And yet the story of Soviet architectural psychotechnics is relevant beyond histories of Soviet architecture and interwar European Americanism. Arguing for a psychotechnics-based brigade system of the organization of architectural work, Karra responded not only to the dehumanizing ethos of Taylor and Kahn but also to the humanist attempts of Narkompros to introduce polytechnic education. Although his intent was to overcome alienation by endowing workers with erudition and providing them with a comprehensive, multisided education, as Karra argued in his article, the "polytechnic specialist" had developed in response to the rules of the capitalist labor market, where an ability to perform different tasks guaranteed flexibility and thus survival. In an organically envisioned socialist society, a profession would instead be a "social function," whose regulation and distribution would be based exclusively on "social purposefulness."[88] The humanist intentions of a flexible and multisided work environment, Karra explained, did not prevent it from paving the way for new forms of exploitation. Although formulated in support of an organicist version of state capitalism, Karra's argument anticipated the effects of the new form of labor management that emerged in the 1970s and has since the 1990s been known as post-Fordism. Based on the myth of making work pleasurable and blurring the division between work and leisure, post-Fordism masks and intensifies rather than overcomes alienation, extending it into the sphere of private and emotional life.

FOUR

Process

Organicist Aesthetics of Soviet Standardization

In *The Technical Everyday and Contemporary Art* (1928), designer and theorist Alexander Toporkov gave an excited description of *Doryphoros,* a celebrated sculpture of a young athlete by Polykleitos, whose lost original dated back to the fifth century BC. The appearance of *Doryphoros* in a work of modernist theory might seem surprising—but no less unusual was Toporkov's reading of it, for he was little interested in the particulars of the classical canon. Rather, in Toporkov's eyes, *Doryphoros* appeared as an early example of standardization:

> Greek sculpture sought the canon, it strove to develop a norm and a standard. . . . Especially telling is the canon of Polykleitos. His Young Athlete truly presents an image of the standardized human. He is normal in this special sense that we today to some extent know from management. The Young Athlete of Polykleitos is well-organized and purposeful, he is practical *[delovit],* he will not fail at a difficult moment. He will complete his mission. He has a purposeful setup. He resembles an object more than a human, at least in the Kantian sense of the word; at least his purpose lies not in himself but rather the opposite: this purpose, to which he is oriented and to which he is suited like a key to the lock, is outside [of himself]. He is full and complete and at the same time presupposes an environment.[1]

Like the ideal human, Toporkov further argued, architecture had to become typical—responding, through its "purposeful setup," to its age and society just as Polykleitos responded to his. Creating such architecture was to become the task of Soviet standardization, a project that preoccupied architectural functionalists in the late 1920s.

Presenting the human as the ultimate subject of standardization, Toporkov's reading of *Doryphoros* anchors this modernist discussion in such publications

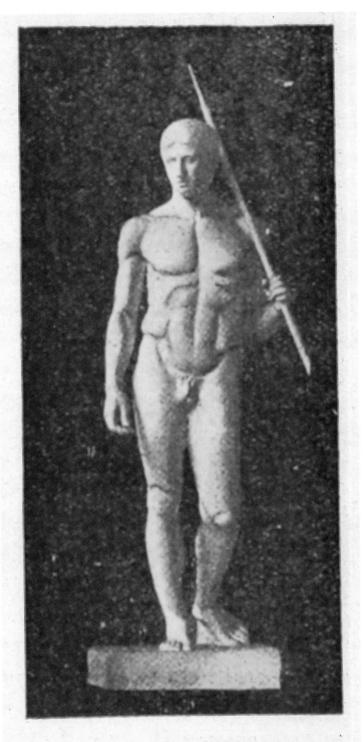

Поликлет. Дорифор.

Figure 4.1. Alexander Toporkov considered *Doryphoros* by Polykleitos (lost original fifth century BC) to be an example of standardization. This image, used by Toporkov as an illustration to his book, is of the bronze cast (made after marble original from Pompeii) of *Doryphoros* in the Pushkin Museum, Moscow. Reproduced in Aleksandr Toporkov, *Tekhnicheskii byt i sovremennoe iskusstvo* (Moscow: Gosudarstvennoe izdatel'stvo, 1928), 135.

as Johannes Bochenek's nineteenth-century treatise on the geometrical normalization of the body (see Figure 1.5).[2] The standardization of architecture, furthermore, mirrored the efforts of modern physiologists at standardizing laboratory animals.[3] "Technical standards *also* serve a normalizing function. Conventions that govern the dimensions of bricks also shape understandings of the bodily politics," argues Nader Vossoughian, examining the work of Ernst Neufert, the German champion of standardization.[4] What remained a hidden agenda in Germany became an overt mission in the USSR. Soviet architecture required a development of a set of normalizing instruments and necessitated a reflection about their formative effect on architecture and the human. Unpacking the constellation of notions that were mobilized for this goal—organization, type, process, function, and setup, among others—this chapter highlights their roots in life sciences in order to examine the bilateral process of simultaneous naturalization (and thus purported humanization) of architecture and the objectification of nature and the human. Unlike the geometric beauty of Bochenek's normalized human, the functionalist, evolutionist beauty of Toporkov's *Doryphoros* changed in response to environmental conditions, thereby endowing architecture with the agency of shaping it.

From Organization to Standardization

On May 30, 1910, St. Petersburg celebrated the birthday of the city's founder, Tsar Peter the Great, by opening a new, state-of-the-art hospital, which, accommodating two thousand patients, became the largest in the city. Although the hospital buildings were designed in romanticized neo-Dutch style associated with the figure and times of Tsar Peter, their arrangement, developed by architects in consultation with medical experts, embodied modern principles of efficiency and hygiene. The plan of the hospital campus was carefully zoned and calculated to segregate the three types of its inhabitants (patients, employees, and corpses) from the rest of the city and from each other. Administration services faced the entrance, welcoming legitimate visitors and guarding off the undesired ones; the gynecological ward was nearby to facilitate emergency admission for women in labor; wards for people with nervous and contagious diseases were isolated from the rest of the hospital to enable quarantining and peace. Inside the pavilions, the depth and width of the rooms were carefully calibrated, their diagonals oriented along a north–south axis to guarantee an even and long-lasting exposure to the sun, and all rooms were equipped with water closets, separated by vestibules for better

Figure 4.2. In their early and at first sight traditional project, Hospital of Peter the Great (1910) in St. Petersburg, architects Alexander Klein, Alexander Rozenberg, and Lev Ilyin tested the principles of nascent functionalism. Stemming from the requirements of the hospital as a type of architecture that deals with body and life, organicism remained a vital, if concealed, part of later functionalism. This general view of the hospital (most likely by Ilyin) was reproduced in L. Il'in, A. Klein, and A. Rozenberg, *Proekt gorodskoi bol'nitsy imeni imperatora Petra Velikago v S.-Peterburge na 1000 krovatei* (St. Petersburg: Zhurn. "Stroitel'," 1908), 3–4.

ventilation. Taking the human organism as both the object and the model, this project asserts the hospital, rather than the factory or the grain elevator, as the *Ur*-type of functionalist architecture, placing its architects, Alexander Klein, Alexander Rozenberg, and Lev Ilyin, at its origins.[5] Whereas Ilyin was responsible primarily for the hospital's decoration, Klein—soon to obtain fame in Germany (where he would immigrate in 1921) as the author of functional diagrams exploring the effects of the depth–width proportion of spaces—oversaw the project and prepared its masterplan, while Rozenberg focused on the plans of individual pavilions. In both the hospital and their later work, the latter two pioneered an organizational—and organicist—approach to architecture.

Today it is often forgotten that two commonly used terms, *organism* and *organization,* are etymologically and semantically related. The ultimate split between them occurred only during the second half of the twentieth century, when the rise of the computing machine disembodied the idea of knowledge, confining the meaning of "organism" to the world of biology and of "organization" to the domain of management and information science. Instead, Immanuel Kant used the term "organized being" to refer to plants and animals, while German physiologist Johannes Müller in 1837 defined organism as "a governing unity of the whole, which emerges from the coordination of different elements"—"the enduring activity of living organic matter," Müller added, "is also present in the laws of rational purposeful planning."[6] In 1858, Müller's student Rudolf Virchow formulated his influential doctrine of the "cell-state" *(der Zellenstaat),* which was based on an analogy between the biological and the social organism: every animal, according to Virchow, "presents itself as a sum of vital unities, every one of which manifests all the characteristics of life."[7] The cell-state theory remained a part of mainstream biology well into the twentieth century, while Virchow's progressive political activism contributed to its popularity among the revolutionized intelligentsia, particularly in Russia.

In 1866, Virchow's student Ernst Haeckel had suggested another term for his own program of an evolutionist science of organization: "tectology."[8] Every organism, according to Haeckel, was an aggregate of natural bodies of a different hierarchical order: a cell, an organ, an antimere (such as a half), a metamere (such as a segment), a person, or a corm (animal colony). Embracing Haeckel's monism, Alexander Bogdanov applied this method to the entire universe: all natural, cultural, and social phenomena could be viewed, he argued, as organisms. The common ground, which allowed Bogdanov to compare elements of such different nature, was form—the anatomy of an animal, the morphology of a word, or a social structure.[9] In the spirit of Herbert Spencer, Bogdanov considered forms transient and unstable, constantly modifying themselves in response to environmental challenges. This modification activity was none other than organization. Bogdanov's major philosophical work, *Tectology: A Universal Organizational Science* (*Tektologiia: Vseobshchaia organizatsionnaia nauka,* 1913–17), was a metatheory that identified general laws and principles of organic, inorganic, and social worlds—it was, as he called it, "a systematization of organized experience," a universal theory of organization.[10]

Bogdanov conceived of tectology not as a philosophy but as a practical tool for organizing labor.[11] He believed that the entire complex world of culture (language, ideas, and, ultimately, ideology) belonged to a set of tectological instruments, or adaptational mechanisms in the struggle of humans with nature. As an art of creating new usable forms, architecture became for Bogdanov a model of tectological activity:

> [If] it is necessary to build a house—this is achievable only because the necessary elements (i.e., wood, stone, lime, glass, axes, saws, hammers, and other tools, the work force of carpenters, stone-masons, etc.) are present, and is achievable only in such a way that elements are united and separated, brought into novel combinations, and the final result—a building—is characterized by such a link and such a correspondence of its elements that it presents something greater than they originally contained, namely an increase in harmony between people and their natural environment, and consequently presents, from a human point of view, an "organized" system.[12]

The most diligent reader of Bogdanov among architects, Rozenberg conceived his own treatise, *Philosophy of Architecture* (*Filosofiia arkhitektury,* 1923), as a metatheory of the discipline—a taxonomy of categories and a set of universal tectological principles applied to architecture.[13] Like Bogdanov, he saw the taxonomy of form as a reflection of the hierarchy of organizational activity. Comparing "the art of architecture" with the "art of medicine," he divided the kingdom of "architectural structures" into classes, genera, species, subspecies, and types.[14] Class was a category of scale, and the four classes (rooms, buildings, complexes, and settlements) were arranged in a hierarchy of size and complexity. The twelve genera were defined by function. They were subdivided into two groups of six: industrial (mining, processing, retail, storage, transportation, and communication) and civil (residential, hygienic, medical, educational, public, and administrative). Each genus consisted of several species, which were identified according to "the character of the process." The species were further subdivided based on how the process was performed (for example, hygienic buildings were divided into bathhouses, showers, and pools). Finally, type, a category that would soon become important for the theory of standardization, described the relationship between an architectural subspecies and its form.[15]

"Enticing title and . . . complete disappointment," bemoaned the soon-

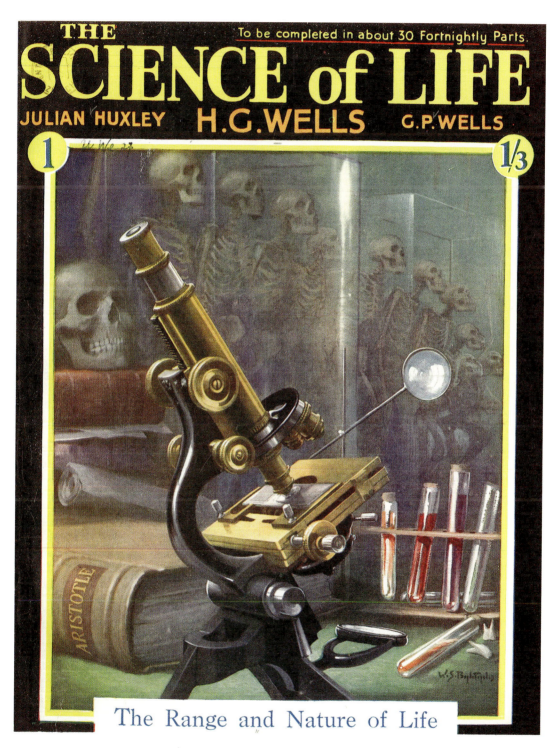

Plate 1. The cover of *The Science of Life* by H. G. Wells, G. P. Wells, and Julian Huxley (1929–30) illustrates the evolutionist notions of life and the human.

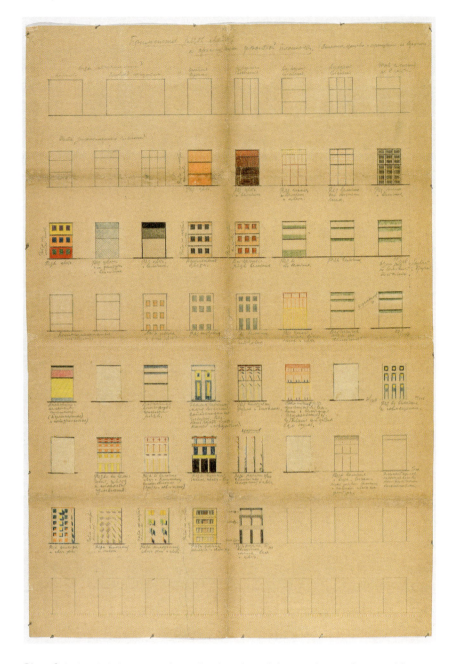

Plate 2. Ladovsky's former students developed an elaborate theory of composition, which was based on an analysis of rows. This unfinished scheme by Viktor Balikhin illustrates "The Application of the Rows of Properties to the Organization of Frontal Plane (Dynamics, Unity, and the Limitations of the Vertical)." The top row illustrates "Types of Relationships" (left to right: equality; the predominance of horizontality; the predominance of verticality; neutral divisions [the next three diagrams]; a two-partite division). The second row illustrates "Types of Regular Divisions" and metric rhythm created by number, size, and color. The third row illustrates metric rhythm created by color and size. In the fourth row, rhythm is created by modifications of intervals and size. The fifth row uses proportion and geometry for the creation of rhythm and introduces elements of dynamic. The sixth row creates rhythm with size, color, and the speed of transformation. The last colored row relies on chiaroscuro and relief. Pencil drawing. Courtesy of the Museum of the Moscow Institute of Architecture.

Plate 3. El Lissitzky's *Tatlin at Work on the Monument to the Third International* (1922) can be read as a symbolic self-portrait that illustrates Lissitzky's views about the relationship between art and mathematics as well as about monocular perspective. The collage was used as an illustration to Ilya Ehrenburg's *Six Stories with Easy Endings* (Il'ia Erenburg, *Shest' povestei o legkikh kontsakh* (Moscow: Gelikon, 1922). Courtesy of the Grosvenor Gallery, London.

Plate 4. The first of the sixteen analytical illustrated tables (posters) that supplemented Georgy Krutikov's VKhUTEIN diploma project "The City of the Future" (1929) explored "The Visual Deformation of a Dynamic Form," showing how movement produced what Lissitzky called imaginary space. Courtesy of the A. V. Shchusev State Museum of Architecture, Moscow (PIa 11200/1).

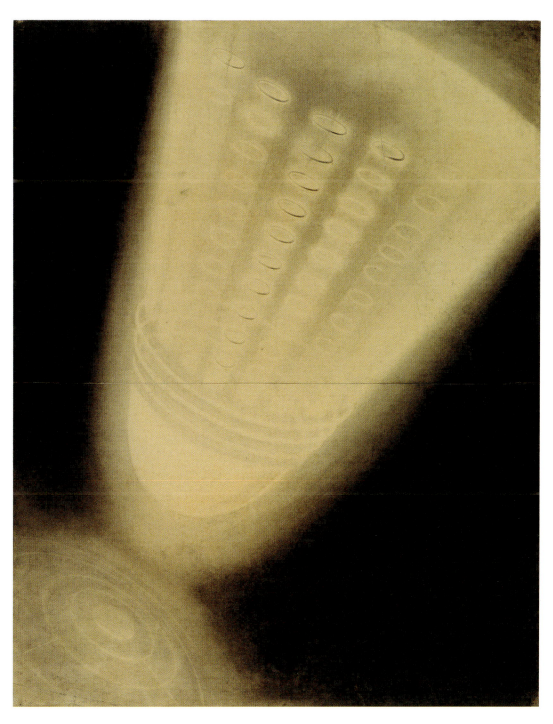

Plate 5. Georgy Krutikov, "General View," part of "The City of the Future," VKhUTEIN diploma project (1929). This rendering of the city of the future seen from space explores Lissitzky's concept of imaginary space and Krutikov's experimental and analytical research of the visual effects of movement and light. Courtesy of the A. V. Shchusev State Museum of Architecture, Moscow (PIa 11201/4).

Plate 6. Lissitzky's color sketch depicting one of the horizontal skyscrapers (to be located at the Nikitsky Gates Square) illustrates his proposition that "the introduction of color for differentiation of each individual skyscraper will enhance its orientational potential" (*Izvestia ASNOVA*, no. 1 [1926]: 3). Courtesy of the State Tretyakov Gallery, Moscow (RS-1923).

Plate 7. Digital model by Pierluigi D'Acunto and Juan José Castellón González illustrates the mechanics of the space-meter's work. Courtesy of the authors.

Plate 8. Visually resembling Klein's diagrammatic multitudes, *Finite Format 04*, a series of watercolors by Mauricio Pezo and Sofia von Ellrichshausen for Chicago Architecture Biennial 2017, similarly erases form while replacing it not by type but by format. Courtesy pezo von ellrichshausen.

Plate 9. Maria Ender's table (Table VI. "The change of color spot and color background in time, within the eyes closed") illustrates her teacher Mikhail Matyushin's theory of the linking color. Courtesy of the State Museum of the History of St. Petersburg (80449/12-osn).

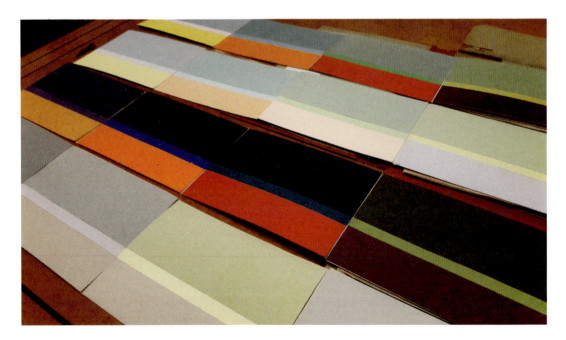

Plate 10. In his hand-colored set of tables, *The Handbook of Color: A Pattern of the Convertibility of Color Combinations* (*Spravochnik po tsvetu: Zakonomernost' izmeniaemosti tsvetovykh sochetanii* [Leningrad: Gosudarstvennoe izdatel'stvo izobrazitel'nykh iskusstv, 1932]), Mikhail Matyushin suggested applying his theory of linking color to interior design. Photograph by the author.

Plate 11. Translated into Russian in 1926, Wilhelm Ostwald's *Farbkunde* (1923) became the standard textbook of color theory at both VKhUTEMAS and Malyarstroy. Pictured here is Ostwald's one-tone triangle from the Russian edition of *Farbkunde*. This color plate was produced at VKhUTEMAS, while the dyes and the printing technique were developed by VKhUTEMAS professor and chemist N. V. Turkin.

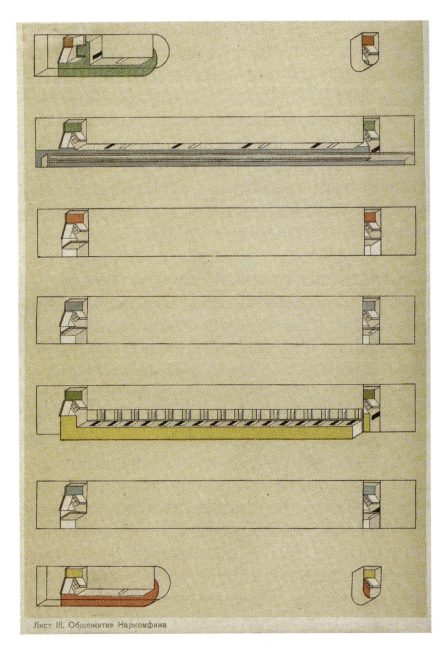

Plate 12. Hinnerk Scheper and Malyarstroy's color scheme for the Narkomfin building circulation areas utilizes the Bauhaus experience of the use of color for orientation (most important, Scheper's color scheme for the Bauhaus building in Dessau). The scheme was published in *Maliarnoe delo* (color supplement to no. 3–4, 1930); original in the Bauhaus-Archiv Berlin. Courtesy of the Bauhaus-Archiv Berlin.

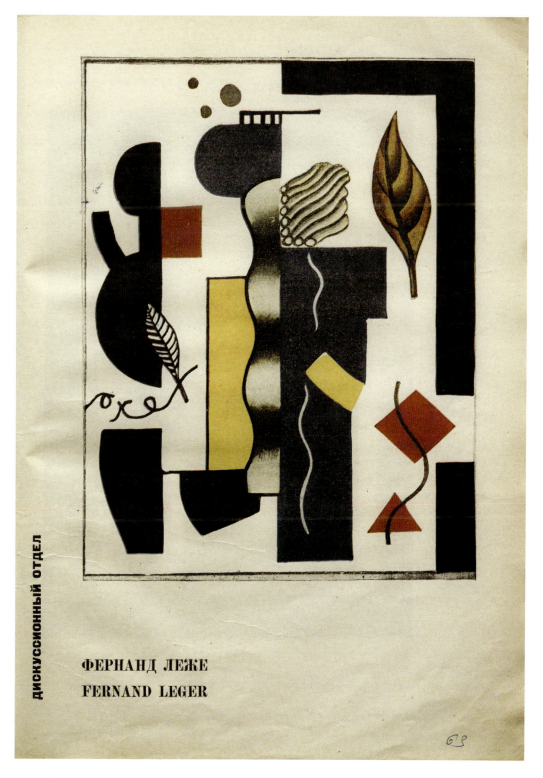

Plate 13. The special issue of the constructivist journal *Sovremennaya arkhitektura* on architectural polychromy (1929) was richly illustrated with the works of Fernand Léger (the only artist whose work was represented in the issue). Ginzburg, the journal's editor, explained that he saw Léger's work not as easel painting but as an analytical exercise in exploring how form can be expressed by color. From *Sovremennaia arkhitektura*, no. 2 (1929): 59.

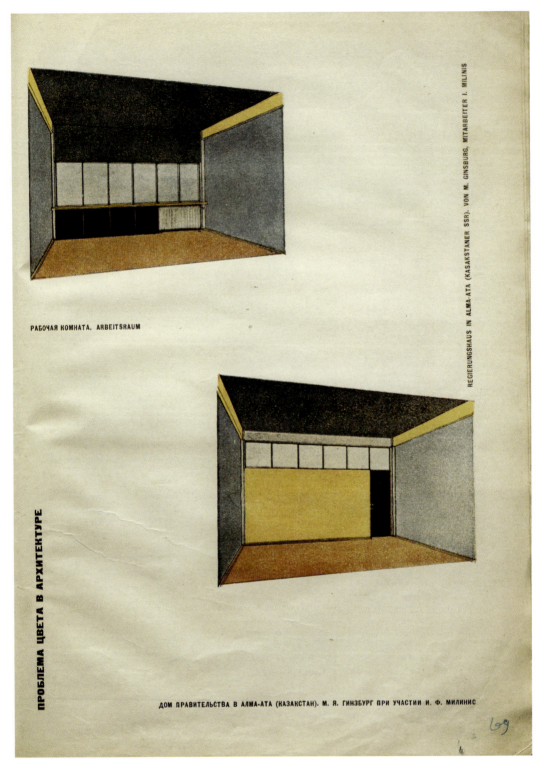

Plate 14. Moisei Ginzburg's early interior color schemes employed a Léger-like palette of contrasting primary colors and black. This project of interior coloration for an office in Ginzburg's Government Building in Alma-Ata (contemporary Almaty, Kazakhstan; together with Ignaty Milinis) demonstrates a black ceiling and a black external wall facing a bright yellow wall, while the two remaining walls are painted blue. Project published in *Sovremennaia arkhitektura,* no. 2 (1929): 69.

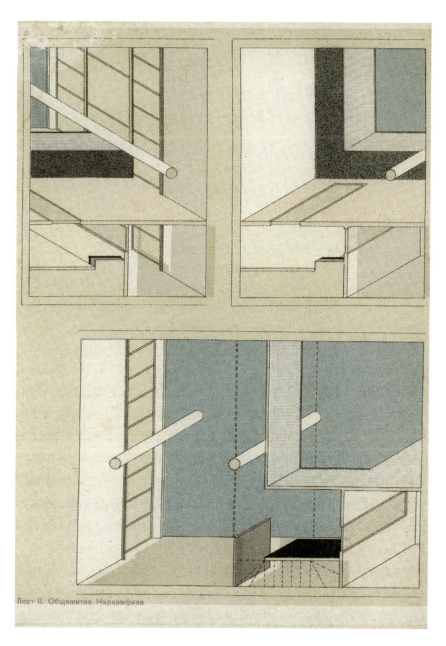

Plate 15. Hinnerk Scheper and Malyarstroy's cold scheme was to be used in apartments of type K: three-room apartments for families with children. The scheme was published in *Maliarnoe delo* (color supplement to no. 3–4, 1930); original in the Bauhaus-Archiv Berlin. Courtesy of the Bauhaus-Archiv Berlin.

Plate 16. A 1979 watercolor drawing by Elena Ovsyannikova shows the dining room in the "penthouse" Narkomfin apartment, which belonged to Ginzburg's patron, the minister of finance Nikolay Milyutin. Courtesy of Elena Ovsyannikova.

Plate 17. The warm scheme was to be applied in the apartments of type F. Scheper presented it with two more traditional central perspectival drawings. The scheme was published in *Maliarnoe delo* (color supplement to no. 3–4, 1930); original in the Bauhaus-Archiv Berlin. Courtesy of the Bauhaus-Archiv Berlin.

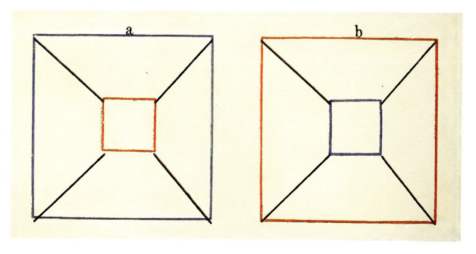

Plate 18. This quasi-perspectival diagrammatic construction was often cited in nineteenth-century psychological literature as an example of a figure that could be read as both pyramidal form and receding space. According to Wilhelm von Bezold, if the smaller square was orange, the figure was perceived as a pyramid, while a blue smaller square turned it into a receding space. Scheper employed the same compositional structure in his drawing for the warm scheme to support the spatial effect of the white outer wall (white was considered by psychologists an equivalent of blue in its potential to expand space). Diagram reproduced in Wilhelm von Bezold, *Die Farbenlehre im Hinblick auf Kunst und Kunstgewerbe* (Braunschweig: George Westermann, 1874), Tafel VI.

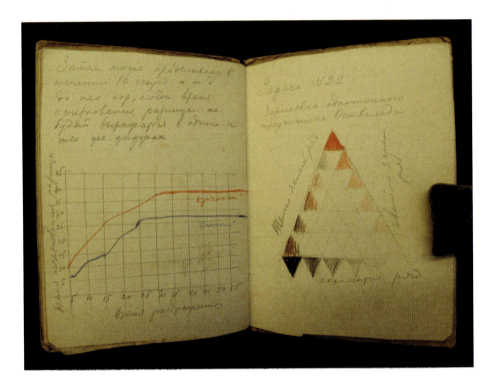

Plate 19. At VKhUTEIN, the notion of fatigue redefined the artistic discourse about color. A "Practicum of Color Theory" student sketchbook by Alexander Lyushin (VKhUTEIN, 1928–30) contains exercises on observing the effects of color fatigue *(left)* and Ostwald's color triangle *(right)*. Author's photograph. Courtesy of the Getty Research Institute, Los Angeles (950052).

Plate 20. An illustrated children's book by artists Valery Alfeevsky and Tatyana Lebedeva (Mavrina) presents an idealized vision of the park as a space of personal activation. This overview shows a variety of activities performed in the park. *Park kultury i otdykha: Risunki Alfeevskogo i Lebedevoi* (Moscow: Gosudarstvennoe izdatel'stvo, 1930).

to-be leader of constructivism Moisei Ginzburg (who at that time was under the sway of Le Corbusier's proselytizing of architecture expressive of *l'esprit nouveau*), reviewing Rozenberg's book in 1923: "On fifty-three little pages [one finds] an endless recapitulation of various schemes and classifications, which give nothing, which explain nothing, and which the author calls 'philosophy' for no apparent reason."[16] As industrialization gained its momentum in the Soviet Union, Ginzburg was to reconsider his opinions. By 1926, he also viewed organism as a model of architectural work:

> Freed from any clichés of the past, from prejudices and superstitions, the new architect analyses all sides of the task, its specificity, he divides it into elements, groups according to functions, and organizes his solution according to these premises. The result is a spatial solution that is similar to any conscious organism, divided into separate organs, receiving this or that development depending on the functions that it performs.[17]

If in the early 1920s Rozenberg could explore organization on a purely theoretical level, toward the end of the decade organizational questions became integrated into a new set of practical and industry-related concerns. The First Five-Year Plan aspired to meet its ambitious economic goals through a centralization of all aspects of economic activity. Standardization, a technique that emerged as both a product and a driver of industrialization, enabled the necessary coordination and centralization of production. Although, in architecture, standardization was not limited to modern construction materials and aesthetics, the new technique quickly captivated the imagination of modernist architects.[18] Detailing a simultaneously Corbusean and evolutionist vision of the house as a "tool for living," El Lissitzky argued that such a tool "requires an elaboration of types and norms, which could be sent to mass factory production and then ordered from a catalog."[19] By 1929, Soviet theoretician of the scientific organization of labor Osip Ermansky could contend that the unavoidable arrival of standardization paved "the ground for mass production, calculation, [and] regulation, informing, thus, the horizontal and vertical growth of rationalization."[20] In Soviet Russia, this standardization remained imbued with the same organicism as Rozenberg's early architectural and theoretical works.

Indeed, while in the second half of the century the notion of standardization became inseparable from the industrial production of building elements, in the 1920s its definition was less precise. Arguing against the French and American authors who equated standardization with rationalization, Ermansky attempted to clarify the term by comparing the nuances of its use in German and Russian languages. Derived from the English word *standard,* the expanded sense of the Russian word *standardizatsiia* (equivalent to the German *Vereinheitlichung*) referred to the unification of production. This broad concept, according to Ermansky's classification, was subdivided into standardization in the narrow sense (German *Normung*)—in turn consisting of two parts, the development of types (typification) and the unification of the sizes of details (German *Normalisierung*; in the Russian-language classification this notion occupied the same hierachical level as standardization in the narrow sense)—and the distribution of these details' production between factories (specialization). Meanwhile, a related term, *norming* (the analog of German *Normierung*), which Ermansky used but considered separate from standardization, addressed the expenditure of material resources and the productivity of labor.[21] Since standardization in its narrow sense required well-developed industrial production and was thus only achieved in the Soviet Union in the late 1950s, during the interwar period, Soviet standardization remained focused on organizational rather than on industrial aspects: not on regulating the factory production of building elements but on controlling a variety of processes connected to architecture as an object of design, construction, and use—in other words, on typification and norming.[22]

In fact, typification and norming had entered the sphere of concern of Russian architecture long before the Soviet revolution. Typification (Russian *tipizatsiia*) relied on the category of type, which was used across biological taxonomy, nascent sociology, and the modern theory of architecture and the arts. What type inevitably demonstrated regardless of the context in which this term was used was the relationship between form and function. Nineteenth-century biologists defined type as a specimen that embodied characteristic features of the species, while realist literature (a tradition that was particularly strong in Russia) relied on type as a character that exemplified its social group. In classicist architecture type was understood as a formal order that expressed the function of the building.[23] By the eighteenth century, when the notion reached Russia, it was redefined as a model design solution appropriate for a particular purpose: sets of state-approved model facades were regularly published from the rule of Peter the Great until the revolution. The Russian imperial *Construction Codex* (*Stroitel'nyi ustav*, 1832) also prescribed the types for state, ecclesiastical, and civil buildings. This codex, furthermore, was supplemented with the *Work Regulation (Urochnoe polozhenie),* which focused on construction. Addressing construction managers, *Work Regulation*

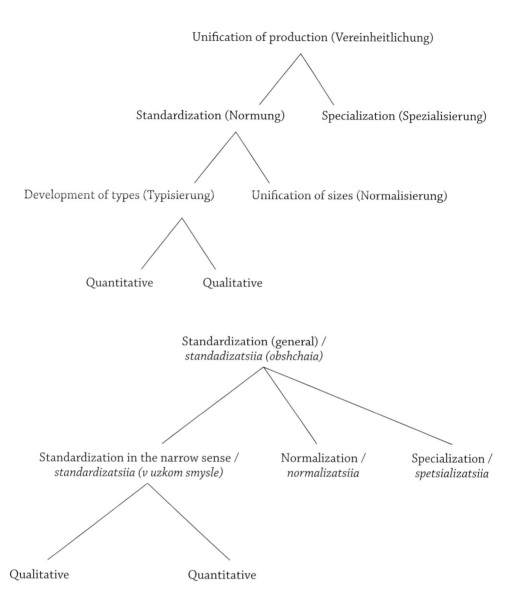

Figure 4.3. These diagrams illustrate the differences in the understanding of the term "standardization" in German *(above)* and Russian *(below)*. Originally published in Russian in Osip Ermanskii, *Teoriia i praktika ratsionalizatsii,* vol. 1 (Moscow: Gosudarstvennoe izdatel'stvo, 1929), 269–70. Redrawn and translated into English by the author.

assisted them with norming—compiling budgets and organizing the work of employees.[24] Closely related, both typification and norming were thus introduced as mechanisms of normalizing architectural work: whereas the former addressed the process of design, the second targeted the process of construction.

World Process and the Process of Construction

In the second half of the 1920s, Rozenberg headed work on *The Set of Industrial Construction Norms* (*Svod proizvodstvennykh stroitel'nykh norm*, 1927–30), a multivolume compendium aimed at replacing the *Work Regulation*.[25] This work gave him an opportunity to continue developing his earlier theory of normalization, which aspired to devise a single methodological foundation for architecture, from its most abstract, organizational principles down to the practical particularities of construction. The term "normalization," for Rozenberg, referred not to industrial details but to processes. To normalize a process was, according to him, to subject it to the energy-economic principle: "to organize it in such a way that it would give the maximum production with the minimal expense of resources and energy."[26] Rozenberg received this approach from Bogdanov as well as from Russian imperial military architect Viktor Sokolsky, whose "economic principle" appears its most immediate source.[27] Whereas nature, Rozenberg stipulated, possessed absolute normalization—the evolution of form in response to the changes in the environment—the normalization of human society was relative as culture diverted the normalizing economic course. In its continuous progress toward more complex organization and fuller normalization, human society was thus simultaneously returning to nature.[28]

Evoking Eduard von Hartmann's and Friedrich Nietzsche's philosophies of history, Rozenberg described the world as "the world process," which encompassed all other processes, including "the all-human process."[29] Every human process, he explained, required three elements: setting (*obstanovka*), which he identified as "the sum of all objects necessary for a normal functioning of the process"; mass, "the sum of all objects and people participating in the process"; and the sequence of the process, "a certain order of the duration of the process."[30] Design, in this picture, emerged as the evolution of the building's shape out of many possibilities as the one most economically responding to its conditions. Such a concept was vividly illustrated by Klein's diagrams examining the relationship between the depth and the width of the room. Publicized and studied in the Soviet Union, they demonstrated the process of finding the balance between hygiene (relatively wide external wall and relatively shallow depth for better insolation) and economy.[31]

Rather than developing several fixed types, Rozenberg proposed creating a single form-generating algorithm, which would regulate, simplify, and demystify the process of design. Beginning with an analysis of the process that takes place inside a room, he proceeded, relying on modern hygienic and economic standards, to calculate the ceiling's height, the room's volume and

Figure 4.4. Reproduced by the constructivist journal *Sovremennaya arkhitektura* shortly after the original publication in German, Alexander Klein's diagrams demonstrated the process of finding the balance between hygiene and economy. *Sovremennaia arkhitektura*, no. 1 (1929): 29.

shape, and the size and location of windows, subsequently uniting rooms in buildings, adding circulation areas, stacking up floors, combining buildings into complexes, complexes into settlements, and settlements into settlement nodes, which could proliferate, forming organic ties with each other. "To normalize a space," Rozenberg elucidated in his *General Theory of Design of Architectural Structures* (*Obshchaia teoriia proektirovaniia arkhitekturnykh sooruzhenii*, 1930), means to establish numerical values for each type of space, according to its "varied character *[velichina]*, for all its characteristic coefficients." Rozenberg formalized this operation of translation with a series of rules and guidelines, which he developed based on Sokolsky's publications. By entering architectural coefficients (volume, perimeter, building surface, width of walls, among others) into numerical relationships, the architect could determine the building's economic indexes: the norm of main areas a (indicating the rationality of the main areas' plan), the coefficient of the breadth (rationality) of solution k (the rationality of the plan of service areas), the coefficient of projectiveness l (the rationality of circulation), the coefficient of constructiveness m (the rationality of the size of the building's footprint). The ultimate parameter—the spatial rationality of the building—was calculated based on the comparison of its volume v and median ceiling height h with the norm a and the coefficients $k, l,$ and m.[32]

Since form would continuously change following the change of parameters, Rozenberg's organic architecture was inherently unstable: the size of a bedroom, for instance, could grow alongside the family, subsequently leading to its split into several bedrooms. Moreover, economic purposefulness, Rozenberg mused, leads "to the necessity of giving the structure only such a robustness" that would guarantee that its "functional (moral) death" would occur simultaneously with its "physical death."[33] Thus expanding the definition of architecture to include not only erection but also maintenance and demolition of buildings, he redefined it as "construction process."[34]

Dedicated to norming, *The Set of Norms* aspired to became a periodic table of elements for this process. Borrowing the system of periodization from *Work Regulation,* its fourteen volumes divided the discipline according to the leading working material and technique: transportation works, earth works, masonry works, ferro-concrete works, wood works, roofs, hearths, plaster works, wall-painting works, metal works, sanitation works, external networks, highway and road works, and hydrotechnical works. Each volume was further organized as a set of normalizing instructions for processes of different hierarchical order: elementary operations, simple works, complex works for parts of buildings, and, finally, norms for complete buildings. If the old *Work Regulation,* Rozenberg explained, had focused on calculations

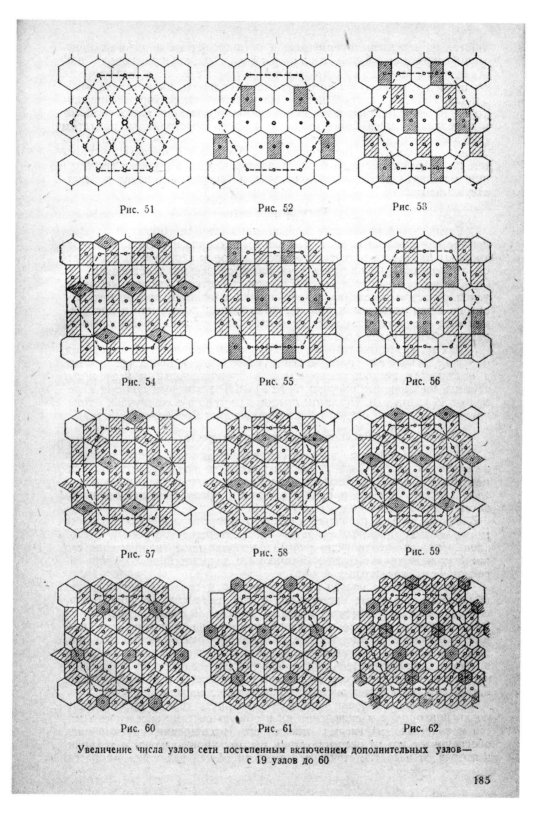

Figure 4.5. Alexander Rozenberg's diagrams illustrate the process of growth of urban nodes. Reproduced in Aleksandr Rozenberg, *Obshchaia teoriia proektirovaniia arkhitekturnykh sooruzhenii* (Moscow: Plankhozgiz, 1930), 185.

of expenses, his *Set of Norms* offered an active, organic approach to the construction process.[35] Alongside norms for work, it provided norms for rest and included the so-called *orgdobavki* (organizational additions), or time "cushions" for possible organizational delays for each type of works.[36] But most important, in addition to providing norms it offered detailed, step-by-step descriptions of each work operation; in other words, it not only normed but also normalized the work of construction. Whereas Rozenberg's earlier philosophical schemes inscribed architecture into a universal taxonomy by linking it to categories of different ontological order, his scientific normalization of construction turned architecture into a mediating mechanism that allowed reconciling the unattainable ideals of modernization and the crude reality of unskilled, technologically backward labor in the interwar Soviet Union, including the latter in the discussion alongside building materials and construction techniques.

Like a Taylorist efficiency engineer, Rozenberg's organizer of architectural work was equipped with a chronometer and a camera for documenting the processes of construction and measuring its outcome. Yet, the difference between Rozenberg's approach and Taylorism was significant: whereas the latter focused on physical movement alone, Rozenberg's normalization aspired to provide a comprehensive account of varied factors that provided the context for labor activity. Illustrating his managerial method of "the documentation of factors" *(fiksazh faktorov)* in another publication, Rozenberg described flooring work as performed on a particular day by two ethnic Russian workers, forty-five and forty-seven years of age and in satisfactory health, both literate and trained as carpenters, one with fifteen years of experience and the other with twenty, one right-handed and the other left-handed. This work, we further find out, took place on a summer Saturday, during the morning and early afternoon hours, when it was hot (30 degrees C) and dry; although the wind was insignificant, the building had drafts. Their tools were the usual: the hammer weighed 1.22 kg and the axe 2.04 kg; the bow saw was 0.7 meter long. The rest of the tools and materials were described just as meticulously, the methods and outcomes of the work documented by drawings.[37] The resulting observations would allow modifying the basic work norm for flooring (as provided in *The Set of Norms*) in accordance with these specific factors. This meticulousness notwithstanding, Rozenberg's "documentation of factors" avoids considering any personal circumstances: where the workers came from, who their friends and families were, what they ate, or what their emotional disposition was that day. The depersonified subjects of the evolutionary process, they existed inasmuch as they reconfigured the environment in accordance with objective environmental factors. This objectification

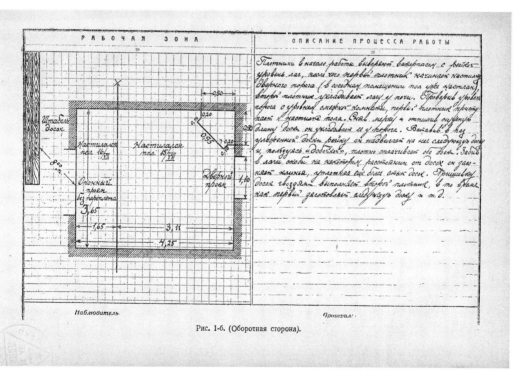

Figure 4.6. The forms for "cards of the documentation of factors" were issued by the State Planning Committee of the Soviet Union as instruments of registering the working environment. Such a form was filled out by Rozenberg to document the process of flooring. (a) verso; (b) recto. Published in Aleksandr Rozenberg, *Teoriia normirovaniia stroitel'nykh protsessov* (Moscow: Aktsionernoe izdatel'skoe obshchestvo, 1928), 40–41.

permitted making their normalized work an element in the great world process, which Rozenberg described as the "normalization of life in general."[38]

Functionalism

Meanwhile, in Moscow, Ginzburg was developing similar ideas. The functional (*funktsional'nyi*) method of architecture, which he developed in 1926–28, can be seen as an attempt at exploring the mechanics of making architecture a tool for the normalization of life. Contrary to the received mechanicist understanding of functionalism, Ginzburg's method was deeply organic. Function, for him (as it also was for Rozenberg), was inseparable from the environment: by paying attention to function, he aspired to achieve a full integration of architecture with life. The term "functionalism" arrived from Germany, where function was identified with the process of everyday life: in 1928, Hannes Meyer (who would soon move to the USSR) famously defined building as an organization of "the processes of life," including personal hygiene, sleep, sex, pets, and car maintenance, and Neufert, in his *Bauentwrufslehre* (1936), would supplement typified plans with drawings of human figures engaged in various activities.[39] Related to Taylorism, which divided work into a series of elemental operations, in the Soviet Union this approach departed from such sociological methods as the time-budget studies of Soviet workers that economist Stanislav Strumilin, a mastermind of the Soviet planning system, had conducted in the early 1920s (and which H. G. Wells and Julian Huxley's PEP repeated during the following decade).[40] "Everyday-life processes, of course, have to be examined with the same scrutiny and attention as industrial," Ginzburg explained, adding that everyday life was to be divided into such functions as sleep, eating, and children's play in the same way that scientific management divided labor into separate physical and intellectual tasks. Opposing the artificial separation of industrial and domestic spheres, Ginzburg proposed, instead, to use a more holistic notion of the "combined industrial-everyday process."[41]

As a method of architectural design, "the functional method," for Ginzburg, was synonymous with evolution as the creative method of nature: "The method of functional creativity . . . leads to a unified, organic creative process, in which one task follows from another with all the logic of natural development. No element, no part of the concept of the architect is arbitrary. Everything finds its explanation and functional justification in its purposefulness."[42] In its strive for organic unity, Ginzburg's method approached psychological functionalism, an antistructuralist program that represented an attempt, on the part of American psychologists such as William James and John Dewey, to reconstitute psychology according to the principles of evolutionary theory. Just as evolutionary theory explored the morphology of the organism as shaped by the functions of its organs, so psychological functionalism examined the functions of thoughts, sensations, and feelings.[43] These and other psychological notions are in reality "distinctions of flexible function only, not of fixed existence," argued Dewey underscoring the transitory and flexible character of function.[44] Dewey's work on pedagogy was influential in Russia due to his support of the Soviet revolution and his much-publicized visit, following an invitation by Anatoly Lunacharsky, in 1928.[45]

The implications of functionalism for aesthetics included the rehabilitation of the aesthetic value of purposefulness, which Kant had previously deemed antiaesthetic. The beautiful, for Kant, was associated with "purposiveness without purpose" *(Zweckmässigkeit ohne Zweck),* which (unlike the purposeless sublime) demonstrated clear organization that did not have a useful end. Instead, the functionalist aesthetics identified beauty with purpose. Function, according to Lissitzky, "in the language of mathematics means dependence. When working on his project a functionalist architect therefore must consider dependences."[46] Bretagne fishermen's houses, his follower Toporkov likewise explained, evolved in the course of their inhabitants' adaptation to climate and available tools and materials—they appeared not accidentally, but as a result of necessity, embodying "only the general, the typical, the transindividual."[47] His *Doryphoros,* "an object more than a human," embodied this transindividuality. Ginzburg, however, objected to any mechanicism and reductivism in functionalist aesthetics. Taking a chair as an example, he warned against its simplistic understanding as an object for sitting on; rather, "only a careful study of all circumstances secondary to this function—an examination of which work the chair is designed for, [for] which space and conditions, from which material [it is made], etc.," he professed, "can give the ultimate and exhaustive material for the design of the chair."[48]

Developing from process to form—"from skeleton to skin" and *"from inside out"*—functional architecture, Ginzburg argued, created a "material formal environment *[oformlenie]* determined by new life conditions." The skeleton, to Ginzburg, was "spatial organization"—unique parameters and their mutual relationships.[49] Any architectural project thus had to start as two diagrams: those of movement and of equipment.[50] Contemporaneous with the movement diagrams of Klein, the diagrams of Ginzburg (who publicized Klein's work in *Sovremennaya arkhitektura*) betray similar intention. As Christoph Lueder demonstrated arguing against the stereotypes associated with Klein's work, his intent was not to contain functions but to create a psychologically therapeutic effect through the economy of movement within the small apartment and the improved spatial experience.[51] The apartment, for Klein, was a "living organism, which needs to reflect the forms of our lives."[52] Likewise, Ginzburg defined the goal of the functional method in organicist and economic terms—as "the economy of space and life energy" and "the hygiene of perception."[53]

A key notion in his functionalist theory, Ginzburg's "purposeful setup" (*tselevaia ustanovka*) developed his earlier notion of purpose orientation (*tselevoe ustremlenie)*, which, he believed, enabled the organic coordination of design processes (such as plan, construction, and decoration).[54] Already in his early *Style and Epoch (Stil' i epokha*, 1924), Ginzburg relied on the work of the head of the Central Institute of Labor Alexey Gastev, who (in turn, rephrasing G. E. Lessing) declared that "what was important was not to possess a machine but to strive toward it."[55] Ginzburg too saw the machine not merely as an exemplification of Zeitgeist but as an ideal to which humanity should aspire, and a metaphor of directed movement: "the essence of any motion in a machine is not a self-contained motion in and of itself, but a *motion generating work in the direction of an axis located beyond that motion and representing an ideal, unrealizable objective.*"[56]

Gastev's scientific organization of labor relied on a psychological concept, *ustanovka* (German *Einstellung*), which, depending on the context, is translated to English as *attitude, setup, disposition,* or *mental set,* and is related to such philosophical ideas as Schopenhauer's principle of will as the world's unconscious driving force. First introduced in the late 1880s by psychophysiologists who studied the impact of prior experience on reaction time, it was later developed by the members of the revisionist Wundtian Würzburg school, such as Karl Marbe and Henry Watt, who believed that human actions were determined by unconscious tendencies.[57] Highlighting the power of the *Einstellung* to control the unconscious, Hugo Münsterberg later argued that *Einstellungen* could be formed by hypnotic suggestion, and the Russian term *ustanovka* was indeed often used as *suggestion*'s synonym.[58] Similarly, appearing with an introduction by Ernst Mach, the influential *Theory of Creative Work (Teoriia tvorchestva*, 1910) by Russian empiriocriticist Peter Engelmeyer analyzed every invention, technological as well as artistic, as a three-part action (*Dreiakt,* in the book's German edition) that consisted of unconscious intuition (will, which is comparable to *Einstellung*), conscious knowledge and analysis (reason), and constructive reification (skill).[59] During the interwar period, in the Soviet Union the theory of *ustanovka* was developed by Wundt's student Dmitry Uznadze at the University of Tbilisi (Georgia), who

Figure 4.7. Stroykom schemes of proportion and movement, which accompanied each of their apartment types (in this example type A-2), illustrate Ginzburg's definition of the functional method as "the economy of space and life energy" and "the hygiene of perception." Published in *Sovremennaia arkhitektura*, no. 1 (1929): 10.

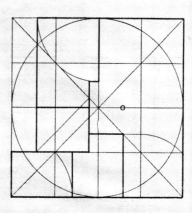
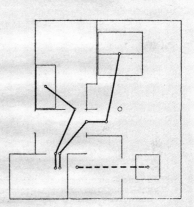

saw *ustanovka* as unconscious preparation of the organism for conscious activity.[60] From psychology, the term entered theories of scientific management and planning, most consequentially, Münsterberg's psychotechnics and Gastev's scientific organization of labor, in which it described both the mental and the physical setup necessary for the successful performance of work.

Despite its association with the unconscious, in translating *tselevaia ustanovka* to German, Ginzburg chose the expression *Zielbewusste Einstellung*: "a setup that is conscious of its goal."[61] According to Ginzburg, his functional method was in need of clearly articulated, practical goals, which he saw aligned with the goals of economic planning.[62] In similar terms, Rozenberg had earlier argued that as a part of material culture architecture can endow unconscious evolution with a conscious goal.

> Creating objects of culture, . . . humanity brought a certain element of consciousness into its biological development. Externalizing its organizational creativity, endowing it with an element of consciousness, humanity accelerated its biological development and, most importantly, widened the scope of foreseeing its future achievements. But this does not mean that inside our organism further organizational changes have stopped: they continue, although outside of our consciousness, but they are set in the closest connection with the material culture.[63]

Entangled within a network of social meanings, architecture, considered as the process of design, required an external setup, while, considered as the material product of design, it created the setup for its users. To put it differently, functionalist architecture was conceived as an instrument of controlling the social unconscious and therefore of regulating social evolution. This ambition remained at the core of the Soviet program of typification.

Type

Headed by Ginzburg, the Section of Typification within the Construction Commission (Stroykom) of the Economic Council of the Russian Republic was founded in 1928, responsible for the development of constructions and standards, experimental construction, and the education of technical specialists.[64] This ambitious mission notwithstanding, it employed only four specialists (the architects Mikhail Barshch, Vladimir Vladimirov, Alexander Pasternak, and Grigory Sum-Shik) and focused only on residential buildings.[65] Its most prominent realized project was the apartment block for the Soviet Ministry of Finance (Narkomfin), designed by Ginzburg and Ignaty Milinis on Novinsky Boulevard in Moscow in 1928 under the patronage of the commissar (minister) of finance, Nikolay Milyutin.[66] The project provided opportunities for discussing the theoretical and practical problems of typification and for collaborating with other designers, most importantly, with Lissitzky (who was also employed by Stroykom, working within the Department of Construction Control) on the standardization of furniture, and with the Bauhaus designer Hinnerk Scheper on standardized interior color schemes.[67]

The Narkomfin belonged to a series of *Existenzminimum* (minimal habitation) projects devised by CIAM, to which Ginzburg was a delegate, in the late 1920s as an application of the economic principle—an attempt to determine the universal formula of the minimal living standard for workers' housing as a balance between its affordability for the masses and the quality of the living environment for the individual occupant.[68] The endeavor seemed vital in the situation of material scarcity faced by the Soviet Union in the 1920s, caused by rapid urbanization and industrialization, which consumed all resources at the expense of the workers' quality of life. Thus, although the official Soviet per capita living standard remained a meager nine square meters, in reality the average was only 5.9 square meters (and even less, 5.2, in Moscow)—in comparison Le Corbusier's minimal individual "biological unit" ("the cell") of fourteen square meters seemed luxurious. The vast majority of the Soviet urban population resided in "communal apartments"—old bourgeois flats shared by several families. There was little hope, architects agreed, that individual two- and three-room apartments would become available to families in any foreseeable future: for many of them, even a one-room individual apartment appeared wishful thinking.[69] Responding to this challenge, Stroykom employed a building plan, based on a wide, naturally lit side corridor, which had initially been elaborated for military barracks and was praised by Sokolsky, who saw it as an exemplification of his economic principle.[70] Stroykom modified the plan, replacing the barracks' rooms with typified individual apartments, which made the critics point out that, despite being designed for families, the apartments would in reality be occupied as communal. Yet, was precisely this seeming oversight that was at the core of Stroykom's program of typification.

Like other Russian theorists of rationalization, Stroykom architects considered typification—associated with evolutionary adaptability—preferable to mechanical standardization. For Sokolsky, typification had been an important instrument of rationalization: type, he argued, was the general design idea, which could be modified depending on local conditions.[71] Even for such

Figure 4.8. Designed by Moisei Ginzburg and Ignaty Milinis in 1928, the apartment block for the Soviet Ministry of Finance (Narkomfin) on Novinsky Boulevard in Moscow was the most prominent realized project of Stroykom's Section of Typification. These photographs by an unknown photographer document the building shortly after its construction. Reproduced in Moisei Ginzburg, *Zhilishche: Opyt piatiletnei raboty nad problemoi zhilishcha* (Moscow: Gosstroiizdat, 1934), 87.

an enthusiast of Taylorism as Gastev, the standard was antagonistic to the idea of evolution, appearing as "a congelation, as it were, of technical progress at a certain stage," which mummified a transient version of adaptation of form to fluctuating environmental conditions.[72] Similarly, Rozenberg warned against "the ossification of norms," contending that building types responded to the infinite variety of processes, whose organization constantly changes in response to the evolution of life.[73] Therefore, Rozenberg argued, each building was unique, and determining precise standards was impossible:

> From the normalization point of view, it would even be uneconomical to determine precise standards for architectural structures. Because a structure in any case will always remain an object that is assembled *(montaged)* from many separate elements, its standardization should be mostly directed toward the standardization of its parts. In regard to the structure in general, standardization will only fix general *characteristic* features of the structure, that is, it will *typify* it, while the actual standardization will be achieved only for the simplest structures.[74]

Refraining from typifying buildings, which would have limited the flexibility of architecture, Ginzburg's team suggested typifying apartments, offering several one-, one-and-a-half-, two-, and three-room versions that could be recombined depending on a particular situation.[75] Two- and three-room ones could initially be "communal," to be converted to individual in the future, while one-room apartments, initially housing families, would later become available to singles and childless couples.

More than simply flexible and growing with the economy, society, and the family, Stroykom's architecture had to lead their growth. Ginzburg's base model—type F, the one-bedroom double-level "residential cell" *(iacheika)* that could be between twenty and thirty square meters in size depending on the building's budget—offered the same minimum amenities as larger apartments, using the free space (primarily the well-lit common corridor, "gained" by lowering the ceilings of bedrooms) for social activities. Its purpose was to inspire residents to move from traditional to socialized living. Type F was simultaneously a conventional minimal apartment and the housing of the future. Its corridors were to function as the spaces of study and recreation, prompting the use of other shared areas, such as the communal kitchen and the dining hall. A complex of type-F apartments, Ginzburg professed, will in the future develop into "a higher form of living": the communal house.[76] Although the architectural details of this house were yet to be discovered

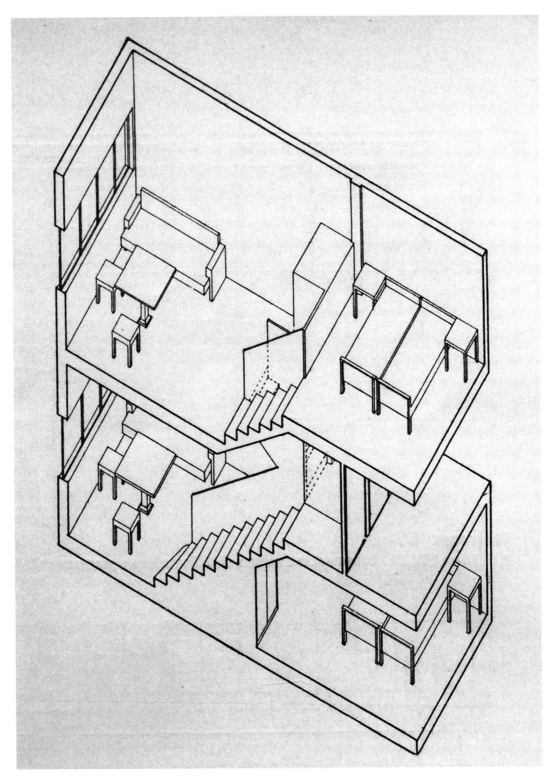

Figure 4.9. The type-F apartment was the minimal, and the base, unit among Stroykom typified plans. This axonometric section by Stroykom was reproduced in V. I. Vel'man, ed., *Tipovye proekty i konstruktsii zhilishchnogo stroitel'stva rekomenduemye na 1930 god* (Moscow: Gosudarstvennoe tekhnicheskoe izdatel'stvo, 1929), 60.

along the path toward socialism, Ginzburg was convinced that this new type would result from the dissolution of the bourgeois family and the collectivization of domestic chores, childrearing, culture, and sports. As more everyday activities came to be socialized, he suggested, the dwelling organism would evolve in the direction of socialization, rather than individualization, of space. Famously defining the task of architecture as the creation of "social condensers" (spaces that transform the personality of its user the way a mechanical condenser transforms vapor into water), Ginzburg designed the Narkomfin as a prototype building "of a transitional type," which inconspicuously stimulated residents accustomed to old, family-based lifestyles to transition to collective modes of living.[77] Rather than forcing people to change their lives, architecture would tacitly provide them with an evolutionary path. As a later proposal specified, assuming a Spencerian tone, "the material-objective environment," which is itself a product of human labor and economic conditions, and as such, is endowed with purpose, "reversely impacts the development of these processes and thus affects the formation of social-everyday skills and the ideology of the human."[78]

The Commissariat of Everyday Life

As a part of an intra-Stroykom collaboration, Lissitzky, who between 1925 and 1930 was the professor of Furniture and Artistic Interior Design at VKhUTEIN, embarked on a project of elaborating principles of standardized furniture, including that for the Narkomfin building.[79] Soviet society, Lissitzky believed, provided unique opportunities for typification because, in contrast to capitalist countries with their "complete anarchy of needs," it unified the needs of its members.[80] Deindividualization opened the door for reconfiguring design according to the economic principle: the normalization of life necessitated the rationalization of architecture, and as a result, the "contemporary apartment must be developed like the best contemporary travel suitcase, considering everything necessary that it must contain and using every square centimeter."[81]

In 1925, Lissitzky had distinguished between the purely economic and technical "American" architectural principles of rationalization, functionality, and hygiene, and "European" social aspirations, manifested through reimagining everyday life.[82] While the changes in the urban sphere were driven by technological invention and were thus guided by the first set of principles, the progress of the domestic sphere was tightly connected with the social and psychological evolution of the human. Yet the two spheres were interconnected.

The theoretician of constructivism Boris Arvatov explained in his essay "Everyday Life and the Culture of the Object," published the same year, that a new, modern relationship between the human and the object first emerged in the industrial city alongside the technological principles of standardization and normalization, subsequently penetrating everyday life. This relationship, which Arvatov classified as monistic, sublated the opposition of naïve materialism and idealism from an evolutionary standpoint: the modern urban environment, built of glass, steel, and concrete, was honest about its material and function, thereby encouraging people to think functionally. This, in turn, changed the relationship between humans and the objects of their everyday use, announcing "a new stage in the evolution of material culture" exemplified by "collapsible furniture, moving sidewalks, revolving doors, escalators, automat restaurants, reversible outfits."[83] Such objects, which purportedly infused the act of use with productivist ethics, attracted the attention of Lissitzky-the-furniture-designer, who was acquainted with Arvatov through the constructivist network. He found examples of such objects in Gerrit Rietveld's Schoeder house in Utrecht, which he had visited in 1926: fascinated with furniture and sliding partitions, he sketched them to use as a teaching material.[84]

Lissitzky's ensuing projects for transformable furniture aspired to engage the user in an active, dynamic relationship with the object. At the 1929 *Hygiene* exhibition in Dresden, he presented a visionary project for an "individual living cell" in a communal house as a full-scale model of a space that could convert from a bedroom to a living room: in the middle was a movable screen-cabinet, one end of which was attached to a wall and the other end rotating to a 90-degree angle; both sides of the cabinet had shelves and foldable elements, including a bed.[85] Lissitzky's other project—modular, or combinable *(kombinatnaia)* furniture—typified not objects but their elements in the same way as Stroykom typified apartments rather than buildings. Its primary unit was a box-case for storing belongings, which, developed into five standardized elements—a nightstand (which could be converted to a rack by adding lower shelves), a cabinet (transformed to a chest when placed horizontally), a wardrobe, a drawer, and a standardized furniture leg—could be turned and recombined to achieve a variety of forms and functions. This uniformity and compatibility, Lissitzky argued, guaranteed aesthetic unity, while at the same time encouraging users' active participation and enabling variety and individual expression as they would be free to recombine the elements.[86]

Although constructivist theory saw physical interaction with furniture as a tool of personal transformation, by the end of the 1920s designers became skeptical of overtly complicated mechanisms, which, they feared, could enslave

Figure 4.10. El Lissitzky's project for the *Hygiene* exhibition in Dresden (1929) featured a project of a transformable apartment in a communal house. The screen-cabinet with a foldable bed could rotate to a 90-degree angle, transforming the space from a bedroom into the living room. Period photograph by unknown photographer. Courtesy of the Getty Research Institute, Los Angeles (950076).

their user.[87] In a 1928 lecture, "The Artistic Preconditions of the Standardization of Civic Individual Furniture," Lissitzky argued against mechanicism and technofetishism in furniture design. Transformable furniture, for him, was interesting not because of its mechanical solutions, but because it possessed a potential for expressing the Zeitgeist. In what at first sight seems a surprising reversal of his earlier maxim, "Man is the measure of all tailors—Measure architecture with architecture" (which was discussed in chapter 2), Lissitzky now called for a return to Protagoras: "The man is the measure of all things. This relation, this scale [*masshtab*] has to be clearly expressed in the shape of furniture."[88] Rather than a rejection of his earlier principles, however, this statement can be read as a warning against their simplistic mechanist understanding: what mattered for Lissitzky in both cases was the relationship between an organism and its environment. In his work for Stroykom,

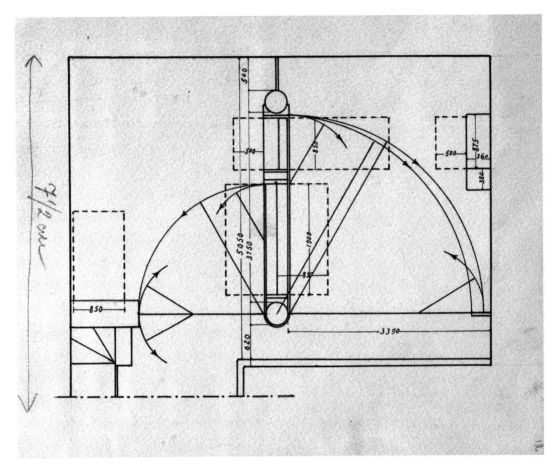

Figure 4.11. El Lissitzky's drawing (1930) demonstrates the mechanics of the transformable apartment. Courtesy of Russian State Archive of Literature and the Arts, fond 2361, op.1, d. 19, l. 16.

no less than in the early 1920s, Lissitzky was preoccupied with the designed environment's evolutionary effect upon the human.

"The word 'art' has to be deleted from the lexicon," Lissitzky explained. "If Lenin was alive today, he would have founded the 'Commissariat of Everyday Life.'"[89] In his design for the interior of the Stroykom type-F apartment, like Ginzburg, Lissitzky attempted to create a normed and normalizing environment that would both respond to the current condition of scarcity and gradually transform this condition—and the apartment's inhabitant as well. This evolution had to be incremental: as a social condenser, furniture was to transform gently and creatively, addressing the immediate needs of the human in the first place. In the words of Arvatov, "Understanding the developing tendencies of material *byt* [everyday life] means being able to direct them, to

Figure 4.12. El Lissitzky's modular, or combinable *(kombinatnaia)*, furniture typified not objects but their elements in the same way as Stroykom typified apartments rather than buildings. This illustration by Lissitzky shows the five elements of combinable furniture at the bottom, while the upper images provide examples of their possible combinations. The top combination consists of the nightstand placed on top of the cabinet and the wardrobe and drawer tilted horizontally (all elements using a set of legs); the desk underneath is assembled of one small set of shelves, two small cabinets, and one horizontal board. Published in V. I. Vel'man, ed., *Tipovye proekty i konstruktsii zhilishchnogo stroitel'stva rekomenduemye na 1930 god* (Moscow: Gosudarstvennoe tekhnicheskoe izdatel'stvo, 1929), 33.

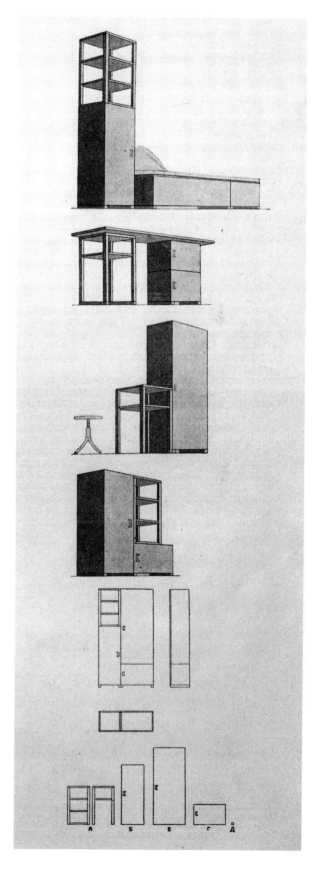

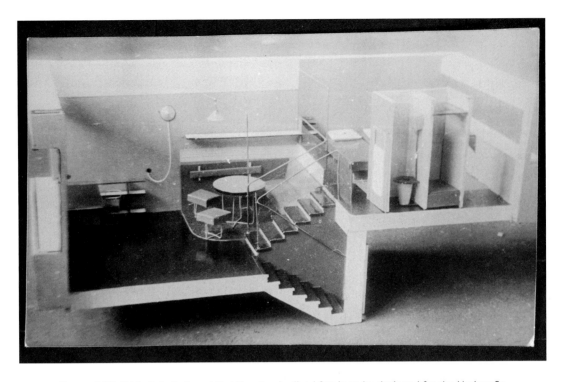

Figure 4.13. El Lissitzky believed that the standardized furniture he designed for the Narkomfin would transform the personalities of its residents. This 1929 photograph (possibly taken by Lissitzky) shows Lissitzky's model of the furnished apartment type F. Courtesy of the State Tretyakov Gallery.

transform them systematically, i.e. to turn *byt* from a conservative force into a progressive one."[90] The space was divided into three functional zones: work, dining (which could become an additional sleeping place at night), and sleeping (which could turn into office space during the day). Built-in standardized furniture would free the worker from the sense of possession, while the round dining table ensured gender and age equality within the family.[91] Meanwhile, the individual kitchen was reduced to a "kitchen-element" (kitchenette), which Lissitzky designed in collaboration with his wife Sophie Küppers.[92] Also combinable, the element consisted of four elements and could be installed fully or partially depending on the availability of space (in its most minimal version occupying only 0.7 square meters of floor space). Intended to breed not bourgeois domesticity but collectivism, it would shrink, rather than grow, with time and eventually be removed altogether.

The regulation of life, understood as humanity's evolutionary process, was the goal of Soviet interwar standardization, which, prioritizing typification, relied not on industrial but on organicist models. For Rozenberg, Ginzburg,

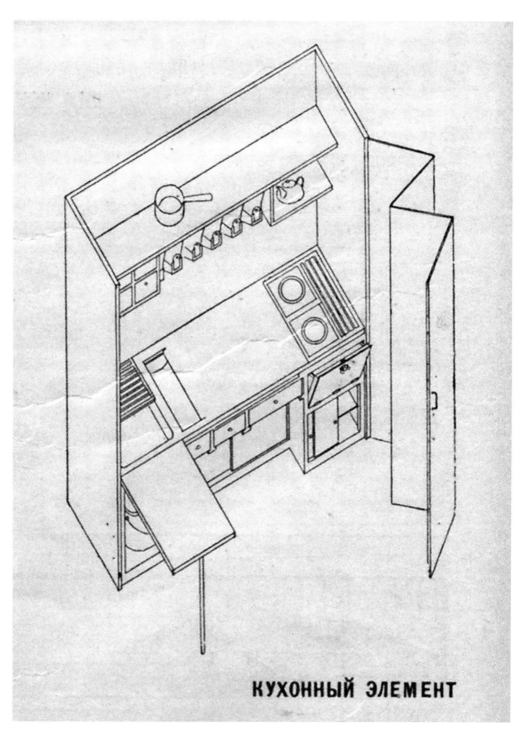

Figure 4.14. The "kitchen-element" designed for the Narkomfin house by El Lissitzky and his wife Sophie Lissitzky-Küppers also relied on the principles of minimalism and combinatorics. It taught the household members to appreciate collective rather than family meals and would be gradually disassembled and eventually removed altogether. Lissitzky-Küppers's coauthorship is acknowledged by Lissitzky in "From a Questionnaire on Furniture" ("Aus einem Fragebogen über Möbel," in *Proun und Wolkenbügel: Schriften, Briefe, Dokumente*, ed. Sophie Lissitzky-Küppers and Jen Lissitzky [Dresden: VEB Verlag der Kunst, 1977], 197). The image was published in *Sovremennaia arkhitektura*, no. 1 (1929): 24.

and Lissitzky, architecture was a process of devising adaptational mechanisms—of transforming the environment in accordance with the purported evolutionary goals of the human. Moreover, no less than architecture and furniture, the human itself became an object of design. In Rozenberg's theory of normalization, the taxonomy of scale ensured the connection between the process of construction and the world process. Similarly, Ginzburg attempted to subordinate architecture to the goals of social evolution (as exemplified in his concept of purposeful setup), by developing the notion of type as a flexible adaptational instrument. The same goal guided Lissitzky's furniture design projects, which saw everyday life as a field of the formation of consciousness. As process, or rather, as a multiplicity of adaptational processes such as those of design, construction, and habitation, their architecture was to be both fluid and regulated.

Taking standardization as an opportunity to make architecture more processual and organic (and thus, to rehumanize it, as expressed explicitly by Lissitzky), Soviet architecture could not help but standardize and deindividualize the human—a problem with modernism that did not go unnoticed by later critics. Kenneth Frampton pointed to this loss of individuality to condemn both suburbanization and postmodernist fascination with infrastructure, which he classified as an architecture of process. Unlike it, the "architecture of object" was guided by "more traditional criteria of worldliness and use."[93] Frampton's argument departed from Hannah Arendt's seminal distinction, in *The Human Condition* (1956), between dull, repetitive labor, necessary for the maintenance of biological life, and creative and fruitful work, whose products were long-lasting and culturally significant. Unlike the Soviet functionalists, for whom process endowed the work of design, construction, and use with goal and, thus, with humanity, both Arendt and Frampton (as well as Giorgio Agamben later) considered natural necessity the opposite of freedom.[94]

The arrival of the informational age resulted in another reevaluation of the opposition of the process and the object. While modernism treated multiplicity as a natural condition, feeling an urge to organize it by typification, the architecture of the informational age, exemplifying the shift from the economy of production to the one of consumption, replaced the organic concept of type with the informational concept of customization. Visually resembling Klein's diagrammatic multitudes, *Finite Format 04,* a series of 729 watercolors by Mauricio Pezo and Sofia von Ellrichshausen (2017), proposes to replace "form by format" and to erase "an ideal object," highlighting, instead, "hereditary metamorphosis within the same family" (Plate 8).[95] In the words of Pier

Vittorio Aurelli, who detected a transition from the early modernist notion of organic process to a new concept of the immaterial process of artificial intelligence in the British architect Cedrik Price's method of "life-conditioning," what is at stake today is no longer the autonomy of architecture from life but the autonomy of life from capitalism.[96]

FIVE

Energy
Soviet Wall-Painting and the Economy of Perception

According to French artist Fernand Léger, he and his friend, Russian revolutionary Leon Trotsky, were the first to elaborate the idea of painting the facades of houses in different colors. The two often talked about "the thrilling problem of a colored city" on their Montparnasse furloughs during the First World War. "The idea of a blue street, a yellow street aroused Trotsky's enthusiasm," recalled Léger, adding that Trotsky wanted him to come to Moscow to implement his colorful vision on its streets.[1] The artist and the revolutionary understood that color could transform the perception of a city; it could affect people's emotions, behavior, and personality. Moreover, as color theorists soon discovered, it could be standardized and—inasmuch as it also affected working productivity—become a powerful weapon in the struggle for industrialization. This chapter traces how these artistic and scientific discoveries were employed by wall-painting, a modern design discipline that emerged in the late 1920s at the crossroads of art, architecture, science, technology, and labor management. Situating wall-painting in the context of Soviet industrialization, it focuses on the activity of one of its main centers (Malyarstroy research and design center in Moscow, which became the site of a dialog between Russian and German approaches to design) and to the subjectivity that it construed.[2]

Expanded Seeing

One day in the early 1920s, while walking along the banks of the Neva in Petrograd (as St. Petersburg was then called) the landscape watercolorist Albert Benois saw a group of people painting the river while facing the opposite direction. Initially convinced that he had encountered a group of lunatics, he soon recognized them as the futurist artist and composer Mikhail Matyushin and his students, who practiced artistic seeing with the backs of their heads.[3, 4] Matyushin's concept of "expanded seeing" (*rasshirennoe smotrenie*) as a fuller kind of visual perception had gestated under the influence of P. D. Ouspensky's theosophy. The 1923 manifesto of Matyushin's group Zorved (from archaic Russian roots "zor," from *zret'*, to see, and "ved," from *vedat'*, to know) professed a "physiological change of . . . the way of seeing"—an incorporation into the field of vision of what had previously remained outside of it.[5] Matyushin developed his concept as the head of the Department of Organic Culture at the State Institute of Artistic Culture (GINKhUK) in Leningrad (as the city was renamed once again), and later, after GINKhUK was incorporated into the State Institute of Art History in 1927, as the head of the Experimental Laboratory of Physical-Physiological Foundations of Fine Arts within the institute.

Matyushin's expanded seeing was based upon the so-called Purkinje effect, a visual phenomenon recorded by the Czech anatomist Jan Evangelista Purkinje in 1825. Purkinje noticed that the colors of the red end of spectrum were perceived as brighter in the light of the day and duller under twilight, while blues, on the contrary, acquired luminosity in the evening until, in darkness, the distinctions of color gave place to the contrast of light and shade. Moreover, if during the day human sight was focused at a 30–60-degree angle, in twilight one could observe a field of 180 degrees. At the end of the century, German physiologist Johannes von Kries explained this effect by proposing that the retina consisted of two types of photoreceptors: cones, which were situated in the center of the eye and were responsible for daytime vision, and peripheral rods, which became active at the lower levels of light. Matyushin suggested combining the two types of seeing and, furthermore, expanding the angle of seeing to a full 360 degrees.[6] To do so, one would have had to see with the back of their head, and indeed, in his own physiological experiments, Matyushin discovered that the occipital part of the brain acted as an independent, nonretinal visual center. Two types of visual centers have been detected by modern psychologists: one in the middle, and the other in the cortex of the brain. Matyushin suggested that the activity of the latter, the lesser-studied cortex centers (which, he discovered, were concentrated in the brain's posterior, occipital part), explains the effect of complementary color.

The psychological phenomenon of complementary color fascinated Matyushin. In a GINKhUK laboratory experiment, he divided a specially constructed black room with a solid screen. In one part of the room, he placed an electric lamp covered with a colored sheet, while in the other, the subject was seated facing away from the screen. The only opening in the screen was a small hole, which was hermetically closed with a hose that ended in a cap on the subject's head. The beam of light from the first part could thus reach only the occiput of the subject, who was asked to describe their impressions. Although compared to experiments with retinal vision, the subjects needed significantly more time to analyze what they perceived, in the end, Matyushin reported, they inevitably succeeded in doing so. Moreover, as he discovered in the course of the experiment, the color perceived by the subject was not the one of the color screen but the one complementary to it.[7] Another, more familiar, manifestation of the same phenomenon was the chromatic visual effect that appeared when one closed their eyes after looking at a colored shape. In this instance, Matyushin discovered, the background acquired the color complementary to that of the object, while a third color appeared around the object as a halo until the main color finally died out. The addition of the third color (which he called the linking [stsepliaiushchii] one) to the dyad of the primary and the complementary was Matyushin's key artistic invention: he believed that it allowed him to overcome the effect of mutual dulling that occurred when contrasting colors were mixed with each other, and thus to establish a visual equilibrium between an object and its context (Plate 9). It was this discovery that allowed him to find an industrial application for his concept—wall-painting. Since 1929, he worked on *The Handbook of Color: A Pattern of the Convertibility of Color Combinations*—a set of tables demonstrating primary, context, and linking colors that were recommended for use on internal and external walls of buildings (Plate 10).[8] Matyushin's color tables offered a universal, standardized recipe for the calculated visual effect of color combinations that always looked brilliant and fresh.

Matyushin's students, most importantly, the four siblings Ender—Boris, Xenia, Maria, and Georgy, descendants of a glass designer from Saxony who had settled in St. Petersburg in the nineteenth century—developed his exploration of nonretinal vision.[9] Boris Ender's theory of "complementary seeing" (*dopolnitel'noe smotrenie*) synthesized Matyushin's "expanded seeing" and his interest in complementary colors. In 1924, Boris Ender conducted a series of experiments that explored the perception of a blindfolded subject. In one of them, he tightly covered his eyes with a kerchief and asked his collaborators to guide him toward the endpoint—a place that he had never seen before. Remaining blindfolded, for half an hour Ender recorded the visual impressions that he received through the back of his head; the blindfold was then removed as he proceeded to record his visual impressions, comparing them with what he had perceived previously. Like his teacher, Boris Ender was eager to find a practical application for his theory. In 1927, he became an assistant at the Committee of Contemporary Artistic Industry, headed by architect Alexander Nikolsky, the leader of the Leningrad section of the constructivist group Organization of Contemporary Architects (Ob'edinenie sovremennykh arkhitektorov, OSA), with whom Maria Ender also collaborated.[10] The same year, Boris Ender moved to Moscow, where he would soon join Malyarstroy, or the State Trust for Wall-Painting Works under the Supreme Council of the People's Economy of the USSR, contributing his expertise in the study of peripheral and nonretinal vision and his experimental approach to its emerging program of wall-painting.

Foreign Expertise

Founded in October 1928, Malyarstroy executed "wall-painting works using contemporary technological achievements."[11] The scope of the organization's activity extended to "all sorts of wall-painting works, the interior and exterior design of residential, industrial, office, cultural, farm buildings, color design of clubs, theaters, palaces of labor and culture, urban architectural complexes, streets, and squares."[12] Explaining the goals and methods of the new organization, the head of Malyarstroy, party official Efim Stokolov, introduced wall-painting as a progressive Western technology necessary for the optimization of social and work processes:

> [In] Europe and America . . . wall-painting is subjected to study, improvement, and rationalization alongside all other processes of building. Inserted into the context of scientific research, comprehensively studied, wall-painting abroad is no longer primitive, but is, as any other branch of construction, subjected to the elements of planning, economic calculation, and scientific substantiation in the application of necessary combinations of colors.
>
> It is therefore natural that in our effort to "catch up and overtake" we cannot leave this important part of construction in a primitive state.[13]

Stemming from Lenin's 1917 article "Imminent Catastrophe and How to Struggle with It," the phrase "to catch up and overtake" (Western countries) acquired a new meaning after the announcement of the First Five-Year Plan in 1928. The goal of the plan, the construction of a centralized industrial economy, required surmounting technological barriers, and many foreign specialists were invited to the USSR to contribute to achieving this task.[14]

In March 1929, a special delegation of the Construction Commission (Stroykom) arrived in Germany to recruit specialists for the Soviet building industry. The committee's head, the engineer Boris Barsky, turned for advice to architect Fred Forbát, who pointed him to Hinnerk Scheper.[15] A Bauhaus graduate, Scheper had been the director of the Bauhaus Workshop of Wall-Painting since 1925 and had executed numerous wall-painting commissions in Germany, including the one for the Bauhaus building in Dessau. As early as July 1929, Scheper moved to Moscow, where he became the head of the Production-Technical Sector of Malyarstroy, a role in which he remained until September 1931.[16] Scheper's presence shaped the brief but vibrant flourishing of wall-painting in the Soviet Union.

The technological breakthrough was not only an economic endeavor but a moral one. V. Sestroretsky (who replaced Stokolov as the head of the trust) and N. Nishenko presented the task of the newly created organization as the battle against the individual craftsman: "The question of the [interior] design of homes, civil and industrial buildings, etc., cannot be excluded from the front of the cultural revolution, cannot be left in the hands of an unorganized initiative—a product of pre-Revolutionary bourgeois tastes and needs."[17] To facilitate technological development, the government created a chain of research centers and institutes, which collaborated, and sometimes conflicted, with each other. Thus, Malyarstroy was paired with Vsekhimprom (All-Union Association of the Chemical Industry); its periodical, *Malyarnoe delo (Wall-Painting)*, published between 1930 and 1932, served both organizations. As a result, some associated wall-painting exclusively with the invention and application of chemical dyes, while others maintained a broader view of Malyarstroy's mission, which included artistic problems.[18] This ambivalence predicated the discussions that were soon to unfold around Malyarstroy.

The design work at Malyarstroy was concentrated in the Office of Design (Proektnoe Byuro, also headed by Scheper), a part of its Production-Technical Sector. Only a few of the twenty-seven people who worked in the Production-Technical Sector under Scheper were affiliated with the Office of Design. Despite its small size, the office undertook multiple commissions—over three hundred in 1931 alone.[19] This work in Moscow, as Scheper's wife Lou (also a Bauhaus graduate) recalled, provided a "tremendous field for experimentation." Among the wall-painting projects were clubs, theaters, factory dining halls, and collective farm buildings, all of which were to become prototypes for later complete or partial reproduction.[20] Most of the members of Malyarstroy's Office of Design were trained artists. In addition to Ender, they included Lev (Leyba) Antokolsky, the eldest member of the team and the deputy editor of *Malyarnoe delo,* who graduated from the Imperial Academy of Arts in St. Petersburg, studied decorative art in Hamburg, and worked as a portraitist and monumental painter in Moscow. In 1930, immediately after graduating from the Bauhaus, Scheper's student, the Neue Sachlichkeit painter Erich Borchert (who, unlike Scheper, was a member of the Bauhaus Communist

Figure 5.1. Malyarstroy's Office of Design became a space where Mikhail Matyushin's theory of color met with the German Bauhaus wall-painting tradition. This 1929 photograph shows *(lower row, left to right)* Boris Ender, Sophia Matveeva, Hinnerk Scheper, unidentified person (possibly Ender's wife), Erich Borchert; *(upper row, left to right)* Lev Antokolsky, Igor Budkevich, Vladimir Zhuravlev. Courtesy of the Bauhaus-Archiv Berlin.

Party cell), joined him in Moscow as his assistant.[21] Borchert's Bauhaus graduation certificate praised the successful results of his "experiments in all spheres of research of color and light on the basis of the psychology of their perception."[22] After Scheper's return to Germany, Borchert became the head of the Office of Design. Finally, most VKhUTEIN students who graduated in monumental painting in 1929 and 1930 received internships at Malyarstroy, and some (like Borchert's soon-to-be wife Sofia Matveeva) transitioned to permanent positions. As all of its key members were fluent in German, the design office became one of the hubs of Soviet Germanophonic culture (cooperating with its other prominent members, including Moisei Ginzburg and El Lissitzky) and a site of Soviet-German intellectual exchange.[23] Describing his approach to wall-painting in 1935, Boris Ender could boast, "My work on the art of wall-painting possesses two particular qualities: on the one hand, I ground my work on color scientifically (something that even the Germans, for instance Scheper, do not do); on the other hand, I put the gradations of color (color tones) directly into production (this I have learned from Scheper)."[24]

Malyarstroy was modeled after such organizations as the Hamburg-based Union for Furthering Color in the Cityscape, which brought together administrators, town planners, chemists, artists, and architects, and after Scheper's Workshop of Wall-Painting at the Bauhaus.[25] Collaborating with the National Research Association for Efficiency in Construction and Housing, the Bauhaus workshop experimented with different spraying machines, the chemical properties of dyes, and methods of their mixing and application, seeking to integrate wall-painting into the program of standardization.[26] As Scheper later argued, "One has to decisively turn to a mass production of new, standardized, and cheap materials, to their factory production, partially directly on the construction site, in order to use them most fully and to economize on transport."[27] Color, moreover, became an object of standardization. In 1927, Scheper's Bauhaus workshop hosted a lecture by the color theorist and chemist Wilhelm Ostwald, the second president of the German Monist League and an early enthusiast of standardization.[28] Unlike the earlier color systems, Ostwald's system was based on the psychological perception of color. Four basic colors—the three primary plus sea green—and their gradations formed the twenty-four-color wheel, to which a gray scale was added to account for the effect of light; the resulting triangles had the achromatic scale as one of their edges and a chromatic color as the vertex facing it: all colors thus emerged as combinations of a pigment and a shade of gray. Appearing with a preface by VKhUTEMAS/VKhUTEIN pedagogue and psychologist Sergey Kravkov, Ostwald's *Farbkunde* (1923) was translated into Russian in 1926, immediately becoming the standard textbook of color theory at both VKhUTEMAS and Malyarstroy, which likewise aspired to use color as an instrument of standardization (Plate 11).[29]

Invisible Colors

In 1930, Scheper received an opportunity to further explore the affinity between color and standardization when Malyarstroy was invited to collaborate with the Section of Typification of Stroykom, headed by Ginzburg, on the design of its experimental residential block of the Narkomfin, which was intended to become a prototype model of typified housing. As was discussed in the previous chapter, in the Narkomfin, Ginzburg viewed the challenges of standardization through the lens of his concept of the social condenser. Accordingly, whereas some of the problems he and Scheper faced in the interior design were also pertinent for architectural modernism elsewhere, others were unique to the Narkomfin social program.

Orientation belonged to the former set of concerns. "With color, you accentuate, you classify, you clarify, you disentangle," Le Corbusier would urge architects in 1938.[30] Classifying and grouping through color coding typified information. This idea had been explored by the Viennese Verein Ernst Mach (Ernst Mach Society), whose members, including the logical positivists Rudolf Carnap and Otto Neurath (who were invited to lecture at the Bauhaus by Hannes Meyer), aimed to apply the methodology of empiriocriticism to a design of "life."[31] Since 1928, Neurath had been developing his system of orientation, which later became known as ISOTYPE (International System of Typographic Picture Education), as a new international language. In the early 1930s he was a frequent guest in Moscow, where he continued the collaboration with Meyer. From 1931 to 1934, with graphic designer Gerd Arntz, Neurath participated in the creation of the Moscow Institute of Statistics (Izostat). His standardized pictorial signs represented concepts metonymically, operating on the level of the automatic. This approach informed *Signaletik,* a German term for a system of architectural prompts that facilitated orientation within a building with the help of bright contrasting colors, such as those that Scheper used in the Bauhaus building in Dessau. In large buildings, he explained, "separate colors or colorful objects and their elements might be used for orientation. Specific spaces might be colored according to their purpose, depending on their location."[32] Ginzburg, who had visited the Bauhaus in 1927, acknowledged the importance of this precedent. As in the Bauhaus building, the staircase for each level in the Narkomfin block received a distinctive color—orange, light blue, green, cobalt, vermillion (red), and Veronese green (emerald)—so that "ascending a staircase, a person could immediately orientate himself and wouldn't accidentally end up one floor too high or too low."[33] Meanwhile, the ceilings in the two common corridors were painted gray and lemon. Furthermore, like in the Dessau house of Oskar Schlemmer, alternating doors in the Narkomfin corridors were painted black or white to be immediately distinguishable and, like in the Kandinsky/Klee house, the vertical surfaces of staircases were white and the horizontal ones black (Plate 12).

Spatial perception of architecture was another problem often associated with color by the modernists. Echoing August Schmarsow's famous definition of architecture as the *Raumgestalterin,* Le Corbusier called colors "the creators of space." Color, he argued, could make planes look closer or farther away, dissolve architecture within the landscape, and destroy the weight and density of volumes.[34] By identifying architecture with color, the Swiss architect reconstituted it as a psychological phenomenon: "An architect may thus work with color as he works with proportions, or rather . . . as he would work with the geometric relations between surfaces or volumes," he exhorted students at the Kyiv Institute of Construction in 1932.[35] Similarly, in a special issue on architectural polychromy of *Sovremennaya arkhitektura (Contemporary Architecture),* richly illustrated with the works of Léger, Ginzburg, the journal's editor, explained that he saw Léger's work not as easel painting but as an analytical exercise in exploring the spatial and surface role of color (Plate 13). Beginning with the impressionists, artists had been eager to redefine painting as an expression of form through color until cubism recuperated the former; purism—an artistic "-ism" developed by Léger, Le Corbusier, and Amédée Ozenfant—then rejected the cubist dulled palette without sacrificing its concern with form.[36] In Ginzburg's classroom at the Moscow Higher Technical College (where he taught in the first half of the 1920s), the black color of the external wall, through contrast, enhanced the luminosity of the windows; the bright lemon yellow on the opposite wall, reflecting light, became an additional source of illumination; the orange of the two remaining walls contributed warmth to the room and accentuated its spatial properties, while the black on the ceiling masked the vaults.[37] Similarly, a scheme proposed for an office in Ginzburg's Government Building in Alma-Ata (contemporary Almaty, Kazakhstan; Ginzburg worked on this project with Ignaty Milinis between 1927 and 1931) had a black ceiling and a black external wall facing a bright yellow wall, while the two remaining walls were painted blue (Plate 14).

However, by the time he began working on the Narkomfin building, Ginzburg was more interested in the physiological than in the aesthetic effects of design. From his earlier fascination with purism, he moved toward Scheper's vision of wall-painting as "being directly *subordinated* to architecture." For Scheper, wall-painting served to give architecture "maximum external expressivity," elevated it, and was therefore "able to indirectly reorganize it."[38] Ginzburg now admitted that although his earlier color schemes succeeded in correcting the conditions of lighting and space, the brightness of coloration exerted a tiring effect on the perceiver and destroyed the three-dimensionality of space.[39] Accordingly, not aesthetic effect, but the perceiver's psychological and physiological well-being became Ginzburg's and Scheper's prime concern at the Narkomfin. Since most everyday activities of its residents, including eating and recreation, were to be socialized, the purpose of apartments (or residential cells, as they were called) was reduced to rest, or restoring productive energy.

In the Soviet Union, rest and leisure were valorized as productive in their own right. "No such thing as absolute rest exists," explained an architect named Kuzmin in 1930 on the pages of *Sovremennaya arkhitektura*: "A person is constantly working (even when he is asleep)."[40] Such a program was realized, for instance, by Konstantin Melnikov in his project for the Green City (1930), a vacation town near Moscow that he interpreted as a "sleeping sonata," a factory that would physically and mentally transform people through sleep. This explains what might have otherwise seemed paradoxical: in general, Malyarstroy's activity concentrated on producing color schemes not for factories but for spaces associated with workers' leisure, such as homes, clubs, canteens, theaters, and cinemas. Evoking the work of French physiologist Charles Féré to explain his understanding of how color could become an instrument of psychological influence and social transformation, Ginzburg detailed: "From the colored discs of Féré [we have to move to] color screens (i.e., large surfaces of color) and from color screens to their spatial combinations, enclosing the perceiving subject."[41]

In the Narkomfin building, Malyarstroy tested two schemes of such spatial combinations of color screens, the warm and the cold.[42] An oblique axonometric projection illustrates the cold scheme, to be applied in apartments of type K: three-room apartments for families with children (Plate 15). Axonometric projection was Malyarstroy's preferred method of representation, even though it remained unpopular in the Soviet Union because of its illegibility for anyone unfamiliar with its conventions. Defending axonometry, Borchert argued that it was the most economic technique of representation, which enabled simultaneous depiction of several spaces.[43] Malyarstroy's drawing illustrating the type-K apartment color scheme is indeed difficult to read. It presents the space as if viewed through the floor, showing the apartment's internal partitions and supporting columns suspended in the air. The ceiling is shown as a large area of bright blue, while the internal partition walls are given a light blue-grayish color. This scheme was partially realized in the "penthouse" apartment of the building's commissioner, the minister of finance Nikolay Milyutin (Plate 16).

Two more traditional central-perspectival drawings illustrate the warm palette applied to a small, studio-like F unit, an apartment for singles and childless couples (Plate 17). The identical composition of these drawings is based on a square within which, slightly off-center, is inscribed another, smaller, square. This composition repeats the perspectival diagrammatic construction that was often cited in nineteenth-century psychological literature as an example of a figure that could be read as both pyramidal form and receding space.[44] Charles Wheatstone was the first to use this diagram within a stereoscopic pair, and Mach was the first who used it as a single image. Psychologists gave different interpretations of what made the subject perceive the figure as solid or void. For Wheatstone, this depended on the location of the small square; for Wilhelm Wundt on whether one focused attention on the small or the large square; and for Wilhelm von Bezold on the color of the squares. Bezold observed that if the smaller square was orange the figure was perceived as a pyramid, while a blue smaller square turned it into a receding space (Plate 18).[45] These studies were well known to early twentieth-century art theorists, including Jacques-Louis Sorel, Broder Christiansen, and Viktor Shklovsky, and the two drawings published in *Malyarnoe delo* indeed seem to be exploring different psychological effects of color on the perception of space.[46] The first shows a pale-beige ceiling and a blue wall of the bedroom in the background, relying on the potential of white and blue to visually expand space. The other drawing seems to be contradicting the principles of the psychology of architecture. In it, the ceilings are orange and lemon yellow, while the walls are white or near-white. Why did this scheme—just as the cold scheme for the type-K apartment—depart from the convention of white ceilings, approved by psychologists? And what does this departure reveal about Ginzburg's rejection of Léger's bright palette?

To use the language of modern psychology, Ginzburg's design preferences shifted from film to surface colors. This distinction was discussed in the same 1929 issue of *Sovremennaya arkhitektura* by psychologist Boris Teplov, whose article focused on color typology. Following the German psychologist David Katz, Teplov divided colors into surface *(poverkhnostnye),* film *(besfakturnye),* and spatial *(rasprostranennye)* color.[47] Whereas the last category encompassed transparent colors, rarely encountered in life, the first two groups, distinguished through brightness and saturation, appeared frequently and were important for architecture. Bright and saturated film colors were glossy, immaterial, and abstract, while surface colors were material and solid, connected to the object they covered. Following Ostwald's color theory, Katz saw surface colors as mixed with gray and, due to their light-absorbent quality, able to convey such architectural properties as facture, form, and distance. The unobtrusive quality of these slightly off-white hues emphasized the utter subordination of color to architecture. Asserting the status of architecture as an art of form and space, the surface colors used in the Narkomfin building rendered both the making and the perception of this art invisible.

Bright colors, while generally avoided in interiors, could nevertheless be found in one area: on ceilings. Scheper advocated for colorful ceilings as more appropriate for domestic spaces than sterile white. He also used the combination of nearly white walls and bright ceilings at the Bauhaus building.[48] This solution acquired a new meaning for Ginzburg, who noticed that the surface of ceilings "penetrated into the consciousness only in individual, separate visual images," which were registered by peripheral vision.[49] Color, which otherwise would provoke a strong nervous agitation, should enter perception in small doses, not unlike those used by Borchert in a psychiatric hospital in Berlin, where he suggested curing mentally ill patients by prescribing small doses of bright colors.[50] The brief glances that one threw on a ceiling, in other words, were too short for the color to enter the cognitive sphere and thus make one tired. Unlike ceilings, walls constantly remained in one's field of central vision and were thus to be given an "invisible coloration" *(nevidimaia rastsvetka)* that was perceived by the subject without consciously registering it. This effect was achieved by means of subtle, "almost imperceptible spatial-color shades of the same, almost monochrome, gamut." In an example suggested by Ginzburg—and indeed followed in the Narkomfin block—a room with a light-blue ceiling could have walls of cool white, pale gray, or pale yellow, while a greenish ceiling could be accompanied with mostly white, slightly greenish walls with a subtle shade of warm brown or cool white tones. If one paid a short visit to such a room, Ginzburg continued, the color of the walls would remain almost unnoticeable and the room would seem white. However, if someone remained subjected to the effect of the walls for a longer period of time, the color began "deeply, almost half-consciously to penetrate, without any noticeable visual irritation, into the sensation of the living [subject], becoming not so much a factor of color as such, but a sort of purely spatial sensation."[51]

Ginzburg used the word "half-consciously" *(polusoznatel'no)* to describe how the "invisible . . . but sensible" *(nevidimaia, no oshchushchaemaia)* coloration entered the mind of the subject unregistered by consciousness. This concept was pertinent for both Matyushin's theory of expanded seeing and the mainstream physiological research of unconscious perception employed by Scheper and Borchert. The perception of color, Borchert argued, was unconscious and thus pertinent to humans and animals alike:

> People, animals, [and] plants experience the impact of color and light. This impact is usually manifested in this or that primitive reaction on a certain color environment, be it a green spring, a yellow-golden fall, or a moon-bluish light. People mostly unconsciously perceive the impact of colored light in an interior, such as a lamp with a green shade in the office or a pink lantern in the bedroom; this is similar to the unconscious agitation of a bull or a turkey cock when they see a red cloth. Color affects human body

not only as the color effect of surrounding nature, but also as the effect of the chromatic solution of an interior space.[52]

Having removed the perception of wall-painting into the domain of the unconscious, Malyarstroy's program culminated in its dissolution as art. Its color schemes were intended to remain unseen and unappreciated by the viewer, who was to respond to them—not aesthetically but psychologically and physiologically—by sensing spatial form and experiencing relaxation. The subject, not the building, was the ultimate object of Malyarstroy's design.

Ergographic Wall-Painting

As Anson Rabinbach detailed in his study of modern subjectivity as "the human motor," the concept of energy appeared in European philosophical discourse as one of its foundational notions following the developments in thermodynamics in the mid-nineteenth century.[53] Energy was interpreted as the source of all mechanical, and eventually human, work. The first law of thermodynamics declared that the amount of energy possessed by a system always remained a constant: energy could be transformed but not created. The discovery of the second law of thermodynamics in the 1860s added a pessimistic note to this idea. The law postulated an inevitable loss of energy during the process of its conversion: energy was now understood as a scarce and ever-diminishing resource that had to be economized. As a result, the concepts of energy and fatigue (or, the loss of energy) became tropes of nineteenth-century psychology and physiology. Richard Avenarius's principle of the least measure of force and Ostwald's "energetic imperative" were only two of the most influential applications.[54] Academic disciplines and practical methods of organizing industrial work turned to color as a tool of economizing energy. Rephrasing Avenarius, Scheper urged, "We have to use all achievements of technology, the laws of functionality, [and] the principle 'of maximum effect under the least measure of force' in order to build dwellings, which play such an important role in our life."[55]

In 1884, Angelo Mosso, a physiologist from Turin, invented the ergograph, an instrument that measured fatigue in the forearms after lifting or pulling a weight.[56] This invention stimulated the emergence of a new science, ergography, in the 1900s. Ergography explored how external and internal physiological factors (such as temperature, rhythm, and blood chemistry) contribute to fatigue. Particularly well known in Russia were the ergographic studies of Charles Féré. In *Sensation and Movement* (1900), the French physiologist

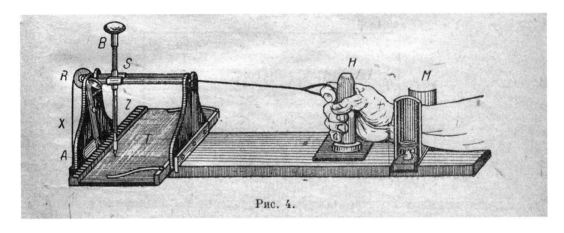

Figure 5.2. Charles Féré's ergograph was well known to Soviet designers. This drawing from a Soviet publication on the use of color in architecture explains the principles of its work. Reproduced in S. S. Alekseev, *Tsvet v arkhitekture* (Moscow: Gosstroiizdat, 1934), 21.

described the "dynamogenity" of colors, or their effect on muscular work. His dynamometer measured the muscle strength of the arm of a subject positioned in front of a colored screen—red, orange, green, yellow, or blue. Féré's other device, a modification of Mosso's ergograph, recorded working energy by marking the height at which a weight could be lifted; the results were then considered to exemplify any type of muscular work.[57]

Other psychological studies revealed that red, yellow, and orange intensified the activity of the circulatory system, strengthened breathing, and increased the heartbeat, while blue and violet depressed physiological processes.[58] Labor psychologists established that precise color vision was a necessary prerequisite for many working-class occupations, such as those related to factory production and transportation (where signaling systems were often based on color).[59] They also gave architects practical suggestions regarding the noticeability of colors, the use of colored light, and the use of color as a background for work processes. *Malyarnoe delo* enthusiastically reported about the experience of American shoe factory Doherty and Donovan and of rubber and tobacco factories in Hamburg, where bright colors used in the interiors allegedly aroused workers' enthusiasm and inspired tidiness, and about the example of the Montreal Industrial Painting Company, which publicized its campaign for an introduction of color in factories with a poster depicting spoilage, fatigue, depression, sickness, eye strain, and accidents flying out of the factory with the arrival of wall-painters, who carry paint buckets that bring "visibility," "energy," "accuracy," "efficiency and increased output," and ultimately "reduced insurance."[60] According to Sofia Belyaeva-Ekzemplyarskaya, who

Figure 5.3. This image, originally published in New York in *The Painters Magazine* (June 1931): 11, was an advertisement for the Montreal Industrial Painting Company. It depicts spoilage, fatigue, depression, sickness, eye strain, and accidents flying out of the factory with the arrival of wall-painters, who bring "visibility," "energy," "accuracy," "efficiency and increased output," and ultimately "reduced insurance." Reproduced in *Maliarnoe delo*, no. 4 (1931): 59. As the journal explained in relationship to this image, if in the capitalist "West" color was introduced to industrial spaces in pursuit of profit, in the Soviet Union it could be used for "strengthening our industrial tempos." Courtesy of Kansas State University Libraries.

lectured at the Higher Institute of Architecture and Construction (VASI, as VKhUTEIN was renamed after the reorganization of 1930), fatigue was most easily provoked by violet, followed by red, while the least tiring color was green.[61] Researchers also established that green was the best color for stimulating work, whereas red, increasing energy at first, soon induced fatigue, and blue and violet exerted a depressing effect.[62] At VKhUTEIN, the notion of fatigue redefined the artistic discourse about color: whereas Matyushin had discussed colors in terms of their dullness and luminosity, in his classes, the psychologist Kravkov explained these effects through such concepts as color fatigue and the processes of color adaptation.[63] A student sketchbook on color theory preserves an exercise on observing, measuring, and comparing the effects of color fatigue: the students were asked to take two pieces of paper, one chromatic (red or blue) and another black; they were then to cover half of the colored sheet with the black paper and look at it for several seconds;

after removing the black sheet they were to observe that the part that was covered seemed brighter than the part that was not (Plate 19).[64]

In 1929, with the support of the Institute for Mass Psychology, Ladovsky planned to start an "experimental investigation of the role of color in interior architecture" in his Psychotechnical Laboratory at VKhUTEIN, in particular, of the "psychophysiological impact of color" and color's "spatial role."[65] Ladovsky's focus on testing and experiment came close to the constructivists' investigation of spatial properties of color. Mikhail Barshch, Ginzburg's former student and a Stroykom employee, became Ladovsky's doctoral student at VKhUTEIN. Barshch's dissertation aimed to develop "such a [working] environment and such methods of work that would ensure the maximum productivity of labor without jeopardizing the health of the worker."[66] Outlining a program for a broader use of the physiology of color perception in architecture, Barshch argued that the discoveries of Féré were applicable to several types of labor—receptor (perception-based, such as the labor of an accountant or a typesetter), effector (physical work), and cerebral—and to several environmental factors: the dimensions and the shape of the room, the shape and location of light openings, and the color and facture of walls. The architect, Barshch contended, was responsible for the optimal functioning of bodily, mental, and perceptive processes in order to economize the physiological energy of the user.[67] Barshch defined the scope of his research as a study of the psychophysiological impact of color on work productivity, which he saw occurring on several levels: associative (such as feelings of order, disorder, neatness, or dirt), acoustic (silence, noise, or rhythm), and optical (the form, size, and illumination of the room).[68] Although Barshch examined different experiments of Féré, such as the dynamogenic effects of alternating colored and white light and the relationship between the dynamogeneity of colors and the time of the day, he was particularly interested in ergography, hoping to offer Soviet architects a system of dynamogenic properties of colors.[69] Red, he established, was the most dynamogenic at the beginning, but then quickly lost its power; orange and yellow had a constant and permanent effect; green provided moderate stimulation at the beginning and maintained a steady positive effect afterward; blue and violet initially exerted a depressing effect but could defer fatigue if used for a long period of time.

Barshch's research complemented the exploration of the psychological effects of color that Scheper and Borchert had conducted in Germany.[70] But whereas the German designers initiated the standardization and rationalization of wall-painting, defining its subject as physiological, Barshch's program integrated their program with labor management: by reacting to the "color screens," the dweller of the Narkomfin was conducting an economically important work. The difference between the Germans' mechanicism and the more holistic and simultaneously economic aspirations pertinent to Soviet functionalism was only the first among a series of tensions that would soon lead to Scheper's departure and the dissolution of Malyarstroy as an independent artistic center.

The Limits of Objectivity

The so-called *Typen-Streit*, a formative debate for modernist architecture between Hermann Muthesius, who was supported by Ostwald, and Henry van der Velde at the 1914 meeting of the German Werkbund, had raged around the question of whether architecture should embrace standardization or remain an individual, artistic work.[71] Remaining true to the principles of Muthesius and Ostwald, Scheper believed that standardization became a weapon in the ethical and aesthetic crusade against individualism and, consequently, against individual creativity—in short, against the traditional notion of art, whose definition and very existence it challenged. As he had earlier done in his Bauhaus workshop, Scheper reoriented Malyarstroy's approach to a modern synthesis of art and technology, and turned its production toward standardizable and mass-producible schemes. In 1930, in an open letter to the students of VKhUTEIN, where he taught in the academic year of 1930/31, Scheper asserted:

> *New necessities will create the new art. . . .* Because this is what your construction needs: architects, wall-painters, furniture designers, weavers, that is, constructors, material workers, designers of form, makers of objects, the virtuosos of form—of function-related form. . . . You cannot paint academic nudes and construct *the* chair for *the* house, for *the* masses at the same time. You cannot allow your formal education, which you consider to be the foundation of your education in new painting, to be affected by old traditional principles, while you think about the satisfaction of new, nontraditional demands. Your formal education must be organized according to new methods that familiarize you with the elements of your work: materials, functions, the laws of color.[72]

This program repelled some VKhUTEIN students. P. F. Katichev, who had graduated from the painting department in 1930 and immediately began to work at Malyarstroy, quickly lost his initial enthusiasm.[73] In January 1931, he initiated a public attack on Malyarstroy on the pages of the journal *Za proletarskoe iskusstvo (For the Proletarian Art)*. In an article titled "A Functionalist Sway," Katichev elaborated his program of technologization without standardization, summoning Soviet muralists to use paint-sprayers while working on unique projects (not unlike today's graffiti artists). Borchert responded on the pages of *Malyarnoe delo,* accusing Katichev of individualism and technological and ideological incompetence: "We need people that, first of all, think rationally, economically and, of course, 'functionally.' Those whose working field is limited by a low horizon, dreamer-romantics that fuss over their petty 'I' (the price of which we know all too well), cannot be of any use to us."[74] The "functionalist" ideology of Malyarstroy, based on the principles of economy and rationality, left no place for individualism, Borchert went on, whether for the designer or for the user of architecture:

> The design office of Malyarstroy develops its color schemes on the basis of scientifically verified conclusions of lighting engineering, physiology, and psychology. Departing from the data [received by] technical devices, the design office researches the basic demands of the human in the colored environment and follows them in its design work. The projects are executed with those methods that are most understandable for the builder, give the best general color impression, and are executed rationally, with the least expenditure of resources and time. It is not an "abstract play of colored planes" . . . but quite a real work, based on really existing prerequisites, because the rules of every design, and of color design in particular, are based on the needs of a human organism viewed in connection to the given means.[75]

In August 1931, *Za proletarskoe iskusstvo* published the article "Architecture and *Tsvetopis'"* by young artist Vladimir Kostin, written in collaboration with Hungarian-born art critic János Mácza (spelled as Ivan Matsa in Russian), renowned for his sociological perspective.[76] It began by redefining wall-painting as a new artistic genre: *tsvetopis'*. "If one takes painting as the art of color, in a room we will have perhaps the most 'pure,' abstract kind of painting. It would be best to call this kind of painting *tsvetopis'*." Combining the roots *tsvet* (color), and *pis'* (from *pisat',* to write or paint), this term was coined by Kostin as a counterpart to *zhivopis',* painting (a word that is etymologically connected to *zhizn',* life, and thus literally means "a depiction of life") to signify a non-figurative art whose medium was not paint but color, and thus whose result was not material but psychological.[77] Kostin's *tsvetopis'* echoed *fotopis'*, a new photographic genre based on the photogram, which was invented by El Lissitzky in the late 1920s. *Fotopis'* had freed photography from its narrative content, thereby distilling it to its medium-specific core and elevating it to the status of a "true art."[78] As art, *fotopis'* was "another means of affecting our conscious and our senses"—a function identical to that of interior color, which, as Lissitzky noted quoting physiologist Nikolay Pomortsev when discussing furniture design, affects cerebral visual centers and, through them, the entire body with a variety of its functions.[79] Hailing Ginzburg's definition of architecture as a combination of color screens enclosing the perceiving subject, Kostin likewise defined *tsvetopis'* as a means of attaining psychological affect.[80]

However, Kostin went further, supplementing this psychologism with Mácza's Marxist sociological aesthetics. Each social group, Kostin argued, had its own psychological response to color, based on its ethical values and ideological associations. Thus, a pink room and an orange lampshade "arouse in a philistine a certain feeling of satisfaction, coziness and repose, whereas in a person with a stronger ideological mindset the same room provokes only a feeling of contempt—not to mention that the color of the red flag agitates the fascist like a lash of whip, whereas in a proletarian it arouses the feeling of class solidarity and might." Moreover, a color could evoke conflicting connotations even within the same group: "the same fascist, for example, could very much like the red wallpaper of a female boudoir or the red blouse of his mistress."[81] This approach had been promoted by Vladimir Friche's influential *Sociology of Art* (1930), whose chapter on color in art, in turn, extensively drew on Ostwald Spengler's observations in *The Decline of the West,* about the connection between the culture of the epoch and the chromatic choices of painters.[82] Yet, neither reliance on Friche nor Mácza's revisions could help the article's fate. It was declared "a characteristic document of mechanistic views in art criticism, right opportunism in left clothing, theoretical substantiation of the replacement of art with technology."[83] In August 1931, Stalinist critic I. Amov closed the debate by returning wall-painting to individual artistic work and even unskilled craftsmanship: Kostin's deliberations about the psychological and physiological effects of color were, he declared, "completely scholastic and bourgeois." Instead, wall-painting had to express "a concrete idea"—or simply cover the building's walls.[84]

Back in Leningrad, in 1932, Maria Ender made an attempt to salvage Matyushin's physiological theory of color combinations in the preface that she wrote for his *Handbook of Color,* which came out that year.[85] Spengler-Friche's theory, she argued, treated color as an isolated and simplified phenomenon: for example, when associating yellow and red with festivity and the market.

Meanwhile, in painting, the color of the used pigment was often different from the perceived color of the depicted object, and this psychological impression was frequently determined by the chromatic context. It was this understanding of the context that the color theories of Ostwald and Friche missed, and that, she hoped, secured the relevance of Matyushin's work even within the changed political and aesthetic conditions. Although her call for the appreciation of the chromatic *environment* (*sreda*, a notion rooted in life sciences, from which it was borrowed by social critique) was repeated by Mácza the following year, the importance of the hand-painted *Handbook*, which came out with a minimal print run, and with it, of Matyushin's color theory, for the practice of Soviet wall-painting remained marginal.[86]

Despite the fact that the debate ended with a seeming victory of figurative monumental art, the concept of wall-painting as a field endowed with an economic purpose (and consequently, of the perceiving subject as bio-economic), which was developed at Malyarstroy, persisted—moreover, the economic perspective on wall-painting informed later Soviet aesthetics. As new, social, approaches to psychology gained importance in the Soviet Union, physiological and cerebral functions came to be seen in their more holistic context. One such influential approach, activity theory, was initiated by the circle of Lev Vygotsky and continued in the 1930s by the Kharkiv school of psychology (most notably, by Alexey Leontyev), exploring hierarchies of psychological processes.[87] According to Leontyev, "the concept of activity is necessarily bound up with the concept of motive. . . . 'Unmotivated' activity is not activity that has no motive, but activity with a subjectively and objectively hidden motive."[88] Connecting all physical and mental phenomena into a unified system oriented toward the end goal, Leontyev's hierarchy began as activity at the most general and conscious level; it was subdivided into actions consisting of operations, which in turn were divided into functions. Similarly, when in 1933 Mácza published his own article on color in painting, he argued that the formal and material aspects of color are explained through its role as an instrument of solving social problems.[89] It was such social potential that now endowed wall-painting with the status of art and that—in contrast to the Bauhaus's mechanism—imbued it with a humanist content. In a lecture that he gave to a group of wall-painters in 1936 Boris Ender highlighted the connection between the unconscious, physiological process of color perception and higher, conscious, and socially meaningful activity:

> My duty to you, specialists dealing with color, is to help you eliminate the colorful chaos, with which our life is still littered. . . . Let color become a building material in our construction of socialism.

Imagine that in a factory, walls, machines, production clothes are not only given a special color, but these colors are combined in a way that increases working productivity. Imagine that in hospitals walls, curtains, blankets, furniture are harmonized in such a way that the patient cures sooner and better. That in a theater, the impression increases due to color design in a way that is not yet practiced. The same in a book, in a First-of-May rally, on a railway station, in the metro. I argue that you must organize color.[90]

This organizing potential remained wall-painting's most long-lasting legacy.

This potential was last explored in 1935–38 in the work of the Laboratory of Color Perception under the Narkompros (directed by Nikolay Norman [Troitsky] and patronized by the secretary of the Union of Soviet Architects Vladimir Dedyukhin), which employed the psychologist and author of books on color in architecture Sergey Alekseev. Collaborating with several schools in Moscow and Podolsk, the laboratory's specialists painted the walls of classrooms in particular colors and later subjected the students to "a comprehensive medical examination." After that, using "specially developed methods and forms, psychologists conducted conversations and interviews with teachers and students of [all] grades from the first to the tenth. Their opinions and impressions were processed, analyzed, and discussed with specialists in pedagogy." This work subsequently turned into "a broad study, delegated to a whole range of research institutions."[91] The introduction of the second, sociological step of data analysis revealed the desire to overcome the mechanicism of the "German" approach—yet it, too, did little to help wall-painting's fate. The second, physical, defeat of Soviet wall-painting research proved to be final: in 1938, both Dedyukhin and Norman were subjected to repression.[92] Finally, Borchert, who became a Soviet citizen, was arrested in 1942, during the Second World War, to die in a labor camp two years later.

From Matyushin's eccentric experiments in expanded seeing to Malyarstroy's interest in ergography, wall-painting (just like standardization, as discussed in the previous chapter) in industrially backward Russia developed as a more theoretical, perception-oriented discipline than its international counterparts, which were immediately related to industrial production. Even as a tool of standardization, as the example of the Narkomfin shows, Soviet wall-painting focused on regulating of subjectivity rather than on the unification of production. Ironically, this theoretical bias and this focus on psychological perception was a reversal of the program of industrialization, which had led to the invitation of the German specialists to Moscow. But while, helpless in the face of Russia's technological backwardness, the "German" modernist approach to wall-painting as the standardization of colors and their relationships did not last long, the organizational concerns that were developed at Malyarstroy persisted well into the 1930s.

Although the painting schemes, as well as the residential Narkomfin block, remained experimental models, the story of wall-painting as an instrument of psychological control did not end. In the late 1960s, it was revived in the wake of the emergence of environmental psychology and still continues to inform architecture.[93] Today, the seeds sown by the Narkomfin building ripened not only in the architecture of the "neo-avant-garde," but in such ostensibly architecturally insignificant projects as schools, hospitals, and prisons, as scientists continue to explore the potential of color for improving outcomes in learning, healing, and correction.[94] Famously, the Baker-Miller pink color is still used in detention centers across the globe (most recently, in the German-speaking countries). It is named after the directors of the Naval Correctional Facility in Seattle, where in the 1970s the psychologist Alexander Schauss conducted research on the impact of color upon human emotions and claimed that pink exercises a calming effect.[95] The importance of color for these canonic examples of what Michel Foucault called disciplinary institutions—modern spaces of normalization—reveals the disciplining aspirations in both Malyarstroy's social utopia and contemporary society. And yet, an important difference pertains: whereas the use of color in contemporary institutions is limited to optimizing physiological and behavioral functions, for Malyarstroy, scientifically determined color opened a path to imbuing behavior with an external, universally significant goal.

SIX

Personality

Gorky Park as a Factory of Dealienation

On July 23, 1934, after visiting the Central Park of Culture and Leisure in Moscow in the company of his son and coauthor of *The Science of Life* G. P. Wells, H. G. Wells left an excited note in the park's guestbook: "When I die to capitalism and rise again in the Soviet Heaven, may I wake up first place in the Park of Culture and Rest—perhaps attended . . ."[1] He added a sketch of an angel welcoming him to that better world. As the director of the park Betty Glan later claimed, the angel was none other than her, and the note originally ended with words ". . . by the charming Betty Glan."[2] Only thirty years old when she welcomed the Wellses in Moscow (and twenty-five when she assumed the directorship of the park), Glan was indeed charming: cheerful, energetic, and enthusiastic, she was known as "as a real Komsomol person, who could inspire people and raise them for great work."[3] In a subsequent letter thanking her for the tour of the park, Wells wrote, "I sincerely congratulate you. You are the director of the factory of happy people."[4] As this chapter argues, developing the Wellses' and Julian Huxley's monistic humanism, Moscow Central Park of Culture and Leisure (Tsentral'nyi park kul'tury i otdykha) was indeed a machine for the production of the modern subject, for which Glan provided an embodied model.[5] As Fabiola López-Durán recently demonstrated, the program of modern metropolitan parks in Europe and Latin America was informed by neo-Lamarckian evolutionism, which suggested the genetic improvement of the population through the design of the environment.[6] Carrying a similarly evolutionist program, the design of Soviet parks reconciled Lamarckism with vitalist Marxism, focusing not only on health but on the integral personality of the human and on its production by social means. From its origins in Glan's vision for the Central Park of Culture and Leisure, inspired by Lunacharsky's thought, the Soviet public park was conceived as a heterotopia where the alienating effects of the division of labor—reinforced elsewhere in the Soviet Union during the First Five-Year Plan—were overcome. Paradoxically, this endeavor relied on

Figure 6.1. H. G. Wells was excited to visit Gorky Park and meet Betty Glan. In this photograph, he is seen with Glan and his son and coauthor of the *Science of Life,* zoologist G. P. Wells, in the park. Also published is the note Wells sent to Glan in the aftermath of the visit, which reads: "When I die to capitalism and rise again in the Soviet Heaven, may I wake up first place in the Park of Culture and Rest—perhaps attended..." (as Glan later claimed, the note originally ended with "...by the charming Betty Glan"). Published in *USSR in Construction,* no. 9 (1934): 28.

the organizational solutions of the industrial age: dialectically sublated in socialism, alienation was to turn into dealienation, producing the better and happier humans of the future, while this dealienation, in turn, was to spur industrial productivity.

Leisure

The Moscow Central Park of Culture and Leisure opened in August 1928 on the site of the 1923 All-Russian Agricultural and Artisanal–Industrial Exposition, whose layout it incorporated. As its name betrays, the immediate goal of the park was to make the leisure of the working class cultured—to teach the newly urbanized population that arrived to work on the construction sites of the First Five-Year Plan the habits of urban life, simultaneously preparing unskilled workers for acquiring qualifications demanded by industry. The idea was first introduced by the chairman of the Moscow Council, Konstantin Ukhanov. Anatoly Lunacharsky, who became the deputy head of the commission for the foundation of the park, elaborated on it, as later did his protégé Glan.[7] According to Ukhanov, who in March 1928 announced the park's creation in the party newspaper *Pravda,* "the battle for culture" in the park was a part of the "cultural revolution," intended to "reconstruct the everyday life of a worker and a peasant, fill it with new content, adequate for the socialist essence of our construction."[8] The park had to replace the old, "unorganized" outdoor sites of the individual leisure of the workers, where on weekends they "walked or sat on the grass in a narrow circle of friends," where vodka and beer "abounded, an accordion creaked, tipsy couples danced, and fortune-tellers moved to and fro."[9] Instead, Ukhanov stipulated, the new park was to become a collective cultural entertainment complex, in which a worker could find everything for a day off: cinema, theater, circus, radio, music, fields for sports, playgrounds, attractions, exhibitions, newspaper kiosks, dining rooms, cafés, and milk and grocery stands.[10] Along the same lines, professor of "resort medicine" Georgy Danishevsky, who developed the park's hygienic program, distinguished between two forms of leisure: one was "idle and dumb," the other "correctly organized" and able to "fully activate the worker and the peasant and strengthen their will to socialist labor."[11]

This program was elaborated in response to the two existing types of modern working-class outdoor recreation spaces: the urban public park and the entertainment park.[12] While the former served a moral and hygienic purpose, helping urbanites to reunite with nature, the latter, downplaying these goals, indulged the city sensibility of the workers by providing them with

Figure 6.2. The Moscow Central Park of Culture and Leisure opened in 1928 on the site of the 1923 All-Russian Agricultural and Artisanal–Industrial Exposition. This photograph by Shalashov (first name unknown) documents the park in 1936. Courtesy of the State Central Museum of Contemporary History of Russia (13409/33).

nervous stimulation and easy gratification. Rather than simulating nature in the manner of nineteenth-century metropolitan parks, the Central Park of Culture and Leisure was to become an industrial-like space for the utilization of natural hygienic resources; rather than catering to the emerging mass culture, it was to make high culture accessible to the masses (Plate 20).

In other words, the Park of Culture and Leisure, which was to be visited in the immediate aftermath of factory work, aimed to restore all that divided labor, as Karl Marx vividly demonstrated, alienated from the workers: their health, their sense of collectivity, and their moral, cultural, and intellectual integrity. Indeed, Marx's view of industrial labor, unlike that of some of his followers, was far from romanticizing: for him, labor was a hard, monotonous, and debilitating physical activity.[13] Whereas the craftsman had control over the entire process of production, the capitalist manufacturing process and, even more so, the Fordist assembly line made the worker responsible for only a fragmented operation repeated over and over again.[14] This work, as Wells illustrated in his gruesome neo-Lamarckian image of Martians in *War of the Worlds* (1898), threatened the genetic evolution of humanity, leading to biological simplification—a monstrous reversal of the evolutionary strive to complexity: "To me it is quite credible that the Martians may be descended from beings not unlike ourselves, by a gradual development of brain and hands (the latter giving rise to the two bunches of delicate tentacles at last) at the expense of the rest of the body."[15] The result of this development was repulsive:

> They were huge round bodies—or, rather, heads—about four feet in diameter, each body having in front of it a face. This face had no nostrils—indeed, the Martians do not seem to have had any sense of smell, but it had a pair of very large dark-colored eyes, and just beneath this a kind of fleshy beak. . . . The internal anatomy . . . was almost equally simple. The greater part of the structure was the brain, sending enormous nerves to the eyes, ear, and tactile tentacles. Besides this were the bulky lungs, into which the mouth opened, and the heart and its vessels. . . . And this was the sum of the Martian organs. . . . Entrails they had none. They did not eat, much less digest. Instead, they took the fresh, living blood of other creatures, and *injected* it into their own veins.[16]

Marx's solution to the problem of alienation was to redistribute all types of work among everyone. In *The German Ideology* he foresaw a society in which one would "hunt in the morning, fish in the afternoon, breed cattle in the evening, criticize after dinner."[17] But as such an egalitarian redistribution of tasks proved to be unachievable (in postrevolutionary Russia, no less than elsewhere, social stratification based on training and occupation persisted), leisure emerged as a way of restoring the soul just as rest ensured the recuperation of the body.

Famously distinguishing between labor, which belonged to the domain of necessity, and work, which, as creative and socially meaningful action, belonged to freedom, Hannah Arendt noted that in ancient Greece, labor was delegated to slaves, whose dehumanization was the sole attainable means of ensuring the humanity of citizens. Humanness, which was inseparable from freedom, originated not in labor, but in its absence.

> Contempt for laboring, originally arising out of a passionate striving for freedom from necessity and a no less passionate impatience with every effort that left no trace, no monument, no great work worthy of remembrance, spread with the increasing demands of *polis* life upon the time of the citizens and its insistence on their abstention *(skhole)* from all but political activities, until it covered everything that demanded an effort.[18]

As Arendt did later, Lunacharsky, in *The Foundations of Positive Aesthetics* (1903), praised this idea of *skhole* as the source of human dignity:

> Σχολή *[skhole]*—idleness—is the mother of all sciences. With a class that did not have to struggle constantly for survival, there emerged a new mighty stimulus of human progress. Idle people could better develop their organs, from muscles to brain, because they could play: this was their freedom; the [Russian] word "slavery" *[rabstvo]* stems from the word "work" *[rabota]*: art and science were inaccessible for a slave *[rab]* [or] a worker *[rabochii]*. Play gave a tremendous strength to the aristocracy, because it not only exercised the body and brain of the representatives of the upper classes, but gave them an opportunity to transfer a concrete struggle into the sphere of abstraction: they could combine, daringly generalize generations' experience, they could pose questions in the most general, abstract terms.[19]

Today, the root of the Greek word *skhole* survives in the word "school." In its original meaning of "leisure, free time," *skhole* was identified with "time used for intellectual discussion," and then came to mean the place where such discussions were conducted. Like the Greek *skhole,* the Roman *otium* was a concept associated with intellectual, contemplative leisure, which allowed the patricians—attended by slaves and temporarily relieved from daily political obligations—to engage in scholarly activity and to reunite with nature.[20] The concept of *otium* led to the emergence of an architectural type, the suburban villa. Both *otium* as a concept and the villa as its architecturalization were embraced by Renaissance humanists; as a bourgeois architectural type, the villa persisted, almost unchanged, until this day.[21] For one, in his *News from Nowhere* (1890), illustrated with an image of his suburban villa at Kelmscott, British romantic socialist William Morris endowed leisure with a prominent role in the society of the future: guaranteeing the dignity and humanity of the citizens of the ideal London and thus enabling happiness, pleasure, self-fulfillment, creativity, and beauty.

Resembling Arendt's later distinction between labor and work, another distinction can thus be detected in the thought of the Soviet park theorists: the one between rest and leisure. If the English word "leisure," stemming from Latin *licere* ("to be allowed"), originally meant an opportunity afforded by freedom from necessity (thus related in its meaning to *skhole* and *otium*), "rest" is related to Old Norse *rost* ("distance after which one rests") and Old Saxon *resta* (burial place) and is thus associated with immobility. In a similar manner, contemporary German distinguishes between *Muße* and *Ruhe*; French between *loisir* and *repos*; and Russian between *dosug* and *pokoi*. In other words, whereas the body requires rest to return to labor, the mind needs leisure to be able to work. In Russian, furthermore, both meanings are subsumed under the umbrella of *otdykh* (originating from *dyshat'*, to breath—a moment when one takes a breath from work), which is accordingly subdivided as passive or active.[22] This word was used in the park's title. Its ambiguity elucidates the program of the "Park of Culture and *Otdykh*" as the site for both rest and leisure, but with a priority, strengthened by the addition of "culture," assigned to the latter. In the words of the hygienist Danishevsky, "the primacy of the social in the unity of the biological and the social" comprised the principle of the park's work: only departing from the social, "can the organization of mass leisure, activating and strengthening *homo corporalis* and supporting, in every possible way, the harmonic development of his physical and intellectual forces in its form and content, be subordinated to the decisive task—the improvement of the productivity of labor for the struggle for socialist construction and the defense of its heroic participant—*homo socialis*."[23]

Like Morris, Lunacharsky believed that creativity (which, for him, constituted the essence of humanity) was a fruit of leisure, an active and meaningful use of free time. Such active and productive leisure emerged not as the opposite of work but as a precondition for it. Applying his teacher Richard Avenarius's philosophy to aesthetic thought, Lunacharsky argued that everything that increased the amount of energy *(affektsional)* in an organism was "aesthetic," while everything that decreased it was "antiaesthetic."[24] However, a simple accumulation of energy was no less harmful than its excessive loss because it led to energetic "obesity": passivity, laziness, and weakness. What was needed instead was a balance of two processes: assimilation, or the acquisition of energy from the external environment, and deassimilation, the loss of energy of the organism to that external environment.[25] From a more vitalist perspective, Alexander Bogdanov, developing what he called "psycho-energetics," postulated that the principle of organic development presupposed neither an accumulation of energy nor its prudent expenditure but rather the use of energy for brave, audacious deeds.[26] In a socialist society (which, for him, was the natural direction of social evolution, artificially impeded by capitalism), selection would lead to the survival of those "who possess maximum vitality, that is, the greatest sum of energy along with the maximum flexibility and diversity of organic adaptation."[27] Following Lunacharsky's and Bogdanov's long-time associate and Wells's old friend, the writer Maxim Gorky had earlier condemned the capitalist entertainment park as "the kingdom of boredom," where "the person is immediately stupefied, his consciousness squashed by its gleam, thought expelled from it, and personality turned into a fragment of the crowd"; Glan called for the Soviet park to become "the city of cheerfulness."[28] In 1931, Gorky's name was given to the Park of Culture and Leisure, which has been known as Gorky Park ever since. The addition emphasized the park's vitalist and collectivist agenda, exemplified in its mission to become the proletarian villa.

In accordance with this program, Glan based her project of transforming workers' personality on "the principle of the activation of visitors" *(printsip aktivizatsii posetitelei)*.[29] The visitors were, for instance, invited to take part in the experiments of the Timiriazev Biological Museum within the park and in the demonstrations of machinery in the park's Village of Science and Technology.[30] Moreover, mass singing, dancing, and the reciting of rhythmic poetry engaged thousands of people every day, leading to the emergence of a new position, which became crucial for the functioning of the park: "mass organizer." Several hundred volunteers specialized in activating the masses. Like Glan, they were "young cheerful [people]" who "possess a wonderful quality . . . the special capacity to organize and lead the masses, to draw them into singing, dance, play, to give it a free and easy merry disposition."[31] The significance of such collective activities within the park's program overshadowed the role of aesthetic spatial experience: in essence, the park was not a site but a mobile activity infrastructure, which could be brought to factories and workers' clubs by "touring brigades."[32] The lengthy and excited testimony left by Julian Huxley, the coauthor of *The Science of Life,* who visited the park with a group of British scientists in 1931, provides a personal glimpse of how this program of energizing the workers was realized in the park:

> The biggest park in Moscow is called "the Park of Culture and Rest." At the far end is the Rest section, with abundance of deck-chairs, and little open-air libraries at which you may borrow books. Towards the city, there are side-shows, restaurants, theatres, cinemas. There is a band-stand, surrounded with huge hoardings on which are painted propaganda cartoons. There is an exhibition of machinery. There are courts for volley-ball, open-air gymnastic apparatus, places where the novice can be instructed in fencing, bayonet practice, athletics (the coaches all giving their time voluntarily).
>
> Community singing is always going in two or three places, very efficiently run by young women. And community dancing is also much in vogue. Every day there are small dancing circles, but sometimes the big central square is given over to this. The band

Figure 6.3. Personal development and self-education were indispensable parts of the Soviet concept of leisure. This photograph by an unknown photographer documents combine harvesters exhibited in the Central Park of Culture and Leisure (likely in the park's Village of Science and Technology) in 1930. Courtesy of the State Central Museum of Contemporary History of Russia (8596/16).

plays the tune; the conductor, through a microphone, explains the dance and tells those who want to take part to form a circle; then the instructors—a dozen pairs of young girls—demonstrate the dance; the public try the steps, first slowly, then faster; and finally they dance for some ten minutes, then beginning on another set of steps. Our party happened to be there on an evening of this sort, and insisted on joining the fun. And all of us, from medical students to Harley Street specialists and scientific professors, experienced a real exhilaration from our brief immersion in this organized mass activity shared with four or five hundred other human beings. . . .

Almost every day the central square is the seat of different activity. Once I saw a big demonstration of physical exercises by boys and girls; once a parade of trained Alsatian dogs; and once there was an enormous anti-gas demonstration, staged as a mimic gas-attack from the air. Five airplanes came across from the aerodrome; mimic bombs were exploded all over the park, scaring up a protesting flock of rooks. Men and women lay down, pretending to be casualties. Fire-engines and ambulances with all the personnel in gas-masks drove up and rescued the "casualties." Hand-carts which sprayed anti-gas chemicals were wheeled up and down. To add as much verisimilitude as possible, the men with the "bombs" would often throw them right up against the crowd, which hastily scattered before the explosion could take place; and the fire-engines were deliberately driven through the masses of people, ringing their bells and hooting. I do not know whether this was Culture or Rest, but it certainly proved a very popular spectacle.[33]

Huxley's and his colleagues' "exhilaration" from their brief immersion into an "organized mass activity" shared with hundreds of other bodies summarizes the collectivist dialectic of the park: to flourish, individuality required collectivity. The rest of this chapter will examine how this dialectic was architecturalized by the park's designers.

The Individual and the Collective

Both a laboratory and a showcase of the socialist park, Gorky Park included its own Scientific-Methodological Center (Nauchno-metodicheskii tsentr), which employed theater directors and education specialists who developed its program, and the Office of Design and Planning (Proektno-planirovochnyi otdel), responsible for elaborating design principles for Soviet public parks. This office was directed by Konstantin Melnikov in 1928–29, El Lissitzky in 1929–32, and later by Alexander Vlasov.[34] At the same time, the park served as the largest recreational facility in the country: in 1932, it was visited by eight million people.[35] The two aspects of the park's program—its giant scale and its use as a base for research and theorization—overlapped, as the mass character was precisely what, according to its theorists, defined the socialist park of the future.

The park's collectivist program relied on the philosophy of "god-building" (bogostroitel'stvo), which Gorky and Lunacharsky had developed in the 1900s.

Blending turn-of-the-century Orthodox "god-seeking" with socialism, the god-builders deified the people: God cannot be found, they claimed, but can be built by a collective effort of people—and moreover, the people itself, when consolidated into the collective, became the god. In the aftermath of the revolution, Lunacharsky evoked this agenda when elaborating a program for mass celebration as the new, proletarian, type of art, which transubstantiated individuals into the people:[36]

> In order for the masses to make themselves felt, they must outwardly manifest themselves, and this is possible only when, to use Robespierre's phrase, *they are their own spectacle*. If *organized masses* march to music, sing in unison or perform some extensive gymnastic maneuvers or dances, in other words, organize a kind of parade, then those other, unorganized masses clustering round on all sides of the streets and squares where the festival takes place, will merge with the organized masses, and thus, one can say: the whole *people manifests its soul to itself*.[37]

In 1929, the artist L. Roshchin based a scenario for mass celebrations upon this principle, suggesting enhancing the dramatic potential of the rally by choreographing the flow of its movement. "Let [demonstrating] columns face [demonstrating] columns along the entire length of streets. . . . Let enthusiasm multiply enthusiasm, joy [multiply] joy, sounds [multiply] sounds, colors [multiply] colors, political slogans [multiply] political slogans!" he called, adding that this spectacle would finally eliminate the boundary between the participants and the viewers, achieving, as it were, the ambition of the avant-garde theater.[38]

This call inspired the proposal for Gorky Park that was defended as a diploma project by Ladovsky's student Mikael Mazmonyan in 1929. The project made the demonstrating procession the backbone of its design. Arriving via the "report alley," flanked by tribunes from which the representatives of public organizations reported to the passing citizens, the procession moved into the park through the ceremonial entrance. This was a broad, meandering ramp, on which the procession would ascend to enjoy the panorama of the park while simultaneously providing spectacle for the others.[39] As Mazmonyan explained, whereas the "triumphal arch of the past," a product of absolutism, dominated over the spectator, the (socialist) ramp-arch of Gorky Park remained architecturally incomplete without the participation of the masses. Evoking modern highway intersections developed around the same time, more immediately, his theatrical project relied on Lissitzky's 1926 unrealized

Figure 6.4. In his VKhUTEIN diploma project (1929), Ladovsky's student Mikael Mazmonyan explored the idea of turning the demonstrating procession into a key design element of the park. The procession's movement was orchestrated by the entrance ramp as the triumphal arch of the socialist future. As head architect of the park, Lissitzky enthusiastically supported the idea of turning the park into a "system of paths and levels, moving along which the mass would self-organize and turn into an animated form." Reproduced in *Stroitel'stvo Moskvy,* no. 10 (1929): 15.

stage-set for Vsevolod Meyerhold's Theater and on Frederick Kiesler's Endless Theater (1924), both of which employed a set of intersecting ramps.[40] Praising Mazmonyan's project, Lissitzky noted that it blended the bodies of workers into the great transindividual subject, giving each of them a jolt of energy ("high charge," *vysokaia zariadka,* as Lissitzky called it). The park, for him, was defined through its mass character: "*The entire class, the mass, the collective* is the master of the park." The park thus had to become a "*system of paths and levels,* moving along which the mass would self-organize and turn into an animated form."[41] Several arteries would lead from the city to the park, where they merged into a large thoroughfare. Within the park, this thoroughfare would symbolically narrate the story of humanity's evolution—in society, labor, and culture—from the primitive to advanced stages. Ironically, when the formal idea of intersecting ramps would finally be realized, under the patronage of Huxley, by a former VKhUTEMAS student Berthold Lubetkin as the penguin pavilion in the London Zoo (1933), it proved to be not an animal habitat but a theatrical setting, which, as Hadas Steiner remarks, "dic-

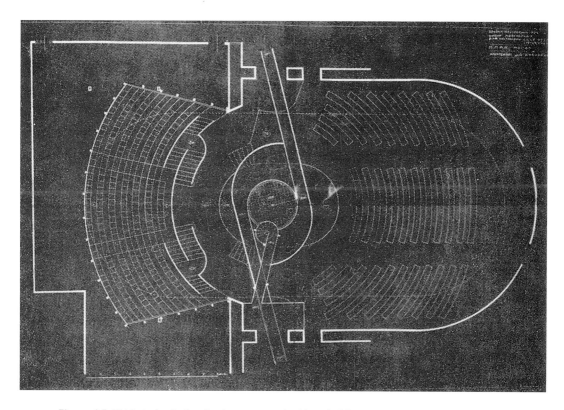

Figure 6.5. El Lissitzky, design for the stage set for Meyerhold's production of Tretyakov's *I Want a Child* (1926), drawing. Mazmonyan's project related landscape architecture to theater design, using this stage-set design as a model for the entrance ramp. Location unknown; image in the public domain.

tated that penguins, birds that move gracefully through water, awkwardly plod up and down ramps," as if showcasing their evolutionary primitivism that precluded them from forming a collective.[42]

Even when acting individually, the imagined visitors to the Soviet park were far from the presumed weak and debilitated benefactors of European and Latin American progressivist programs—rather, they were seen as the best specimens of the modern type. The park's utopian goal was not to prevent genetic degeneration but to take humanity to the next level of its evolutionary development: it heroicized the individual body and challenged its physical abilities, accelerating, as it were, the biological evolution of the human species. Its most popular attractions were athletic, such as the popular Spiral Slide, the ski-jumping hill, and the sled track. A simplified version of László Moholy-Nagy's Kinetic Construction System (1922), the Spiral Slide (whose idea, and likely design, can be attributed to Lissitzky) presented a tower from whose top one could slide down a spiraling furrow, which was

175

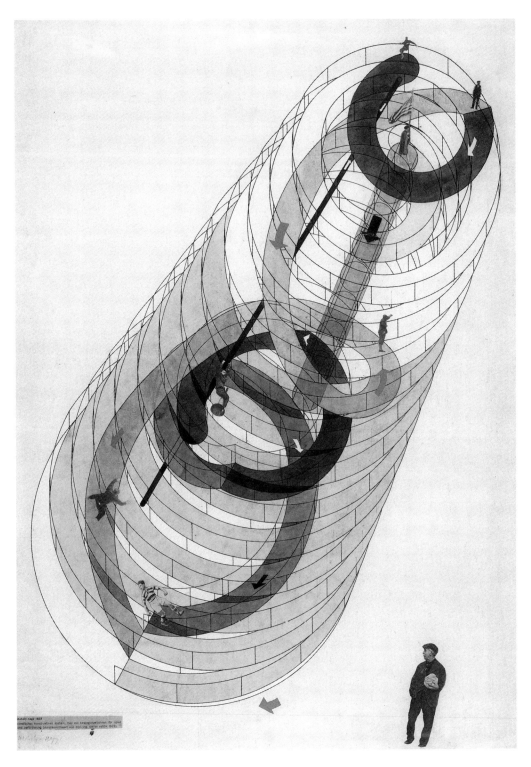

Figure 6.6. László Moholy-Nagy, Kinetic Construction System (1922). The structure contains two alternative spiral ramp systems. The first, the outer spiral, is for general use; it is less steep and is equipped with a guard rail, and at the top it opens into a platform that has access to an elevator shaft. The second, a steep inner spiral, is for the use of the athletes and has no rail. At the top, it has access to a slide pole, which runs down in parallel to the elevator shaft. Published in László Moholy-Nagy, *Von Material zu Architektur* (Munich: Langen, 1929), 204.

Figure 6.7. A version of László Moholy-Nagy's Kinetic Construction System, the Spiral Slide (likely designed by El Lissitzky) was a tower from whose top one could slide down a steep spiraling ramp. After 1933, it was used as a parachute tower. It is documented here on a 1930s postcard. Courtesy of Museum-Preserve "Alexandrovskaya Sloboda," Alexandrov, Russia (AMKP: 3977/8).

filled with water in the winter, turning into an ice slide. Because the athletic visitors found the sliding angle not steep enough, after 1933 the tower was used for jumping down with a parachute.[43] Similarly, the forty-meter-high ski-jumping tower, for which Lissitzky designed a poster, made the skier fly in the air. This thrilling experience was echoed by the kilometer-long sled track, whose design was suggested by the celebrated athlete brothers Kharlampiev, that started at the tip of the high Vorobyovy Hills on the opposite bank of the river and continued into the park.[44] Breathtaking perspectives were also promised by Lissitzky's (unrealized) cable car that was to connect the entrance and the rally field on the low bank of the Moscow River to the Vorobyovy Hills.[45]

Developing its program for individual rest, the park collaborated with the Institute of Resort Studies *(kurortologiia)*, which employed both architects and medical doctors, including its director Danishevsky and Alexander Orlyuk, the author of *How to Use Sun, Air, and Water* (1930) and other brochures on preventive medicine.[46] In 1930, Lissitzky and Orlyuk developed a program for a "complex *[kombinat]* for regaining energy *[vosstanovleniia sil]* and mass health"—an "experimental base of rest," which would provide up to seven hundred workers with several hours of rest every day.[47] The unrealized "factory of health" (to use Orlyuk's expression), designed by Lissitzky, was an industrial-like, one- to two-story structure whose central area housed an athletic hall as well as areas for leisure and interest clubs *(kruzhki),* while the functions of hygiene and dining were placed in protruding side wings.[48] Visitors would enter through the central foyer, leaving their coats and their children (to be taken care of in a separate wing), and proceed to the showers to clean themselves after a day of work. The open space of the south-facing athletic hall could be easily separated by movable glass screens that reduced the noise while preserving collectivity and the unity of space, and could thus be used for afternoon naps. Passing through the athletic hall and the dressing rooms, the visitor would exit to one-story verandas for sunbathing—two long narrow structures, one for men and another for women, surrounded by lawns and sports grounds and topped with roof gardens. A similar wing for children was located on the side opposite the entrance.

Even while taking care of individual bodies, the Soviet park did not lose sight of the collective as its ultimate subject. The curved plan of the verandas in Lissitzky's project would ensure collectivity during sunbathing, enabling each person to see their neighbor without turning their head. During the summer, the glass walls of the verandas could be opened, merging the interior with nature, and visitors could pass through the lawns and to the glass hall filled with plants—the winter garden—where people would lie naked beneath bedsheets. On gloomy days, instead of the winter gardens, the visitors of both

Figure 6.8. Designed by El Lissitzky in consulation with hygienist Alexander Orlyuk of the Institute of Resort Studies, the project for the complex of one-day rest was an industrial-like, one- to two-story structure whose central area was devoted to leisure, while hygiene and dining were housed in protruding side wings. Courtesy of the State Tretyakov Gallery, Moscow (p.101729).

genders would meet in the domed planetarium-like hall, which connected the male and female wings, to enjoy the rays of an artificial sun."[49]

The Principle of Switching

The competition for Gorky Park's general layout, announced in 1931, specified that the park had to become "a powerful cultural [production] complex [*kul'turnyi kombinat*] combining mass political, scientific–popular, art spectacle, and physical culture and health work, intended to attract tens and hundreds of thousands of workers throughout the year."[50] The exhaustive list of required functions and facilities encompassed physical, intellectual, and political needs of the Soviet worker: kindergartens with kitchen gardens and flowerbeds, athletic halls, libraries, and theaters for adults and children; food facilities and spaces for quiet rest; grounds for sports and military training. The park's evolutionist program was to be reinforced by ethnographic, botanical, and zoological exhibits.[51] Among the ten projects submitted for the competition, two, by Melnikov and Moisei Ginzburg, relied on zoning as the primary design strategy, imagining the park as a modern city within the city.[52] By the time of the competition, zoning had emerged as the principle of modernist urbanism, which subordinated the city to the logic of the division of labor. It would be codified during the fourth conference of CIAM (1933), devoted to the "Functional City," which was originally scheduled to take place in Moscow. One among the four main functional zones of the city, the green space was a type of social infrastructure that contained kindergartens, schools, and other community programs.[53] Reinforcing the zonal approach, Melnikov and Ginzburg postulated it as the principle of the design of these green spaces themselves.

In Melnikov's project, zoning was solidified by canals, which, radiating from the central stadium, divided the low bank of the river into functionally defined sectors. Unlike Melnikov, Ginzburg, a Soviet delegate to CIAM, was concerned not with isolating zones but with connecting them. He envisioned a developed circulation system, which included the railroad, pedestrian and bicycle paths, streetcar and bus routes, water transportation, and a "tank way." Ginzburg divided the park into a series of long narrow stripes that, following the curve of the river, housed the multiplicity of its sections. Those were sliced by perpendicular pedestrian alleys, which would allow visitors, depending on their goals and expectations, to either explore one zone in detail or to receive an experience across all of the zones.[54] Ginzburg's design evokes the "linear city," concurrently developed by Stroykom's patron, the minister of finance Nikolay Milyutin, who proposed a "flowing functional assembly-line system" to rationalize production processes in the factory and the city alike. In Milyutin's vision, functionally similar zones would be placed next to each other, ensuring minimal distances and the easy flow of the workforce.[55] Just as the development of the modern factory followed the conveyor belt, Milyutin explained, urbanism followed the factory, and the park followed the city. In Ginzburg's project, the zones were situated in a sequence whose logic was defined by function, one following another in a series of narrow, gently curving stripes: exhibition zone, science zone, "advanced work zone," mass-sportive zone, military zone, botanical and zoological zones, zone of water sports, spectacle zone, preventive medicine zone, zone of quiet rest, and children's zone.

Glan welcomed zoning as the method that helped visitors develop their individuality by structuring the park according to their possible interests.

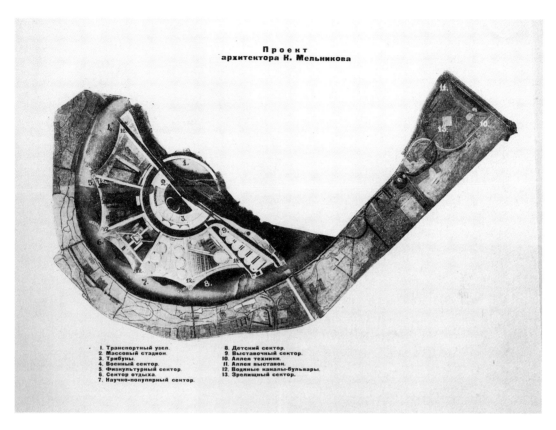

Figure 6.9. Like most other entries, the competition project for the Central Park of Culture and Leisure (1931) by Konstantin Melnikov, who had been the park's chief designer in 1928–29, is based on zoning. Radiating from the central stadium, "water canal-boulevards" divide the low bank of the river into functionally defined sectors. Reproduced in Betti Glan, *Za sotsialisticheskii park: Obzor proektov general'nogo plana* (Moscow: Izdatel'stvo Mosoblispolkoma, 1932).

Like Ginzburg, she sought to mitigate zonal divisions by asking architects to devote special attention to boundaries and the spaces between the zones so that "a correct transition of the worker from one activity to another" would be guaranteed.[56] Thus, in the work of Gorky Park's Office of Design and Planning, the principle of zoning was supplemented with "the principle of switching." According to Glan, "It is unquestionable that the park must not continue working processes, that it has to accommodate a pause in labor; however, the energy of the visitor to the park must be not be switched off but rather redirected to other activities, which due to the very fact of this voluntary switching offers rest after previous work."[57] The idea of switching energy from one activity to another was inspired by the first law of thermodynamics, which stated that energy in a system was constant: it could be transformed from one form to another, but not be created or destroyed. This law

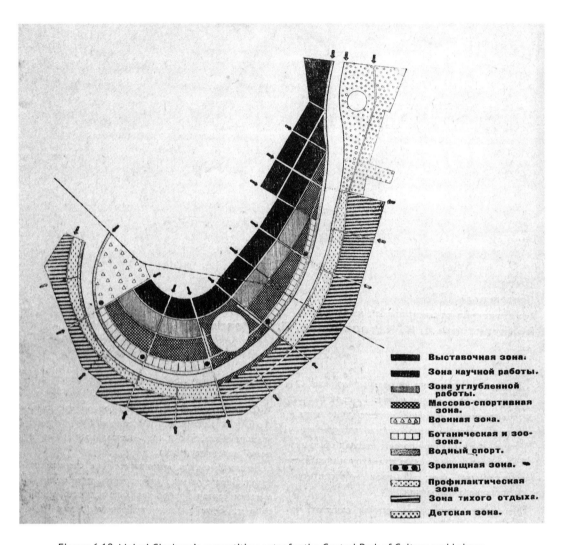

Figure 6.10. Moisei Ginzburg's competition entry for the Central Park of Culture and Leisure (1931) is also based on zoning and contains a Zoning Scheme (pictured here). The ribbons of Ginzburg's zones evoke the "linear city" ideal of his patron, the minister of finance Nikolay Milyutin. The zones are defined by functional sequence, which encourages transition from one to another: exhibition zone, science zone, "advanced work zone," mass-sportive zone, military zone, botanical and zoological zone, zone of water sports, spectacle zone, preventive medicine zone, zone of quiet rest, and children's zone. Reproduced in Betti Glan, *Za sotsialisticheskii park: Obzor proektov general'nogo plana* (Moscow: Izd. Mosoblispolkoma, 1932), 28.

was psychologized by Ernst von Brücke, whose science of psychodynamics presented organisms as energetic systems, and by Brücke's student Sigmund Freud in his concept of sublimation. Similarly, for Danishevsky, "The positive, refreshing, invigorating impact of switching from one type of activity to another is well known and, in many instances, has been experimentally

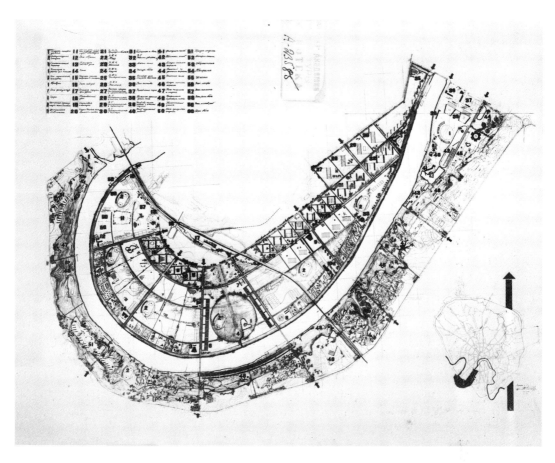

Figure 6.11. Unlike Melnikov, Ginzburg was more concerned with connecting than with isolating the zones. His general layout of the Central Park of Culture and Leisure (1931, competition project) demonstrates how circulation paths organize the complexity of function, relief, and vegetation. Photograph of the original plan (photographer unknown). Courtesy of the A. V. Shchusev State Museum of Architecture, Moscow (XI 28441).

confirmed." Alternating between intellectual and physical activity, he argued, had a positive effect upon general work productivity, reducing the urotoxic coefficient (the toxicity of urine, whose increase pointed to liver dysfunction) by 33 percent.[58]

Lissitzky, who had by then long pursued an interest in the unconscious mechanisms of orientation (as was examined in chapter 2), became the architect who theorized the notion of switching as a way of linking urbanism and landscape architecture that was complementary to zoning. Like Ginzburg, he supported an easy and smooth flow of visitors between zones, stimulated not by conscious decision but by the surrounding environment. Tacitly prompting visitors to explore all zones rather than remain limited to just one, architecture was to ensure the completeness of the park's "ideological effect": beginning their movement at the zone of their particular interest, visitors would then find themselves in a neighboring area, from which they would move to the next one, thus becoming subjected to the "combined effect of all forms of the park's work." In 1931, in a project for the park of culture and leisure in Sverdlovsk (today, Ekaterinburg) in the Ural Mountains, Lissitzky and Andrey Korobov developed a program of "a gradual switching of the visitor from one activity to another, which enables the complex impact of all forms of the park's work."[59] Here, similar zones were adjacent to each other, and the borders between them, which could have otherwise hindered the movement of visitors, were made transparent: following each other thematically, zones merged into a unified contourless landscape, across which the visitors seamlessly flowed.

From the park's opening, sociologists in its team studied how it was navigated by the visitors. In their interview-based analysis of the visitors' budget of time and means (1928), Iosif Blinkov and Vladimir Altman noted that the workers spent more time looking for entertainment than getting it, and argued that it was necessary to install information stands at the park's entrances.[60] This recommendation was later elaborated by architects as the concept of the "switching zone," which developed the principle of switching. In 1934, this concept was proposed by a Gorky Park architect (and Ladovsky's and Melnikov's former student) Militsa Prokhorova in her project for the park of culture and leisure in Tula, an old industrial city to the south of Moscow. The scheme, Prokhorova's largest independent project of that time, significantly enlarged the preexisting park, which was now to occupy one and a half square kilometers and, to use her expression, could "suck in" 10 percent of the city's population (twenty to thirty thousand people) on weekends and holidays. Whereas zoning allowed the even distribution of the masses throughout the park, the circulation of visitors was made possible by the carefully arranged and porous sequence of zones. Thus, the Children's Village bordered the sector for school-age children, while the theater was to be located on the border with the "adult" zone in order to be accessible to those children who visited the park with their parents. This system was supplemented by a new way of facilitating the navigation between the zones—the switching zone (*zona perekliucheniia*), located at the main entrance to the park. Like a factory planning department, it guaranteed the organization and coordination of the park's work. Here, visitors received initial information about the park's zonal division and could independently develop their personal programs of leisure and routes through the park. A project for such an information stand was prepared by V. Tarasov, an architect employed at the Institute of Resort Studies. Meanwhile, the other zones, each allocated to a specific activity or targeting a particular group of visitors,

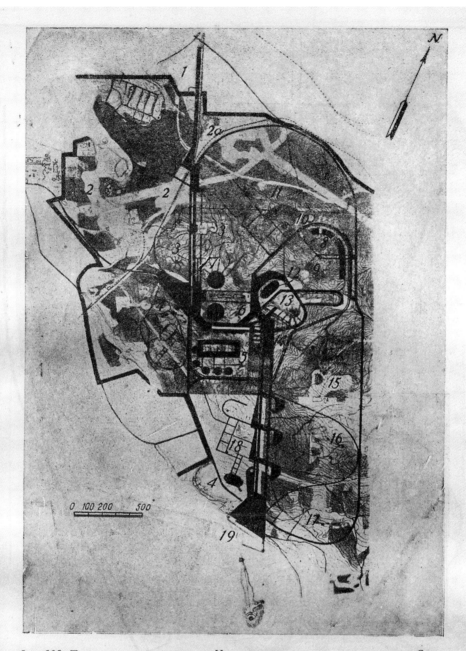

Рис. 225. Планировка всей территории Центрального парка культуры и отдыха Свердловска по проекту арх. Лисицкого Л. М. и Коробова А. С.: 1 — главный вход в парк; 2 — этно-зоопарк; 3 — птичий заповедник; 4 — ботанический парк; 5 — детский сектор; 6 — научно-популярный сектор; 7 — сектор выставок; 8 — макет «Большой Урал»; 9 — сектор оборонной пропаганды; 10 — лагеря военизированного отдыха; 11 — сектор зрелищ; 12 — зеленый театр; 13 — областной стадион; 14 — поле массовых действ; 15 — городок национальностей; 16 — горный городок отдыха; 17 — зона тишины; 18 — городок отдыха; 19 — физкультурный сектор; 20 — водная станция.

Figure 6.12. In their project for the park of culture and leisure in Sverdlovsk (today, Ekaterinburg) in the Ural Mountains (1931), El Lissitzky and Andrey Korobov elaborated the principle of "a gradual switching of the visitor from one activity to another, which enables the complex impact of all forms of the park's work." Reproduced in L. B. Lunts, *Parki Kul'tury i Otdykha* (Moscow: Gosstroiizdat, 1935), 267.

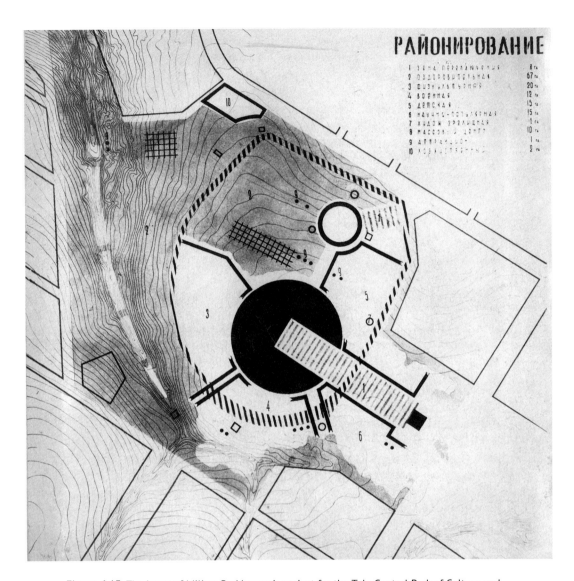

Figure 6.13. The heart of Militsa Prokhorova's project for the Tula Central Park of Culture and Leisure (1934) is the Switching Zone (marked as 1), where visitors receive initial information about the park's zonal division and consciously develop their personal programs of leisure and their routes through the park. Pictured here is the Zoning Scheme for the project. Courtesy of the A. V. Shchusev State Museum of Architecture, Moscow (OF 4761-044).

were separated by paths and hedges, forming segments of a circle centered on the park's main square, not unlike Melnikov's solution for Gorky Park.

In contrast to the earlier projects of Ginzburg and Lissitzky, Prokhorova's partial reinstatement of boundaries and the introduction of the switching zone as the space where the visitor would consciously analyze the park's layout and develop an individual program of movement construed the subject

Figure 6.14. Exhibition stand by architect V. Tarasov (Institute of Resort Studies) accompanied his project for a base of rest. It could have also been used as an information stand. Reproduced in G. M. Danishevskii, *Problemy massovogo otdykha v SSSR* (Moscow: Profizdat, 1934), 63.

as the manager of their own time. The project signaled a forthcoming shift in Soviet landscape architecture, and culture in general, from form, and thus unconscious perception, to content—a shift that would eventually be exemplified by the arrival of socialist realism. Before this shift would happen, however, another attempt was made to organize the navigation of visitors through the park with the help of experimental psychology.

Vertical Development

In 1930, Lunacharsky proposed a novel science, anthropagogy *(antropagogiia),* which was devoted to the education of adults just as pedagogy studied the education of children. Lunacharsky saw the goal of anthropagogy in "unfolding all possibilities hidden in a human," or the creation of what he called a polytechnic personality—a person of broad interests and erudition, physically, intellectually, ethically, and aesthetically developed.[61] Only such multifaceted personalities, which used all of their talents to their maximum potential, could, according to Lunacharsky, consciously and energetically participate in the construction of the new society. Glan developed this idea when she defined the park as "a giant factory of *the transformation of human* consciousness, the rebuilding of everyday life, a giant agitator, under the most immediate guidance of the party conducting a huge work of the political and cultural reeducation of millions."[62]

The challenge of the anthropagogical program, as the park's theorists soon realized, was that most visitors resisted this transformation, preferring entertainment to culture. As a social condenser, the park had to respond tacitly and incrementally, without forcing anyone into the new selfhood. In Danishevsky's words, the visitor had to possess "full freedom in choosing occupation, entertainment, labor processes (no elements of compulsion!) under the guiding educational impact of the organizers of leisure and the organization of the entire environment."[63] To this end, Glan proposed a program of personal transformation as a movement "from accordion and guitar—to sophisticated symphony music; from primitive physical exercises—to ski-jumping from a forty-meter-high springboard and skiing roped to a motorcycle," "from a simple choral song—to concerts of the best masters of singing and stage," "from amateur propaganda brigade—to a giant performance at the mass theater on the Smychka Square [Unification Square, the central square of the park used for rallies and mass spectacles]."[64] The mission of the park was to trigger this upward development: to make the visitors recognize the seeds of talent and interest within them to nourish them into a beautiful tree. To do so, the park had to offer everyone, independent of their level of culture, something that responded to their taste and interests: these interests could then be developed, skills improved, and knowledge expanded.

In 1935, Glan invited the Psychological Brigade of the All-Union Institute of Experimental Medicine, headed by Alexey Leontyev (whose activity theory was examined in chapter 5), to conduct two and a half months of research in the park.[65] Glan's program of shaping human personality by external, often unconscious stimuli corresponded with Leontyev's interest in Kurt Lewin's

Figure 6.15. At the core of Gorky Park's program was Anatoly Lunacharsky's *anthropagogy*. In Glan's words, the park was a "factory of the transformation of human consciousness," achieved according to the scheme "from—to." The park aimed to awaken the workers' interest in science and technology. In this 1933 photograph by Evzerikhin (first name unknown), worker S. S. Valdner demonstrates a model "aerotrain" that he designed at the Park. Courtesy of the State Central Museum of Contemporary History of Russia (10986/63).

field theory, which postulated the foundational role of a social and material environment (the field) in the formation of the human psyche.[66] Leontyev reformulated Glan's program for the development of the visitors' personality as "the formula 'from—to': from the elementary, the superficial, and the accidental to deeper, more developed and stable."[67] He called this type of personal development "vertical movement," comparing it with the visitor's physical movement in the park. Progressing from a curiosity about an amusing physical phenomenon to learning the science of physics, or from a jump from the parachute tower to parachuting as a serious sport, the visitor was transformed into "a free and multisided, harmonically developed personality." For the psychologist, the park was first and foremost "an institute that unfolds

Figure 6.16. The Bolshoi Theater section during the exhibition "Art at the Service of Lenin's Party" (1930) at the Park of Culture and Leisure aimed at explaining to the workers the theater's social role: supporting sowing campaigns (by performing for agricultural workers), conducting antireligious events, carnivals, and concerts, participating in the May Day demonstrations. Photographer unknown. Courtesy of the State Central Museum of Contemporary History of Russia (6065/7a).

Figure 6.17. In the words of psychologist Alexey Leontyev, who worked in the park in 1935, objects had to become "organizers of personality." Much of Leontyev's team work aimed to improve the Park's Children's Village. Depicted here is the Technical Station in the Children's Village prior to Leontyev's arrival. Postcard, 1931. Courtesy of the State Museum of the History of St. Petersburg (372248/853).

personality during the time of leisure."[68] It was this unfolding environment—understood as a system of objects—that Leontyev studied in the park in lieu of (human) laboratory subjects, because the visitors were too many to be examined empirically: "As the subject of our research, we had to take objects that reveal themselves in a moving flow; that is, we had in fact to experiment with an object that we plunged into the human flow."[69] Based on his research at the park, Leontyev concluded that the park had to offer what he called a system of verticals, which provided the visitor with a choice of opportunities. Such a vertical system, however, began with a number of horizontal moves, from the attraction of one thematic cycle to that of another, in which the vertical movement could begin from any point of the horizontal row.[70]

Leontyev entered into polemics with Dmitry Uznadze, the author of one of the original Soviet theories of *ustanovka* ("setup").[71] Whereas Uznadze maintained that the setup was primary to activity, Leontyev and his school believed in the primacy of activity, arguing that setups were formed within it. Accordingly, the park's targets were not those visitors who had a preexisting interest (the setup), but rather those who came to the park without any particular reason, in order to simply stroll or rest. As a system of objects, the park captured those people, attracted them to its educational centers, and prompted to explore their content; they would ultimately leave with a new interest and a determination to explore it deeper. According to Leontyev:

> A person does not come to the Park to become this or that or to receive such and such knowledge; he comes not to become a fully developed member of society, but to have rest; thus, [our] task is to make him, having come to the Park and having freely surrendered himself to the Park—that is, being moved by the system of objects, or, to be more precise, by the system of situations that these objects create—to perform the program of development that forms the social-pedagogical task of the Park.[72]

The psychologists observed that coming to the park without any plan or "cultural" purpose, the visitors tended to avoid walking to reach particular points of interest, preferring, instead, to concentrate in the zones adjacent to the entrance and to float from one zone to the next. To change these patterns, attracting visitors to educational centers, Leontyev developed a program that he, like Glan, called their activation. Thus, in the course of an experiment at the Aviation Laboratory in the Children's Village, Leontyev's team succeeded in reducing the percentage of "specialists" (children who came to the park with the purpose of improving their preexisting knowledge of model-making) from 65 to 9 percent, whereas the percentage of those who came to explore this unfamiliar topic and those who came without any particular purpose increased from 15 to 44 percent and from 17 to 43 percent respectively. In the vertical of personal development, the child began at the most amusing, entertaining exhibit (the object that, in Lewin's terminology, created the strongest *Druck* [tension], such as an airplane model), subsequently moving to the exhibits that did not possess an immediate attractive force (such as the demonstration of the principles of aerodynamics). One of the most successful innovations of the psychologists in the work of the Aviation Laboratory was allowing children to engage with exhibition objects directly, which, they discovered, helped children overcome their inclination to steal; objects were thus transformed, to use Leontyev's language, from "objects-'disorganizers'" to the organizers of personality.[73]

Leontyev's theory developed the neo-Lamarckian cultural-historical theory of his mentor, social psychologist Lev Vygotsky. As Vygotsky postulated, the process of evolution unfolded in two stages: the first, biological, stage was described by Darwinism, the second, human, by Marxism. The man, according to the psychologist, developed biologically from animal to "the primitive" and the child, and then to the (Western) adult, and would continue developing. As he argued in "The Socialist Alteration of Man" (1930), the social transformation of humans was a key to their biological evolution:

> A human being evolves and develops as a historical, social being. Only a raising of all humanity to a higher level in social life, the liberation of all humanity, can lead to the formation of a new type of man.
>
> However . . . this change of the human personality, must inevitably lead to further evolution of man and to the alteration of the *biological type of man*. Having mastered the processes which determine his own nature, man, who is struggling with old age and diseases, undoubtedly will rise to a higher level and transform the very biological organization of human beings. But this is the source of the greatest historical paradox of human development, that this biological transformation of the human type which is mainly achieved through science, social education, and the rationalization of the entire way of life, does *not represent a prerequisite, but instead is a result of the social liberation of man*.[74]

The same idea had earlier been supported by Leon Trotsky, according to whom, "Life, even if purely physiological, will become collective-experimental. The humankind, the frozen *Homo sapiens,* will again go into active reworking and will become—under its own fingers—an object of the most complex methods of artificial selection and psychophysical training."[75]

Like the French and Latin American hygienists and architects discussed by López-Durán, the creators of Gorky Park treated the urban public park, due to its association with nature, as the architectural type designated for evolutionary progress. While elsewhere, however, the goal of conservative eugenic programs of such parks was to restore the nation's gene pool, Soviet psychologists and designers believed in the necessity of stimulating the evolutionary progress of *Homo sapiens*. This program was simultaneously totalitarian and humanist, racist and universalist, elitist and democratic. As Rene Van der Veer and Jaan Valsiner observed, Vygotsky formulated an image of man as "a rational being taking control of his own destiny and emancipating himself from nature's restrictive bounds"—even though rooted in the philosophy of

Francis Bacon, Spinoza, and Marx, "above all, of course, this was an image of man Vygotsky believed in, a belief that was very common along the people of his time and in the country he lived."[76]

The story of Gorky Park challenges the myth of Soviet modernization (and the First Five-Year Plan as its epitome) as based solely on the state-capitalist ethos of productivist self-sacrifice. Unlike the other stories examined in this book, the concept of the park of culture and leisure served not to intensify but to counterbalance exploitation in the same manner as this was done by philanthropic (and often eugenic) public parks elsewhere. Yet, due to Lunacharsky's collectivist agenda at its core, the Soviet park differed from its international neo-Lamarckian analogs in that it focused not on individual health but on social evolution, which it aspired to guide. The influence of Lunacharsky's ideas, which in many ways prefigured later humanist Marxism, reveals the complexity of the Soviet monistic modernist discourse, in which humanism and productivism became intrinsically intertwined.[77] Collective leisure promised to overcome the predicament of industrialization, healing the debilitating effects of divided factory labor at a time when the development of technology did not yet allow the move to the next step of social relationships of production. To use Arendt's terms, leisure was to transform labor into work. These utopian hopes were crashed in the purges of 1937. That year, Milyutin lost his political influence (although he was never arrested), while Mazmonyan was arrested and exiled to the Arctic city of Norilsk. Most tragically, Glan was subjected to repression following the execution of her husband, the head of the Communist Party of Yugoslavia Milan Gorkić.[78] However, she was to reemerge in 1954 and to resume playing a leading role in Soviet culture, from which the influence of Lunacharsky's romantic socialism never fully disappeared. The hope of humanist productivism would wither away under very different political circumstances.

In contrast to the eugenic programs of Western parks, it was labor— understood as the humanist work on oneself—that was seen as the key to evolutionary progress in the Soviet Union. Furthermore, in the end, the development of personality was none other than cultivating superb laboring abilities. Lunacharsky's and Glan's ambitions notwithstanding, in reality, humanist concerns about individuality and creativity became managerial instruments that intensified exploitation. The opposition of productivism and humanism was eventually resolved in favor of the former. In this sense, the Soviet concept of productive leisure presaged the ethics of post-Fordism, a still-prevalent managerial approach that aspired to rehumanize work without sacrificing—and, in fact, while intensifying—productivity. Although some specific concerns of Soviet architecture, such as forging the collective subject and, most importantly, accelerating and directing social evolution, have been rejected, almost a century after the opening of Gorky Park, architecture is still trying to rationalize, optimize, mitigate, humanize, and otherwise improve productivity rather than abolish it. In the words of Kathy Weeks, "metaphysics and moralism of work require a more direct challenge than the critique of alienation and humanist work ethics are capable of posing. The struggle to improve the quality of work must be accompanied by efforts to reduce its quantity."[79]

CONCLUSION

History

From the Monistic to the Terrestrial

In the aftermath of the Second World War, tainted partially by its implicit and explicit ties with racism, the bioeconomic concept of humanness lost its validity. More than a rejection of particular "pseudo-sciences" with which it was associated, its discreditation led to the decline of life sciences as the universal epistemological paradigm and to the resultant dissolution of the entire set of principles and values associated with it. Belief in economic planning and organization was replaced by the revival of the nineteenth-century ideal of the free market; liberal democracy was recognized as the only ethical political model; imperialism as a way of governing nature and populations was shattered by the postwar decolonization movements; existentialism and humanist Marxism questioned evolutionarily interpreted life as the ultimate philosophical and ethical category; the modernist epistemological model of truth as single and verifiable was replaced by relativism and pluralism. Despite the fact that as an organized movement and ideology, monism was dissipated by the totalitarian regimes shortly before the Second World War, it was itself proclaimed totalitarian.[1] Writing during the 1950s, Russian emigrant liberal philosopher Isaiah Berlin distinguished between two types of thinkers: the monistic "hedgehogs," who "relate everything to a single central vision, one system . . . a single, universal, organizing principle in terms of which alone all that they are and say has significance," and the pluralist "foxes," who "pursue many ends, often unrelated and even contradictory . . . , related to no moral or aesthetic principle."[2] By doing so, Berlin highlighted the political implications of the philosophical concept of monism. He thus presaged the work of later liberal political theorists, who condemned the monistic philosophical approach to life sciences as misguided because it postulated collectivist rather than individual subjectivity.[3] Yet the story of monism as an epistemological paradigm was not over. The ecological disaster that only accelerated in the aftermath of the Cold War compromised the myth of unrestricted individual freedom (the freedom that had too often been defined in the economic terms of production and consumption) and monistic ideas return to discussion as a part of ecologically minded critical theory, which reintegrates natural and social sciences on the basis of such principles as life, process, and organism.[4]

This reintegration has informed the "planetary" shift in historical research recently announced by Dipesh Chakrabarty, who sees it as an antidote to historical Hegelianism.[5] From Hegel and Benedetto Croce to Karl Marx and the German Neo-Kantians to R. G. Collingwood, modern philosophers saw an unbridgeable chasm between history, as a humanistic discipline that studies society, on the one hand, and natural sciences, including geology and evolutionary theory, which study the nonhuman environment, on the other. Croce was influenced by the subjectivism of Ernst Mach and Henri Poincaré (which was discussed in chapter 1): just as Mach postulated that the objective physical world is always perceived as a sum of subjective sensations, the Italian philosopher believed that "there is no world but the human world," since "existence" is a concept that has "meaning only within a context of human concerns and purposes."[6] For Collingwood, the follower of Croce and author of *The Idea of History* (1946), a historian "would not be interested in the fact that men eat and sleep and make love and thus satisfy their natural appetites" but rather "in the social customs which they create by their thought as a framework within which these appetites find satisfaction in ways sanctioned by convention and morality."[7] The similarity between Collingwood's description of "non-historical" biological processes and human "functions," for which modern architecture (as was discussed in chapter 4) had to provide is striking. And indeed, just as the approach of Croce and Collingwood reminds of the rationalist philosophy of architecture, the "functionalists" were likely readers of Collingwood's intellectual adversary, the theorist of life, biologist J. B. S. Haldane—a communist with connections both in the USSR and among radical cultural intelligentsia elsewhere—who suggested blurring the boundary between natural and human histories to enable writing the history of nonhuman nature. Judging from the vantage point of today, Chakrabarty proclaims Haldane the winner in the debate.

Soviet interwar architecture can similarly be viewed as a series of historical propositions—attempts at reifying competing versions of history, which occupied different positions along the materialism–idealism scale. Yet, unlike the historians, Soviet interwar architects inevitably aimed to sublate the opposition between nature and culture. While contemporary critical theory is unambiguous in its repudiation of anthropocentrism, interwar monism's relationship with it (as discussed in chapter 2 and elsewhere in this book) was more complicated. The human was the ultimate subject of Soviet interwar modernism, yet this subject was defined collectively, from a perspective that was both scientific and managerial: as simultaneously a part and the master of nature. In this monistic economy, a materialist concept of nature collided with teleology—the desire to direct history's course by the power of will and reason.

An ill-defined and ambiguous notion, teleology has often been associated with Abrahamic theologies and with Hegelian philosophy, which posit that events unfold toward a preexisting end goal. Thus understood, teleology has been the target of countless criticisms, most recently from the perspective of postcolonial theory, which associated it with white Euro-American political hegemony, and from the perspective of geocentered critical theory, which related it to the careless ravaging of natural resources and disregard for the well-being of the planet. For Bruno Latour, one of the foremost critics representing the latter perspective, teleology is a "drive toward some Omega point," an imperative of historical movement toward an external goal.[8]

Yet teleology has been also linked to a number of materialist, first of all, biological, theories, which Russian social democratic philosopher Sergey Suvorov in 1904 had described as immanently teleological in contrast to transcendentally teleological idealist worldviews.[9] Among these theories were those of Jean-Baptiste Lamarck and Herbert Spencer, who considered the inheritance of adaptational changes to be the mechanism of evolution: they believed that the species demonstrates a teleological striving toward greater perfection. And even though Darwin's theory of "the survival of the fittest" presented biological life as blind and irrational, unfolding without goal or direction, this blind evolution created such regularities as species.[10] In the words of Russian empiriocriticist philosopher Peter Engelmeyer (writing in 1910), Darwin's greatest contribution was that he provided logic to a concept that had previously seemed impossible: "purposefulness in the absence of goals"; for Darwin, "purposefulness is a result of life selection and is secured genetically through natural selection."[11] Still routinely used by biologists, such evolutionist concepts as function and purpose (for instance, of an organ) also betray a teleological reasoning, causing debates among theorists of biology.[12]

When Eduard von Hartmann elevated the notion of the unconscious to a major philosophical principle in his *Philosophy of the Unconscious* (*Philosophie des Unbewussten*, 1869), he nevertheless argued against Darwin's vision of natural selection as the prime mechanism of evolution, supporting, instead, a neo-Lamarckian theory of adaptation. If Darwinism, for him, professed a "mindless causality," effectively denying adaptation, Hartmann's unconscious provided evolution with a teleological guiding channel, through which the genus could move toward its biological goal.[13] Not chance, but logics, even if unconscious, directed evolution. Unlike the same concept in Freud's interpretation, Hartmann's unconscious existed not at the bottom of an individual psyche, but as a locus of collective will independent of individual subjects: "When we . . . view the world as a whole, the expression 'the unconscious' acquires the force not only of an *abstraction* from all unconscious individual functions and subjects, but also of a *collective,* comprehending the foregoing both extensively and intensively."[14] Just like instinct united birds into complex flock formations, not consciousness, but the instinctive and the unconscious enabled individuals to act as a species, in coordination with one another. This interpretation ultimately prompted Hartmann in later editions of his work to replace the term *das Unbewusste* with *das Überbewusste* (superconscious), highlighting the role of the unconscious in the process of individual interiorization of collective goals.

The ambiguous relationship between determinism and the freedom of will posed a problem for Marxism, which was simultaneously an analytical theory and an activist platform: if social relationships are always a consequence of objective technological development, then any social revolution that is not preceded by a technological one is destined for failure. This problem, which became particularly vexing for Russian revolutionary Marxists, has been interpreted in the light of Marx's seemingly ambiguous attitude to teleology: while his ideal of communism is usually seen as the end goal of historic process, some critics noticed that his vision of history lacked a conscious subject.[15] Sean Sayers explained this paradox as resulting from Marx's vision of history as a process of increasing self-consciousness: its first stage, "the prehistory," was defined by an unconscious evolutionary development toward greater consciousness; this stage would be overcome with the arrival of communism, which would become the beginning, rather than the end, of the real historic process.[16] Immanent "prehistorical" teleology was to leave a place for teleology in the more common, idealist, sense of the word.

Since the mid-nineteenth century, both immanent and transcendental teleologism informed radical Russian culture, which was equally fascinated with natural sciences and Hegelian philosophy: whereas science provided it with an areligious model of the world, the legacy of Hegel, received through the Left Hegelians and Marx, became the point of departure for political radicalism. The first—Lamarckian—teleological model was famously articulated by Leo Tolstoy, who argued against the concept of history as shaped by heroic figures. Describing how the Russian marshal Kutuzov orders his army to enter the Battle of Tarutino against his will, his passage from *War and Peace* (1865–69) conveys a sense of historic inevitability:

> The Cossack's report, confirmed by horse patrols who were sent out, was the final proof that events had matured. The tightly coiled spring was released, the clock began to whirr and the chimes to play. Despite all his supposed power, his intellect, his experience, and his knowledge of men, Kutuzov—having taken into consideration the Cossack's report, a note from Bennigsen who sent personal reports to the Emperor, the wishes he supposed the Emperor to hold, and the fact that all the generals expressed the same wish—could no longer check the inevitable movement, and gave the order to do what he regarded as useless and harmful—gave his approval, that is, to the accomplished fact.[17]

Giving in to the inevitable or, to put it in Spinozian terms, finding freedom in the understanding of necessity, Kutuzov could not impose his will and instead surrendered to forces greater than it. This determinism appalled postwar liberal thinkers, who equated freedom with individual agency. For Berlin, Tolstoy was a hedgehog, who "advocated a single embracing vision; he preached not variety but simplicity, not many levels of consciousness but reduction to some single level."[18]

Meanwhile, to Russian early twentieth-century social democrats, the evolutionism of Tolstoy's model proposed a temporality whose slowness was incompatible with the urgency of their task—political and social revolution. Turning away from Tolstoy's determinism, they proposed a revision to Marx's vision of history: blind evolution had to be transformed into history here and now, not as a result but as the prerequisite for the arrival of communism. The revolutionaries turned to Hegelian idealism, such as the work of Anatoly Lunacharsky's Zurich friend, Rudolf Maria Holzapfel, a fellow student of Richard Avenarius and a fellow social-democrat.[19] Holzapfel delineated a theory of "panidealism" as an all-encompassing philosophic (and eventually spiritual) worldview.[20] Holzapfel's book *Panideal: A Psychology of Social Feelings* (*Panideal: Psychologie der sozialen Gefühle,* 1901; Russian translation 1909) was popular among international social-democratic and scientific circles.[21] Written in Ukraine, where Holzapfel lived at that time, it appeared with a preface by Mach; its enthusiastic readers included French writer Romain Rolland, a correspondent of Freud and a future excited visitor to Gorky Park. Holzapfel used Avenarius's epistemology as the foundation for a practical philosophy of action and value, mirroring his teacher's hierarchy of elements of cognition with a hierarchy of core human feelings, states, and activities: loneliness, yearning, hope, prayer, fight, consciousness, art, world, and, finally, ideal. Unlike individual ideals, the panideal served everything, everybody, and on all levels: practical and theoretical, logical and psychological, economic and artistic, individual and social. The panideal enabled the maximum development of individual creative personality—and thus of life.

Liberal political and cultural theory has defined such interiorized externality as totalitarianism.[22] Boris Groys famously described the Stalinist Soviet Union as an aesthetic project, a *Gesamtkunstwerk* in which every process was coordinated, aestheticized, and subordinated to the totalizing logic of the whole. Socialist realism, for him, emerged not as a falsification of reality but as a depiction of *telos*: "Socialist realism is oriented toward that which has not yet come into being but which should be created, and in this respect it is the heir of the avant-garde, for which aesthetics and politics are also identical."[23] What I have suggested in this book is that rather than identifying aesthetics and politics, Soviet culture saw both as a manifestation of a larger concern: as a *historical* project, Soviet interwar modernism vacillated between materialist determinism and idealist teleology. When Soviet architects meticulously calculated the expected physiological and psychological effects of form, space, and color, or when they aspired to formalize the processes of design and construction, they sought to not only exert political power but to use that power to help the human psyche catch up with its own historic and urban environment, to facilitate psychological hygiene, and eventually to regulate and direct the social evolution of *Homo sapiens*. While architecture was undisputedly among the key tools of this regulation, its methods remained a matter of debate.

Although Russian revolutionaries, who remained intellectual heirs to nineteenth-century radical intelligentsia, religiously adhered to scientific materialism as a worldview, they simultaneously espoused a Hegelian ambition of making history. Similarly, Soviet architects struggled to apply their scientific worldview and methods to their ambition of using architecture for formulating historic goals and directing social evolution. The dominant approach to teleology in Soviet Russia could be seen as changing from immanent in the early 1920s to predominantly idealist a decade later. The two approaches, however, were not simply opposite, but also tightly intertwined within the monistic search for a compromise between the human and nature. Subordinating architecture to historic goals (which have been often wrongly dismissed as utopian in historiography), all projects discussed in this book demonstrate such an entanglement of immanent and transcendental approaches to teleology. Their ultimate *telos* was not the dictatorship of the proletariat or its party, the revolution, or even communism—this ultimate *telos* was *life*.

Discussed in chapter 1, Nikolay Ladovsky's Machism made ASNOVA the target of frequent accusations of idealism.[24] Although inevitably dismissed by the group's members, these accusations do not appear entirely ungrounded: after all, Mach's subjectivist philosophy of science was the same theory that inspired Croce's philosophy of history and Holzapfel's idealist philosophy of action. But although Ladovsky's theory dissolved the material world in the mosaic of human sensations, thereby making architecture anthropocentric, it simultaneously reconstituted this *anthropos* as the subject of the psychological laboratory. This definition found its application in the space-meter (the subject of chapter 3) as the instrument for directing the process of the natural selection of architects. Ladovsky's students and colleagues departed from this immanent toward a more idealist teleology, dedicating themselves to the development of the theory of rhythm as an instrument of imbuing perception with an external goal. Likewise, as chapter 2 delineated, Ladovsky's associate El Lissitzky and their student Georgy Krutikov, interested in studies of perception, applied them not to design, but to speculating about the future evolution of cities, arguing that their investigations would help architects in their everyday work. Furthermore, as demonstrated in chapter 4, both Alexander Rozenberg's program of normalization and Moisei Ginzburg's program of typification presented attempts at channeling the development of architecture into its "natural" course, just like the revolution seemingly channeled history into its right direction. Even Ginzburg's functionalism—its very name, its preoccupation with processuality, and its declared materialism notwithstanding—relied on the teleological theory of "purposeful setup," which aimed to direct architecture from without: the setup, however, remained a psychological and intellectual disposition rather than an explicitly postulated goal. Similarly, as discussed in chapter 5, it was the teleological component that Soviet designers such as Boris Ender perceived as missing from Hinnerk Scheper's objectivist approach to wall-painting, which they eventually enriched with Alexey Leontyev's activity theory. The most explicitly teleological of all, the program of the Central Park of Culture and Leisure (the subject of chapter 6) was preoccupied with building the energetic builder of the future. In all these examples, architecture was reinterpreted as the psychological interface that enables unconscious interiorization of collective goals and thereby allows adapting to, regulating, or directing history—understood as social evolution.

Although contemporary critical theory has been unequivocal in rejecting the teleology that Suvorov called transcendental, its relationship with immanent teleology has been more complex. It has accepted Walter Benjamin's concept of "weak messianic power" based on the present anticipation of the future, as well as such Lamarckian theories as Louis Marin's concept of utopia as horizon, which is inevitably rooted in the present, and Jacques Derrida's suggestion to substitute eschatology, in which history unfolds toward a "future that cannot be anticipated," for teleology, which "locks up, neutralizes, and finally cancels historicity."[25] Tolstoy's concept of history thus once again becomes relevant today. To Latour, it offers a model of agency that is shared between the individual and the environment. Discussing Tolstoy's same portrayal of Kutuzov that Berlin condemned, Latour concludes that the Russian marshal appears not as a human actor but as the personification of "forces that have entirely different characteristics."[26] He explains the marshal's reasoning through a neo-Spinozian dialectics of freedom and necessity: "To be a subject is not to act autonomously in front of an objective background, but *to share agency with other subjects that have also lost their autonomy*."[27] Furthermore, Latour advocates not only limiting the agency of individual humans but also endowing the Earth—that which the modernist managerial culture had considered a mere resource for human use—with an agency of her own.[28] Following scientist James Lovelock, Latour calls her Gaia, using the name of the ancient Greek primordial force (unlike Ernst Haeckel, Latour nevertheless insists on Gaia's secular character). Gaia, he contends, is a "full-fledged actor" in "geostory," a notion that should replace the human-centered and teleological "history."[29] By positing Gaia as a (nonorganismic and devoid of consciousness) system that actively responds to disturbances, he achieves a monistic dissolution of the boundary between nature and culture.

While Latour elaborates the concept of shared agency, McKenzie Wark, in *Molecular Red: Theory for the Anthropocene* (2016), suggests replacing individual agency with the concept of "intra-action" as an effect of the context and situation.[30] This platform allows Wark to transition "from molar to molecular perceptions of experience": from the "drama of events . . . where big-bodied entities clash, antagonist against protagonist" to "subtle and imperceptible" "interesting processes."[31] Wark replaces Hegelian teleology with an evolutionary vision of history: "History is Lamarckian," he says, quoting science fiction writer Kim Stanley Robinson; "History is *directing* evolution."[32] Sidelining the subjectivist side of Alexander Bogdanov's empiriomonism (a program that was heavily dependent on the empiriocriticism of Mach and Avenarius), Wark finds the philosophical and activist platform of the Russian revolutionary to be the closest precedent for his theory for the Anthropocene. He embraces Bogdanov's humanism as well as what he calls his "labor point of view" (the aspiration to put theory into practice), his tectology (which he values for its practical orientation), and what he calls "proletkult" (Proletkult theory of culture, which merged art and life). Empiriomonism not only offers Wark a model for integrating Marxism with natural sciences, but also allows questioning the modern subject-object dichotomy, suggesting an example of carving new, collective, forms of agency out of the predicament of the dissolution of individual subjectivity by science. Mach's self-portrait, in which his body, as a visual sensation, merges with the environment, could be a metaphor for such dissolution, just as Alexander Rozenberg's method of the documentation of factors, which treated labor productivity as a function of objective circumstances (these two examples are discussed in chapters 1 and 4 respectively).

Bogdanov's tectology, which is today recognized as a forerunner of systems theory, is certainly not incompatible with Lovelock's vision of Gaia as "the totality constituting a feedback or cybernetic system which seeks an optimal physical and chemical environment for life on this planet."[33] Postulating homeostasis as Gaia's goal, the Gaia theory elaborates a sort of "immanent teleology"; to survive, humanity (and by extension, architecture) has no other way but to move forward with Gaia. This movement can only be described negatively, in such categories as resistance, counteraction, or slowing down. Such a "Lamarckian" (to use Wark's description) theory of history focuses not on the distant but on the near, not on the big but on the incremental—not on building but on maintenance. Accordingly, the new organicist architecture cancels its autonomy and once again questions the authority of the designer.

In their collection of *Geostories* (series of conceptual drawings comprised of research visualizations and utopian renderings, which were created for several architecture biennials between 2015 and 2018) Rania Ghosn and El Hadi Jazairy of the architectural office Design Earth explicitly refer to Latour's writing.[34] These stories upset temporalities common for architecture and architectural history: they are case studies that not only show how the Earth has been recently exploited by capital, but also examine how its "resources" were formed in the course of millions of years. Viewed from this perspective, the Earth emerges not as a passive object but as the creative subject. The Koolhaas- and Archigram-inspired ironic proposals of Ghosn and Jazairy, which are simultaneously utopian and dystopian, show impossible man-made interventions in the natural landscape. These interventions reuse products of human civilization—waste and architecture alike; their impossibility makes them a warning more than the end goal. The concept of history that emerges in these proposals remains cautious: avoiding formulating positive ideals, Design Earth finds a way to discuss the future through negation. To use Ginzburg's terms, they give architecture a setup—to think about the consequences of design for the planet—without prescribing a course of action. But even though doing it negatively, they assert the Earth as the new subject

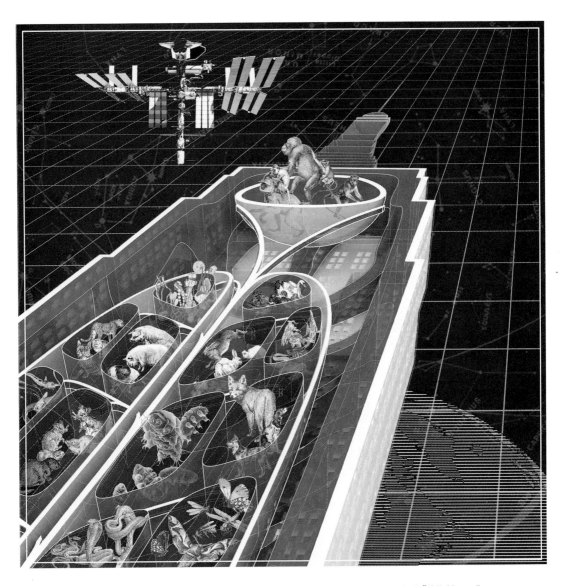

Figure C.1. In this drawing by Design Earth (Rania Ghosn and El Hadi Jazairy), "(All Aboard) the Cosmic Architekton: The Multi-species Architekton Embarks on Its Cosmic Journey" from the *Cosmorama* series (United States Pavilion at the Venice Biennale, *Dimensions of Citizenship*, 2018), the Empire State Building, the symbol of modern rationalization (and of international Americanism), is transformed into Noah's Ark that must save the Earth's biodiversity from the disaster inflicted by none other than this rationalization. Along its cosmic way, the Empire State Building discovers itself as Kazimir Malevich's *arkhitekton*. Both an homage to Rem Koolhaas's *Delirious New York* and a critique of its romanticization of accumulation, this work can also be read as a critique of the futility of teleological ambitions of both the Russian "avant-garde" and Western capitalism. Courtesy of Design Earth.

of architecture and *her* life as its goal. This "life" is no longer the abstract ideal of monistic modernism but the very material ground underneath our feet—a new regime of historicity that Latour defines as "the terrestrial."

What can the builders of the terrestrial learn from Soviet monistic architecture, which was guided by a concept of history that was simultaneously materialist and teleological? One lesson, perhaps, is that just as it defies binary philosophical, political, and ethical oppositions, Soviet monistic modernism also demonstrates the impossibility of drawing a neat boundary between the managerial, exploitative (civilizational, in Latour's terms) modernist attitude to nature on the one hand and materialism and organicism on the other.[35] The roots of the terrestrial lie at the very heart of the civilizational—and perhaps it is precisely in this conflation where the clues to resistance could be found.

ACKNOWLEDGMENTS

Writing requires time, space, archives, and intellectual dialog, and I am immensely thankful to everyone who provided me with that: to those on whose research I relied and by which I was inspired, to librarians and archivists, and to my children's caregivers. And of course, my deepest gratitude goes to institutions and individuals who generously supported my research with funding, material, work space, and feedback.

This project began as a dissertation at the MIT History, Theory, and Criticism of Architecture and Art program. I am deeply indebted to my inspirational dissertation advisor, Mark Jarzombek, and the thoughtful dissertation readers, Caroline A. Jones and Danilo Udovički-Selb, as well as to my other teachers, including Erika Naginski, Kristel Smentek, and David Friedman. At MIT, I was lucky to meet a cohort of fellow students, a dialog with whom proved to be equally formative: Tijana Vujošević, Ana Maria Leon, Rebecca Uchill, Nicola Pezolet, Christian Hedrick, Sarah Katz, Shiben Banerji, Ateya Khorakiwala, Jordan Kauffman, Razan Francis, Mohammed Alkhabbaz, Farshid Emami, Azra Dawood, and Yavuz Sezer, among others. The memory of Yavuz, who left us too early, lives in our hearts.

This project has since traveled between institutions and continents, supported by a Social Science Research Council Dissertation Proposal Development Grant, the Graduate Research Fellowship from the Canadian Center for Architecture, the Getty Research Institute Pre-Doctoral Fellowship, a Dumbarton Oaks Research Library Junior Fellowship, a Swiss Government Excellence Scholarship, and membership at the Institute for Advanced Study in Princeton. Working with Philip Ursprung and his team at the ETH Zurich provided an invaluable and fruitful experience. I also benefited from the financial and institutional support of my employers, the ETH, Illinois Institute of Technology, and Kassel University. I would like to thank Provost Peter Kilpatrick at IIT, and President Reiner Finkeldey and Dean Uwe Altrock at Kassel University in particular. I am also deeply grateful to my students at the ETH, IIT, and the University of Kassel who became fellow riders on this intellectual journey.

My mentors (in alphabetical order) Edward Dimendberg, Laurent Stalder, and Danilo Udovički-Selb were instrumental in nourishing my thinking and bringing this project to life. This book would not have been possible without the support of and scholarly exchange with many, including (in alphabetical order) Haseeb Ahmed, Maria Ametova, Rahman Azari, Daniel Barber, John Beardsley, Philipp Blom, Anna Bokov, Benedikt Boucsein, Annie Bourneuf, Aaron Butts, Juan José Castellón, Paroma Chatterjee, Peter Christensen, Jean-Louis Cohen, Leah Comeau, Pierluigi D'Acunto, Nasrin Davatgar, Paola De Martin, Maryana Demchenko, Nikolay Erofeev, Martin Frimmer, Ron Henderson, Daniel Hershenzon, Max Hirsh, Gordon Hughes, Dora Imhof, Leslie Johnson, Elisabet Jönsson Steiner, Jennifer Josten, Harald Kegler, Sean Keller, Nikita Kharlamov, Igor Khristoforov, Tim Klauser, Heike Klussmann, Valérie Kobi, Anne Kockelkorn, Katharina Kucher, Vladimir Kulić, Torsten Lange, Jennifer Dorothy Lee, Michael Lee, Ayala Levin, Tatyana Levina, Benjamin Lytal, David Mather, Ákos Moravánszky, Alona Nitzan-Shiftan, Ginger Nolan, Esen Ogus, Alexander Ortenberg, Michael Osman, Philipp Oswalt, Elena Ovsyannikova, Nancy Perloff, Tobias Pohlmann, Ekaterina Pravilova, Wiebke Reinert, Sophia Rochmes, Michelangelo Sabatino, Sabine Sarwa, Brett Savage, Emily E. Scott, Alexa Sekira, Alexandra Selivanova, Maria Silina, Andrey Smirnov, Kim Soss, Martino Stierli, Adrian Täckman, Misha Tsodyks, Noa Turel, Philip Ursprung, Nikolai Vassiliev, Catherine Wetzel, Mechtild Widrich, Mantha Zarmakoupi, and Nina Zschocke.

I am particularly thankful to the leaders and participants of the Art History and History of Science seminars at the IAS, who provided insightful feedback on chapter drafts: Yve-Alain Bois, Charlotte Denoël, Heidi Gearhart, Marius Hauknes, Clémence Imbert, Frances Jacobus-Parker, Isabelle Marchesin, Anthony Petro, and Laura Weigert; Myles Jackson, Sarah Dry, Rob Iliffe, Deirdre Loughridge, Gabriela Soto Laveaga, Marion Thomas, and Glen Van Brummelen. Megan Eardley, Adam Jasper, Serguei Oushakine, and Georgi Parpulov also provided helpful comments on drafts of the chapters. Presenting different parts of this project at conferences, workshops, and as invited lectures at the Getty Research Institute, Dumbarton Oaks, and the IAS helped me strengthen the argument. I sincerely thank Michael Osman, Simon Baier, Kenny Cupers, Eva Ehninger and Julia Bryan-Wilson, Zeynep Çelik Alexander, Adam Jasper, Vladimir Kulić, Edward Dimendberg and Steven Jacobs, Lorens Holm and John Hendrix, Dale Allen Gyure, Samia Henni, Anna-Maria Meister, Benedikt Boucsein, and Torsten Lange and Dietrich Erben for the invitations.

This work would have been impossible without the help of archivists and librarians at the Russian State Library, the State A. V. Shchusev Museum of Architecture, the Russian State Archive of Literature and Arts, the Russian State Archive in Samara, the Dumbarton Oaks Research Library, the Getty Research Institute Library and Special Collections, Kansas State University

Libraries, among other collections, particularly to Maria Ametova, Irina Finskaya, Anna Stoiko, Larisa I. Ivanova-Veen, and Tatiana Lysova.

My infinite gratitude goes to the University of Minnesota Press, in particular to Pieter Martin for his interest, engagement, and patience, to Deborah Oosterhouse for her careful reading of the text, as well as to Anne Carter and Ana Bichanich for their support. I am deeply indebted to the manuscript's anonymous readers for their thoughtful and helpful reviews, to Lenore Hietkamp, whose skillful editing improved the manuscript in innumerable ways, and to Douglas Easton, who prepared the index. I would also like to thank Laura Jung, who assisted with obtaining illustrations, and Fee Huschenbeth, who helped with administrative matters.

Last but not least, I am beyond indebted to my family, which had to share the burden of writing. I am infinitely grateful to my mother, Olga Vronskaya, for her unconditional support, to Igor Demchenko for taking on much more child-sitting than he had ever imagined while engaging in discussions about Soviet architecture, and to Stanislav and Vladimir, who arrived with the dissertation and grew with the book, for making this world brighter and livelier. I dedicate this book to the memory of my father, Genrikh Vronsky, who taught me to love history and care for old buildings.

NOTES

Introduction

1. Stanford Anderson, "The Fiction of Function," *Assemblage,* no. 2 (February 1987): 19.
2. Henry-Russell Hitchcock and Philip Johnson, "The Extent of Modern Architecture," in *Modern Architecture: International Exhibition, New York, February 10 to March 23, 1932* (New York: Museum of Modern Art, 1932), 21.
3. This opposition has been pertinent to architectural criticism that focused on modernism. Among its more recent examples are publications by Alan Colquhoun, Giorgio Ciucci, Oscar Newman, and Sarah Goldhagen. See Juliana Maxim, *The Socialist Life of Modern Architecture: Bucharest, 1949–1964* (London: Routledge, 2019), 65 n.105.
4. Morphology had been a key preoccupation of ecological thought since Ernst Haeckel's *Generelle Morphologie der Organismen* (1866), in which he introduced the term "ecology." The discussion by biologist D'Arcy Thompson in *On Growth and Form* (1917) was particularly influential within artistic circles. See Philip Steadman, *The Evolution of Designs: Biological Analogy in Architecture and the Applied Arts* (1979; repr., London: Routledge, 2008), 12–13.
5. Stephen Jay Gould, *Ontogeny and Phylogeny* (Cambridge, Mass.: Harvard University Press, 1977), and Lynn Nyhart, *Biology Takes Form: Animal Morphology and the German Universities, 1800–1900* (Chicago: University of Chicago Press, 1995).
6. Their influence has been well studied. See, for instance, Oliver Botar, "Prolegomena to the Study of Biomorphic Modernism: Biocentrism, László Moholy-Nagy's 'New Vision,' and Erno Kállai's *Bioromantik*" (PhD dissertation, University of Toronto, 1998); Detlef Mertins, "Architecture, Worldview, and World Image in *G*," in *G: An Avant-Garde Journal of Art, Architecture, Design, and Film, 1923–1926* (Los Angeles: Getty Research Institute, 2010); Charissa N. Terranova, *Art as Organism: Biology and the Evolution of the Digital Image* (London: I. B. Tauris, 2016); Oliver Botar and Isabel Wünsche, eds., *Biocentrism and Modernism* (London: Ashgate, 2011).
7. Adolf Behne, *The Modern Functional Building,* trans. Michael Robinson (Santa Monica: Getty Research Institute, 1996), 128–30.
8. Behne's *Modern Functional Building* was written in 1923 and published in 1926. Lissitzky's translation, which he expected to be published by ASNOVA, remained unpublished. It can be accessed at the Russian State Archive of Literature and the Arts, fond 2361 (El Lissitzky), op. 1, ed. khr. 29. Lissitzky intended to supplement Behne's text with his own chapter, devoted to modern architecture in Russia. See his letter to Jacobus Oud (1925), published in El Lissitzky, *Proun und Wolkenbügel: Schriften, Briefe, Dokumente,* ed. Sophie Lissitzky-Küppers and Jen Lissitzky (Dresden: VEB Verlag der Kunst, 1977), 131.

9. The First Five-Year Plan addressed the period between October 1, 1928, and October 1, 1933. The project was approved at the Sixteenth Conference of the All-Union Communist Party of Bolsheviks in April 1929, and in the Fifth Congress of the Soviets in May 1929. The plan was completed ahead of schedule in four years and three months (by the end of 1932). These complexities explain the inconsistency of dating the plan in historiography.

10. Solomon Lisagor died in incarceration in 1937; Mikhail Okhitovich was executed in 1937; Vladimir Dedyukhin, who headed the Design Department of Mossoviet (Moscow Council of Workers' Deputies) was executed in 1938. The rector of the Academy of Architecture Mikhail Kryukov was subjected to repression in 1938 (he died in the GULAG in 1944) following the execution of vice-rector Alexander Alexandrov in 1936; academic secretary and later vice-rector Genrikh Lyudvig was incarcerated between 1938 and 1956; architect Oleg Vutke was executed in 1938. Somewhat better was the fate of architects Mikael Mazmonyan (whose work is examined in chapter 6) and Gevorg Kochar, who in 1937 were arrested and sent to the Arctic city Norilsk, where they, alongside a number of other incarcerated architects, remained until after their rehabilitation in 1954.

11. V. Koval', "No iarkikh krasok bol'she u sud'by" [Interview with Betty Glan], *Komsomol'skaia Pravda,* unknown issue. Central Moscow Archive-Museum of Private Collections, fond L-33, op. 1, d. 217.

12. As Loren Graham notes, the two books most important for the Marxist concept of nature and life—Friedrich Engels's *Dialectics of Nature* and Lenin's *Philosophical Notebooks*—had not yet been published at that time. Loren Graham, *Science, Philosophy and Human Behavior in the Soviet Union* (New York: Columbia University Press, 1987), 73.

13. Danilo Udovički-Selb, *Soviet Architectural Avant-Gardes: Architecture and Stalin's Revolution from Above, 1928–1938* (London: Bloomsbury, 2020), 168. The event singled out by Udovički-Selb is an anonymous article in the party newspaper *Pravda* published on February 20, 1936.

14. Udovički-Selb, *Soviet Architectural Avant-Gardes,* 45–46.

15. For a discussion of such binarism, see chapter 1, "Binary Socialism," in Alexei Yurchak, *Everything Was Forever, Until It Was No More: The Last Soviet Generation* (Princeton, N.J.: Princeton University Press, 2005).

16. In architecture, the symbolic break between the two periods has typically been associated with the 1932 competition for the Palace of the Soviets in Moscow. For a discussion of this approach, see Alla Vronskaya, "Deconstructing Constructivism," in *Re-framing Identities: Architecture's Turn to History, 1970–1990,* ed. Ákos Moravánszky and Torsten Lange (Basel: Birkhäuser, 2016), 149–63.

17. For a similar argument, see Peder Anker, *From Bauhaus to Ecohouse: A History of Ecological Design* (Baton Rouge: Louisiana State University Press, 2010), 4.

18. It must be noted that Kloppenberg does not use the term "monism" in the same sense as I do in this book: instead, he refers to "via media" or "social democracy" (James Kloppenberg, *Uncertain Victory: Social Democracy and Progressivism in European and American Thought, 1870–1920* [Oxford: Oxford University Press, 1986], 3, 5–6). During the 1920s, via media became a rhetorical trope widely

used in art and architecture criticism. Adolf Behne believed that German architectural culture could build its identity around overcoming the split between the totalizing collectivity of "the East" and the individualism of "the West" (Behne, *Modern Functional Building,* 119–20); Ladovsky, musing about the future of skyscraper construction in Russia, argued for a middle ground between the pragmatic American approach and the idealist German one (Enael [N. A. Ladovskii], "Neboskreby SSSR i Ameriki," *Izvestia ASNOVA,* no. 1 [1926]: 6); Sergei Eisenstein argued for overcoming the dualism of "emotion" and "reason" (Sergei Eisenstein, "Perspektivy," *Iskusstvo,* no. 1–2 [1929]: 116–22); and as late as 1938, Mies van der Rohe declared his ambition to unite materialism and idealism (Ludwig Mies van der Rohe, "Inaugural Address as Director of Architecture at Armour Institute of Technology," in Fritz Neumeyer, *The Artless Word: Mies van der Rohe on the Building Art,* trans. Mark Jarzombek [Cambridge, Mass.: MIT Press, 1991], 316–17).

19. Cathy Gere, *Knossos and the Prophets of Modernism* (Chicago: University of Chicago Press, 2009), 6. See also Jeffrey Herf's influential book *Reactionary Modernism: Technology, Culture, and Politics in Weimar and the Third Reich* (1984; repr., Cambridge: Cambridge University Press, 2003), which argues that "modernism is not a movement exclusively of the political Left or Right" (12), and that German modernity presented a cultural paradox: "the embrace of modern technology by German thinkers who rejected Enlightenment reason" (1). Significantly, among the latter were engineers.

20. Giorgio Agamben, *Homo Sacer: Sovereign Power and Bare Life* [1995], trans. Daniel Heller-Roazen (Stanford, Calif.: Stanford University Press, 1998), 4.

21. Agamben, *Homo Sacer,* 10. The notion of biopolitics was first developed by Michel Foucault, who juxtaposed biopolitics with politics in his *History of Sexuality* (1984).

22. On Huxley's involvement with modernist architecture, see Anker, *From Bauhaus to Ecohouse,* 23–35; Hadas Steiner, "Life at the Threshold," *October* 136 (Spring 2011): 133–55; and Lucia Allais, *Designs of Destruction: The Making of Monuments in the Twentieth Century* (Chicago: University of Chicago Press, 2018), 19.

23. Julian Huxley, "Scientific Humanism," in *The Uniqueness of Man* (London: Readers Union, 1943), 260. Huxley elaborated his evolutionist vision of humanism in *The Humanist Frame,* ed. Julian Huxley (New York: Harper and Brothers, 1961) and elsewhere.

24. Written from a vitalist position was Gustav Bunge, *Vitalismus und Mechanismus: Ein Vortrag* (Leipzig: F. C. W. Vogel, 1886), while Otto Bütschli, *Mechanismus und Vitalismus* (Leipzig: Engelmann, 1901) defended mechanicism. Both works were translated into Russian as appendixes to Isidor Rozental', *Obshchaia fiziologiia: Vvedenie v izuchenie estestvoznaniia i meditsiny,* trans. from German by S. S. Salazkin (St. Petersburg: Brokgauz-Efron, 1902). Many of Wundt's works were translated into Russian.

25. Alfred North Whitehead, *Science and the Modern World* (New York: Macmillan, 1925), 58. On the notion of life, see, in particular, J. H. Woodger, *Biological Principles: A Critical Study* (London: Routledge & Keegan Paul, 1929); J. B. S. Haldane, "The Origin of Life" [1929], in *Science and Life: Essays of a Rationalist,*

intro. J. Maynard Smith (London: Rationalist Press, 1968), 1–11; Lancelot Hogben, *The Nature of Living Matter* (London: K. Paul, Trench, Trubner, 1930).

26. Haeckel's monism and the concept of evolution became the subject of multiple Russian-language publications and public discussions. Russian translations of Haeckel's works include his seminal book about art and architecture *Kunstformen der Natur* (1904 [1899]), *Der Kampf um den Entwickelungsgedanken* (1909 [1905]), as well as *Natürliche Schöpfungsgeschichte* (1914 [1899]), *Anthropogenie oder Entwicklungsgeschichte des Menschen* (1919 [1910]), and *Indische Reiserbriefe* (1925 [1882]). In this and subsequent endnotes citing translations, the date of the translation is given first, followed by the date of original publication.

27. Many of Spencer's works were translated into Russian, such as *Principles of Biology* (1870 [1864]), *Essays: Scientific, Political, and Speculative* (1874 [1858]), *The Inadequacy of Natural Selection* (1894 [1893]), *Principles of Psychology* (1898 [1855]), *Principles of Ethics* (1899 [1884]), and *Facts and Comments* (1903 [1902]).

28. Louis Sullivan, "The Tall Office Building Artistically Considered" [1896], *Kindergarten Chats and Other Writings* (New York: George Wittenborn, 1947), 208.

29. J. Arthur Thomson and Patrick Geddes, *Evolution* (New York: Henry Holt, 1911), 184.

30. Many of the supporters of Mendelian eugenics, however, maintained close relationships with the Soviet Union, among them Huxley, Geddes, Shaw, Karl Pearson, J. B. S. Haldane, H. J. Muller (who worked in the USSR during the 1930s), and Paul Kammerer (whose intention to move to the Soviet Union was prevented only by his death). Kammerer's life and suicide were glorified by Lunacharsky in the scenario for the 1928 film *Salamander.* On eugenics in Russia, see Mark B. Adams, "Eugenics in Russia, 1900–1940," in *The Wellborn Science: Eugenics in Germany, France, Brazil, and Russia,* ed. Mark B. Adams (Oxford: Oxford University Press, 1990), 153–215.

31. Having grown up in Riga, Latvia, where he also began his academic career, Ostwald was fluent in Russian and maintained personal ties with his Russian followers (he was, for example, a foreign corresponding member of the Russian Academy of Sciences). The translations of his works include *Grundlinien der anorganischen Chemie* (1902 [1900]), *Vorlesungen über Naturphilosophie* (1903 [1902]), *Die Schule der Chemie* (1904 [1903]), *Prinzipien der Chemie* (1910 [1907]), and *Die Farblehre* (1926 [1918]). In *Materialism and Empirio-Criticism* (1908), Lenin called Ostwald "a big chemist but little philosopher," remaining skeptical about his energeticism (which he associated with the empiriocriticism of Avenarius). As a result, Ostwald's philosophical (though not scientific) works were not published in Russia after the revolution, although his ideas continued to be disseminated through the influence of Bogdanov and Lunacharsky.

32. Niles R. Holt, "Wilhelm Ostwald's 'The Bridge,'" *British Journal for the History of Science* 10, no. 2 (July 1977): 146–50. The members of the Bridge included, among others, Henri Poincaré and Russian zoologist Ilya Mechnikov (while Ernst Mach declined Ostwald's invitation to join). See also Nader Vossoughian, "On the Organization of geistige Arbeit: Historical Reflections on Die Brücke," *Library Trends* 62, no. 2 (2013): 478–88; Markus Krajewski, *World Projects: Global*

Information before World War I (Minneapolis: University of Minnesota Press, 2014), 33–92.

33. Hannah Arendt, *The Human Condition* (Chicago: University of Chicago Press, 1958), 89–90.

34. Karl Marx, *Capital,* vol. 1, trans. Ben Fowkes (London: Penguin, 1990), 283; Karl Marx, *Wage-Labour and Capital* [1847] (New York: International Publishers, 1933), 19.

35. Quoted in Igor Polianski, "Between Hegel and Haeckel: Monistic Worldview, Marxist Philosophy, and Biomedicine in Russia and the Soviet Union," in *Monism: Science, Philosophy, Religion, and the History of a Worldview,* ed. Todd H. Weir (London: Palgrave Macmillan, 2012), 197.

36. Hermann Reinheimer, *Evolution by Co-Operation: A Study in Bio-Economics* (New York: Dutton, 1913), 1.

37. Ernst Haeckel, *Generelle Morphologie der Organismen: Allgemeine Grundzüge der organischen Formen-Wissenschaft, mechanisch begründet durch die von Charles Darwin reformierte Descendenz-Theorie* (Berlin: G. Reimer, 1866), 8.

38. Donald Worster, *Nature's Economy: A History of Ecological Ideas* (Cambridge: Cambridge University Press, 1977).

39. Georges-Louis Leclerc Buffon, "When the Powers of Man Assisted Those of Nature," in *Natural History: General and Particular,* vol. 9 (London: W. Strahan and T. Cadell, 1761), 404. Writing from a critical perspective, historian Peder Anker demonstrated how ecological reasoning was subsequently mobilized by modern colonial powers to justify their rule. Peder Anker, *Imperial Ecology: Environmental Order in the British Empire, 1895–1945* (Cambridge, Mass.: Harvard University Press, 2001).

40. Herbert Wells, *The Work, Wealth, and Happiness of Mankind* (London: William Heinemann, 1932), 84–117.

41. Alexander Etkind, *Internal Colonization: Russia's Imperial Experience* (Cambridge: Polity, 2011).

42. Linking the economic theories of planning with modern utopian thought, Manfredo Tafuri famously argued that the turn of modernist architects toward urban planning in the late 1920s represented the pinnacle of utopian tradition, after which "the utopia of the plan" became dissolved in the reality of the plan, i.e., in Keynesian economic politics. Manfredo Tafuri, *Architecture and Utopia: Design and Capitalist Development,* trans. Barbara Luigia La Penta (1973; repr., Cambridge, Mass.: MIT Press, 1976).

43. Michael Osman, *Modernism's Visible Hand: Architecture and Regulation in America* (Minneapolis: University of Minnesota Press, 2018), xxii.

44. The PEP manifesto is cited in Anker, *From Bauhaus to Ecohouse,* 27.

45. Anker, *From Bauhaus to Ecohouse,* 32. On Huxley's political views, see his *Democracy Marches* (London: Chatto and Vindus, 1941). As Anker's pioneering study of the role of ecological thought in modernist architecture demonstrates, Huxley's support for modernism was an outcome of his social biologism.

46. Gerald Young, ed., *Origins of Human Ecology* (Stroudsburg, Penn.: Hutchinson Ross, 1983). For more on Wells's human ecology, see Anker, *From Bauhaus to Ecohouse,* 24–36.

47. H. G. Wells, Julian Huxley, and G. P. Wells, *The Science of Life,* vol. 3 (Garden City, N.Y.: Doubleday, Doran, 1931), 641. On the ecologization of society, see Lynn K. Nyhart, *Modern Nature: The Rise of the Biological Perspective in Germany* (Chicago: University of Chicago Press, 2009), 251–92.

48. Many of the NOT enthusiasts were later subjected to repression or otherwise persecuted, including Trotsky, Gastev, Klutsis, Zalkind, Spielrein, and Blonsky.

49. For a detailed account of the circle, its approach to architecture, and its repercussions during the second half of the century in the United States, see Anker, *From Bauhaus to Ecohouse,* and Avigail Sachs, *Environmental Design: Architecture, Politics, and Science in Postwar America* (Charlottesville: University of Virginia Press, 2018).

50. Both the founder of Russian materialist aesthetics Nikolay Chernyshevsky and the leading Marxist theoretician Georgy Plekhanov considered themselves Spinozians. This importance was solidified by a Russian translation of Spinoza's *Ethics* in 1886, followed by a host of other translations. See A. D. Maidanskii, *Benedikt Spinoza—pro et contra: lichnost' i tvorchestvo B. Spinozy v otsenkakh russkikh myslitelei i issledovatelei. Antologiia* (St. Petersburg: Izdatel'stvo Russkoi khristianskoi gumanitarnoi akademii, 2012), 9. Radical scientism was promoted by authors like the scientist and writer Mikhail Filippov, who until his death during a chemical experiment was the editor of *Nauchnoe obozrenie* (Scientific Review, 1894–1903), a journal that published, alongside Mach, Helmholtz, and Bekhterev, the works of Lenin, Plekhanov, and other Bolsheviks. For an overview of monism in Russia, see Polianski, "Between Hegel and Haeckel."

51. G. V. Plekhanov, *The Development of the Monist View of History,* vol. 1 of *Selected Philosophical Works,* trans. Andrew Rothstein and A. Fineberg (Moscow: Progress Publishers, 1974). V. I. Lenin, *Polnoe sobranie sochinenii,* vol. 19 (Moscow: Izdatel'stvo politicheskoi literatury, 1968), footnote on p. 313.

52. V. I. Lenin, "O karikature na marksizm i ob imperialisticheskom ekonomizme" [1916], in *Polnoe sobranie sochinenii,* vol. 30 (Moscow: Institut Marksizma-Leninizma, 1958), 108.

53. Quoted in Polianski, "Between Hegel and Haeckel," 197. Gorky also applauded Ostwald's "fertile, productive idea of organization" (quoted in Holt, "Wilhelm Ostwald's 'The Bridge,'" 148).

54. Anatolii Lunacharskii, "Vospominania iz revolutsionnogo proshlogo" [1919], *Nasledie A. V. Lunacharskogo,* September 5, 2019, http://lunacharsky.newgod.su/lib/vospominaniya-i-vpechatleniya/vospominania-iz-revolucionnogo-proslogo/.

55. Lunacharskii, "Vospominania iz revoliutsionnogo proshlogo."

56. Anatolii Lunacharskii, "Osnovy pozitivnoi estetiki," in *Ocherki realisticheskogo mirovozzrenia* (St. Petersburg: Izdatel'stvo S. Dorovatovskogo i A. Charushnikova, 1903), 51.

57. Anatolii Lunacharskii, "Meschanstvo i individualizm," in *Ocherki filosofii kollektivizma* (St. Petersburg: Izdanie tovarischestva "Znanie," 1909), 91. Compare Lunacharsky's exaltation of the fight as the highest manifestation of life with Donna Haraway's seminal analysis of Carl Akeley's nearly simultaneous taxidermic dioramas in the New York Museum of Natural History, which

present manhood, identified with the fight, as the highest manifestation of life (Donna Haraway, "Teddy Bear Patriarchy: Taxidermy in the Garden of Eden, New York City, 1908–1936," *Social Text,* no. 11 [Winter 1984–85]: 20–64).

58. Lunacharskii, "Meschanstvo i individualism," 335. For more on Lunacharsky's Nietzscheanism, see Alla Vronskaya, "From the Aesthetics of Life to the Dialectics of Collectivity: Anatoly Lunacharsky, Alexander Bogdanov, and Maxim Gorky, 1905–1917," in *Productive Universals—Specific Situations: Critical Engagements in Art, Architecture, and Urbanism,* ed. Anne Kockelkorn and Nina Zschocke (Berlin: Sternberg, 2019), 316–35.

59. Aleksandr A. Bogdanov, *Empiriomonizm: Stat'i po filosofii,* vol. 2 (Moscow: Izdatel'stvo S. Dorovatovskago i A. Charushnikova, 1905), 186. The German-Austrian psychiatrist Theodor Meynert believed brain anatomy to be the key to treating psychological disorders.

60. S. Suvorov, "Osnovy filosofii zhizni" [1904], in *Ocherki realisticheskogo mirovozzreniia: Sbornik statei po filosofii, obshchestvennoi rabote i zhizni* (St. Petersburg: Izdatel'stvo Dorovatskogo i Charushnikova, 1905), 79, 94.

61. The influence of Bogdanov's thought on Russian postrevolutionary culture has been acknowledged by multiple scholars; for example, Isabel Wünsche, "Organic Visions and Biological Models in Russian Avant-Garde Art," in Botar and Wünsche, *Biocentrism and Modernism,* 127–52; Barbara Wurm, "Factory," in *Revoliutsiia! Demonstratsiia! Soviet Art Put to the Test,* ed. Matthew Witkovsky and Devin Fore (Chicago: Art Institute of Chicago, 2017), 218–25; Dmitri V. Sarabianov and Natalia Adaskina, *Popova* (New York: Harry N. Abrams, 1990); and Devin Fore, "The Operative Word in Soviet Factography," *October* 118 (Fall 2006): 95–131.

62. Three out of eight key presentations at the First All-Russian NOT Conference were made by Proletkult members, including Bogdanov. Georgii Gloveli and Nadezhda Figurovskaia, "Tragedia kollektivista," in Aleksandr Bogdanov, *Voprosy sotsializma: Raboty raznykh let* (Moscow: Politizdat, 1990), 23 n. 123.

63. See V. Kemenov, "Dovol'no metafiziki! (Protiv idealizma Novitskogo)," *Za proletarskoe iskusstvo,* no. 11–12 (1931): 8–12, and Charlotte Douglas, "Mach and Malevich: Sensation, Suprematism, and the Objectless World," *The Structuralist* 49/50 (2009): 58–65.

64. See Mark Crinson, *Rebuilding Babel: Modern Architecture and Internationalism* (London: I. B. Tauris, 2017); David Ayers, *Modernism, Internationalism, and the Russian Revolution* (Edinburgh: Edinburgh University Press, 2018).

65. The postrevolutionary wave of "Russophilia" was carefully cultivated by the Soviet government. See Michael David-Fox, *Showcasing the Great Experiment: Cultural Diplomacy and Western Visitors to the Soviet Union, 1921–1941* (Oxford: Oxford University Press, 2012).

66. Those who traveled in Russia at the invitation of the Soviet government included Behne, Theodore Dreiser, Dewey, Wells, Keynes, Shaw, Huxley, Diego Rivera, Knud Lönberg-Holm, Stefan Zweig, Romain Rolland, André Gide, Walter Benjamin, and Bruno Taut, as well as those architects who received commissions or were employed by the Soviet government.

67. Oliver Botar, "Defining Biocentrism," in Botar and Wünsche, *Biocentrism and*

Modernism, 31. *Lebensphilosophie* is a term retrospectively applied to a set of philosophies (including Friedrich Nietzsche, Wilhelm Dilthey, Bergson, and Georg Simmel) that opposed positivism and asserted, instead, the irrationality of life.

68. Polianski, "Between Hegel and Haeckel," 212–13.
69. Huxley criticized Lysenko's ideas in *Soviet Genetics and World Science: Lysenko and the Meaning of Heredity* (London: Chatto and Vindus, 1949). On Lysenko's Lamarckism, see Loren Graham, *Lysenko's Ghost: Epigenetics and Russia* (Cambridge, Mass.: Harvard University Press, 2016).
70. A. Toporkov, *Tekhnicheskii byt i sovremennoe iskusstvo* (Moscow: Gosudarstvennoe izdatel'stvo, 1928), 223.
71. Spinoza, *Ethics,* IVD1 and IVD2.
72. John Bernal, "The Freedom of Necessity" [1942], in *The Freedom of Necessity* (London: Routledge and K. Paul, 1949), 8.
73. Agamben, *Homo Sacer,* 181–82.

1. Space

1. Selim O. Khan-Magomedov, *Ratsionalizm (ratsio-arkhitektura) "Formalizm"* (Moscow: Arkhitektura-S, 2007), 140–43.
2. Selim Khan-Magomedov, *Mikhail Korzhev* (Moscow: Russkii Avangard, 2009), 32.
3. Anatolii Lunacharskii, "Doklad na III sessii VTsIK 7-go sozyva" [1920], in *O vospitanii i obrazovanii* (Moscow: Pedagogika, 1986), 78.
4. V. Petrov, "ASNOVA za 8 let," *Sovetskaia arkhitektura* 1–2 (1931): 49. In 1929, the "collective method of pedagogy" was defined as a combination of the collective elaboration of programs and methods, collective conversations with students and field trips, collective reviews of student projects, and collective research: "Obshchaia programma raboty Osnovnogo Otdeleniia" (Moscow, 1929), cited in Khan-Magomedov, *Ratsionalizm,* 140–43; Khan-Magomedov, *Mikhail Korzhev,* 360.
5. Khan-Magomedov, *Ratsionalizm,* 146.
6. Formed in 1919 (and disbanded in 1920), the group was first known as Sinskul'ptarkh (Synthesis of Sculpture and Painting). A thorough account of Zhivskulptarkh and INKhUK discussions and their role in the formation of rationalist theory is given in Anatole Senkevitch, "Aspects of Spatial Form and Perceptual Psychology in the Doctrine of the Rationalist Movement in Soviet Architecture in the 1920s," *VIA* 6 (1983): 78–115.
7. Accordingly, the program of the INKhUK Group of Objective Analysis aimed at an "analysis of elements and the laws of their organization in works of art" (the definition of Varvara Bubnova [1920]; quoted in Maria Gough, *The Artist as Producer: Russian Constructivism in Revolution* [Berkeley: University of California Press, 2005], 32).
8. Nikolai Dokuchaev, "Poiasnitel'naia zapiska k kursu 'Iskusstvo arkhitektury' dlia khudozhestvennykh tekhnikumov," in *Sbornik materialov po khudozhestvennomu obrazovaniiu* (Moscow: Gosudarstvennoe izdatel'stvo, 1927), 79. The course "Space" was first offered in 1923.
9. Similarities between the Bauhaus and VKhUTEMAS pedagogy have been noted

by many, leading to the popular curatorial branding of VKhUTEMAS as "the Russian Bauhaus." The role of psychological techniques in the pedagogical curriculum of the two schools provides another ground for comparison. On the role of psychological ideas at the Bauhaus, see Oliver Botar, "Prolegomena to the Study of Biomorphic Modernism: Biocentrism, Laszlo Moholy-Nagy's 'New Vision,' and Erno Kállai's *Bioromantik*" (PhD dissertation, University of Toronto, 1998), and Zeynep Çelik Alexander, *Kinaesthetic Knowing: Aesthetics, Epistemology, Modern Design* (Chicago: University of Chicago Press, 2017).

10. For more on VKhUTEMAS, see Anna Bokov, *Avant-Garde as Method: Vkhutemas and the Pedagogy of Space, 1920–1930* (Zurich: Park Books, 2021).

11. In addition to Ladovsky and Krinsky, participants in the debate included the artists Varvara Bubnova, Alexander Drevin, Karl Ioganson, Ivan Klyun, Konstantin Medunetsky, Nadezhda Udaltsova, brothers Vladimir and Georgy Stenberg, as well the sculptors Aleksey Babichev and Boris Korolev and the art critic Nikolay Tarabukin. On the debate, see Gough, *Artist as Producer,* 21–59.

12. P. N. Medvedev [identified as Mikhail Bakhtin], "Uchenyi sal'erizm (o formal'nom (morfologicheskom) metode)," in *Freidizm. Formal'nyi metod v literaturovedenii. Marksizm i filosofiia iazyka. Stat'i* (Moscow: Labirint, 2000), 8.

13. Khan-Magomedov, *Ratsionalizm,* 107.

14. See "Minutes of the meeting of the Working Group of Architects in INKhUK" ("Protokol zasedaniia rabochei gruppy arkhitektorov INKhUKa," in Khan-Magomedov, *Ratsionalizm,* 108).

15. Ladovsky's personal profile at VKhUTEMAS. Russian State Archive of Literature and the Arts (RGALI), fond 680, op. 2, ed. khr. 2597. The same document mentions his conversion from Judaism to Lutheran Protestantism. Cited after Margarete Vöhringer, *Avantgarde und Psychotechnik: Wissenschaft, Kunst und Technik der Wahrnehmungsexperimente in der frühen Sowjetunion* (Göttingen: Wallstein Verlag, 2007), 52.

16. Khan-Magomedov, *Ratsionalizm,* 127; Vladimir Krinskii, "Otchet o teoreticheskoi rabote gruppy arkhitektorov IkhUK," in Khan-Magomedov, *Ratsionalizm,* 126–27. K. Pirson, *Nauka i obiazannosti grazhdanina,* trans. K. Timiriazev (Moscow: I. N. Kushnerov, 1905); K. Pirson, *Grammatika nauki,* trans. V. Bazarov and P. Iushkevich (n.p.: Shipovnik, n.d.).

17. Besides Ladovsky, among ASNOVA's founding members were Krinsky, Dokuchaev, the dean of the VKhUTEMAS Architecture Department Aleksey Rukhlyadev, Ladovsky's first students Sergey Mochalov and Viktor Balikhin, and architects Efimov and Vladimir Fidman. Not a prolific writer, Ladovsky preferred to disseminate his ideas through teaching and conversation. Alongside publications by his associates (most notably Dokuchaev), documents related to Ladovsky's pedagogical activity offer the best insight into the theory of rationalism.

18. Quoted in Alexey Alexeyevich Kurbanovsky, "Freud, Tatlin, and the Tower: How Soviet Psychoanalysts Might Have Interpreted the Monument to the Third International," *Slavic Review* 67, no. 4 (Winter 2008): 895. The Russian Psychoanalytical Society functioned between 1922 and 1930, and numerous translations of Freud were published both before and after the revolution of 1917. On psychoanalysis in Russia, see Alexander Etkind, *The Eros of the Impossible: The*

History of Psychoanalysis in Russia (Boulder: Westview Press, 1997), and Martin A. Miller, *Freud and the Bolsheviks: Psychoanalysis in Imperial Russia and the Soviet Union* (New Haven, Conn.: Yale University Press, 1998).

19. On the role of psychoanalysis in the thought of Vygotsky and Luria, see René Van der Veer and Jaan Valsiner, *Understanding Vygotsky: A Quest for Synthesis* (Oxford: Blackwell, 1991), 78–111.

20. B[ernard] Bykhovskii, "O metodologicheskikh osnovaniiakh psikhoanaliticheskogo uchenia Freida," *Pod znamenem Marksizma* 11–12 (1923): 166.

21. Aleksandr Luria, "Psikhoanaliz kak sistema monisticheskoi psikhologii," in *Zigmund Freid, psikhoanaliz i russkaia mysl'*, ed. V. M. Leibin (Moscow: Respublika, 1994), 193–94.

22. On the economic potential of libido, see also Tijana Vujošević, *Modernism and the Making of the Soviet New Man* (Manchester: Manchester University Press, 2017), 58–61.

23. Giese's prolific work was well known to the Bauhaus designers (and likely to their Soviet colleagues) due to his friendship with László Moholy-Nagy. Moholy-Nagy authored the entry "The Work of the Bauhaus" in the *Dictionary of Work Science: Handwörterbuch der Arbeitswissenschaft,* ed. Fritz Giese, 2 vols. (Halle, 1927–30), 1:654–66. In 1926 psychotechnics ventured into architectural pedagogy: while Hannes Meyer introduced it to the curriculum of the Bauhaus (where it focused on advertisement psychology), Ladovsky opened the Psychotechnical Laboratory at VKhUTEIN.

24. Richard Avenarius, *Philosophie als Denken der Welt gemäß dem Prinzip des kleinsten Kraftmaßes: Prolegomena zu einer Kritik der reinen Erfahrung* (Leipzig: Fues's Verlag, 1876), iii.

25. Anatolii Lunacharskii, "Vospominania iz revolutsionnogo proshlogo" [1919], in *Vospominania i vpechatlenia* (Moscow: Sovetskaia Rossia, 1968), 19–20; R. Avenarius and A. Lunacharskii, *R. Avenarius, Kritika chistogo opyta v populiarnom izlozhenii A. Lunacharskogo. Novaia teoria pozitivnogo idealizma (Holzapfel, Panideal). Kriticheskoe izlozhenie A. Lunacharskogo* (Moscow: Izd. Dorovatskogo i Charushnikova, 1905).

26. Anatolii Lunacharskii, *Osnovy pozitivnoi estetiki* (1903; repr., Moscow: Gosudarstvennoe izdatel'stvo, 1923), 23.

27. Lunacharskii, *Osnovy pozitivnoi estetiki,* 13–19.

28. Dmitrii Ovsianiko-Kulikovskii, "Vvedenie v nenapisannuiu knigu po psikhologii umstvennogo tvorchestva (nauchno-filosofskogo i khudozhestvennogo", in N. V. Os'makov, *Psikhologicheskoe napravleneie v russkom literaturovedenii* (Moscow: Prosveschenie, 1981), 111.

29. Fedor Kalinin, "Proletariat i tvorchestvo," *Proletarskaia Kul'tura* 1 (1918): 10. For the original account of Poincaré's story, see Henri Poincaré, *Science and Method* (London: T. Nelson & Sons, 1914). On the notion of the unconscious in Soviet criticism, see John Fizer, "The Problem of the Unconscious in the Creative Process as Treated by Soviet Aesthetics," *Journal of Aesthetics and Art Criticism* 21, no. 4 (Summer 1963): 399–406.

30. Whereas Ladovsky used the terms "rational architecture" or "ratio-architecture," the term "rationalism" was coined as a counterpart to "constructivism" by historian Selim Khan-Magomedov. See Vöhringer, *Avantgarde und Psychotechnik,* 42.

31. Nikolai Ladovskii, "Osnovy postroeniia teorii arkhitektury (pod znakom ratsionalisticheskoi estetiki)," *Izvestia ASNOVA* 1 (1926): 3.

32. Fritz Giese, "Rationalisierung," in *Handbuch der Arbeitswissenschaft*, vol. 1 (Halle: Carl Marhold, 1930), 3622. For an example of an application of this principle to design, see, for instance, August Schirmer, "Handwerk und Rationalisierung," *Schweizerischen Maler- und Gipsermeister-Zeichnung* 7 (1929): 125–27.

33. O. A. Ermanskii, *Teoriia i praktika ratsionalizatsii,* vol. 1 (Moscow: Gosudarstvennoe izdatel'stvo, 1929), 134–35. Like Lunacharsky, Ermansky studied in Zurich, graduating from Zurich Polytechnic Institute in engineering in 1895 (the year Lunacharsky began his studies). It is unclear whether or not Ermansky could have studied with Avenarius. For more on NOT, see the introduction to this book.

34. Ermanskii, *Teoriia i praktika ratsionalizatsii,* 133.

35. [ASNOVA's manifesto], *Izvestia ASNOVA,* no. 1 (1926): 1.

36. In its modernist self-reflexivity, the parallelepiped presages Peter Eisenman's reading of Le Corbusier's Maison Dom-Ino (1914–15) (Peter Eisenman, "Maison Dom-Ino and the Self-Referential Sign," *Oppositions* 15/16 [1979]: 189–98), although unlike the latter, it reveals not the process but the product of design.

37. Johannes Bochenek, *Die männliche und weibliche Normal-Gestalt nach einem neuen System* (Berlin: A. Haak, 1875), 15.

38. Khan-Magomedov, *Ratsionalizm,* 112–14. According to the minutes of the meeting published by Khan-Magomedov, Petrov's quote from Mayakovsky's poem "Ulichnoe" (Streetways, 1913) was imprecise. Petrov's position evokes the argument made by Roman Jacobson the same year (Roman Iakobson, "Noveishaia russkaia poezia. Nabrosok pervyi: Podstupy k Khlebnikovu" [1921], in Serguei Oushakine, *Formal'nyi metod: Antologiia russkogo modernizma,* vol. 3 [Ekaterinburg: Kabinetnyi uchenyi, 2016], 246–304).

39. Khan-Magomedov, *Ratsionalizm,* 113. The importance of Worringer's book for Russian formalism was noted by Aage A. Hansen-Löve, *Russkii Formalizm* [1978] (Moscow: Iazyki russkoi kul'tury, 2001), 70.

40. N. Dokuchaev, "Osnovy iskusstva arkhitektury: Kurs dlia khudozhestvennykh tekhnikumov," in *Sbornik materialov po khudozhestvennomu obrazovaniiu* (Moscow: Gosudarstvennoe izdatel'stvo, 1927), 90.

41. Adolf von Hildebrand, *Das Problem der Form in der bildenden Kunst* (Strasbourg: J. H. E. Heitz, 1893); A. Hildebrand, *Problema formy v izobrazitel'nom iskusstve,* trans. N. B Rozenfel'd and V. A. Favorskii (Moscow: Musaget, 1914). Hildebrand's book was translated to Russian by N. B. Rozenfel'd and graphic designer Vladimir Favorskii, the rector of VKhUTEMAS between 1923 and 1926. The book is cited by Dokuchaev ("Osnovy iskusstva arkhitektury," 88) and Aleksei Mikhailov, *Gruppirovki sovetskoi arkhitektury* (Moscow: OGIZ-IZOGIZ, 1932), 44.

42. Adolf Hildebrand, "The Problem of Form in the Fine Arts," in *Empathy, Form, and Space: Problems in German Aesthetics, 1873–1893,* trans. Harry Francis Mallgrave and Eleftherios Ikonomou (Santa Monica, Calif.: Getty Center for the History of Art and the Humanities, 1994), 235, 245. A similar understanding of art was suggested by Pearson: "The single statement, a brief formula, the few words of which replace in our minds a wide range of relationships between isolated phenomena, is what we term a scientific law." Art, for Pearson, allowed

one to find "concentrated into a brief statement, into a simple formula or a few symbols, a wide range of human emotions and feelings." Karl Pearson, *The Grammar of Science* (London: A. and C. Black, 1900), 31, 35.

43. Hildebrand, "The Problem of Form in the Fine Arts," 233. An artist, according to Hildebrand, operated with effective form, creating not objects, but phenomenal impressions. Architects of Renaissance Genoa, for instance, solved the problem of narrow streets by leaning cornices down and making them shorter, which created the effect of a regular cornice observed from a distance. Hildebrand, "Anhand zur 6. Auflage. Nachträgliche Aufsätze zum *Problem der Form,*" in *Das Problem der Form in der bildenden Kunst,* 130–36. Hermann von Helmholtz, *Handbuch der Physiologischen Optik* (Leipzig: Voss, 1867).

44. Ladovskii, "Osnovy postroeniia teorii arkhitektury (pod znakom ratsionalisticheskoi estetiki)," 4.

45. Ladovskii, "Osnovy postroeniia teorii arkhitektury (pod znakom ratsionalisticheskoi estetiki)," 4. *Petrov* is a common Russian surname, and it remains unclear whether V. Petrov, the author of the project praised by Ladovsky, was the same person as the member of the Working Group of Architects A. Petrov. The difference in initials, likely suggesting that they were two different people, might also be a result of a typographic mistake.

46. Viktor Balikhin, "Programma prostranstvennogo konstentra Osnovnogo Otdeleniia VKhUTEMAS," quoted in Selim Khan-Magomedov, *Viktor Balikhin* (Moscow: Russkii avangard, 2009), 83–86.

47. Ernst Mach, *Contributions to the Analysis of the Sensations* [1886], trans. C. M. Williams (Chicago: Open Court Publishing, 1897), 22.

48. Mach, *Contributions to the Analysis of the Sensations,* 2–3.

49. Mach, *Contributions to the Analysis of the Sensations,* 16.

50. [El Lissitzky and] Adolf Behne, "Sovremennaia tselesoobraznaia arkhitektura," unpublished manuscript, RGALI, fond 2361, op. 1, ed. khr. 59, l. 27.

51. Nikolay Ladovsky, "Osnovy postroeniia teorii arkhitektury (pod znakom ratsionalisticheskoi estetiki)," unpublished draft of *Izvestia ASNOVA,* no. 1 (1926), RGALI, fond 2361, op. 1, ed. khr. 59, l. 33. The sentence was deleted from the published version of the article.

52. Quoted in Khan-Magomedov, *Ratsionalizm,* 119.

53. "Protokol zasedaniia rabochei gruppy arkhitektorov INKhUKa," March 26, 1921, 108–9.

54. "Protokol zasedaniia rabochei gruppy arkhitektorov INKhUKa," 108.

55. Carl Stumpf, *Über den psychologischen Ursprung der Raumvorstellung* (Leipzig: S. Hirzel, 1873), 278. Translated in Harry Francis Mallgrave and Eleftherios Ikonomou, "Introduction," in *Empathy, Form and Space,* 60. Stumpf's 1907 book *Erscheinungen und Funktionen* was translated into Russian in 1913 (Karl Stumpf, "Iavleniia i psikhicheskie funktsii," *Novye idei v filosofii* 4 [1913]: 50–101).

56. Khan-Magomedov, *Ratsionalizm,* 385.

57. Sergei Eisenstein, "Montage and Architecture," introduction by Ive-Alain Bois, *Assemblage,* no. 10 (December 1989): 101–31, and Martino Stierli, *Montage and the Metropolis: Architecture, Modernity, and the Representations of Space* (New Haven, Conn.: Yale University Press, 2018), 180–92.

58. V. Kalmykov, "Avtostroi," *Sovetskaia arkhitektura* 1–2 (1931): 22–26.

59. After graduating from VKhUTEMAS in 1926, Korzhev, Balikhin, and Turkus spent the summer developing the course as a theory of architectural composition. They rented a house in a village near Moscow, where Petrov, Spassky, and Lamtsov visited them. For more on "the summer in Kriushi," see Khan-Magomedov, *Mikhail Korzhev,* 84–90. The diary documenting the theoretical work of Balikhin, Korzhev, and Turkus in Kriushi in 1926 was published by Khan-Magomedov (*Mikhail Korzhev,* 143–71).

60. Nikolai Dokuchaev, "Sovremennaia russkaia arkhitektura i zapadnye paralleli," *Sovetskoe Iskusstvo,* no. 2 (1927): 13.

61. Dokuchaev, "Sovremennaia russkaia arkhitektura i zapadnye paralleli," 12–13.

62. Vladimir Krinskii, Ivan Lamtsov, and Mikhail Turkus, *Elementy arkhitekturno-prostranstvennoi kompozitsii* (Moscow: Stroiizdat, 1934). The second edition came out in 1938 (Lamtsov and Turkus, *Elementy arkhitekturnoi kompozitsii* [Moscow: Glavnaia redaktsia stroitel'noi literatury, 1938]). Reprinted in 1968, it remained a key textbook on architectural composition for generations of Soviet students (Krinskii, Lamtsov, and Turkus, *Elementy arkhitekturno-prostranstvennoi kompozitsii* [Moscow: Stroiizdat, 1968]). Moreover, in 1962, Lamtsov, Krinskii, and Turkus, together with V. S. Kolbin and N. V. Filasov, published another book, *Vvedenie v arkhitekturnoe proektirovanie* (Moscow: Gosudarstvennoe izdatel'stvo po literature i stroitel'stvu), which partially drew upon *Elements of Architectural-Spatial Composition.*

63. Anatolii Lunacharskii, "Formalizm v nauke ob iskusstve," *Pechat' i revoliutsiia* 5 (1924): 19–32; accessed online: http://lunacharsky.newgod.su/lib/ss-tom-7/formalizm-v-nauke-ob-iskusstve/.

64. Moskovskii Gosudarstvennyi Vysshii Khudozhestvenno-Tekhnicheskii Institut, *Programma raboty osnovnogo otdeleniia* [1929], reproduced in Khan-Magomedov, *Ratsionalizm,* 361.

65. Technical requirements specified that the elevator had to be divided into several areas for grain storage; grain was to be received through pouring reservoirs and lifted to the upper level where it would pass through purifying devices and then pour back down. Architectural requirements stated that the form of the elevator had to be revealed and expressed as a holistic volumetric structure. Nikolai Dokuchaev, "Programma na izuchenie form dlia II-oi gruppy Osnovnogo otdeleniia Ob'edinennykh masterskikh VKhUTEMASa," quoted in Khan-Magomedov, *Mikhail Korzhev,* 56–57, and Khan-Magomedov, *Ratsionalizm,* 165–67.

66. Moskovskii Gosudarstvennyi Vysshii Khudozhestvenno-Tekhnicheskii Institut, *Programma raboty osnovnogo otdeleniia,* 362.

67. Michael Golston, "'Im Anfang war der Rhythmus': Rhythmic Incubations in Discourses of Mind, Body, and Race from 1850–1944," *Stanford Electronic Humanities Review* 5, Supplement (December 1996): Cultural and Technological Incubations of Fascism; accessed online at https://web.stanford.edu/group/SHR/5-supp/text/golston.html. See also his *Rhythm and Race in Modernist Poetry and Science* (New York: Columbia University Press, 2008).

68. Fritz Giese, *Girlkultur, vergleiche zwischen amerikanischem und europäischem rhythmus und lebensgefühl* (Munich: Delphin-Verlag, 1925), 25.

69. As Peter Michael Mowris has demonstrated, they were influenced by experimental psychology, in particular, the work of Wilhelm Wundt (Mowris, "Nerve Languages: The Critical Response to the Physiological Psychology of Wilhelm Wundt by Dada and Surrealism," PhD dissertation, University of Texas at Austin, 2010). Kandinsky's second cousin, the psychiatrist Viktor Kandinsky, was among the first translators of Wundt's work to Russian (Wundt's *Principles of Physiological Psychology* [1874] was published in his translation in 1880–81). See also Robin Veder, *The Living Line: Modern Art and the Economy of Energy* (Hanover, N.H.: Dartmouth College Press, 2015).

70. Lunacharskii, *Osnovy positivnoi estetiki,* 70.

71. Lunacharskii, *Osnovy positivnoi estetiki,* 115–18; Stierli, *Montage and the Metropolis,* 191.

72. Friedrich Nietzsche, "Sämtliche briefe: Kritische Studienausgabe in 8 Bänden," in *Friedrich Nietzsche,* ed. Giorgio Colli and Mazzino Montinari, vol. 8 (Munich: Deutscher Taschenbuch Verlag, 1986), 1975–84; Moisei Ginzburg, *Ritm v arkhitekture* (Moscow: Sredi kollektsionerov, 1922), 9.

73. Ginzburg, *Ritm v arkhitekture,* 7–9.

74. Golston, *Rhythm and Race in Modernist Poetry and Science*, 7. On the use of psychoanalysis for consumer and political propaganda, see Stuart Ewen, *Captains of Consciousness: Advertising and the Social Roots of the Consumer Culture* (1976; repr., New York: Basic Books, 2008), and *PR! A Social History of Spin* (1996; repr., New York: Basic Books, 2003).

75. Fritz Giese, *Psikhoanaliz i psikhotekhnika,* trans. A. A. Goriainov (Leningrad: Sovremennik, 1926), 17.

76. "It is necessary to introduce visual spatial rhythms (rise, beat, fall) to support and facilitate the perception of a topic," stipulated a guide for the decorators of mass celebrations. A. Kuznetsova, A. Magidson, and Yu. Shchukin, *Oformlenie goroda v dni revoliutsionnykh prazdnenstv* (Moscow: Izogiz, 1932), 66.

77. For more on Lunacharsky's concept of mass spectacle, see Alla Vronskaya, "Objects-Organizers: The Monism of Things and the Art of Socialist Spectacle," in *A History of Russian Exposition and Festival Architecture, 1700–2014,* ed. Alla Aronova and Alexander Ortenberg (London: Routledge, 2018), 151–67.

78. Viktor Kalmykov, "Arkhitekturnye problemy parkov (Doklad po pervomy etapu raboty nad temoi)," 1936, 2; manuscript in the collection of Russian State Archive in Samara.

79. Bachelard's essay "Le Surrationalisme" opened the sole issue of *Inquisitions* (1936), a review edited (among others) by Louis Aragon and Tristan Tzara.

80. Gaston Bachelard, *The Dialectic of Duration* [1936], trans. Mary McAllester Jones (Manchester: Clinamen Press, 2000), 21. The notion of rhythmanalysis was first introduced by the Brazilian philosopher Lucio Alberto Pinheiro dos Santos. *La Rythmanalyse* was published by the Rio de Janeiro Psychological and Philosophical Society in 1931.

81. Henri Lefebvre, *Rhythmanalysis: Space, Time, and Everyday Life* [1992], trans.

Stuart Elden and Gerald Moore (London: Continuum, 2004), 15. Only the triad "time-space-energy," he believed, could adequately analyze reality.

82. Lefebvre, *Rhythmanalysis,* 16–17.

2. Orientation

1. *Izvestiia ASNOVA,* no. 1 (1926). In February 1923, Ladovsky had sent Lissitzky a written invitation to join ASNOVA, and in February 1924 welcomed him, also by mail, as a member (El Lissitzky, *Proun und Wolkenbügel: Schriften, Briefe, Dokumente,* ed. Sophie Lissitzky-Küppers and Jen Lissitzky [Dresden: VEB Verlag der Kunst Dresden, 1977], 177). As late as November 1928, Lissitzky represented ASNOVA at the discussion of Ginzburg's report on the typification of housing at the Gosplan (State Planning Committee) of the Russian Federative Republic. *Sovetskaia arkhitektura* 1 (1929): 26.

2. On Soviet Americanism, see Jean-Louis Cohen, *Building a New New World: "Amerikanizm" in Russian Architecture* (New Haven, Conn.: Yale University Press, 2020).

3. El [El Lissitzky], "Chelovek—mera vsekh portnykh," *Izvestiia ASNOVA,* no. 1 (1926): 10.

4. R[oman] Ia. Khiger, *Puti arkhitekturnoi mysli, 1917–1932* (Moscow: OGIZ-IZOGIZ, 1933), 49.

5. Khan-Magomedov believed that what Lissitzky suggested measuring in architecture was the strength of the psychological effect (Selim Khan-Magomedov, *Lazar' Lissitzky* [Moscow: Russkii Avangard, 2011], 239). Vöhringer saw the clue to the photo collage in the arrow pointing to the pattern and a picture of a boy: a comparison with architecture, she argued, made one recognize the smallness of the human (Margarete Vöhringer, *Avantgarde und Psychotechnik: Wissenschaft, Kunst und Technik der Wahrnehmungsexperimente in der frühen Sowjetunion* [Göttingen: Wallstein Verlag, 2007], 44–46).

6. See, for instance, Alan C. Birnholtz, "El Lissitzky, the Avant-Garde, and the Russian Revolution," *Artforum* 11, no. 1 (1972), 71–76; Werner Hofmann, "Sur un Auto-Portrait de El Lissitzky," *Gazette des beaux-arts* 107 (1986), 39–44; Joachiim Heusinger von Waldegg, "El Lissitzky *Der Konstrukteur* (Selbstbildnis) von 1924: Künstlerbildnis zwischen Funktionalismus und Utopie," *Pantheon: Internationale Jahreszeitschrift für Kunst* 50 (1992): 125–34.

7. See Paul Galvez, "Self-Portrait of the Artist as a Monkey-Hand," *October* 93 (Summer 2000): 109–37; and the section "Hand-Eye" (articles by John Bowlt, Margarita Tupitsyn, and Leah Dickerman) in *Situating El Lissitzky: Vitebsk, Berlin, Moscow,* ed. by Nancy Perloff and Brian Reed (Los Angeles: Getty Research Institute, 2003).

8. Leah Dickerman, "El Lissitzky's Camera Corpus," in Perloff and Reed, *Situating El Lissitzky,* 153–76.

9. El Lissitzky, "The Film of El's Life" [1928], in Sophie Lissitzky-Küppers, *El Lissitzky: Life, Letters, Texts* (New York: Thames and Hudson, 1968), 325.

10. Lissitzky studied at Riga Polytechnic during the First World War, when it was evacuated to Moscow.

11. The sketches of the emblem by Georgy Mapu are reproduced in Selim O.

Khan-Magomedov, *Ratsionalizm (ratsio-arkhitektura) "Formalizm"* (Moscow: Arkhitektura-S, 2007), 29.

12. Giorgio Vasari, *The Lives of the Artists,* trans. Julia Conaway Bondanella and Peter Bondanella (Oxford: Oxford University Press, 1991), 472. For an example of citing this phrase in the Soviet context, see V. E. Bykov, "Kak rabotal Mel'nikov" [1969], in *Konstantin Stepanovich Mel'nikov,* ed. by A. A. Strigalev (Moscow: Iskusstvo, 1985), 241. Here, the saying is wrongly attributed to Leonardo da Vinci.

13. Khan-Magomedov, *Lazar' Lissitzky,* 89–90. For more on the INKhUK debate, see chapter 1.

14. Lissitzky's letter to Küppers, December 12, 1924, Getty Research Institute, cited in Galvez, "Self-Portrait of the Artist as a Monkey-Hand." Friedrich Engels, *The Part Played by Labor in the Transition from Ape to Man* [1876] (New York: International Publishers, 1950).

15. Ernst Kapp, *Elements of a Philosophy of Technology: On the Evolutionary History of Culture* [1877], trans. Lauren K. Wolfe (Minneapolis: University of Minnesota Press, 2018), 19, 35.

16. The photograph had already been used by Lissitzky in 1924 in a Pelican Drawing Ink advertisement.

17. El Lissitzky, "A. and Pangeometry" [1925], in Lissitzky-Küppers, *El Lissitzky: Life, Letters, Texts,* 348.

18. Lissitzky, "The Film of El's Life," 325.

19. El' Lisitskii, "Glaz arkhitektora (izlozhenie knigi E. Mendel'sona)," *Stroitel'naia promyshlennost',* no. 2 (1926); Erich Mendelsohn, *Amerika: Bilderbuch eines Architekten* (Berlin: Rudolf Mosse, 1926). On Lissitzky's reading (and looking at) *Amerika,* see Cohen, *Building a New New World,* 215–26.

20. El Lissitzky, "Die künstlerischen Voraussetzungen zur Standardisierung individueller Möbel für die Bevölkerung: Vortrag für die Sektion Standardisierung NTU VSNCh" [1928], in *Proun und Wolkenbügel.* Russian-language original at the Russian State Archive of Literature and the Arts, fond 2361.

21. Lissitzky, "Die künstlerischen Voraussetzungen zur Standardisierung individueller Möbel für die Bevölkerung," 93.

22. Friedrich Nietzsche, *Beyond Good and Evil* [1886], trans. R. J. Hollingdale (London: Penguin, 1990), 162. Quoted in Bryan L. Moore, *Ecological Literature and the Critique of Anthropocentrism* (London: Palgrave Macmillan, 2017), 20.

23. These ideas were developed by such nineteenth-century art theorists as Adolf Zeising, who suggested the ancient theorem of the golden section as the standard of beauty present in all things natural, including the human.

24. Yve-Alain Bois, "El Lissitzky: Radical Reversibility," *Art in America,* April 1988, 174.

25. Based on the observations collected during two field trips to central Asia in 1931–32, Luria discovered the absence of visual illusions in "primitive" Uzbek people, entering into debate with Kurt Koffka, who argued for the universality of core illusions. A. Yasnitsky, "Kurt Koffka: 'U uzbekov EST' illuzii: zaochnaia polemika mezhdu Luriei i Koffkoi," *Dubna Psychological Journal,* no. 3 (2013): 1–25.

26. Lissitzky, "A. and Pangeometry," 349. See Yve-Alain Bois, "From -∞ to +∞: Axonometry, or Lissitzky's Mathematical Paradigm," in *El Lissitzky, 1890–1940: Architect, Painter, Photographer, Typographer* (Eindhoven: Van Abbe Museum, 1990), 31.

27. Jean Arp, *On My Way: Poetry and Essays, 1912–1947,* trans. Ralph Manheim (New York: Wittenborn, Schultz, 1948), 35. Lissitzky and Arp collaborated on the publication of *Die Kunstismen / Les ismes de l'art / The Isms of Art* (Zurich: Eugen Rentsch Verlag, 1925).

28. Arp, *On My Way,* 91.

29. El Lissitzky and Kurt Schwitters, *Merz,* no. 8–9 (April–July 1924), cover page.

30. Peter Nisbet, "An Introduction to El Lissitzky," in *El Lissitzky, 1890–1941: Catalogue for an Exhibition of Selected Works from North American Collections, the Sprengel Museum Hanover, and the Staatliche Galerie Moritzburg Halle,* ed. by Peter Nisbet (Cambridge, Mass.: Harvard University Art Museums, Busch-Reisinger Museum, 1987), 28–30. Lissitzky and Schwitters were particularly influenced by Francé's books *Die Pflanze als Erfinder* (1920) and *Bios: Die Gesetze der Welt* (1921).

31. Karl Culmann, *Die graphische Statik* (Zurich, 1866). Culmann's discovery was discussed by Kapp (*Elements of a Philosophy of Technology,* 82–84) and D'Arcy Thompson (D'Arcy Wentworth Thompson, *On Growth and Form* [1917; repr., Cambridge: Cambridge University Press, 1945], 976–78). In Russian, it was discussed in detail in P. K. Engelmeier, *Teoriia tvorchestva* (St. Petersburg: Obrazovanie, 1910), 168–72.

32. Kapp, *Elements of a Philosophy of Technology,* 163. On measure, see John Harwood, "The Interface: Ergonomics and the Aesthetics of Survival," in *Governing by Design: Architecture, Economy, and Politics in the Twentieth Century* (Pittsburgh: University of Pittsburgh Press, 2012), 74–83.

33. Cantor's discoveries were popularized in Russia by theologian and theoretician of perspective Pavel Florensky, who used them as evidence against the claims of perspective to truthfulness. Pavel Florenskii, "Obratnaia perspektiva" [1919], *Sochineniia v 4kh tomakh* vol. 3(1) (Moscow: Mysl', 2000), 81–83.

34. El Lissitzky, "Der Suprematismus des Schöpferischen" (originally published as "Suprematizm tvorchestva," *Al'manach Unovis,* no. 1 [1920]), in *Proun und Wolkenbügel,* 19.

35. Nisbet, "An Introduction to El Lissitzky," 29.

36. Jeffrey Herf, *Reactionary Modernism: Technology, Culture, and Politics in Weimar and the Third Reich* (1984; repr., Cambridge: Cambridge University Press, 2003), 49–69.

37. Herf, *Reactionary Modernism,* 62.

38. The collage was used as an illustration to Ilya Ehrenburg's book *Six Stories with Easy Endings.* Il'ia Erenburg, *Shest' povestei o legkikh kontsakh* (Moscow: Gelikon, 1922).

39. Adolf Behne, "Biologie und Kubismus," *Der Sturm,* no. 11–12 (September 1915): 71.

40. Jonathan Crary, *Techniques of the Observer: On Vision and Modernity in the Nineteenth Century* (Cambridge, Mass.: MIT Press, 1990), 128. For more on Crary's interpretation, see chapter 3, "Fitness."

41. David Brewster, *The Stereoscope: Its History, Theory, and Construction* (London, 1856), 53. Quoted in Crary, *Techniques of the Observer,* 120–22.

42. Adolf von Hildebrand, *Das Problem der Form in der bildenden Kunst* (Strasbourg: J. H. E. Heitz, 1893). The book was translated into French (1893), English (1907), and Russian (1914) and was often cited by the rationalists. For more on the rationalists' reading of Hildebrand, see chapter 1.

43. Adolf von Hildebrand, *The Problem of Form in Painting and Sculpture* [1893], trans. Max Meyer and Robert Morris Ogden (New York: G. E. Stechert, 1907), 229–36, 251–60. For a discussion of Hildebrand's planar concept of space in the context of stereoscopic photography, see Richard Difford, "In Defense of Pictorial Space: Stereoscopic Photography and Architecture in the Nineteenth Century," in *Camera Constructs: Photography, Architecture and the Modern City*, ed. Andrew Higgott and Timothy Wray (Farnham: Ashgate, 2014), 295–312.

44. Crary, *Techniques of the Observer*, 125.

45. Gilles Deleuze and Félix Guattari, *A Thousand Plateaus: Capitalism and Schizophrenia*, trans. Brian Massumi (Minneapolis: University of Minnesota Press, 1987), 485. Quoted in Crary, *Techniques of the Observer*, 126.

46. Königsberg, then in East Prussia, is Kalingrad, Russia, today.

47. Martino Stierli, *Montage and the Metropolis: Architecture, Modernity, and the Representation of Space* (New Haven, Conn.: Yale University Press, 2018), 174–75.

48. Lissitzky, "A. and Pangeometry," 350.

49. Auguste Choisy, *Histoire de l'architecture* (Paris: Gauthier-Villars, 1899). As Robin Evans ironically remarked, by making parallel lines converge, perspectival representation in fact broke the laws of Euclidian geometry; while aspiring to get rid of Euclidian geometry, modernist artists introduced something that was even more like it. Robin Evans, *The Projective Cast: Architecture and Its Three Geometries* (Cambridge, Mass.: MIT Press, 2000), 62.

50. Lissitzky, "A. and Pangeometry," 350–51. For more on this diagram, see Bois, "From -∞ to +∞."

51. Linda Dalrymple Henderson, *The Fourth Dimension and Non-Euclidean Geometry in Modern Art* (Princeton, N.J.: Princeton University Press, 1983); Lynn Gamwell, *Mathematics and Art: A Cultural History* (Princeton, N.J.: Princeton University Press, 2016).

52. Malevich's letter to Mikhail Matyushin, June 1913, cited in Evgenii Kovtun, "Kazimir Malevich: His Creative Path," in *Kazimir Malevich, 1878–1935: Works from the State Russian Museum, Leningrad, the State Tretiakov Gallery, Moscow* (Amsterdam: Stedelijk Museum, 1988), 154. See also Peter Michael Mowris, "Nerve Languages: The Critical Response to the Physiological Psychology of Wilhelm Wundt by Dada and Surrealism" (PhD dissertation, University of Texas at Austin, 2010), 172–86.

53. El Lissitzky, "Proun: Nicht Weltvisionen, sondern–Weltrealität," *De Stijl* 5, no. 6 (1922): 83.

54. Ladovsky's interest in set theory arose from his work on standardization: the problem that he hoped to resolve was the combination of standardized architectural modules and details. Similarly, around the same time, Lissitzky was engaged in designing furniture that was "combinable" from standardized parts. For more on standardization, see chapter 4, "Process."

55. See, for instance, the widespread Minnesota Spatial Relations Test, developed

prior to 1930. D. G. Peterson et al., *Minnesota Mechanical Ability Tests* (Minneapolis: University of Minnesota Press, 1930). As early as 1910, Russian "testologist" Grigory Rossolimo suggested testing "the ability of combination" with a puzzle-like test that asked the subject to combine two-dimensional shapes into a geometric figure. G. I. Rossolimo, *Psikhologicheskie profili: Metod kolichestvennogo issledovaniia psikhicheskikh protsessov v normal'nom i patologicheskom sostoianii* (St. Petersburg: M. A. Aleksandrov, 1910), 38.

56. Wilhelm Ostwald, *Die Welt der Formen,* vols. 1–4 (Leipzig: Unesma, 1922–25). See Thomas Hapke, "Wilhelm Ostwald's Combinatorics as a Link between Information and Form," *Library Trends* 61, no. 2 (2012): 286–303.

57. N[ikolai] Ladovskii, introduction to G[eorgii] Krutikov, "Prilozhenie teorii soedinenii k issledovaniiu i izmereniiu sposobnosti prostranstvennogo kombinirovaniia," *Arkhitektura i VKhUTEIN,* no. 1 (1929): 5.

58. Hermann Maertens, *Der Optische-Maassstab, oder, Die Theorie und Praxis des ästhetischen Sehens in den bildenden Künsten: Auf Grund der Lehre der physiologischen Optik* (Bonn: Max Cohen & Sohn, 1877). For a discussion of Maertens's book, see Albert Erich Brinckmann, "Der Optische Maßstab für Monumentalbauten im Stadtbau," *Wasmuths Monatshefte für Baukhunst* 2 (1914): 57; Ákos Moravánszky, "The Optical Construction of Urban Space: Hermann Maertens, Camillo Sitte and the Theories of 'Aesthetic Perception,'" *Journal of Architecture* 17, no. 5 (2012): 655–66.

59. Lisitskii, "Glaz arkhitektora." Here cited after: El Lissitzky, "Das Auge des Architekten," in *Proun und Wolkenbügel,* 64.

60. Dziga Vertov, "The Council of Three" [1923], in *Kino-eye: The Writings of Dziga Vertov,* trans. Kevin O'Brien, ed. by Annette Michelson (Berkeley: University of California Press, 2008), 17. Similar ideas were simultaneously explored by Alexander Rodchenko in his photographic work.

61. El' Lisitskii, "Arkhitektura zheleznoi i zhelezobetonnoi ramy," *Stroitel'naia promyshlennost',* no. 1 (1926): 63.

62. "Here the 250-meter aerial masts stand in one spot," Lissitzky had earlier written about the transmitting station in German Nauen. "The Egyptian Pyramid is obsolete" (Lissitzky, "Wheel—Propeller and What Follows" [1923], translated in Lissitzky-Küppers, *El Lissitzky: Life, Letters, Texts,* 349). The image resembled the so-called spherical perspective (invented by artist Kuzma Petrov-Vodkin shortly earlier), which employed a high horizon line recessing toward the edges of the painting and making horizontal surfaces convex.

63. Lissitzky, "Das Auge des Architekten," 67. Although this building by architect Ernest R. Graham, photographed by Knud Lönberg-Holm, was reproduced in Mendelsohn's book, Lissitzky used another image in the *Izvestia ASNOVA* photo collage.

64. Commercial sewing patterns proliferated in Europe and the United States from the 1860s on. Joy Spanabel Emery, *A History of the Paper Pattern Industry: The Home Dressmaking Fashion Revolution* (London: Bloomsbury, 2014), 29–34.

65. Maria Gough, "Constructivism Disoriented: El Lissitzky's Dresden and Hannover *Demonstrationsräume,*" in Perloff and Reed, *Situating El Lissitzky,* 77–125.

66. El Lissitzky, "Proun: Not World Visions, BUT—World Reality" [1920], in Lissitzky-Küppers, *El Lissitzky: Life, Letters, Texts*, 343.

67. Lissitzky, "A. and Pangeometry," 352.

68. László Moholy-Nagy, *The New Vision* [1928], trans. Daphne M. Hoffmann (New York: Wittenborn, Schultz, 1947), 57.

69. Sigfried Giedion, "Lebendige Museen," *Der Cicerone* 21, no. 4 (1929): 105–6. Translated in Lissitzky-Küppers, *El Lissitzky: Life, Letters, Texts*, 379.

70. Maria Gough, "Lissitzky on Broadway," in *Modern Photographs: The Thomas Walther Collection 1909–1949*, ed. Mitra Abbaspour, Lee Ann Daffner, and Maria Morris Hambourg (New York: Museum of Modern Art, 2014), https://www.moma.org/interactives/objectphoto/assets/essays/Gough.pdf. ASNOVA's project—the major practical preoccupation of the association—remained unrealized.

71. Mendelsohn, *Amerika*, 44.

72. For accounts of the project and its reception in English, see Selim Khan-Magomedov, *The Flying City and Beyond*, trans. Christina Lodder (Barcelona: Tenov Books, 2015), and Alla Vronskaya, "Two Utopias of Georgii Krutikov's City of the Future," in *Writing Cities: Working Papers*, vol. 2, *Distance and Cities: Where Do We Stand?*, ed. Gunter Gassner, Adam Kaasa, and Katherine Robinson (London: London School of Economics and Political Science, 2012), 46–56.

73. "Dela Asnovy," *Izvestia ASNOVA*, no. 1 (1926): 6 (the article mentions that the work on the architectural design of Tsiolkovsky's dirigible was conducted by Lissitzky and Krutikov in collaboration with engineer Vinogradov [first name unknown]); Selim Khan-Magomedov, *Georgii Krutikov* (Moscow: Russkii Avangard, 2008), 118–30.

74. The Archive of the A. V. Shchusev State Museum of Architecture, Moscow, Georgy Krutikov's collection, KPof 5291/131.

75. The first table explored the situation in which the moving object and its trajectory visually merged, creating, as it were, a new body endowed with new physical qualities: examples included lightning, a flying airplane, a falling meteorite, and long-exposure photography. The second table described connections between static and vertical compositions (such as a skyscraper) on the one hand, and between dynamic and horizontal compositions (such as a profile of a city) on the other. In the third table, Krutikov presented the discovery he made in the laboratory: "when moving, two equal forms are perceived as having different sizes depending on their location on the axis of movement."

76. Heinz Rasch and Bodo Rasch, *Wie bauen? Materialien und Konstruktionen für industrielle Produktion* (Stuttgart: Wedekind, 1928), 156–57. Lönberg-Holm's membership in ASNOVA is mentioned in *Izvestia ASNOVA*, no. 1 (1926): 1. From 1929, Lönberg-Holm was also an American delegate to the International Congresses of Modern Architecture (Congrès internationaux d'architecture moderne, CIAM). At least two meetings between Lissitzky and Lönberg-Holm are documented in the latter's archive (letter to Til Brugmann, 1923; I am indebted to Adrian Täckman for this information). Lönberg-Holm, Fuller, and Frederick Kiesler befriended each other in 1929 and met often, elaborating a "functionalist" concept of modernism that they juxtaposed to Philip Johnson's "interna-

tional style." See Suzanne Strum, *The Ideal of Total Environmental Control: Knud Lönberg-Holm, Buckminster Fuller, and the SSA* (London: Routledge, 2018).

77. Georg Simmel, "Metropolis and Mental Life" [1903], in *The Blackwell City Reader,* ed. Gary Bridge and Sophie Watson (Malden, Mass.: Blackwell, 2002), 11. Simmel's text was well known in Russia. It was discussed in detail, for example, by Alexander Toporkov in *Tekhnicheskii byt i sovremennoe iskusstvo* (Moscow: Gosudarstvennoe izdatel'stvo, 1928).

78. Erich Mendelsohn, Erich Mendelsohn's "Amerika": 82 Photographs [1926] (New York: Dover, 1993), 56.

79. Michael K. Hays, *Modernism and the Posthumanist Subject* (Cambridge, Mass.: MIT Press, 1992), 192–94.

80. El Lissitzky, *Russia: An Architecture for World Revolution* [1930], trans. Eric Dluhosch (Cambridge, Mass.: MIT Press, 1970), 62.

81. El Lissitzky, "Suprematism in World Reconstruction," in Lissitzky-Küppers, *El Lissitzky: Life, Letters, Texts,* 328.

82. Lissitzky, "Suprematism in World Reconstruction," 329.

83. In 1914, Brinckmann elaborated Hildebrand's parenthetical idea that optical scale could be used for an analysis of buildings' visual proportional relationships. In "Optical Scale for Monumental Structures in City Planning," he introduced a new set of concepts, such as the visual effect of buildings' scale, the *Leitlinie* (optical transition between scales), and an expression of scale through an articulation of surface (Brinckmann, "Der Optische Maßstab für Monumentalbauten im Städtebau"). Brinckmann's article was cited by N. Dokuchaev in "Osnovy iskusstva arkhitektury: Kurs dlia khudozhestvennykh tekhnikumov," in *Sbornik materialov po khudozhestvennomu obrazovaniiu* (Moscow: Gosudarstvennoe izdatel'stvo, 1927), 97.

84. N. Dokuchaev, "Arkhitektura i planirovka gorodov," *Sovetskoe Iskusstvo,* no. 6 (1926): 14.

85. Enael [N. A. Ladovskii], "Neboskreby SSSR i Ameriki," *Izvestia ASNOVA,* no. 1 (1926): 5–6.

86. El' Lisitskii, "Seria neboskrebov dlia Moskvy: WB 1 (1923–1925)," *Izvestia ASNOVA,* no. 1 (1926): 2–3. Lissitzky discussed the structural aspects of the project with Swiss architect Emil Roth. See Christoph Bürkle and Werner Oechslin, *El Lissitzky: Der Traum vom Wolkenbügel. El Lissitzky-Emil Roth-Mart Stam* (Zurich: gta Ausstellungen, 1991), and Samuel Johnson, "El Lissitzky's Other *Wolkenbügel*: Reconstructing an Abandoned Architectural Project," *Art Bulletin* 99, no. 3 (September 2017): 147–69.

87. Lisitskii, "Seria neboskrebov dlia Moskvy," 2. In this sense, the *Wolkenbügels* presaged Lissitzky's later work on developing color schemes for Kuznetsky Most and Dzerzhinsky streets in Moscow, which (alongside several other artists, who were responsible for other streets) he conducted following Leiba Antokolsky's recommendations to code the city by color whose intensity increased proportionately to the centrality of the area, inducing people to move in that direction.

88. El' Lisitskii, "Amerikanizm v evropeiskoi arkhitekture," *Krasnaia Niva,* no. 49 (1925): 1189.

89. Toporkov, *Tekhnicheskii byt i sovremennoe iskusstvo,* 80.

90. Toporkov, *Tekhnicheskii byt i sovremennoe iskusstvo,* 100.

91. Lisitskii, "Amerikanizm v evropeiskoi arkhitekture," 1189; Lisitskii, "Arkhitektura zheleznoi i zhelezobetonnoi ramy," 61–62.

92. Standardized and prefabricated parts were to be assembled on site without the use of scaffolding. Lisitskii, "Seria neboskrebov dlia Moskvy," 3.

93. See Lissitzky, "Proun Room, Great Berlin Art Exhibition" [1923], in Lissitzky-Küppers, *El Lissitzky: Life, Letters, Texts,* 361.

94. El Lissitzky, "Exhibition Rooms," in Lissitzky-Küppers, *El Lissitzky: Life, Letters, Texts,* 362.

95. Gough, "Constructivism Disoriented," 93.

96. In the words of Martino Stierli, these representations invited the viewer "to walk around the structure in his or her imagination and gain a more complete idea of the building than a single representation can provide." Stierli, *Montage and the Metropolis,* 101.

97. Lissitzky, "Proun," 343. On the affinity between the Prouns and the W2 *Wolkenbügel,* see Johnson, "El Lissitzky's Other *Wolkenbügel.*"

98. Hays, *Modernism and the Posthumanist Subject,* 6.

99. Moore, *Ecological Literature,* 19–20; H. P. Blavatzky, *The Secret Doctrine: The Synthesis of Science, Religion, and Philosophy,* vol. 2 (1888; Theosophical University Press Online Edition, https://www.theosociety.org/pasadena/sd-pdf /SecretDoctrineVol2_eBook.pdf), 684, 197–201.

100. Lissitzky, "Der Suprematismus des Schöpferischen," 20.

3. Fitness

1. The anecdote is reported by Margarete Vöhringer after Selim Khan-Magomedov's words. Margarete Vöhringer, *Avantgarde und Psychotechnik: Wissenschaft, Kunst und Technik der Wahrnehmungsexperimente in der frühen Sowjetunion* (Göttingen: Wallstein Verlag, 2007), 35.

2. Richard Difford, "Infinite Horizons: Le Corbusier, the Pavillon de l'Esprit Nouveau Dioramas and the Science of Visual Distance," *Journal of Architecture* 14, no. 3 (2009): 295–323.

3. See Mary Nolan, *Visions of Modernity: American Business and the Modernization of Germany* (Oxford: Oxford University Press, 1994). On Americanism in Soviet architecture, see Jean-Louis Cohen, *Building a New New World: "Amerikanizm" in Russian Architecture* (New Haven, Conn.: Yale University Press, 2020), and Danilo Udovički-Selb, *Soviet Architectural Avant-Gardes: Architecture and Stalin's Revolution from Above, 1928–1938* (London: Bloomsbury, 2020).

4. Siegfried Kracauer, "The Salaried Masses: Duty and Destruction in Weimar Germany" [1930], in *Class: The Anthology,* ed. Stanley Aronowitz and Michael J. Roberts (London: Wiley Blackwell, 2018), 223.

5. Michael Osman, *Modernism's Visible Hand: Architecture and Regulation in America* (Minneapolis: University of Minnesota Press, 2018), 131.

6. Sonia Melnikova-Raich, "The Soviet Problem with Two 'Unknowns': How an American Architect and a Soviet Negotiator Jump-Started the Industrialization of Russia, Part I: Albert Kahn," *Journal of the Society for Industrial Archeology* 36,

no. 2 (2010): 57–80; Christina E. Crawford. "From Tractors to Territory: Socialist Urbanization through Standardization," in "Second World Urbanity," special issue, *Journal of Urban History* 44, no. 1 (2017): 54–77; Cohen, *Building a New New World,* 144–307.

7. See Claire Zimmerman, "The Labor of Albert Kahn," Aggregate, December 12, 2014, http://www.we-aggregate.org/piece/the-labor-of-albert-kahn.

8. On Fordism in Russia, see Cohen, *Building a New New World,* 133–44.

9. Henry-Russell Hitchcock, "The Architecture of Bureaucracy and the Architecture of Genius," *Architectural Review,* January 1947, 3–6, quoted in Zimmerman, "The Labor of Albert Kahn."

10. Nikolai Il'inskii, "Vziat' vse luchshee is amerikanskogo proektirovaniia, *Stroitel'stvo Moskvy,* no. 11 (1931): 25.

11. Melnikova-Raich, "The Soviet Problem," 62–63.

12. *Torgovo-promyshlennaia gazeta,* June 12, 1929, quoted in I. A. Kazus', *Sovetskaia arkhitektura 1920-kh godov: Organizatsiia proektirovaniia* (Moscow: Progress-Traditsiia, 2009), 141.

13. Mary McLeod, "'Architecture or Revolution': Taylorism, Technocracy, and Social Change," *Art Journal* 43, no. 2 (Summer 1983): 137.

14. For discussions of Gastev's scientific organization of labor, see Devin Fore, "The Operative Word in Soviet Factography," *October* 118 (Fall 2006): 95–131; Barbara Wurm, "Factory," in *Revoliutsiia! Demonstratsiia! Soviet Art Put to the Test,* ed. Matthew S. Witkovsky and Devin Fore (Chicago: Art Institute of Chicago, 2017), 218–25, particularly the discussion of Gastev's "visual interface" *(zritel'naia ustanovka),* which subjected the eye to the same mechanizing training as other body elements and their movements (222–23); and Cohen, *Building a New New World,* 101–8, 117–33.

15. See Julia Kursell, "*Piano Mécanique* and *Piano Biologique*: Nikolai Bernstein's Neurophysiological Study of Piano Touch," *Configurations* 14, no. 3 (Fall 2006): 245–73. I am thankful to Myles Jackson for this reference.

16. Andrey Smirnov, *Sound in Z: Experiments in Sound and Electronic Music in Early-20th-Century Russia* (London: Sound and Music and Koenig Books, 2013), 115–32.

17. For an analysis of stereophotogrammetry in the work of Marcel Duchamp, see Penelope Haralambidou, "Stereoscopy and the Architecture of Visual Space," in *Camera Constructs: Photography, Architecture and the Modern City,* ed. Andrew Higgott and Timothy Wray (Farnham: Ashgate, 2014), 313–30.

18. Aleksandr Bogdanov, "O tendentsiiakh proletarskoi kul'tury (Otvet A. Gastevu)," *Proletarskaia Kul'tura* 9–10 (1919): 46.

19. V[ladimir] Lenin, "'Nauchnaia' sistema vyzhimaniia pota" [1913], in *Polnoe sobranie sochinenii,* vol. 23 (Moscow: Izdatel'stvo politicheskoi literatury, 1973), 18; V[ladimir] Lenin, "Sistema Teilora—poraboshchenie cheloveka mashinoi" [1914], in *Polnoe sobranie sochinenii,* vol. 24 (Moscow: Izdatel'stvo politicheskoi literatury, 1973), 369.

20. Andrei Burov, *Pis'ma. Dnevniki. Besedy s aspirantami. Suzhdeniia sovremennikov* (Moscow: Iskusstvo, 1980), 35, cited in Kazus', *Sovetskaia arkhitektura 1920-kh godov,* 141.

21. Anatolii Lunacharskii, "Chto takoe obrazovanie" [1918], in *O vospitanii i obrazovanii* (Moscow: Pedagogika, 1986), 356.

22. In 1930, VKhUTEIN was again reorganized, as VASI (Vysshii Arkhitekturno-Stroietel'nyi Institut, Higher Institute of Architecture and Construction). Bruno Taut, "Spetsialisty," *Russko-germanskii vestnik nauki i tekhniki* 3 (1931): 49–50, cited in Kazus', *Sovetskaia arkhitektura 1920-kh godov,* 143. A similar adherence to holism and humanistic education *(Bildung)* was demonstrated by László Moholy-Nagy. See Zeynep Çelik Alexander, *Kinaesthetic Knowing: Aesthetics, Epistemology, Modern Design* (Chicago: University of Chicago Press, 2017), 183–84.

23. Cited in Andreas Killen, "Weimar Psychotechnics between Americanism and Fascism," in "The Self as Project: Politics and the Human Sciences," special issue, *Osiris* 22, no. 1 (2007): 50.

24. See Annette Mülberger, "Mental Association: Testing Individual Differences before Binet," *Journal of the History of the Behavioral Sciences* 53, no. 2 (Spring 2017): 176–98; Benoît Godin, "From Eugenics to Scientometrics: Galton, Cattell, and Men of Science," *Social Studies of Science* 37, no. 5 (2007): 691–728.

25. Translations included the works of Münsterberg and Fritz Giese, and such books as Georg Schlesinger *Psychotechnik und Betriebswissenschaft* (1922 and 1925 [1920]), and Franciszka Baumgarten, *Psychotechnics* (translation of her essays, 1922 and 1926). Among the original publications were S[olomon] G. Gellerstein, *Psikhotekhnika* (Moscow: Novaia Moskva, 1926); N[ikolai] D. Levitov, *Psikhotekhnika i professional'naia prigodnost': Problemy i metody* (Moscow: Mozdravotd., 1924).

26. For more on psychotechnics in Russia, see Franciska Baumgarten, *Arbeitswissenschaft und Psychotechnik in Russland* (Munich: R. Oldenbourg, 1924); Paul Devinat, *Scientific Management in Europe* (Geneva: International Labor Office,1927); N. S. Kurek, *Istoria likvidatsii pedologii i psikhotekhniki v SSSR* (St. Petersburg: Alteiia, 2004); Marcel Turbiaux, "Sous le drapeau rouge: La conférence internationale de psychotechnique de Moscou de 1931," *Bulletin de psychologie* 5, no. 527 (2013): 417–35; 6, no. 528 (2013): 513–26.

27. In 1901, Alexander Nechaev founded the Laboratory for Experimental Pedagogical Psychology, where he designed a set of simplified experimental devices and testing cards for the use of school teachers. As early as the 1910s, the founder of "characterology" (character studies) Alexander Lazursky and neuro- and development pathologist Grigory Rossolimo had developed a method of graphic representation of the psychological profile of a child. See Valerii Kadnevskii, *Istoriia testov* (Moscow: Narodnoe obrazovanie, 2004), and Andy Byford, "The Mental Test as a Boundary Object in Early-20th-Century Russian Child Science," *History of the Human Sciences* 27, no. 4 (2014): 22–58.

28. See, for instance, I. V. Aevergetov, *Vvedenie v eksperimental'nuiu pedagogiku* (Leningrad: 1-aia Tip. Transpechati NKPS im. Vorovskogo, 1925).

29. Quoted in Gellerstein, *Psikhotekhnika,* 27–28.

30. Tijana Vujošević, *Modernism and the Making of the Soviet New Man* (Manchester: Manchester University Press, 2017), 37–38.

31. Quoted in Sonia Moore, "The Method of Physical Actions," *Tulane Drama Review* 9, no. 4 (Summer 1965): 92. See also O. V. Aronson, "Neokonchennaia polemika:

Biomekhanika Meierkhol'da ili psikhotekhnika Stanislavskogo?," *Russkaia antropologicheskaia shkola. Trudy* 4, no. 1 (2007): 410–23.

32. Konstantin Stanislavskii, "Rabota aktera nad soboi," in *Sobranie Sochinenii v 8mi tt.* (Moscow: Iskusstov, 1954–61), vol. 3, 316.

33. For more on the collectivist roots of this program, see chapter 1 of this book.

34. Nikolai Ladovskii, "Psikhotekhnicheskaia laboratoriia arkhitektury"; selection translated from Russian by Anatole Senkevitch Jr., "Trends in Soviet Architectural Thought, 1917–1932: The Growth and Decline of the Constructivist and Rationalist Movements" (PhD dissertation, Cornell University, 1974), 335–36. Hugo Münsterberg, *Grundzüge der Psychotechnik* (Leipzig: Barth, 1914), 610.

35. Georgii Krutikov, "Arkhitekturnaia nauchno-issledovatel'skaia laboratoriia pri Arkhitekturnom fakul'tete Moskovskogo Vysshego Khud.-Tekhnich. Instituta," *Stroitel'naia promyshlennost'*, no. 5 (1928): 374.

36. Aleksandr Karra, "Za sotsialisticheskuiu ratsionalizatsiiu proektnykh kontor," *Stroitel'stvo Moskvy*, no. 4 (1930): 2–5, quoted in Kazus', *Sovetskaia arkhitektura 1920-kh godov*, 143–44. For the ensuing discussion (responses by A. V. Fridliand and N. A. Krapukhin), see Fridliand, "Kak ratsionalizirovat' proektirovanie?," *Stroitel'stvo Moskvy*, no. 7 (1930): 17–20; Krapukhin, "Struktura proektnoi kontory," *Stroitel'noe proektirovanie* 1 (1931): 13–17.

37. The Dalton Plan was introduced to Soviet Russia in 1923 and was actively used until its condemnation by the decree of the Central Committee of the Communist Party in August 1932.

38. Quoted in Kazus', *Sovetskaia arkhitektura 1920-kh godov*, 142. See also I. S. Cheredina and P. P. Zueva, "Eshche odna stranitsa v istorii russkoi arkhitektury sovetskogo perioda," in *Arkhitektura mira: Materialy konferentsii "Zapad-Vostok: Lichnost' v istorii arkhitektury*," vol. 4 (Moscow: Arkhitektura, 1995), 151–56. Meyer also testified that "his" projects were in fact results of the collective work of a group of people from different backgrounds and with different areas of expertise ("Kak ia rabotaiu," *Arkhitektura SSSR* 6 [1933]: 34–35).

39. Lewis Siegelbaum, "Production Collectives and Communes and the 'Imperatives' of Soviet Industrialization, 1929–1931," *Slavic Review* 45, no. 1 (Spring 1986): 65–84.

40. Karra, "Za sotsialisticheskuiu ratsionalizatsiiu proektnykh kontor," 4.

41. For a similar scheme of American factory organization, see Osman, *Modernism's Visible Hand*, 155.

42. Quoted in Kazus', *Sovetskaia arkhitektura 1920-kh gorov*, 73.

43. Anatolii Lunacharskii, "Iskusstvo slova v shkole" [1928], in *O vospitanii i obrazovanii*, 467.

44. Karra, "Za sotsialisticheskuiu ratsionalizatsiiu proektnykh kontor," 4.

45. G. T. Krutikov, "Arkhitekturnaia nauchno-issledovatel'skaia laboratoriia pri Arkhitekturnom fakul'tete VKhUTEIN," *Arkhitektura i VKhUTEIN*, no. 1 (1929): 2–4.

46. Krutikov, "Arkhitekturnaia nauchno-issledovatel'skaia laboratoriia pri Arkhitekturnom fakul'tete Moskovskogo Vysshego Khud.-Tekhnich. Instituta," 375.

47. Hugo Münsterberg, *Vocation and Learning: A Popular Reading Course. Part IV. Vocation* (St. Louis, Mo.: Lewis Publishing Company, 1916), 241–44.

48. Krutikov, "Arkhitekturnaia nauchno-issledovatel'skaia laboratoriia pri Arkhitekturnom fakul'tete VKhUTEIN": 2.

49. G. I. Rossolimo, *Psikhologicheskie profili: Metod kolichestvennogo issledovaniia psikhicheskikh protsessov v normal'nom i patologicheskom sostoianii* (St. Petersburg: M. A. Aleksandrov, 1910). The work of Rossolimo and his colleague Fedor Rybakov pioneered psychological testing and was highly esteemed by Giese.

50. Gellerstein, *Psikhotekhnika,* 12.

51. See Hermann von Helmholtz, *Handbuch der Physiologischen Optik* (Leipzig: L. Voss, 1867); Paul Kramer, "Anmerkungen zur Theorie der räumlichen Tiefenwahrnehmung," *Jahresbericht des Königlich Preuß. Gymnasiums zu Schleusingen,* 1872: 3–38; Carl Stumpf, *Über den psychologischen Ursprung der Raumvorstellungen* (Leipzig: S. Hirzel, 1873).

52. Editor, "What Does Anschauung Mean?," *The Monist* 2, no. 4 (July 1892): 530. Albert E. Brinckmann, *Plastik und Raum als Grundformen künstlerischer Gestaltung* (Munich: R. Piper, 1922).

53. See Vladimir Krinskii, "Otchet o teoreticheskoi rabote gruppy arkhitektorov IKhUK," in Selim O. Khan-Magomedov, *Ratsionalizm (ratsio-arkhitektura) "Formalizm"* (Moscow: Arkhitektura-S, 2007), 126–27, and N. Dokuchaev, "Osnovy iskusstva arkhitektury: Kurs dlia khudozhestvennykh tekhnikumov," in *Sbornik materialov po khudozhestvennomu obrazovaniiu* (Moscow: Gosudarstvennoe izdatel'stvo, 1927), 97.

54. Dokuchaev, "Poiasnitel'naia zapiska k kursu 'iskusstvo arkhitektury' dlia khudozhestvennykh tekhnikumov," in *Sbornik materialov po khudozhestvennomu obrazovaniiu,* 79.

55. Among the publications that attracted his interest and were, he believed, worth studying by architects were Edgar Pierce, "Aesthetics of Simple Forms (I): Symmetry," *Psychological Review* 1 (1894): 483–96; Ethel D. Puffer, "Studies in Symmetry," *Harvard Psychological Studies* 1 (1903): 467–541; Rosewell Parker Angier, "The Aesthetics of Unequal Division," *Harvard Psychological Studies* 1 (1903): 541–64; Eleanor Harris Rowland, "The Aesthetics of Repeated Space Forms," *Harvard Psychological Studies* 2 (1906): 193–269.

56. Wilhelm Wundt, *Vorlesungen über die Menschen- und Tierseele* (Leipzig: Voß, 1863), 164.

57. Hugo Münsterberg, *Business Psychology* (Chicago: La Salle Extension University, 1915), 13–14.

58. Selim O. Khan-Magomedov, *Georgii Krutikov* (Moscow: Russkii Avangard, 2008), 39–40.

59. See, for instance, E. Zimmermann, *Psychologische und Physiologische Apparate: Liste 50* (Leipzig, 1928).

60. Georgy Krutikov described the set of devices for assessing visual estimation in "Arkhitekturnaia nauchno-issledovatel'skaia laboratoriia pri Arkhitekturnom fakul'tete VKhUTEIN," 2–4, and publicized them in "Arkhitekturnaia nauchno-issledovatel'skaia laboratoria pri Arkhitekturnom fakul'tete Moskovskogo Vysshego Khud.-Tekhnich. Instituta," 372–75.

61. A. I. Tupikova-Fraishtadt, "Apparat dlia ispytaniia lineinogo staticheskogo glazomera," in *Voprosy somaticheskogo i psikhotekhnicheskogo profpodbora voditelei mestnogo transporta* (Leningrad: Transportnoe upravlenie Lensoveta, 1936), 195–96.

62. These tests were common in measuring intelligence and had a wider application; for example, the "Alpha Test" was developed by American psychologist Robert Yerkes to select recruits for the United States Army during the First World War.

63. See R. S. Turner, *In the Eye's Mind: Vision and the Helmholtz-Hering Controversy* (Princeton, N.J.: Princeton University Press, 1994).

64. For more on this concept of Ladovsky, see chapter 1.

65. P. A. Rudik, *Standarty psikhotekhnicheskikh ispytanii* (Leningrad: Prakticheskaia meditsina, 1926), 8.

66. Krutikov, "Arkhitekturnaia nauchno-issledovatel'skaia laboratoriia pri Arkhitekturnom fakul'tete Moskovskogo Vysshego Khud.-Tekhnich. Instituta," 374–75.

67. Rudik, *Standarty psikhotekhnicheskikh ispytanii,* 7–8.

68. I am deeply indebted to the participants of the seminar "Curating *1917: The Architecture of the Russian Revolution*" at the ETH Zurich (in particular, to Pierluigi D'Acunto and Juan Jose Castellon Gonzalez) and to my co-teacher Torsten Lange for helping me analyze the mechanism of its work.

69. Krutikov, "Arkhitekturnaia nauchno-issledovatel'skaia laboratoriia pri Arkhitekturnom fakul'tete Moskovskogo Vysshego Khud.-Tekhnich. Instituta," 374–75.

70. Ewald Hering, "Der Raumsinn und Bewegungen des Auges," in *Handbuch der Physiologie,* ed. Ludimar Hermann (Leipzig: Vogel, 1879–80), 3.1:343–601 (translated into Russian in 1888). In Russian, see G. Chelpanov, *Problema vospriiatiia prostranstva v sviazi s ucheniem ob aprionosti i vrozhdennosti* (Kyiv: I. N. Kushner, 1896), Part 1 "Predstavlenie prostranstva s tochki zreniia psikhologii," 250–327. A similar but enclosed device was used by Edward Titchener ("Photograph Album on Psychological Instruments," 1895, Collection Rand B. Evans; published online at http://vlp.uni-regensburg.de/library/data/lit13651/index_html?pn=31&ws=1.5).

71. Fritz Giese, *Psychotechnische Eignungsprüfungen an Erwachsenen* (Langensalza: Wendt & Klauwell, 1921), 15–16.

72. Giese, *Psychotechnische Eignungsprüfungen an Erwachsenen,* 16.

73. I am deeply indebted to Martin Frimmer for helping me understand the work of the space-meter's optical part.

74. As early as 1856, British scientist Robert Hunt reported that "the stereoscope is now seen in every drawing room; philosophers talk learnedly upon it, ladies are delighted with its magic representations, and children play with it." "The Stereoscope," *Art Journal* 18 (March 1856): 118.

75. This stereoscope is currently on display at Gorki house-museum (Moscow region, Russia).

76. Jonathan Crary, *Techniques of the Observer: On Vision and Modernity in the Nineteenth Century* (Cambridge, Mass.: MIT Press, 1990), 129–32.

77. Like other techniques of viewing, stereographs were used in both science and

entertainment. The fact that any attempts to retouch the image inevitably led to the visual effect of "floating" of the modified part gave stereography an air of truthfulness, contributing to its documentary credibility. See Robert J. Silverman, "The Stereoscope and Photographic Depiction in the 19th Century," in "Biomedical and Behavioral Technology," special issue, *Technology and Culture* 34, no. 4 (1993): 729–56.

78. Ernst Mach, "On the Stereoscopic Application of Roentgen's Rays," *The Monist* 6, no. 3 (April 1896): 321–23.

79. S. Kravkov, *Glaz i ego rabota* (Moscow: Meditsina, 1932). Kravkov taught at VKhUTEMAS/VKhUTEIN between 1924 and 1928.

80. See G. I. Chelpanov, "Obzor noveishei literatury po voprosu o vospriiatii prostranstva," *Voprosy filosofii i psikhologii* 37 (1897): 276–87.

81. S. Kravkov, *Glaz i ego rabota,* 2nd ed. (Moscow: Meditsina, 1945), 292; N. D. Levitov, "Problemy, metody i osnovnye vyvody issledovaniia po difpodboru v FZU po kholodnoi obrabotke metalla," in *Differentsial'nyi podbor v shkoly FZU metallopromyshlennosti,* ed. N. D. Levitov and V. N. Skorsyrev (Moscow: Tsentr. nauch.-issl. in-t okhrany zdorov'ia detei i podrostkov, 1935), 22.

82. Eduard von Hartmann, "Die Stellung der Baukunst in der modernen Ästhetik," *Westermanns Illustrierte Deutsche Monatshefte* 59 (1886): 744.

83. Adolf von Hildebrand, *The Problem of Form in Painting and Sculpture* [1893], trans. Max Meyer and Robert Morris Ogden (New York: G. E. Stechert, 1907), 241.

84. Seeing, for example, could be "linear" or "painterly." Heinrich Wölfflin, *Kunstgeschichtliche Grundbegriffe: Das Problem der Stilentwicklung in der neueren Kunst* (Munich: H. Bruckmann, 1921), 11–12. See Çelik Alexander, *Kinaesthetic Knowing,* 63–96.

85. Khan-Magomedov, *Ratsionalizm,* 371. No images or descriptions of this device have been preserved.

86. Çelik Alexander, *Kinaesthetic Knowing,* 89.

87. Alfred North Whitehead, *Science and the Modern World* (New York: Macmillan, 1925), 59, quoted in Donald Worster, *Nature's Economy: A History of Ecological Ideas* (Cambridge: Cambridge University Press), 316.

88. Karra, "Za sotsialisticheskuiu ratsionalizatsiiu proektnykh kontor," 2.

4. Process

1. A. Toporkov, *Tekhicheskii byt i sovremennoe iskusstvo* (Moscow: Gosudarstvennoe izdatel'stvo, 1928), 132–33.

2. Johannes Bochenek, *Die männliche und weibliche Normal-Gestalt nach einem neuen System* (Berlin: A. Haak, 1875).

3. See Karen Rader, *Making Mice: Standardizing Animals for American Biomedical Research, 1900–1955* (Princeton, N.J.: Princeton University Press, 2004). I am thankful to Marion Thomas for this reference.

4. Nader Vossoughian, "Standardization Reconsidered: Normierung in and after Ernst Neufert's *Bauentwurfslehre* (1936)," *Grey Room,* no. 54 (Winter 2014): 35. See also John Harwood, "The Interface: Ergonomics and the Aesthetics of Survival," in *Governing by Design: Architecture, Economy, and Politics in the Twentieth Century* (Pittsburgh: University of Pittsburgh Press, 2012), 70–92.

5. L. Il'in, A. Klein, and A. Rozenberg, "Poiasnitel'naia zapiska k proektu gorodskoi bol'nitsy imeni Petra Velikago pod devizom 'Zelenyi krug," *Zodchii,* no. 47 (1906): 473–78, 483–86; Il'in, Klein, and Rozenberg, *Proekt gorodskoi bol'nitsy imeni Petra Velikago v S.-Peterburge na 1000 krovatei* (St. Petersburg: Zhurn. "Stroitel'," 1908); and Il'in, Klein, and Rozenberg, *Sovremennoe bol'nichnoe stroitel'stvo v sviazi s postroikoi gorodskoi bol'nitsy imeni Petra Velikogo* (St. Petersburg: Gosudastvennaia Tipografia, 1911).

6. J. Müller, *Handbuch der Physiologie des Menschen* (1837), quoted in Tobias Cheung, "From the Organism of a Body to the Body of an Organism: Occurrence and Meaning of the Word 'Organism' from the Seventeenth to the Nineteenth Centuries," *British Journal for the History of Science* 39, no. 3 (September 2006): 337.

7. Rudolf Virchow, *Cellular Pathology as Based upon Physiological and Pathological Histology,* trans. from 2d ed. of the original by Frank Chance (London: John Churchill, 1860), 13–14. I am thankful to Myles Jackson and the participants of the History of Sciences seminar at the Institute for Advanced Study for this reference.

8. Ernst Haeckel, *Generelle Morphologie der Organismen: Allgemeine Gründzüge der organischen Formen-Wissenschaft, mechanisch begründet durch die von Charles Darwin reformierte Decendenz-Theorie* (Berlin: G. Reimer, 1866), 1:241.

9. Aleksandr Bogdanov, *Tektologiia: Vseobshchaia organizatsionnaia nauka,* vol. 1 [1913] (Moscow: Ekonomika, 1989), 92, 113–14.

10. The influence of Bogdanov's thought upon Russian postrevolutionary culture has been acknowledged by multiple scholars. See, for example, Isabel Wünsche, "Organic Visions and Biological Models in Russian Avant-Garde Art," in *Biocentrism and Modernism,* ed. Oliver Botar and Isabel Wünsche (London: Ashgate, 2011), 127–52; Barbara Wurm, "Factory," in *Revoliutsiia! Demonstratsiia! Soviet Art Put to the Test,* ed. Matthew Witkovsky and Devin Fore (Chicago: Art Institute of Chicago, 2017), 218–25; and Devin Fore, "The Operative Word in Soviet Factography," *October* 118 (Fall 2006): 95–131.

11. Bogdanov, *Tektologiia,* 1:141. Bogdanov's points of reference included Serbian mathematician and inventor Mihailo Petrović and German sociologist Johann Plenge in addition to the work of such theorists of technology as Ludwig Noiré. For more on Bogdanov's theory and its roots, see the Introduction to this book.

12. Bogdanov, *Tektologiia,* 1:48.

13. Biographical information about Alexander Rozenberg (1877–1935) is scarce, as his work has been missing from accounts of modernist architecture. Together with Klein and Ilyin, he won the competition for the Hospital of Peter the Great in 1906. In 1908, the three conducted a trip to Germany to study modern hospital construction. In 1922, Rozenberg developed the Regional Construction Plan for the Petrograd region. In the 1920s, he was an editor of *Zodchii (The Architect),* the journal of the Leningrad Society of Architects, and a professor at the Technical-Pedagogical Institute in Leningrad. In 1926, he again visited Germany to learn about the practice of organization of the architectural profession, industry, and architectural competitions. In the late 1920s, he worked for the Union of Architects. The only critical text that tackles Rozenberg's legacy is a short "Zabytaia tektologiia arkhitektury: Malen'kii traktat A. V. Rozenberga

'Filosofiia arkhitektury' 1923 goda i bol'shoe sovremennoe arkhitekturovedenie" by Andrei Puchkov published in *Suchasni problemy doslidzhennia, restavratsii ta zberezhennia kul'turnoi spadshchini / IPSM AMU* (Kyiv: Khimdzhest, 2010), 7:279–317.

14. Aleksandr Rozenberg, *Filosofiia arkhitektury* (Petrograd: Nachatki znanii, 1923), 5.

15. Aleksandr Rozenberg, *Obshchaia teoriia proektirovaniia arkhitekturnykh sooruzhenii* (Moscow: Plankhozgiz, 1930), 15, 27–28.

16. M. G. [Moisei Ginzburg], "'Filosofiia arkhitektury,' arkhitektor Rozenberg," *Arkhitektura: Ezhemesiachnik MAO*, no. 3–4 (1923): 66.

17. Moisei Ginzburg, "Novye metody arkhitekturnogo myshleniia," *Sovremennaia arkhitektura*, no. 1 (1926): 3.

18. The first standardized architecture, American "balloon-frame" construction, was wooden, and a factory for standardized wooden houses, perhaps the earliest standardization experiment in Russia, functioned in Moscow in the early 1920s. It succeeded, standardization enthusiasts proudly reported, in reducing the cost of labor by 78 percent. See V. Lazarev, *Standardizatsiia: Populiarnyi ocherk* (Moscow: NKRKI SSSR, 1925), 60. The book explains that overall, standardization reduced the cost of labor by 30 percent, largely because standardized elements could be assembled by less expensive unskilled labor.

19. El' Lisitskii, "Amerikanizm v evropeiskoi arkhitekture," *Krasnaia Niva*, no. 49 (1925): 1188.

20. O. A. Ermanskii, *Teoriia i praktika ratsionalizatsii*, vol. 1 (Moscow: Gosudarstvennoe izdatel'stvo, 1929), 270.

21. Ermanskii, *Teoriia i praktika ratsionalizatsii*, 269–71. Standardization in the narrow sense was pioneered by such organizations as the German Die Brücke. Different aspects of standardization in Germany have been covered in publications by Nader Vossoughian, Markus Krajewski, and Anna-Maria Meister.

22. For a discussion of the technical backwardness of the Soviet state in the context of standardization, see V. I. Vel'man, ed., *Tipovye proekty i konstruktsii zhilishchnogo stroitel'stva rekomenduemye na 1930 god* (Moscow: Gosudarstvennoe tekhnicheskoe izdatel'stvo, 1929), 77–136.

23. On the notions of type and typification in the context of the postwar Soviet Bloc, see Juliana Maxim, *The Socialist Life of Modern Architecture: Bucharest, 1949–1964* (London: Routledge, 2019), 67–115.

24. The *Work Regulation* had been repeatedly published and updated since 1811 (most important, in 1843). In 1869 it was rewritten by Nicholas de Rochefort, and subsequent editions relied on this version. In 1894, the government recognized the necessity of revising the document again. Unfinished by the time of the revolution, in its aftermath the work was continued by Rozenberg and his team.

25. The group working on revising the *Work Regulation* included V. Bashinsky, S. Bashinsky, S. Beknev, I. Braginsky, L. Budnevich, N. Bykovsky, N. Galler, V. Gulyaev, N. Dikov, I. Dubinkin, A. Dykhovichny, A. Zubritsky, B. Ivinsky, S. Kazakov, A. Kirshon, A. Kiselev, P. Porfiriev, P. Sidorenko, N. Sobolev, P. Sokolov, A. Sushkov, among others. A[leksandr] V. Rozenberg, *Teoriia*

normirovaniia stroitel'nykh protsessov (Moscow: Aktsionernoe izdatel'skoe obshchestvo, 1928), 5. The introduction to *New Work Regulation* (1931) mentions the following list of authors: S. I. Aslanov, V. N. Afonsky, A. M. Bogoslovsky, N. N. Bukharev, N. A. Butsenin, P. I. Vasilyev, P. I. Vinogradov, M. G. Ginodman, A. M. Gonyaev, V. P. Gorozhansky, N. N. Grigoryev, A. A. Egorova, N. N. Ivanovsky, I. N. Krotov, Kruglikov [*sic*], B. P. Lavrovsky, P. A. Mamatov, I. L. Mittelman, N. V. Mordovin, A. V. Pozdnyakov, A. N. Ponomareva, A. V. Rozenberg, M. S. Rudominer, K. A. Rusakov, B. I. Tatarinov, Tumolsky [*sic*], Iu. I. Fidrus, V. S. Florinsky, L. L. Shapiro, and L. S. Yanovich.

26. Aleksandr Rozenberg, "K peresmotru urochnogo polozhenia," *Zodchii,* no. 1 (1924): 35.

27. Viktor Sokol'skii, *Printsipy ekonomichnosti i ikh vyrazhenie v sovremennom stroitel'stve* (St. Petersburg: Tip. Shtaba otdel'nogo korpusa pogran. strazhi, 1910). Among Rozenberg's other sources was the work of engineer Vladimir Glazyrin on railroad construction (*Osnovy proektirovaniia zheleznodorozhnykh grazhdanskikh sooruzhenii* [St. Petersburg: Institut inzhenerov putei soobshcheniia imperatora Aleksandra I, 1918]). Rozenberg, *Obshchaia teoriia proektirovaniia,* 4.

28. Rozenberg, *Obshchaia teoriia proektirovaniia,* 5.

29. Eduard von Hartmann, *Philosophie des Unbewussten* (Berlin: Carl Dunckers, 1871), and Friedrich Nietzsche, *On the Advantage and Disadvantage of History for Life* [1874], trans. Peter Preuss (Indianapolis: Hackett, 1980). In Russian, a discussion of Hartmann's theory as a philosophy of world process was offered in A. A. Kozlov, *Sushchnost' mirovogo protsessa, ili 'Filosofia bessoznatel'nogo' E. von Gartmana,* vols. 1–2 (Moscow: Tip. Gracheva, 1873–75).

30. In an example suggested by Rozenberg, at a school, the classroom with all the equipment represented the environment; the students, the teacher, and all their belongings comprised the mass; and all their activity in its logical order was the sequence. See Rozenberg, *Filosofiia arkhitektury,* 8.

31. Vel'man, *Tipovye proekty i konstruktsii,* 26–28; "Issledovanie glubiny korpusa," *Sovremennaia arkhitektura,* no. 1 (1929): 29.

32. Rozenberg, *Obshchaia teoriia proektirovaniia,* 195–96.

33. Rozenberg, *Obshchaia teoriia proektirovaniia,* 15, 191.

34. Rozenberg, *Obshchaia teoriia proektirovaniia,* 15.

35. Rozenberg, "K peresmotru urochnogo polozheniia," 35.

36. Rozenberg, *Teoriia normirovaniia stroitel'nykh protsessov,* 20–70.

37. Rozenberg, *Teoriia normirovaniia stroitel'nykh protsessov,* 40–41.

38. Rozenberg, *Obshchaia teoriia proektirovaniia,* 192.

39. Hannes Meyer, "Building" [1928], in *Hannes Meyer, Bauten, Projekte und Schriften / Buildings, Projects and Writings,* ed. Claude Schnaidt, trans. D. Q. Stephenson (Teufen: Niggli, 1965), 95–107.

40. On Strumilin's time budgets, see also Tijana Vujošević, *Modernism and the Making of the Soviet Man* (Manchester: Manchester University Press, 2017), 65–68. See also John Bernal, "Architecture and Science" [1946], in *The Freedom of Necessity* (London: Routledge & K. Paul, 1949), 206–7.

41. Moisei Ginzburg, "Tsvet v arkhitekture," *Sovremennaia arkhitektura,* no. 2

(1929): 74; M. Ia. Ginzburg, "Tselevaia ustanovka v sovremennoi arkhitekture," *Sovremennaia arkhitektura,* no. 1 (1927): 5.

42. Ginzburg, "Novye metody arkhitekturnogo myshlenia," 4.

43. Christopher Green, "Darwinian Theory, Functionalism, and the First American Psychological Revolution," *American Psychologist* 64, no. 2 (2009): 75–83.

44. John Dewey, "The Reflex Arc Concept in Psychology," *Psychological Review* 3 (1896): 364.

45. See John Dewey, *Impressions of Soviet Russia and the Revolutionary World* (New York: New Republic, 1929).

46. El Lissitzky, "Idole und Idolverehrer," in *Proun und Wolkenbügel: Schriften, Briefe, Dokumente,* ed. Sophie Lissitzky-Küppers and Jen Lissitzky (Dresden: VEB Verlag der Kunst, 1977), 46–47 (originally published in *Stroitel'naia promyshlennost',* no. 11–12 [1928]).

47. Toporkov, *Tekhnicheskii byt i sovremennoe iskusstvo,* 147.

48. Moisei Ginzburg, "Funktsional'nyi metod i forma," *Sovremennaia arkhitektura,* no. 4 (1926): 90.

49. Ginzburg, "Novye metody arkhitekturnogo myshleniia," 3.

50. On Ginzburg's interest in Taylorism and Fordism, see Jean-Louis Cohen, *Building a New New World: "Americanizm" in Russian Architecture* (New Haven, Conn.: Yale University Press, 2020), 236–45.

51. Christoph Lueder, "Evaluator, Choreographer, Ideologue, Catalyst: The Disparate Reception Histories of Alexander Klein's Graphical Method," *Journal of the Society of Architectural Historians* 76, no. 1 (March 2017): 82–106.

52. Alexander Klein, "Grundrißbildung und Raumgestaltung von Kleinwohnungen und neue Auswertungsmethoden," in *Technische Tagung in Berlin 1929* (Berlin: RFG, 1929), 4. Quoted in Lueder, "Evaluator, Choreographer, Ideologue, Catalyst," 94–95.

53. Ginzburg, "Tselevaia ustanovka," 10.

54. Ginzburg, "Tselevaia ustanovka," 4–10; Ginzburg, "Novye metody arkhitekturnogo myshlenia," 1.

55. Gotthold Ephraim Lessing's original phrase (from *Anti-Goeze,* 1778) was "The true value of a man is not determined by his possession, supposed or real, of Truth, but rather by his sincere exertion to get to the Truth." A. Gastev, *Kak nado izobretat'* (Moscow: Izd-vo TsIT, 1922).

56. Moisei Ginzburg, *Style and Epoch* [1924], trans. Anatole Senkevitch (Cambridge, Mass.: MIT Press, 1983), 91.

57. Ludwig Lange, "Neue Experimente über den Vorgang der einfachen Reaction auf Sinneseindrücke: Erster Artikel," *Philosophische Studien,* no. 4 (1888): 479–510; Karl Marbe, "Über Unfallversicherung und Psychotechnik," *Praktische Psychologie* 4 (1923): 257–64; Karl Marbe, "Theorie der motorischen Einstellung und Persönlichkeit," *Zeitschrift für Psychologie* 129 (1933): 305–22. Later on, the idea was applied to social psychology by American scholars Florian Znaniecki and William Thomas, who defined attitude as "a process of individual consciousness which determines real or possible activity of the individual in the social world." Florian Znaniecki and William I. Thomas, *The Polish Peasant in Europe and America* (Boston: Richard Badger, 1918–20), 22.

58. Hugo Münsterberg, *Grundzüge der Psychotechnik* (Leipzig: Barth, 1914), 152; Aron Zalkind, *Zhizn' organizma i vnushenie* (Moscow: Gosudarstvennoe izd-vo, 1927).

59. P. K. Engelmeier, *Teoriia tvorchestva* (St. Petersburg: Obrazovanie, 1910); P. K. von Engelmeyer, *Der Dreiakt als Lehre von der Technik und der Erfindung* (Berlin: Carl Heymann, 1910).

60. Uznadze's first experimental study of *ustanovka,* published in 1931, slightly postdated the use of this term by Ginzburg. A. A. Leont'ev, *Deiatel'nyi um (Deiatel'nost', znak, lichnost')* (Moscow: Smysl, 2001), 127.

61. Ginzburg, "Tselevaia ustanovka," 4.

62. Ginzburg, "Tselevaia ustanovka," 10.

63. Rozenberg, *Filosofia arkhitektury,* 25–26.

64. Stroykom (Stroikom) was created in January of 1928 for "general regulation and rationalization of construction on the territory of RSFSR." It was headed by economist Vladimir Velman. I. A. Kazus', *Sovetskaia arkhitektura 1920-kh godov: Organizatsiia proektirovaniia* (Moscow: Progress-Traditsiia, 2009), 293. Translating the section's title to German, Ginzburg used the term *Typenbildung,* "the development of types." Moisei Ginzburg, "Problemy tipizatsii zhil'ia v SSSR," *Sovremennaia arkhitektura,* no. 1 (1929): 4.

65. Vladimirov had studied architecture at the Institute of Civil Engineers in St. Petersburg, where Rozenberg was a professor. In 1930, Ginzburg's group was expanded and reorganized as the Section of Socialist Settlement under the State Planning Committee (Gosplan) of the Russian Federative Republic. It was not the only group engaged in developing techniques of standardized construction in the Soviet Union: in March 1931, Soiuzstandartzhilstroi (from [All-]Union Standard Residential Construction) was founded to develop both standardized dwellings and new towns throughout the country. This was a much bigger organization than the Section of Typification, employing over six hundred specialists (among them, foreign experts such as Ernst May) in 1933. Kazus', *Sovetskaia arkhitektura 1920-kh godov,* 157–59.

66. Five other buildings using the same typified plans were built in Moscow, Sverdlovsk, and Saratov.

67. For more on Scheper's color schemes for the Narkomfin building, see chapter 5, "Activity."

68. The CIAM conference on *Existenzminimum* was held in Frankfurt in 1929 at the initiative of Ernst May, who would move to the USSR in 1930, remaining in the country until 1933.

69. See the discussion of Stroykom's project in *Sovremennaia arkhitektura,* no. 2 (1929), especially the responses of Serk, Voeykov, Kopelyansky, and Venderov.

70. Viktor Sokol'skii, *Printsipy ekonomichnosti v stroitel'nom dele* (St. Petersburg: Tip. Usmanova, 1912), 180.

71. Sokol'skii, *Printsipy ekonomichnosti v stroitel'nom dele,* 115–16.

72. Aleksei Gastev, *Kak nado rabotat': Prakticheskoe vvedenie v nauku organizatsii truda* (1921; repr., Moscow: Ekonomika, 1972), 197. See also A[leksei] Gastev, *Normirovanie i organizatsiia truda (Obshchee vvedenie v problemu)* (Moscow: VTsSPS, 1929).

73. Rozenberg, "K peresmotru urochnogo polozhenia," 36.

74. Rozenberg, *Obshchaia teoriia proektirovaniia*, 192.

75. For a similar approach by Austrian modernist Margarete Schütte-Lihotzky (to work in the USSR between 1930 and 1937), see Sophie Hochhäusl, "From Vienna to Frankfurt Inside Core-House Type 7: A History of Scarcity through the Modern Kitchen," *Architectural Histories,* no. 1 (2013), Art. 24: 1–19.

76. Ginzburg, "Problemy tipizatsii zhil'ia v SSSR," 5.

77. Moisei Ginzburg, *Zhilishche: Opyt piatiletnei raboty nad problemoi zhilishcha* (Moscow: Gosstroiizdat, 1934), 82–96. The expression "social condenser" was introduced by Ginzburg to describe the mission of socialist housing. Redaktsiia, "Desiatiletiiu Oktiabria," *Sovremennaia arkhitektura,* no. 4–5 (1927): 111, and Ginzburg, "Tselevaia ustanovka," 7. See also Michał Murawski, "Introduction: Crystallising the Social Condenser," *Journal of Architecture* 22, no. 3 (2017): 372–86. See also Ginzburg, "Problemy tipizatsii zhil'ia v SSSR," 5; Ginzburg, *Zhilishche,* 68.

78. A. Chaldymov, "K voprosy sozdaniia zhilishcha rekonstuktivnogo perioda," in *Doma-Kommuny,* ed. by E. Vernik et al. (Leningrad: Kubuch, 1931), 5.

79. Lissitzky was instrumental in opening the Laboratory of Furniture within the Institute of Timber in 1929, although it is not clear whether he became affiliated with it. The laboratory is mentioned in D[avid] Arkin, "Stroitel'stvo i 'mebel'naia problema,'" *Stroitel'stvo Moskvy,* no. 10 (1929): 7. For a discussion of Lissitzky's organicist theory of urbanism, see chapter 2, "Orientation."

80. El Lissitzky, "Wohnkultur," in *Proun und Wolkenbügel,* 56 (originally published in *Stroitel'naia promyshlennost',* no. 12 [1926]).

81. Lissitzky, "Wohnkultur," 56–57.

82. Lisitskii, "Amerikanizm v evropeiskoi arkhitekture," 1189.

83. Boris Arvatov, "Everyday Life and the Culture of the Thing (Toward the Formulation of the Question)" [1925], trans. Christina Kiaer, *October* 81 (Summer 1997): 126–27.

84. Sophie Lissitzky-Küppers, "Life and Letters," in Sophie Lissitzky-Küppers, *El Lissitzky: Life, Letters, Texts* (New York: Thames and Hudson, 1968), 81. Lissitzky described the house in detail in his article "Kul'tura zhil'ia," *Stroitel'naia promyshlennost',* no. 12 (1926): 877–81.

85. These ideas inspired Toporkov (who, having graduated from VKhUTEMAS in 1921, had since then been teaching decorative art) to design transformable furniture, such as a collapsible chair and a cabinet whose door, when unfolded, became a desk.

86. Concurrently, and likely in collaboration with Lissitzky, Georgy Krutikov was conducting research on architectural combinatorics. For more on this, see chapter 2, "Orientation."

87. Toporkov, *Tekhnicheskii byt i sovremennoe iskusstvo,* 44; Vel'man, *Tipovye proekty i konstruktsii,* 32. See also Vujošević, *Modernism and the Making of the Soviet Man,* 72–81.

88. El Lissitzky, "Die künstelerischen Voraussetzungen zur Standardisierung individueller Möbel für die Bevölkerung: Vortrag für die Sektion Standardisierung NTU WSNCh," in *Proun und Wolkenbügel,* 101, 107. The Russian-language original is in the Russian State Archive of Literature and Arts, fond 2361 (El Lissitzky), op. 1, ed. khr. 30.

89. El Lissitzky, "Protokoll des Gesprächs Meyerholds mit dem Architekten Lissitzky," in Lissitzky, *Proun und Wolkenbügel,* 201.

90. Arvatov, "Everyday Life and the Culture of the Thing," 121.

91. [El' Lisitskii], "Oborudovanie zhil'ia mebel'iu," in Vel'man, *Tipovye proekty i konstruktsii,* 31–35.

92. El Lissitzky, "Aus einem Fragebogen über Möbel," in *Proun und Wolkenbügel,* 197.

93. Kenneth Frampton, "The Status of Man and the Status of His Objects: A Reading of *The Human Condition*" [1979], in *Architecture Theory since 1968,* ed. by Michael Hays (Cambridge, Mass.: MIT Press, 1998), 370.

94. Frampton, "The Status of Man and the Status of His Objects," 370.

95. Interview by designboom. Available online at https://www.designboom.com /architecture/chicago-architecture-biennial-pezo-von-ellrichshausen-watercolors -finite-format-09-15-2017/.

96. Pier Vittorio Aurelli, "Labor and Architecture: Revisiting Cedric Price's Potteries Thinkbelt," *Log* 23 (Fall 2011): 108.

5. Energy

1. Fernand Léger, "Modern Architecture and Color" [1946], in *Functions of Painting,* trans. Alexandra Anderson (New York: Viking Press, 1973), 152. The same anecdote is repeated in Léger's "A New Space in Architecture" [1949], in *Functions of Painting,* 158.

2. The LoC transliteration is *Maliarstroi* for the institution and *Maliarnoe delo* for the title of its journal.

3. A. P. Ostroumova-Lebedeva, *Avtobiograficheskie Zapiski,* vol. 3 (Moscow: Izdatel'stvo Akademii khudozhestv, 1951), 20.

4. Matyushin was the composer of "Victory over the Sun" (1913) (libretto written by Aleksey Kruchenykh, and costumes and stage set designed by Kazimir Malevich).

5. Mikhail Matiushin, "Ne iskusstvo, a zhizn'," *Zhizn' iskusstva,* no. 20 (1923): 15. English translation in Margareta Tillberg, *Coloured Universe and the Russian Avant-Garde: Matiushin on Colour Vision in Stalin's Russia, 1932* (Stockholm: Stockholm University, 2003), 140.

6. See Tillberg, *Coloured Universe and the Russian Avant-Garde,* 152–54.

7. Larisa Zhadova, "Tsvetovaia sistema M. Matiushina," *Iskusstvo,* no. 8 (1974): 38–42.

8. M. V. Matiushin, *Spravochnik po tsvetu: Zakonomernost' izmeniaemosti tsvetovykh sochetanii* (Leningrad: Gosudarstvennoe izdatel'stvo izobrazitel'nykh iskusstv, 1932).

9. All the members of the Ender family were educated in the German Petersschule in St. Petersburg and were fluent in German.

10. In 1928, at the Leningrad Institute of Civil Engineers, Nikolsky created a Scientific-Research Cabinet and, within it, a Laboratory of Color, which was headed by Maria Ender. Vera Shueninova-Nikolskaya, the architect's wife, was a volunteer there, focusing on the problem of the relationship between color and form and the principles of exterior coloration of buildings.

11. "Ustav Gosudarstvennogo tresta po proizvodstvu maliarnykh rabot VSNKh

SSR" (Statutes of Malyarstroy) [1928], in Igor A. Kazus', *Sovetskaia arkhitektura 1920-kh godov: Organizatsiia proektirovaniia* (Moscow: Progress-Traditsiia, 2009), 244.

12. E. Stokolov, "Ot redaktsii," *Maliarnoe delo,* no. 1–2 (1930): 1–2; Kazus', *Sovetskaia arkhitektura 1920-kh godov,* 244.

13. Stokolov, "Ot redaktsii," 1–2.

14. Antony C. Sutton, *Western Technology and Soviet Economic Development* (Stanford, Calif.: Hoover Institution Press, 1968); Anatole Kopp, "Foreign Architects in the Soviet Union during the First Two Five-Year Plans," in *Reshaping Russian Architecture: Western Technology, Utopian Dreams,* ed. William C. Brumfield (Cambridge: Cambridge University Press, 1990), 176–214; Kurt Junghanns, "Deutsche Architekten in der Sowjetunion während der ersten Fünfjahrpläne und des Vaterländischen Krieges," *Wissenschaftliche Zeitschrift der Hochschule für Architektur und Bauwesen Weimar* 29 (1983): 121–40; and, in Russian, publications by Evgeniya Konysheva, Mark Meerovich, and Dmitrij Chmelnizky.

15. For more on the Construction Commission, see chapter 4. Hungarian-born Alfréd (Fred) Forbát taught at the Weimar Bauhaus from 1920 to 1922; in 1933, he moved to the USSR, where he joined the "brigade" of Ernst May. See Renate Scheper, *Vom Bauhaus geprägt: Hinnerk Scheper: Farbgestalter, Fotograf, Denkmalpfleger* (Bramsche: Rasch, 2007), 92, n. 2.

16. Scheper stayed in Moscow from July 1929 to July 1930, October 1930 to March 1931, and May to September 1931.

17. V. Sestroretskii and N. Nishenko, "Puti pazvitiia maliarnogo dela v SSSR," *Maliarnoe delo,* no. 1–2 (1930): 2.

18. Vsekhimprom, or Vsesoiuznoe ob'edinenie khimicheskoi promyshlennosti (All-Union Association of the Chemical Industry), existed under the Supreme Council of People's Economy of the USSR from 1929 to 1931. For conflicting opinions about Malyarstroy's mission see, for instance, A. V. Shchusev, "Stroitel'stvo novykh gorodov i massovaia okraska zdanii," *Maliarnoe delo,* no. 1–2 (1930): 8–9, and Igor Grabar', "Soiuz iskusstva i remesla," *Maliarnoe delo,* no. 1–2 (1930): 8.

19. Kazus', *Sovetskaia arkhitektura 1920-kh godov,* 244.

20. Lou Scheper, "Retrospective," in *Bauhaus and Bauhaus People: Personal Opinions and Recollections of Former Bauhaus Members and Their Contemporaries,* ed. Eckhard Neumann, trans. Eva Richter and Alba Lorman (New York: Von Nostrand Reinhold, 1993), 125. The projects prepared by the Office of Design included the Club of Railroad Workers at Lyublino station (within contemporary Moscow), the Club of Factory No. 12 at Elektrostal' station (near Moscow), a cinema in the residential complex of the All-Russian Central Executive Committee in Moscow, the dining hall of the Moscow Union of Consumption Associations, and several buildings for a collective farm near Rostov-on-Don.

21. In Moscow, Erich Borchert designed color schemes for Lyublino Club of Railroad Workers, the Government Building, the Institute of Electric Energy, the Central Aviation and Hydrodynamics Institute, pavilions of the All-Union Agricultural Exposition (currently the Exhibition of Achievements of National Economy) (together with another Bauhaus graduate, Max Krajewski),

and a project for painting the city of Gorky (today, Nizhny Novgorod). "Erich Willi Borchert. Biografia," in *Erikh Borkhert v Rossii* (Moscow: Izdatel'stvo im. Sabashnikovykh, 2008), 18–19.

22. Astrid Volpert, "Bez vozmozhnosti vozvrata," in *Erikh Borkhert v Rossii,* 11.

23. In 1936–37, Malyarstroy also employed the German sculptor Will Lambert.

24. Larisa Zhadova, "B. V. Ender o tsvete i tsvetovoi srede," *Tekhnicheskaia Estetika,* no. 11 (1974): 6.

25. Der Bund zur Förderung der Farbe im Stadtbild (1926–37) published the journal *Die farbige Stadt* and included such architects as Ernst May and Paul Schultze-Naumburg. Its work was discussed in Malyarstroy (L. M. Antokol'skii, "O planovoi okraske gorodov," *Maliarnoe delo,* no. 3 [1931]: 5–13).

26. Scheper, *Vom Bauhaus geprägt,* 148n11. See also Scheper, *Vom Bauhaus geprägt,* 24–25.

27. G. L. Sheper, "Arkhitektura i tsvet," *Maliarnoe delo,* no. 1–2 (1930): 12–15. English translation: Morgan Ridler and Natasha Kurchanova, *West 86th* 25, no. 1 (2018): 89–96. My quotations of this article are based on the original Russian-language publication.

28. See W. Ostwald, "Normen," *Jahrbuch des Deutschen Werkbundes,* no. 3 (1914): 77–86; Thomas Hapke, "Wilhelm Ostwald's Combinatorics as a Link between In-formation and Form," *Library Trends* 61, no. 2 (2012): 286–303.

29. V. Ostvald, *Tsvetovedenie,* trans. Z. O. Mil'man (Moscow: Promizdat, 1926). Ostwald's color theory departed from the Weber-Fechner law, the work of Ewald Hering and Ernst Mach, and other discoveries of modern psychophysiology.

30. Mark Wigley, *White Walls, Designer Dresses: The Fashioning of Modern Architecture* (Cambridge, Mass.: MIT Press, 1996), 205.

31. See Peter Galison, "Aufbau/Bauhaus: Logical Positivism and Architectural Modernism," *Critical Inquiry* 16, no. 4 (Summer 1990): 720.

32. Sheper, "Arkhitektura i tsvet," 14.

33. Moisei Ginzburg, "Tsvet v arkhitekture," *Sovremennaia arkhitektura,* no. 2 (1929): 75.

34. Letter to Italian architect Piero Bottoni (1928), quoted in Wigley, *White Walls, Designer Dresses,* 217; August Schmarsow, "The Essence of Architectural Creation" [1893], in *Empathy, Form, and Space: Problems in German Aesthetics, 1873–1893,* trans. Harry Francis Mallgrave and Eleftherios Ikonomou (Santa Monica, Calif.: Getty Center for the History of Art and the Humanities, 1994), 287.

35. Letter to Viktor Nekrasov, quoted in S. Frederick Starr, "Le Corbusier in the USSR: New Documentation," *Oppositions* 23 (1981): 132. The letter was sent in response to the students' assurances of solidarity after the announcement of the results of the first round of the Palace of the Soviets competition.

36. Redaktsia, "Pochemu my pomeshchaem zhivopis' Lezhe," *Sovremennaia arkhitektura,* no. 2 (1929): 58. At VKhUTEMAS, the Cezannists Alexander Osmerkin and Alexander Drevin taught courses on the relationship between color and form: "Expression of Form through Color" (Osmerkin) and "Simultaneity of Color and Form" (Drevin). The constructivist Gustav Klutsis, who taught the propaedeutic discipline "Color" between 1924 and 1930, explored the interaction of color with planar and volumetric form and the surface of the material.

37. Moisei Ginzburg, *Zhilishche: Opyt piatiletnei raboty nad problemoi zhilishcha* (Moscow: Gosstroiizdat, 1934), 93–94.
38. Sheper, "Arkhitektura i tsvet," 13.
39. Ginzburg, *Zhilishche,* 92–94.
40. Arkhitektor Kuz'min, "Problema nauchnoi organizatsii byta," *Sovremennaia arkhitektura,* no. 3 (1930): 14.
41. Ginzburg, "Tsvet v arkhitekture," 74.
42. Both were published in *Maliarnoe delo,* color supplement to no. 3–4 (1930); the originals are kept at the Bauhaus-Archiv Berlin.
43. E. Borkhert, "Metody proektirovaniia maliarnykh rabot," *Maliarnoe delo,* no. 2 (1931): 48–51.
44. On the history of this diagram, see Robin Rehm, "Die 'Einsicht des Blickes': Das Perspektivschema in der Wissenschaft des 19. Jahrhunderts und das Sich-Zeigen des Raumes," in *Zeigen: Die Rhetorik des Sichtbaren,* ed. Gottfried Boehm, Sebastian Egenhofer, and Christian Spies (Munich: Wilhelm Fink, 2010), 46–67.
45. Wilhelm von Bezold, *Die Farbenlehre im Hinblick auf Kunst und Kunstgewerbe* (Braunschweig: George Westermann, 1874), 281–82, Tafel VI. In a similar manner, a contemporary study in the psychology of architecture points out that color affects how we perceive this diagram as space: whereas white makes its "ceiling" look higher, black makes it seem lower; blue makes the walls seem further away and orange makes them seem closer. Jörg Kurt Grütter, *Grundlagen der Architektur-Wahrnehmung* (Wiesbaden: Springer, 2015), 328–29.
46. I am indebted to Yve-Alain Bois for drawing my attention to Shklovsky's article "Space in Painting and the Suprematists" (1915), which discusses the diagram.
47. David Katz, *Die Erscheinungsweisen der Farben und ihre Beeinflussung durch die individuelle Erfahrung* (Leipzig, 1911), 1–30; English translation 1935. In his article "Prostranstvennye i 'vesovye' svoistva tsveta," *Maliarnoe delo,* no. 2 (1931): 5–8, Boris Teplov referred to *Raumfarben* as *prostranstvennye.*
48. Scheper, "Arkhitektura i tsvet," 14; Renate Scheper, *Farbenfroh! Die Werkstatt für Wandmalerei am Bauhaus* (Berlin: Bauhaus-Archiv, 2005), 84–88.
49. Ginzburg, *Zhilishche,* 94.
50. E. Borkhert, "Okraska bol'nits i sanatorii," *Maliarnoe delo,* no. 4 (1931): 25. Borchert suggested replacing gray hues, which provoked depression, with light chromatic colors, and painting walls of patient rooms with calm tones, leaving bright color (usually red) only for therapeutic use in the neuropathological department, where its dose was to be regulated by a system of special screens.
51. Ginzburg, *Zhilishche,* 94–95.
52. E. Borkhert, "Krasochnoe oformlenie zhilishch," *Maliarnoe delo,* no. 1 (1931): 8.
53. Anson Rabinbach, *The Human Motor: Energy, Fatigue, and the Origins of Modernity* (New York: Basic Books, 1990).
54. For more on energeticism, see the Introduction and chapter 1, "Space."
55. Sheper, "Arkhitektura i tsvet," 13.
56. A. Mosso, *Fatigue,* trans. Margaret Drummond and William B. Drummond (New York: G. P. Putnam's Sons, 1904), 82–88. Among other first ergographers was Charles Henry, one of the founders of psychophysical aesthetics. See Rabinbach, *The Human Motor,* 133–42.

57. Charles Féré, *Travail et Plaisir* (Paris: Alcan, 1904).

58. F. Stefănescu-Goangă, *Experimentelle Untersuchungen zur Gefühlsbetonung der Farben* (Leipzig: Wilhelm Engelmann, 1911).

59. Jordanna Bailkin, "Color Problems: Work, Pathology, and Perception in Modern Britain," *International Labor and Working-Class History,* no. 68 (Fall 2005): 93–111.

60. "Vliianie okraski fabriki na proizvoditel'nost' truda rabochikh," *Maliarnoe delo,* no. 2 (1931): 69 (the text is a summary of articles in the German newspaper *Malerzeitung,* October 25, 1930, 450, and in the journal *Werkleiter,* no. 3 [1929]: 62; its author is not credited); B. Shn., "Tsvetovoe oformlenie fabrichnogo oborudovaniia," *Maliarnoe delo,* no. 4 (1931): 58–60.

61. S. Beliaeva-Ekzempliarskaia, "K voprosu o vybore tsvetov dlia okraski rabochikh pomeshchenii," *Maliarnoe delo,* no. 5–6 (1932): 9–11. Lissitzky also discussed the effects of various colors upon the physiological activity of the human (El Lissitzky, "Die künstlerischen Voraussetzungen zur Standardisierung individueller Möbel für die Bevölkerung. Vortrag für die Sektion Standardisierung NTU WSNCh," in *Proun und Wolkenbügel: Schriften, Briefe, Dokumente,* ed. Sophie Lissitzky-Küppers und Jen Lissitzky [Dresden: VEB Verlag der Kunst, 1977], 111).

62. A. M. Lukina, "Vospitanie sochetatel'nogo refleksa na slozhnyi tsvetovoi razdrazhitel'," in *Novoe v refleksologii i fiziologii nervnoi sistemy,* ed. V. M. Bekhterev (Moscow: Gosizdat, 1925). Cited in Beliaeva-Ekzempliarskia, "K voprosu o vybore tsvetov dlia okraski rabochikh pomeshchenii," 9.

63. S. V. Kravkov, "Ob adaptatsii glaza k tsvetnym razdrazhiteliam," *Zhurnal prikladnoi fiziki* 5, no. 2 (1928): 105–15.

64. Aleksandr Liushin, "Practicum of Color Theory," exercise 21, unpublished manuscript, Getty Research Library, VKhUTEMAS collection, accession no. 950052.

65. The program of research was subdivided into several steps: "1. The impact of color upon the process of muscle labor (the method of ergographic curves). 2. The impact of color upon cerebral work (the method of constant tests under changing irritants, recording of the speed of associations, etc.). 3. Testing the dependence of the received results upon color combinations of varied quality and quantity. 4. An investigation of the relationship of color and form. The change of spatial qualities of form [depending on the] color of its surfaces (the method of repeated introspective observation with the help of a specially constructed device)." G. T. Krutikov, "Arkhitekturnaia nauchno-issledovatel'skaia laboratoria pri Arkhitekturnom fakul'tete VKhUTEIN," *Arkhitektura i VKhUTEIN,* no. 1 (1929): 4.

66. Mikhail Barshch, "Vliianie zritel'nykh vpechatlenii na trudovye protsessy," *Sovremennaia arkhitektura,* no. 2 (1928): 72.

67. M[ikhail] O. Barshch, "Tsvet i ego rabora," *Sovremennaia arkhitektura,* no. 2 (1929): 77–79.

68. Barshch, "Vliianie zritel'nykh vpechatlenii na trudovye protsessy," 72.

69. Barshch, "Tsvet i ego rabora," 77–79.

70. In 1925, in a project for the university hospital in Münster, Scheper suggested painting the operating room off-white to avoid blinding the surgeon, and the

X-ray room dark red to help the eye adapt to darkness after the light was turned off. Scheper, *Vom Bauhaus geprägt,* 22–23.

71. Joan Campbell, *The German Werkbund: The Politics of Reform in the Applied Arts* (Princeton, N.J.: Princeton University Press, 1978), 57–79.

72. The letter appeared in the German-language Moscow newspaper *Moskauer Rundschau.* H. Scheper and L. Scheper, "Offener Brief an die Schüler des 'WCHUTEIN," *Moskauer Rundschau,* no. 4 (January 30, 1930).

73. In September 1930, he published an enthusiastic article about its technical achievements, such as a machine for the pneumatic spraying of paint. P. Katichev, "Khudozhnik-stroitel," *Iskusstvo v massy* 9, no. 17 (1930): 14.

74. E. Borkhert, "Funktsionalistskoe zasil'e (v poriadke polemiki)," *Maliarnoe delo,* no. 3 (1931): 38.

75. Borkhert, "Funktsionalistskoe zasil'e," 34.

76. Vladimir Kostin was an artist and an art critic for the newspaper *Komsomol'skaia Pravda.* As he acknowledged, after submitting the article to the journal, he reworked it with the help of Mácza.

77. V. Kostin, "Arkhitektura i tsvetopis'," *Za proletarskoe iskusstvo,* no. 8 (1931): 4.

78. El' Lisitskii, "Fotopis'," *Sovetskoe foto,* no. 10 (May 15, 1929): 311.

79. Lissitzky, "Die künstlerischen Voraussetzungen zur Standardisieurung indivi-dueller Möbel für die Bevölkerung," 111.

80. Kostin, "Arkhitektura i tsvetopis'," 4.

81. Kostin, "Arkhitektura i tsvetopis'," 5.

82. V. Friche, *Sotsiologiia iskusstva* (Moscow: Gosudarstvennoe izdatel'stovo, 1926), 183–89.

83. Although after submission, Kostin asked the editors to withdraw his article, they still published it, supplementing with a scathing preface. "Ot redaktsii," *Za proletarskoe iskusstvo,* no. 8 (1931): 4.

84. I. Amov, "Taktika klassovogo vraga na izofronte", *Za proletarskoe iskusstvo,* no. 8 (1931): 9.

85. Maria Ender, "Predislovie," in M. V. Matiushin, *Zakonomernost' izmeniaemosti tsvetovykh sochtanii: Spravochnik po tsvetu* (Moscow: Gos. izd-vo izobrazitel'nykh iskusstv, 1932), 3–10. For an English translation, see Tillberg, *Colored Universe and the Russian Avant-Garde,* Appendix B, 347–54.

86. Due to the difficulty of the technological process, the illustrations to the book had to be hand colored by Matyushin's students. As a result, the *Handbook* had a print run of only four hundred copies. In 1933, Mácza published his opinion on the role of color in art in a lengthy independent article "Problema tsveta v iskusstve," *Iskusstvo,* no. 1–2 (1933): 8–47.

87. Vygotsky studied Alfred Adler's *Praxis und Theorie der Individualpsychologie* (1927), which argued that to understand behavior, a psychologist must de-tect its purpose—the goal to which the organism strives. However, whereas Adler defined this goal as being superior to others, Vygotsky reformulated it as personal development. René Van der Veer and Jaan Valsiner, *Understanding Vygotsky: A Quest for Synthesis* (Oxford: Blackwell, 1991), 65–75.

88. Alexei Leontiev, *Activity, Consciousness, and Personality* [1975], trans. Maris J. Hall (Englewood Cliffs, N.J.: Prentice-Hall, 1978), 6.

89. Matsa, "Problema tsveta v iskusstve," 9.

90. Boris Ender, lecture on wall-painting, unpublished manuscript, 1936, Russian State Archive of Literature and the Arts, Boris Ender collection, fond. 2973, op. 1, ed. khr. 11, l. 29.

91. Nikolai Troitskii, *Ty moe stolet'ie* (Moscow: Rusaki, 2006), 94–95.

92. While Dedyukhin, a prominent party member, was promptly executed, while Norman (born as Troitsky) (1903–2011) was freed the following year and was eventually able to emigrate. His memoir (Troitskii, *Ty moe stolet'ie*) documents his tumultuous life. I am thankful to Dmitrij Chmelnizki for introducing me to Nikolay and Vera Troitsky.

93. See Joy Knoblauch, *The Architecture of Good Behavior: Psychology and Modern Institutional Design in Postwar America* (Pittsburgh: University of Pittsburgh Press, 2020).

94. See, for instance, Peter Barrett et al., "A Holistic, Multi-Level Analysis Identifying the Impact of Classroom Design on Pupils' Learning," *Building and Environment,* no. 59 (2013): 678; Bradley E. Karlin and Robert A. Zeiss, "Environmental and Therapeutic Issues in Psychiatric Hospital Design: Toward Best Practices," *Psychiatric Services* 57, no. 10 (October 2006): 1376–78.

95. Alexander G. Schauss, "Tranquilizing Effect of Color Reduces Aggressive Behavior and Potential Violence," *Journal of Orthomolecular Psychiatry* 8, no. 4 (1979): 218–21.

6. Personality

1. Published in *USSR in Construction,* no. 9 (1934).

2. The first two words are indeed to be seen on the published note. Betty Glan, interview with Viktor Duvakin, December 16, 1980, published in "O sozdanii parka Gor'kogo, ego ozdorovitel'nykh i agitatsionnykh funktsiiakh i znamenitykh posetiteliakh," OUI NB MGU # 781–782 (http://oralhistory.ru/talks/orh-781 -782). Glan was born Berta Mendelzweig (Mendel'tsveig). Her adopted name was an homage to Knut Hamsun's vitalist novel *Pan* (1894), whose hero was named Thomas Glahn (Glan in Russian translation). Katarina Kukher [Kucher], *Park Gor'kogo: Kul'tura dosuga v stalinskuiu epokhu, 1928–1941* (Moscow: Rospen, 2012), 224.

3. Mikhail Korzhev, "Doklad o tvorcheskom puti parkovogo arkhitektora, chlena SSA i chlena sektsii ozeleneniia goroda Moskvy Prokhorovoi Militsy Ivanovny," March 1960, p. 8, unpublished manuscript, Mikhail Korzhev collection, archive of A. V. Shchusev State Museum of Architecture, Moscow. Written at the end of her long and difficult life, her memoir is entitled *Prazdnik vsegda s nami (Holiday That Is Always with Us / We Are Always Celebrating),* an homage to Ernest Hemingway's novel *A Moveable Feast,* whose Russian translation came under the title *Holiday That Is Always with You (Prazdnik, kotoryi vsegda s toboi).*

4. B. N. Glan, *Prazdnik vsegda s nami* (Moscow: Soiuz teatral'nykh deiatelei, 1988), 112.

5. Although Wells used the word "rest" to translate the park's name, I am using "leisure." More on the semantic difference between the two notions will follow.

6. Fabiola López-Durán, *Eugenics in the Garden: Transatlantic Architecture and the Crafting of Modernity* (Austin: University of Texas Press, 2018).

7. In 1920, Lunacharsky met Glan in Kyiv, where she grew up, and, impressed by her knowledge of French and German, invited the sixteen-year-old to join his Narkompros team. After she moved to Moscow the same year, he assumed a paternal role toward her. From Glan, interview with Duvakin.

8. Konstantin Ukhanov, "V bor'be za kul'turu (K organizatsii v Moskve 'Parka kul'tury i otdykha')," *Pravda,* no. 68 (March 21, 1928).

9. Ukhanov, "V bor'be za kul'turu."

10. The park was largely created by the weekend volunteer labor of thousands of Moscow workers, which was conceived and presented as an instrument of personal transformation.

11. G. M. Danishevsky, *Problemy massovogo otdykha v SSSR* (Moscow: Profizdat, 1934).

12. Glan, interview with Duvakin.

13. In *Capital,* Marx quotes from Adam Smith's *The Wealth of Nations*: "The man whose whole life is spent in performing a few simple operations . . . has no occasion to exert his understanding. . . . He generally becomes as stupid and ignorant as it is possible for a human creature to become." Karl Marx, *Capital,* vol. 1 [1867], trans. Ben Fowkes (London: Penguin, 1990), 483.

14. Sigfried Giedion eloquently described how the roots of the assembly line can be traced back to the "disassembly lines," midcentury slaughterhouses in the American Midwest, in *Mechanization Takes Command: A Contribution to Anonymous History* (New York: Oxford University Press, 1948; repr., Minneapolis: University of Minnesota Press, 2013).

15. H. G. Wells, *The War of the Worlds* (1898; repr., Peterborough, Ont.: Broadview Literary Press, 2003), 146.

16. Wells, *The War of the Worlds,* 143–44. Similarly, in *The Time Machine* (1895) Wells describes the evolutionary separation of humanity, under the condition of capitalism, into two new biological species: Eloi (descendants of privileged classes) and Morlocks (descendants of the proletariat).

17. Karl Marx, "The German Ideology" [1845–46], in *Writings of the Young Marx on Philosophy and Society* (Garden City, N.Y.: Anchor Books, 1967), 425. The work, which remained unpublished during the lifetime of Marx and Engels, was first published in Moscow in 1932.

18. Hannah Arendt, *The Human Condition* [1958] (Chicago: University of Chicago Press, 2018), 81.

19. Anatolii Lunacharskii, *Osnovy pozitivnoi estetiki* [1903] (Moscow: Gosudarstvennoe izdatel'stvo, 1923), 26–27.

20. Seneca's *De Otio (On Leisure),* Cicero's *De Officiis (On Duties),* and the letters of Pliny the Younger are the most famous classical celebrations of *otium.* I am thankful to Robert Iliffe for these references.

21. See James Ackerman, *The Villa: Form and Ideology of Country Houses* (1985; repr., London: Thames and Hudson, 1995).

22. On the meaning and etymology of "leisure," see also Danishevskii, *Problemy massovogo otdykha v SSSR,* 8.

23. Danishevskii, *Problemy massovogo otdykha v SSSR,* 145–46. In this passage, Danishevsky refers to the letter from Friedrich Engels to Marx, which discusses Max Stirner's *The Ego and Its Property,* dated November 19, 1844.

24. Lunacharskii, *Osnovy pozitivnoi estetiki,* 13–19.

25. While Avenarius referred to cognitive energy expended during the perceptive process, Lunacharsky spoke about "vital energy."

26. A. A. Bogdanov, *Empiriomonizm: Stat'i po filosofii,* vol. 1 (Moscow: Izdatel'stvo S. Dorovatovskago i A. Charushnikova, 1904), 94–124, and vol. 2 (Moscow: Izdatel'stvo S. Dorovatovskago i A. Charushnikova, 1905), 43–50.

27. A. A. Bogdanov, *Tektologiia: Vseobshchaia organizatsionnaia nauka,* vol. 2 [1917] (Moscow: Ekonomika, 1989).

28. B. N. Glan, *Udarno rabotat'—kul'turno otdykhat'* (Moscow: Mospartizdat, 1933), 15 (quoting Maksim Gorkii, "V Amerike" [1906]).

29. Danishevskii, *Problemy massovogo otdykha v SSSR,* 8.

30. Glan, *Udarno rabotat'—kul'turno otdykhat',* 57–58.

31. Glan, *Udarno rabotat'—kul'turno otdykhat',* 58.

32. L. B. Lunts, *Parki Kul'tury i Otdykha* (Moscow: Gosstroiizdat, 1934), 80.

33. Julian Huxley, *A Scientist among the Soviets* (New York: Harper & Brothers, 1932), 18–21.

34. Glan also notes the role of Ivan Zholtovsky, the architect of the 1923 exposition, in devising the plan of the park (interview with Duvakin). In 1929, Ladovsky used the park as the topic for the diploma projects of his graduating students: Lyubov Zalesskaya, Vitaly Dolganov, Mikael Mazmonyan, Karo Alabyan, Ivan Bolbashevsky, Oganes Balyian, and Sergey Matorin. Some of them (most notably, Zalesskaya and Dolganov) began to work in the park immediately after graduating. Among Ladovsky's other students who worked in the park were Mikhail Korzhev, Militsa Prokhorova, Innokenty Kychakov, and Mikhail Cherkasov. In 1932, Goszelenstroi ("state green building") trust was created under the Russian Commissariat of Infrastructure as a center for developing the methodology for landscape architecture, and most of the members of the Office of Design and Planning moved to the new organization.

35. Danishevskii, *Problemy massovogo otdykha v SSSR,* 56.

36. On god-building, see Alla Vronskaya, "From the Aesthetics of Life to the Dialectics of Collectivity: Anatoly Lunacharsky, Alexander Bogdanov, and Maxim Gorky, 1905–1917," in *Productive Universals—Specific Situations: Critical Engagements in Art, Architecture, and Urbanism,* ed. Anne Kockelkorn and Nina Zschocke (Berlin: Sternberg, 2019), 316–35. On Lunacharsky's concept of the revolutionary spectacle, see Alla Vronskaya, "Objects-Organizers: The Monism of Things and the Art of the Socialist Spectacle," in *A History of Russian Exposition and Festival Architecture, 1700–2014,* ed. Alla Aronova and Alexander Ortenberg (London: Routledge, 2019), 151–67.

37. Anatolii Lunacharskii, "O narodnykh prazdnenstvakh" [1920], in *Lunacharskii o massovykh prazdenstvakh, estrade, tsirke* (Moscow: Iskusstvo, 1981), 85. Partial English translation: "On Popular Festivals," in *Street Art of the Revolution: Festivals and Celebrations in Russia, 1918–1933,* ed. Vladimir Tolstoy, Irina Bibikova, and Catherine Cooke (New York: Vendome Press, 1990), 124.

38. L. Roshchin, "Iskusstvo massovykh prazdnenstv," *Iskusstvo v massy,* no. 5–6 (1929): 28–29.

39. This idea would soon be explored by the ASNOVA brigade in the competition project for the Palace of the Soviets. The project articulated a new, organic, concept of monumentality: what they designed was "not . . . a static monument, but . . . a live, acting organism, living the same life as the demonstrations and revolutionary-political mass celebrations." El' Lisitskii, "Arkhitektura budushchego parka kul'tury i otdykha," *Park kul'tury i otdykha: Gazeta-desiatidnevka,* no. 7 (November 1930): 3; Brigada ASNOVA [Viktor Balikhin, Militsa Prokhorova, Mikhail Turkus, P. V. Budo, Romual'd Iodko, Flora Sevortian], "ASNOVA: Dvorets Sovetov," *Sovetskaia arkhitektura* 4 (1931): 52. For more on this project, see Alla Vronskaya, "Urbanist Landscape: Militsa Prokhorova, Liubov' Zalesskaia, and the Emergence of Soviet Landscape Architecture," in *Women, Modernity, and Landscape Architecture,* ed. John Beardsley and Sonja Duempelmann (London: Routledge, 2015), 60–80.

40. "The stage has to be set up in such a way that one can enter from all sides: from north, east, south, and west; the driveway of the auditorium—a driveway, not just a visitors' entrance—will draw the spectator into the action when the masses 'stream' on the stage," as Lissitzky explained his concept. El Lissitzky, "Protokoll des Gesprächs Meyerholds mit dem Architekten Lissitzky," in El Lissitzky, *Proun und Wolkenbügel: Schriften, Briefe, Dokumente,* ed. Sophie Lissitzky-Küppers and Jen Lissitzky (Dresden: VEB Verlag der Kunst, 1977), 202.

41. Lisitskii, "Arkhitektura budushchego parka kul'tury i otdykha," 3.

42. Hadas Steiner, "For the Birds," *Grey Room,* no. 13 (Autumn 2003): 16.

43. The Kinetic Construction System was published by Moholy-Nagy in *From Material to Architecture (Von Material zu Architektur)* in 1929.

44. Glan described her first emotional ride on the track in her memoirs. Glan, *Prazdnik vsegda s nami,* 54–55.

45. As late as 1971, a cable car was installed in the park of culture and leisure in Kharkiv.

46. A. G. Orliuk, *Kak pol'zovat'sia sol'ntsem, vozdukhom i vodoi* (Moscow: Fizkul'tura i turizm, 1930). The architects the Institute of Resort Studies employed were Alexander Golubev, Vladimir Tarasov, and Dmitry Chernopyzhsky.

47. A. Orliuk, "Fabrika zdorov'ia," *Park kul'tury i otdykha: Gazeta desiatidnevka,* no. 8–9 (December 1930): 5. In the course of his research on the impact of short-term rest in the Central Park of Culture and Leisure on working productivity, Orlyuk discovered that the increase in productivity visibly outweighed its initial loss: the textile workers of Krasnokholmskaya factory, who spent six days in the park in January, improved their productivity by 7 percent, while the productivity of the workers of the factory "Liberated Labor," who spent twelve days in January and February, improved by 10 percent. Danishevskii, *Problemy massovogo otdykha v SSSR,* 57.

48. Unlike its multistory nineteenth-century predecessors, the modern twentieth-century factory was a long, one-story building whose form followed the logic of the conveyor belt. Such factories were advocated, for example, by Nikolay

Milyutin in *Sotsgorod: The Problem of Building Socialist Cities* [1930], trans. Arthur Sprague (Cambridge, Mass.: MIT Press, 1974), 73. Another industrial element was the conveyor belt for food, which connected the kitchen (hidden behind a wall of greenery) to the dining hall.

49. El' Lisitskii, "K proektu 'Gorodka otdykha'," *Park kul'tury i otdykha*: Gazeta-desiatidnevka, no. 8–9 (December 1930): 5.

50. "Vypiska iz protokola No. 132 Zasedaniia prezidiuma Mosoblispolkoma i Moskovskogo Soveta R.K. i K.D. ot 14 sentiabria 1930," quoted in Betti Glan, *Za sotsialisticheskii park: Obzor proektov general'nogo plana* (Moscow: Izd. Mosoblispolkoma, 1932), 3.

51. V. Lavrov, "Park kul'tury i otdykha v Moskve po proektam diplomnikov VKhUTEINa," *Stroitel'stvo Moskvy,* no. 10 (1929): 14–16.

52. The projects were submitted by the Scientific-Technical Society of Construction Workers (NTO Stroitelei): L. E. Biryukov, L. B. Velikovsky, N. S. Zarubin; ARU: V. P. Kalmykov, V. I. Fidman; The Brigade of Central Park of Culture and Leisure: L. S. Zalesskaya, I. P. Kychakov, M. I. Prokhorova; ASNOVA: T. N. Varentsov, S. A. Geldfeld, A. I. Repkin, S. B. Bekker; All-Union Association *(ob'edinenie)* of Proletarian Architects (VOPRA): P. I. Goldenberg and V. I. Dolganov; Architectural-Construction Institute (ASI): A. V. Natalchenko, P. P. Revyakin, K. Ia. Rogov; and SASS (Sector of Architects of Socialist Construction, as OSA was renamed in 1930): I. U. Bronshtein; Moisei Ginzburg; Konstantin Melnikov; I. I. Klang and A. S. Korobov.

53. Le Corbusier, *The Athens Charter* [1933], trans. Anthony Eardley (New York: Grossman, 1973), 69.

54. Lunts, *Parki Kul'tury i Otdykha,* 212. See also L. Lunts, "Opisanie proektov general'nogo plana tsentral'nogo parka kul'tury i otdykha Mossoveta," in Glan, *Za sotsialisticheskii park,* 28–29.

55. Milyutin, *Sotsgorod,* 64–65, 71–72.

56. Glan, *Za sotsialisticheskii park,* 18.

57. Glan, *Za sotsialisticheskii park,* 11.

58. Danishevsky cited French pathologist Charles-Joseph Bouchard, in Danishevskii, *Problemy massovogo otdykha v SSSR,* 9.

59. Lunts, *Parki Kul'tury i Otdykha,* 265.

60. The study is cited in Danishevskii, *Problemy massovogo otdykha v SSSR,* 63.

61. A. Lunacharskii, *Iskusstvo kak vid chelovecheskogo povedenia* (Leningrad: Gosudarstvennoe meditsinskoe izdatel'stvo, 1930), 29–30. For more on the ideal of polytechnic education, see chapter 3, "Fitness."

62. Glan, *Udarno rabotat'—kul'turno otdykhat',* 13.

63. Danishevskii, *Problemy massovogo otdykha v SSSR,* 22.

64. Glan, *Udarno rabotat'—kul'turno otdykhat',* 13.

65. The brigade included A. N. Rosenblium (head of research on the main territory of the park); L. I. Bozhovich (head of research on the visitors of Children's Village); N. N. Kaulina (research in the Aviation Laboratory); G. L. Rosengart (research in the Electrotechnical Laboratory); V. Kh. Kharkevich and N. A. Klevin (research of the flow of visitors to the Children's Village); A. A. Keldysh (research on the main territory of the park); and A. N. Leont'ev, the head of the

project. I am indebted to Nikita Kharlamov for pointing to the brigade's work in the park.

66. The key principle of field theory was described by Lewin as the formula B = f(P, E), in which B stands for behavior, P for person, and E for environment. Lewin's theory rejected the conception of human personality as stable (shaped, for example, by childhood experience or genetics).

67. See A. N. Leont'ev and A. N. Rozenblium, "Psikhologicheskoe issledovanie deiatel'nosti i interesov posetitelei Tsentral'nogo parka kul'tury i otdykha imeni Gor'kogo (Predvaritel'noe soobshchenie)," in *Traditsii i perspektivy deiatel'nostnogo podkhoda v psikhologii: Shkola A. N. Leont'eva,* ed. A. E. Voiskunskii, A. N. Zhdan, and O. K. Tikhomirov (Moscow: Smysl, 1999), 373.

68. Leont'ev and Rozenblium, "Psikhologicheskoe issledovanie," 373.

69. Leont'ev and Rozenblium, "Psikhologicheskoe issledovanie," 375.

70. Leont'ev and Rozenblium, "Psikhologicheskoe issledovanie," 424–25.

71. For more on the psychological notion of setup, see chapter 4, "Process."

72. Leont'ev and Rozenblium, "Psikhologicheskoe issledovanie," 374.

73. Leont'ev and Rozenblium, "Psikhologicheskoe issledovanie," 409–10.

74. Lev Vygotsky, "The Socialist Alteration of Man" [1930], in *The Vygotsky Reader,* ed. René Van der Veer and Jaan Valsiner (Oxford: Blackwell, 1994), 182–83.

75. L. Trotskii, *Literatura i revoliutsiia* (1923; repr., Moscow: Politicheskaia literatura, 1991), 196.

76. René Van der Veer and Jaan Valsiner, *Understanding Vygotsky: A Quest for Synthesis* (Oxford: Blackwell, 1991), 191.

77. See, for instance, Erich Fromm, *Marx's Concept of Man* (1961; repr., London: Continuum, 2003).

78. While Glan was directing amateur clubs in collective farms in Ivanovo and subsequently in Krasnoyarsk in Siberia, Mazmonian headed the planning group in Norilsk.

79. Kathy Weeks, *The Problem with Work: Feminism, Marxism, Anti-Work Politics, and Postwork Imaginaries* (Durham, N.C.: Duke University Press, 2011), 109.

Conclusion

1. In 1933, the Monist League was dissolved by the National Socialists in Germany, while Haeckel's books were not reprinted in the Soviet Union after 1937.

2. Isaiah Berlin, "The Hedgehog and the Fox: An Essay on Lev Tolstoy's View of History" [1953], in *The Proper Study of Mankind: An Anthology of Essays,* ed. H. Hardy and R. Hausheer (New York: Farrar, Straus and Giroux, 1998), 436. For a similar use of this notion in architecture, see Samir Younés, "The Empire of Masks: Pluralism and Monism in Politics and Architecture," *Philosophy* 79, no. 310 (October 2004): 533–51.

3. Robert Hunt Sprinkle, *Profession of Conscience: The Making and Meaning of Life-Sciences Liberalism* (Princeton, N.J.: Princeton University Press, 1994), 78.

4. See, for instance, Jason W. Moore, *Capitalism in the Web of Life: Ecology and the Accumulation of Capital* (London: Verso, 2016), which foregrounds a critique of binary thinking about nature and society.

5. Dipesh Chakrabarty, "The Planet: An Emergent Humanist Category," *Critical Inquiry* 46, no. 1 (Autumn 2019): 1–31.

6. David D. Roberts, *Benedetto Croce and the Uses of Historicism* (Berkeley: University of California Press, 1987), quoted in Dipesh Chakrabarty, "The Climate of History: Four Theses," *Critical Inquiry* 35, no. 2 (Winter 2009): 203.

7. R. G. Collingwood, *The Idea of History,* ed. with an introduction by Jan van der Dussen (1994; repr., Oxford: Oxford University Press, 2005), 212. Cited in Dipesh Chakrabarty, "Emancipatory Histories, a Troubled but Living Legacy—Response to Latour," *Journal of the Philosophy of History* 14, no. 3 (2020): 29. The distinction between the biological process and the historical social custom recalls the nearly contemporaneous distinction between labor and work made by Hannah Arendt (discussed in chapter 6 of this book).

8. Bruno Latour, "Who Needs a Philosophy of History?" *Journal of the Philosophy of History* 14, no. 3 (2020): 8.

9. S. Suvorov, "Osnovy filosofii zhizni" [1904], in *Ocherki realisticheskogo mirovozzreniia: Sbornik statei po filosofii, obshchestvennoi rabote i zhizni* (St. Petersburg: Izd. Dorovatskogo i Charushnikova, 1905), 74–79.

10. The term "the survival of the fittest" was first introduced by Spencer, in his *Principles of Biology* (1864), to describe the difference between his and Darwin's method.

11. P. K. Engelmeier, *Teoriia tvorchestva* (St. Petersburg: Obrazovanie, 1910), 189. Cf. Kant's definition of the beautiful as "purposiveness without purpose" (on the functionalist critique of Kantian aesthetics, see chapter 4).

12. See, for instance Ernst Mayr, "The Multiple Meanings of Teleological," in *Towards a New Philosophy of Biology,* ed. Ernst Mayr (Cambridge, Mass.: Harvard University Press, 1988), 38–66; Ron Amundson and George V. Lauder, "Function without Purpose: The Uses of Causal Role Function in Evolutionary Biology", *Biology & Philosophy* 9, no. 4 (1994): 443–69; Paul Sheldon Davies, *Norms of Nature: Naturalism and the Nature of Functions* (Cambridge, Mass.: MIT Press, 2001); John Zammito, "Teleology Then and Now: The Question of Kant's Relevance for Contemporary Controversies over Function in Biology," *Studies in History and Philosophy of Science Part C: Studies in History and Philosophy of Biological and Biomedical Sciences* 37, no. 4 (2006): 748–70; Colin Allen and Jacob Neal, "Teleological Notions in Biology," in *The Stanford Encyclopedia of Philosophy,* ed. Edward N. Zalta (Spring 2019 Edition), https://plato.stanford.edu/archives/spr2019/entries/teleology-biology/.

13. Eduard von Hartmann, *Philosophy of the Unconscious,* vol. 1 (London: K. Paul, Trench, Trübner, 1893), 44. Hartmann later developed his polemics with Darwinism in *Wahrheit und Irrthum im Darwinismus: Eine kritische Darstellung der organischen Entwickelungstheorie* (Berlin: C. Duncker, 1875; Russian translation, 1906).

14. Hartmann, *Philosophy of the Unconscious,* 1:4–5.

15. Louis Althusser, *For Marx* (London: Allen Lane, 1969).

16. Sean Sayers, "Marx and Teleology," *Science & Society* 83, no. 1 (2019): 37–63.

17. Leo Tolstoy, *War and Peace* (1867), quoted in Bruno Latour, "Agency at the Time

of the Anthropocene," *New Literary History* 45, no. 1 (2014): 7 , and in his *Facing Gaia: Eight Lectures on the New Climatic Regime* (Cambridge: Polity, 2017), 50.

18. Berlin, "The Hedgehog and the Fox," 466.

19. During the 1920s, Holzapfel was several times nominated for the Nobel Prize in Literature. Three of these nominations (in 1925, 1927, and 1928) were submitted by Romain Rolland.

20. Rudolf Maria Holzapfel, *Panideal: Psychologie der sozialen Gefühle,* with a foreword by E. Mach (Leipzig: J. A. Barth, 1901).

21. Lunacharsky published its Russian-language account in 1905. The account appeared in the same volume as that of Avenarius's *Critique of Pure Experience.* R. Avenarius and A. Lunacharskii, *R. Avenarius, Kritika chistogo opyta v populiarnom izlozhenii A. Lunacharskogo. Novaia teoriia pozitivnogo idealizma (Holzapfel, Panideal). Kriticheskoe izlozhenie A. Lunacharskogo* (Moscow: Izd. Dorovatskogo i Charushnikova, 1905).

22. On the notion of totalitarianism, see Slavoj Žižek, *Did Somebody Say Totalitarianism? Five Interventions in the (Mis)Use of a Notion* (London: Verso, 2001). On its use for the analysis of Soviet architecture, see Alla Vronskaya, "Deconstructing Constructivism," in *Re-framing Identities: Architecture's Turn to History, 1970–1990,* ed. Ákos Moravánszky and Torsten Lange (Basel: Birkhäuser, 2016), 149–63.

23. Boris Grois, *The Total Art of Stalinism: Avant-garde, Aesthetic Dictatorship, and Beyond,* trans. Charles Rougle (Princeton, N.J.: Princeton University Press, 1992), 51.

24. R[oman] Khiger, "K voprosu ob ideologii konstruktivizma v sovremennoi arkhitekture," *Sovremennaia arkhitektura,* no. 3 (1928): 92–102; R[oman] Ia. Khiger, *Puti arkhitekturnoi mysli, 1917–1932* (Moscow: OGIZ-IZOGIZ, 1933), 30–51; Aleksei Mikhailov, *Gruppirovki sovetskoi arkhitektury* (Moscow: OGIZ-IZOGIZ, 1932), 40–65.

25. Walter Benjamin, "On the Concept of History," in *Selected Writings,* ed. Howard Eiland and Michael W. Jennings, trans. Edmund Jephcott, vol. 4, *1938–1940* (Cambridge, Mass.: Belknap Press of Harvard University Press, 2003), 390; Louis Marin, "Frontier of Utopia: Past and Present," *Critical Inquiry* 19, no. 3 (Spring 1993): 397–420; Jacques Derrida, *Specters of Marx: The State of the Debt, the Work of Mourning and the New International,* trans. Peggy Kamuf (London: Routledge, 1994), 70, 74. Cited in Simon Choat, *Marx through Post-Structuralism: Lyotard, Derrida, Foucault, Deleuze* (London: Continuum, 2010), 87.

26. Latour, *Facing Gaia*, 51.

27. Latour, "Agency at the Time of the Anthropocene," 5.

28. See Vandana Shiva, "Resources," in *The Development Dictionary: A Guide to Knowledge as Power,* ed. Wolfgang Sachs, 3rd ed. (London: Zed Books, 2019), 228–42.

29. Latour, "Agency at the Time of the Anthropocene."

30. Wark borrows this concept from the philosopher of science Karen Barad. McKenzie Wark, *Molecular Red: Theory for the Anthropocene* (London: Verso, 2015), 162; Karen Barad, *Meeting the Universe Halfway: Quantum Physics and the Entanglement of Matter and Meaning* (Durham, N.C.: Duke University Press, 2007), 178.

31. Wark, *Molecular Red,* xvi.
32. Wark, *Molecular Red,* 200. The words belong to Robinson's character Arkady Bogdanov. In the same passage, Wark specifies that "it won't be a teleology. History has no plan. There is no horizon to orient toward, no line from present to future." Like Derrida, Wark understands teleology in its "hard" definition.
33. James Lovelock, *Gaia: A New Look at Life on Earth* (1979; repr., Oxford: Oxford University Press, 2000), 10.
34. The drawings were exhibited together at *Geostories: Another Architecture for the Environment* exhibition at the Cooper Union, New York (2017) and accompanied by an eponymous catalog (New York: Actar, 2018).
35. Latour, "Who Needs a Philosophy of History?" 11.

INDEX

"A. and Pangeometry" (Lissitzky), 36, 42–43, 43 (fig.), 44, 48

Abstract Cabinet (Lissitzky), 54

activity theory, 160, 188, 203

adaptation, xix, 10, 33, 67, 70, 104, 112, 123, 129, 138, 155, 169, 199

Addams, Jane, xxviii

Adler, Alfred, 252n87

Adorno, Theodor, xvi

aesthetics, 1, 22–23, 25, 28, 90, 104, 132, 160, 202; biology and, 10; positive (Lunacharsky), xxvi–xxvii, 10, 24, 25, 168–70; psychological, 103; psychophysical, 251n56; rationalist, 18; sociological, 159

Agamben, Giorgio, xviii, xxxi, xxxii, 138

Akeley, Carl, 218n57

Akselrod, Pavel, xxvi

Alabyan, Karo, 255n34

Alekseev, Sergey, 161

Alexander III, 50, 53

Alexandrov, Alexander, 214n10

Alfeevsky, Valery: work of, plate 20

"(All Aboard) the Cosmic Architekton" (Ghosn and Jazairy), 206 (fig.)

All-Russian Agricultural and Artisanal-Industrial Exposition, 165, 166

All-Russian Central Executive Committee, 249n20

All-Russian Psychotechnic Society, 80

All-Union Agricultural Exposition, 248n21

All-Union Association of Proletarian Architects (VOPRA), 257n52

All-Union Association of the Chemical Industry (Vsekhimprom), 145, 248n18

All-Union Institute of Experimental Medicine, 188

All-Union Printing Trades Exhibition in Moscow, 54

Altman, Vladimir, 184

America (Mendelsohn), 36, 48, 54, 55, 62

Americanism, 31, 62, 71–77, 79, 81, 104, 206

"Americanism in European Architecture" (Lissitzky), 64

Amov, I., 159

analytical method in art and architecture, 2, 5, 8, 20, 90, 149

Anderson, Stanford, xi

angle-measuring device, 95 (fig.)

Anker, Peder, 217n39

Anschauung, theory of (Brinckmann), 90

anthropagogy, 188

Anthropocene, 204

anthropocentrism, 31, 70, 198, 203

Antokolsky, Lev (Leyba), 145, 146 (fig.), 233n87

apartments, 122, 125, 131, 135 (fig.), 136 (fig.), 149, 246n75; communal, 127, 128 (fig.), 129; transformable, 133–34, 133 (fig.), 134 (fig.); type-F, 129, 130 (fig.), 134, 150; type-K, 150, 151

Architectural Research Laboratory, 84

"Architecture and *Tsvetopis*" (Kostin), 158

Architecture Department (VKhUTEIN), 36, 37, 71, 221n17

Architecture VKhUTEMAS (Lissitzky), 36, 37 (fig.)

Arendt, Hannah, 84, 138, 167, 168, 194, 259n7

Arntz, Gerd, 148

Arp, Jean, 40–41, 229n27

art, 8, 112; monumental, 160; psychological effect of, 22; technology and, 159

"Artistic Preconditions of the Standardization of Civic Individual Furniture, The" (Lissitzky), 133

ARU. *See* Association of Architects-Urbanists

Index

Arup, Ove, xxv
Arvatov, Boris, xxviii, 132, 134
ASNOVA. *See* Association of New Architects
Association of Architects-Urbanists (ARU), 20, 25, 257n52
Association of New Architects (ASNOVA), xxx, 8, 21, 25, 29, 54, 57, 90, 202–3, 213n8, 227n1, 232n70, 233n76, 256n29, 257n52; founding members of, 221n17; members of, xii
Atlas of Forms (Ostwald), 48
Augenmaß. See visual estimation
Augenmassapparat (Münsterberg), 92, 94 (fig.)
Aurelli, Pier Vittorio, 138–39
avant-garde, xvi, xvii, 1, 71, 162, 206
Avenarius, Richard, xx, xxvi, xxvii, 9–10, 153, 201, 255n25; on empiriocriticism, 204, 216n31; philosophy of, 12, 169
Aviation Laboratory, Central Park of Culture and Leisure, Moscow, 192, 257n65
Avtostroy, 20, 21 (fig.)
axonometry, 46, 63, 150

Bachelard, Gaston, 28, 29, 226n79
Bacon, Francis, 194
Bakhtin, Mikhail, 5
Balikhin, Viktor, 2, 21, 221n17; proclamation by, 3 (fig.); work of, plate 2
Balyian, Oganes, 255n34
Barshch, Mikhail, 126, 156
Barsky, Boris, 144
Bauentwurfslehre (Neufert), 122
Bauhaus, xxxi, 72, 82, 127, 144, 145, 147–48, 151, 248n15, plate 12; pedagogy, 220–21n9; theory of color at, 146
Bayer, Herbert, xxv
Bazarov, Vladimir, 8
Behne, Adolf, xii, xiii, xxviii, 17, 45, 213n8, 215n18
Bekhterev, Vladimir, xxv, 218n50
Belyaeva-Ekzemplyarskaya, Sofia, 154–55

Benjamin, Walter, xxviii, 203
Benois, Albert, 141
Bergson, Henri, xix, 220n67
Berlin, Isaiah, 197
Bernal, John, xxv, xxxi
Bernstein, Nikolay, 75, 103; work of, 75 (fig.)
Bezold, Wilhelm von, 151, plate 18
biology, xxxii, 199; aesthetics and, 10
biomechanics, 75, 103
biopolitics, xviii, xxxi, 215n21
Blavatsky, Helena, 69
Blinkov, Iosif, 184
Blonsky, Pavel, xxv, 218n48
Bochenek, Johannes, 12, 13, 109; work of, 13 (fig.)
Bogdanov, Alexander, xxii, xxvii–xxviii, 2, 10, 75–76, 111, 116, 169, 204, 216n31, 241n1, 241n10, 261n32; influence of, 219n61; on tektology, 112, 205
Bois, Yve-Alain, 250n46
Bolbashevsky, Ivan, 355n34
Bolshoi Theater, 190 (fig.)
Borchert, Erich, 145, 146, 146 (fig.), 150, 152, 156, 158, 161, 248n21, 250n50
Botar, Oliver, xxviii
Bouchard, Charles-Joseph, 257n58
Bozhovich, L. I., 257n65
Bragdon, Claude, 46, 48; work of, 49 (fig.)
Bramante, Donato, 34, 35
Breuer, Marcel, xxv
Brewster, David, 45; stereoscope of, 102 (fig.)
brigade method, 81, 82, 83
Brinckmann, Albert Erich, 63, 90, 233n83
Broadway at Night (Lönberg-Holm), 54, 55
Brücke (institute), xx, 242n21
Brücke, Ernst von, 182
Brunelleschi, Filippo, 38
Bubnova, Varvara, 220n7, 221n11
Bücher, Karl, 24
Budkevish, Igor, 146 (fig.)
Buffon, Count de, xxi

Burckhardt, Jacob, 38
Burov, Andrey, 76
Bykhovsky, Bernard, 9

camera obscura, 101
Cantor, Georg, 42, 229n33
Capital, The (Marx), 254n13
Carnap, Rudolf, 148
Castellón Gonzalez, Juan José, 239n68; work of, 99 (fig.), plate 7
Cattell, James McKeen, 79
Çelik Alexander, Zeynep, 103
cell-state theory (Virchow), 111
Central Aviation and Hydrodynamics Institute, 248n21
Central Committee of the Communist Party, 237n37
Central Institute of Labor, xxv, 75, 77 (fig.), 91–92, 124
Central Park of Culture and Leisure, Moscow, xv, xxxi, 163–66, 170–72, 173, 181, 181 (fig.), 182 (fig.), 183 (fig.), 184, 185 (fig.), 186, 190 (fig.), 193–95, 201, 203, 256n47; layout for, 179; opening of, 165, 166; program of, 189
Central Park of Culture and Leisure, Tula, 184, 186 (fig.)
Chakrabarty, Dipesh, 198
Cherkasov, Mikhail, 355n34
Chermayeff, Serge, xxv
Chernyshevsky, Nikolay, 218n50
Chicago Tribune, response to, 67, 69
Children's Village, Central Park of Culture and Leisure, Moscow, 184, 191 (fig.), 192, 257n65
Chmelnizki, Dmitrij, 253n92
Choisy, Auguste, 20, 46
Christiansen, Broder, 151
CIAM, 127, 180, 233n76, 245n68
"City of the Future, The" (Krutikov), 57, 60 (fig.), 61 (fig.), plate 4, plate 5
Ciucci, Georgio, 213n3
civilization, xxi, xxii, 43, 44, 205, 207
Club of Factory No. 12, Elektrostal, 249n20

Club of Railroad Workers, Moscow, 249nn20–21
collective, 28, 104, 166, 178, 200, 203, 215n18, 237n38; individual and, xxvi–xxvii, 172–75, 178–79
Collective Studio of Architecture (SGKhM/VKhUTEMAS), 1–3
collectivism, 136, 197
Collingwood, R. G., 198
colonization, xxii, xxiii
color: combinations, 159; complementary, 142–43; "dynamogenity" of, 154; film, 151; screens, 150; space and, 148; spatial, 151; standardization of, 162; surface, 151; theory, 151, 155
color fatigue, 155, plate 19
Colquhoun, Alan, 213n3
combinatorics, 48, 93, 137, 246n86
Committee of Contemporary Artistic Industry, 143
communism, 200–202
composition, 14, 21, 23, 35, 81, 93, 94, 150, 225n59, 225n62, 232n75; theory of, 22, 25, 26, 28
Concrete Office Building (Mies van der Rohe), 65 (fig.)
consciousness, 10–11, 81, 126, 138, 152, 189, 200, 201; individual, 244n57
construction, 5, 17, 24, 35, 45, 77, 115, 116, 118, 120, 122, 126, 144, 150, plate 18; lightweight, 59; regulation/ rationalization of, 245n64
Construction Codex, 114
Construction Commission (Stroykom), xv, 125 (fig.), 126, 127–28, 129, 130, 132, 134, 144, 147, 156, 180, 245n64, 246n75, 248n15
constructivism, 18; "international," xxviii, 46, 54, 69; in Soviet art and architecture, xii, 5, 46, 72, 76, 80, 132, 143, 156, 222n30
Constructor, The (Lissitzky), 33, 34 (fig.), 36, 38, 40
Contributions to the Analysis of Sensations (Mach), 17; illustration from, 18 (fig.)
"Crane Head and Femur" (Wolff), 41

Index

Crary, Jonathan, 45, 100–101

creativity, 76, 81, 122, 157, 168, 169, 194; architectural, 1, 20; artistic, 10; collective, 84; organizational, 126

critical theory, 198, 199, 203

Critique of Pure Experience, The (Avenarius), 10

Croce, Benedetto, 198, 203

cubism, 2, 44, 149

Culmann, Karl, 42

cultural-historical theory, 192–93, 202

culture, xvi, xvii, xx, 10, 76, 126, 131, 168, 194, 200, 202, 215n18, 241n10; evolutionary history of, 35; leisure and, 166; mass, 166; material, 126, 132

cyclogramometry, 75

D'Acunto, Pierluigi, 239n68; work of, 99 (fig.), plate 7

Dada, 33, 40, 41

daguerreotype, 102

Dalton Plan, 81, 82, 237n37

Danishevsky, Georgy, 165, 178, 182, 188, 255n23, 257n58; on biological/social, 169

Darwin, Charles, 199, 259n10

Darwinism, xviii, xix, 193, 199, 260n13

das Überbewusste/das Unbewusste, 200

Decline of the West, The (Spengler), 43, 159

Dedyukhin, Vladimir, 161, 214n10, 253n92

Deleuze, Gilles: on Riemann space, 45

Delirious New York (Koolhaas), 206

Department of Construction Control, 127

Department of Organic Culture, State Institute of Artistic Culture (GINKhUK),142

depth, estimation of, 96, 98

Dernova-Ermolenko, Avgusta, 80

Derrida, Jacques, 204

Design Earth (Ghosn and Jazairy), 205; drawing by, 206 (fig.)

Development of the Monist View of History, The (Plekhanov), xxvi

Dewey, John, xiv, xxviii, 81, 123

dialectical materialism, xvi, xxvi

Dialectics of Nature (Engels), 214n12

Dickerman, Leah, 33

Dilthey, Wilhelm, 220n67

documentation of factors, 120; cards of, 121 (fig.)

Doesburg, Theo van, 46

Doherty and Donovan (shoe factory), 154

Dokuchaev, Nikolay, xii, 2, 3, 63, 90, 221n17; on aesthetics, 21–22; on structural properties, 12

Dolganov, Vitaly I., 255n34, 257n52

Doryphoros (Polykleitos), 107, 108 (fig.), 109, 123

Drevin, Alexander, 221n11, 249n36

dualism, xix, 215n18

Duchamp, Marcel, 235n17

Duhem, Pierre, xx

dynamism, 23, 56

dynamometer, 154

ecological thought, 213n4, 217n37, 217n45

ecology: economics and, xxi; human, xxi–xxiii, xxv–xxvi; term, 213n4

Economic Council of the Russian Republic, 126

economics, xv, xxv, 118, 125, 127, 129, 144, 157; ecology and, xxi

education: architectural, 86; formal, 157; polytechnic, 76; reforms, 80; theorists, 180

efficiency, 74, 109; industrial, 79

Ehrenburg, Ilya, plate 3

Einstein, Albert, xxviii

Einstellung. See setup

Eisenman, Peter, 223n36

Eisenstein, Sergei, 20, 21, 215n18

Electrotechnical Laboratory, Central Park of Culture and Leisure, Moscow, 257n65

Elements of Architectural-Spatial Composition (Krinsky, Turkus, and Lamtsov), 22

Elements of Rhythmanalysis (Lefebvre), 28

Ellrichshausen, Sofia von: work of, 138, plate 8

emotion, 1, 81, 105, 141, 215n18; James-Lange theory of, xxvii; theory of, 81

Empire State Building, 206

empiricism, xviii, 104

empiriocriticism, 2, 18, 148, 204

empiriomonism, xxvii, 204–5

Ender, Boris, 143, 144, 145, 146 (fig.), 146–47, 160, 203; complementary seeing and, 143

Ender, Georgy, 143

Ender, Maria, 143, 247n10; on color combinations, 159; work of, plate 9

Ender, Xenia, 143

Endless Theater (Kiesler), 174

energeticism, xvii, xx, xxxi, 153, 216n31, 251n54

energy, xxii, 155; fatigue and, 153; productive, 149; psychic, 11; sexual, 9; switching of, 181

energy-economic principle, 9–10

Engelmeyer, Peter, 124, 199

Engels, Friedrich, 35, 214n12, 255n23

Engineer Menni (Bogdanov), xxii (fig.)

environment, 116, 120; chromatic, 159, 160; organism and, 90; social, 189; spatial, 20; urban, 20, 44

epistemology, xxvii, 43–44, 197

Equity Trust Building, New York, 51

ergography, xiv, 153–54, 154 (fig.), 161, 251n56

Ermansky, Osip, 11, 113–15, 223n33

Ethics (Spinoza), 218n50

eugenics, xiv, xx, 23

Euler, Leonhard, 45

Evans, Robin, 230n49

"Everyday Life and the Culture of the Object" (Arvatov), 132

evolution, 42, 57, 166, 193, 199–200, 216n26; biological, 175, 193; psychological, 131; social, xxx, 126, 131, 138, 169, 194, 195, 202, 203

evolutionary theory, xix, xxx, 123, 198

evolutionism, xix; neo-Lamarckian, xvii, xx, 163

Evzerikhin, photo by, 189 (fig.)

Exhibition of Achievements of National Economy, 248n21

Existenzminimum, 127, 245n68

Experimental Laboratory of Physical-Physiological Foundations of Fine Arts within the State Institute of Art History, Leningrad, 142

expressing, method of, 22, 23 (fig.)

Eye and Its Work (Kravkov), 103

Farbkunde (Ostwald), 147, plate 11

fatigue, 155; energy and, 153

Favorskii, Vladimir, 223n41

Fechner, Gustav, 24

Féré, Charles, 153–54, 156; color screens and, 150; ergograph of, 154 (fig.)

Fidman, Efimov, 221n17

Fidman, Vladimir I., 221n17, 257n52

field theory (Lewin), 189, 258n66

Filippov, Mikhail, 218n50

Finite Format 04 (Pezo and Ellrichshausen), 138, plate 8

First All-Russian NOT Conference, 219n62

First Five-Year Plan, xv, xviii, 72, 74, 79, 113, 144, 163, 165, 194, 214n9

Florensky, Pavel, 229n33

"Flying City, The" (Krutikov). *See* "City of the Future, The"

"For a Socialist Reorganization of Design Offices" (Karra), 81

Forbát, Alfréd (Fred), 144, 248n15

Ford, Henry, 24, 72, 73, 75

Fordism, 73, 74, 79, 166

foreign expertise, 74, 144–47

formalism, xi, xiv, xix, 223n39; in aesthetics, 2; in architecture, xii; in literature, 5, 10, 12, 223n39. *See also* rationalism

"Formalism in the Science of Art" (Lunacharsky), 22

form and function, beyond, xi–xii, xiv–xv

Form and Function (Russell), xi

"Form-Making of Dynamic Element, The" (Krutikov), 57

fotopis' (Lissitzky), 159

Foucault, Michel, 162, 215n21

Foundations of Positive Aesthetics, The (Lunacharsky), xxvi–xxviii, 10, 24, 168

Foundations of Psychotechnics (Münsterberg), 79

Foundations of Realist Worldview, The (Bogdanov, Lunacharsky, and Gorky), xxvii

"Foundations of the Philosophy of Life" (Suvorov), xxvii

4D Lightful Tower (Fuller), 59 (fig.), 60 (fig.)

4D Transport (Fuller), 57

Frampton, Kenneth, 138

Francé, Raoul, xii, 42

freedom, xxiv, xxxi, 138, 167; and necessity, 204; of will, 200

"Freedom of Necessity, The" (Bernal), xxxi

Frege, Gottlob, xiv

Freud, Sigmund, xxx, 9, 182, 200, 201

Friche, Vladimir, 8, 159, 221n18

Frimmer, Martin, 239n73

Fuller, Buckminster, 233n76; *4D Lightful Tower,* 59 (fig.), 60; 4D Transport, 57

functionalism, xi, xiv, xix, 110, 122–24, 126, 131, 157, 198; psychological, 122, 123

"Functionalist Sway, A" (Katichev), 158

furniture: modular (combinable), 132, 135 (fig.); standardized, 136, 136 (fig.); transformable, 132–34, 133 (fig.), 134 (fig.)

Gadamer, Hans-Georg, xiv

Gaia, theory of, 204, 205, 261n29

Galton, Francis, 79

Gastev, Alexey, xxv, 75, 76, 77, 80, 102–3, 124, 126, 129, 218n48, 235n14

Gauss, Carl Friedrich, 42, 44

Geddes, Patrick, xx, xxiii, 216n30

Gellerstein, Solomon, 90, 92

General Theory of Design of Architectural Structures (Rozenberg), 118

geometry, 14, 16, 36, 62, 109, 230n49; Euclidian, 44; non-Euclidian, 42, 67

Geostories (Ghosn and Jazairy), 205

Gere, Cathy, xviii

"German Ideology, The" (Marx), 167

German Society of Friends of New Russia, xxviii

Ghosn, Rania, 205; work of, 206 (fig.)

Giedion, Sigfried, 20, 54, 254n14

Giese, Fritz, 24, 25, 98, 222n23, 236n25, 238n49; diagram by, 100 (fig.); "pathological" graphs by, 87 (fig.); psychotechnics and, 9, 11, 86; rationalization and, 11

giftedness: intellectual, 86, 90; intellectual/spatial, 90

Gilbreth, Frank, 11, 75, 79

Gilbreth, Lillian, 75, 79

Ginzburg, Moisei, xii, xvii, xxi, xxx, 113, 123, 125 (fig.), 126, 127, 129, 131, 134, 136, 146, 148, 151, 152, 156, 159, 181, 186, 205, 227n1, 245n65, 257n52, plate 13, plate 14, plate 16; functionalism of, 122, 203; purposeful setup and, 124; rhythm and, 24–25; typification, xxx; work of, 128 (fig.), 149, 182 (fig.), 183; zoning and, 138, 180, 182. *See also* Government Building, Almaty; Narkomfin building, Moscow

Glahn, Thomas, 253n2

Glan, Betty, xvi, 163, 164 (fig.), 165, 170, 180, 194, 254n7, 255n34, 256n44, 258n78; on park, 181, 188, 189

"Glass skyscraper" (Mies van der Rohe), 41, 42, 62, 63

glazomer. See visual estimation

Glazyrin, Vladimir, 243n27

god-building/god-seeking, 172–73

Goldhagen, Sarah, 213n3

Golosov, Ilya, xvii

Gonzalez, Jose Castellon: work of, 99 (fig.)

Gorkić, Milan, xvi, 194

Gorki manor, 100, 239n75

Gorky, Maxim, xxvi, xxvii, xxviii, 169,

170, 218n53, 248n21; god-building and, 172–73

Gorky Park. *See* Central Park of Culture and Leisure, Moscow

Gosproektstroy, 74

Goszelenstroi, 255n34

Gough, Mari, 67

Government Building, Almaty (Ginzburg and Milinis), 149, 248n21, plate 14

Graham, Ernest R., 231n63

Graham, Loren, 214n12

Green City (Melnikov), 150

Gropius, Walter, xxv, 72

Groys, Boris, 202

Grudzinsky, Arkady, 86

Guattari, Félix, 45

GULAG (Main Directorate of Camps), xv, xvi, 214n10

Gulyaev, V., 253n25

Haeckel, Ernst, xii, xix, xxi, xxvi, 204; on monism, 216n26; on tektology, 111

Haldane, J. B. S., xxviii, 198, 216n30

Hamsun, Knut, 253n2

Handbook of Color, The (Matyushin), 143, 159, plate 10

Haraway, Donna, 69, 70, 218n57

Harmon, Arthur Loomis, 50

Hartmann, Eduard von, 9, 65, 103, 116, 199, 200, 260n13

Harvard Psychological Laboratory, 94 (fig.)

Haussmann, Raoul, xxviii

Hayles, N. Katherine, 69, 70

Hays, Michael K., 62, 69, 70

Hegel, G. W. F., 198, 200

Hegelianism, 198, 199, 200

Heinz brothers, 57; work of, 59 (fig.)

Helmholtz, Hermann von, 14, 90, 91, 218n50; Hering and, 96, 97

Hemingway, Ernest, xxviii

Henry, Charles, 251n56

Herbart, Johann Friedrich, 9

Hering, Ewald, 90, 249n29; Helmholtz and, 96, 97; *Tiefenwahrnehmungsapparat* of, 101 (fig.)

Higher Art and Technical Institute (VKhUTEIN), 46, 60, 61, 71, 72, 84, 89, 131, 146, 147, 155, 156, 157, 236n2, plate 18; building, 91, 174 (fig.); Psychotechnical Laboratory at, 222n23

Higher Art and Technical Studios (VKhUTEMAS), xv, 1, 3, 8, 12, 21, 36, 71, 72, 103, 147, 174, 246n85, plate 11; pedagogy, 220–21n9

Higher Institute of Architecture and Construction (VASI), 77, 155, 236n22

Hilberseimer, Ludwig, xxviii, 69

Hildebrand, Adolf von, 14, 103, 223n41, 224n43, 230n43, 233n83

Hinton, Charles Howard, 46, 49

Histoire de l'architecture (Choisy), 20

history, 198; concept of, 205; intellectual, xvi; Lamarckian, 204; natural, 198; teleological, 204; in Marxism, 200

Hitchcock, Henry-Russell, xi, 73

Höch, Hannah, xxviii

Holzapfel, Rudolf Maria, 201, 203, 254n19

homo sacer (Agamben), xviii, xxxi

Homo Sacer (Agamben), xviii

Homo sapiens, xix, xxxi, 193; social evolution of, 202

homo socialis, 169

"horizontal skyscrapers" (Lissitzky). See *Wolkenbügels*

Hospital of Peter the Great, St. Petersburg, 110 (fig.), 242n13

"Hotel-Type Dwelling" (Krutikov), 60 (fig.)

How to Use the Sun, Air, and Water (Orlyuk), 178

Human Condition, The (Arendt), 138

human ecology, xxi–xxiii, xxv–xxvi

humanism, xix, 11, 103, 104, 160, 166, 168, 194, 204; Renaissance, 38; Scientific (Huxley), xxiii

Hunt, Robert, 239n74

Huxley, Julian, xx, xxv, xxviii, 163, 174, 216n30; on Central Park of Culture and Leisure, Moscow, 172;

on humanism, xix; on Lysenko and, 220n69; modernism and, 215n22, 217n45; PEP and, xxiii, 122; on politics, xxiii; Wells and, xxi–xxii
hygiene, 109, 112, 116, 131, 166
Hygiene exhibition, Dresden, 132

idealism, xiv, xvii, xviii, 132, 198, 203; Hegelian, 201; Kantian, 18; materialism and, 215n18
Idea of History, The (Collingwood), 198
If I Were a Dictator (Huxley), xxiii
Illiffe, Robert, 254n20
Ilyin, Lev, 110, 242n13; work of, 110 (fig.)
Ilyinsky, Nikolay, 74
"Imminent Catastrophe and How to Struggle with It" (Lenin), 144
Imperial Academy of the Arts, St. Petersburg, 145
impressionism, 44, 149
individuality, 2, 28, 81, 104, 131; collectivity and, xxvi–xxvii, 172–75, 178–79; loss of, 138; recognition of, 79; socialist, 84
industrialization, xv, xviii, xxiii, xxv, 25, 113, 127, 141, 161, 194
industrial management, 74, 79
INKhUK. *See* Moscow Institute of Artistic Culture
Institute for Advanced Study, 241n7
Institute for Mass Psychology, Moscow, 156
Institute of Electric Energy, Moscow, 248n21
Institute of Resort Studies, Moscow, 178, 179, 184, 256n46
Institute of Timber, 246n79
intellectual exchange, Soviet-German, 146–47
International Congresses of Modern Architecture. *See* CIAM
International Style (exhibition), xi, 233n76
Iskry nauki (Sparkles of Science), 85
ISOTYPE (International System of Typographic Picture Education), 148

I Want a Child (Tretyakov), 175
Izvestia ASNOVA, 31, 50, 53, 63

Jackson, Myles, 241n7
Jacobson, Roman, 12, 223n38
James, William, 123; James-Lange theory of emotion, xxvii
Jaques-Dalcroze, Émile, 24
Jazairy, El Hadi, 205; work of, 206 (fig.)
Johnson, Philip, xi, 233n76

Kahn, Albert, 72, 73, 76, 104; organization of design work and, 74
Kahn, Fritz: homunculus of, 83–84, 85 (fig.)
Kalinin, Fedor: on consciousness, 10–11
Kalmykov, Viktor P., 257n52; Avtostroy and, 20; rhythm and, 25; work of, 21 (fig.), 26–27 (fig.)
Kammerer, Paul, 316n30
Kandinsky, Wassily, 2, 24, 148, 226n69
Kant, Immanuel, 19, 90, 111, 123, 259n11
Kapp, Ernst, 35, 42
Karra, Alexander, 104, 105; brigade method and, 81–84, 83 (fig.)
Katichev, P. F., 157–58
Katz, David, 39, 151
Kaulina, N. N., 257n65
Kazakov, S., 253n25
Keldysh, A. A., 257n65
Keynes, John Maynard, xxviii
Khan-Magomedov, Selim, 33, 222n30, 223n40, 227n5, 234n1
Kharkevich, V. Kh., 257n65
Kharlamov, Nikita, 257n65
Kharlampiev brothers, 178
Kiesler, Frederick, 174, 233n76
Kinetic Construction System (Moholy-Nagy), 175, 176 (fig.), 177 (fig.), 256n43
kitchen-element (Lissitzky and Lissitzky-Küppers), 136, 137 (fig.)
Klee, Paul, 148
Klein, Alexander, 110, 138, 242n13, plate 8; work of, 110 (fig.), 116, 117 (fig.), 123–24

Klevin, N. A., 257n65

Kloppenberg, James, xviii, 214n18

Klutsis, Gustav, xxv, 218n48, 249n36

Kochar, Georg, 214n10

Koffka, Kurt, 229n25

Komsomol'skaia Pravda, 252n76

Koolhaas, Rem, 205, 206

Korobov, Andrey S., 184, 257n52; park of culture and leisure and, 185 (fig.)

Korolev, Boris, 2, 5, 221n11

Korzhev, Mikhail, 21, 22, 255n34

Kostin, Vladimir, 252n76, 252n83; *tsvetopis'* and, 158–59

Kracauer, Siegfried, 72

Krajewski, Markus, 242n21

Krajewski, Max, 248n21

Krasilnikov, Nikolay, 2; proclamation by, 3 (fig.)

Krasnokholmskaya factory, Moscow, 257n47

Kravkov, Sergey, 103, 147, 155

Kremlin, 66, 67, 68

Kries, Johannes von, 142

Krinsky, Vladimir, 2, 3, 5, 22, 221n11, 221n17

Kruchenykh, Aleksey, 247n4

Krupskaya, Nadezhda, xxv

Krutikov, Georgy, 36, 46, 54–57, 86, 94, 97, 203, 232n73, 232n75, 238n60; "The City of the Future," 58 (fig.), 60 (fig.), 61 (fig.), plate 4, plate 5; collaborations with Lissitzky, 54; on combinatorics, 48, 93, 246n86; other work of, 56 (fig.); on panarchitecture, 52, 54, 56, 57, 58

Kryukov, Mikhail, 214n10

Kuktyniksy (artist collective), work of, 78 (fig.)

Kuznetskii Most, Moscow, 233n87

Kychakov, Innokenty P., 255n34, 257n52

Kyiv Institute of Construction, 149

labor, xx–xxi, 23, 79, 81, 154, 165, 167; architectural, 36; division of, 73, 84, 102, 104, 242n18; productivity of, 156, 169. *See also* scientific organization of labor

Laboratory for Experimental Pedagogical Psychology, 236n27

Laboratory of Color Perception, Narkompros, 61, 247n10

Laboratory of Furniture, Institute of Timber, Moscow, 246n79

"Labor Commune, The" (Krutikov), 61 (fig.)

Ladovsky, Nikolay, xvii, 6 (fig.), 12–22, 25, 34, 46, 48, 63, 81, 84, 86, 87, 88, 90, 93, 96, 103, 104, 156, 173, 174, 184, 215n18, 221n11, 221n17, 222n23, 223n40, 224n45; architectural theory of, 2, 13, 14; ASNOVA and, xii, 8, 31; Collective Studio of, 2; on empiriocriticism ("Machism"), 18–19, 202–3; at INKhUK, 5; *liglazomer* of, 91; *oglazomer* of, 96 (fig.); pedagogical method of, 8; *ploglazomer* of, 94; psychoanalytical method and, xxx; psychotechnics and, 9, 71, 91; on rational architecture (rationalism), 11, 104, 222n30; at SGKhM, 2–3; space-meter (*prostrometr*) of, 97, 98, 99–100; Student Profile Form of, 89 (fig.); *uglazomer* of, 95 (fig.); work of, 4 (fig.), 6 (fig.), 7 (fig.), 16 (fig.), 92 (fig.), 93 (fig.), plate 2

Lamarck, Jean-Baptiste, 199

Lamarckism, xxviii, 163

Lambert, Will, 249n23

Lamtsov, Ivan, 21, 22, 225n59

landscape architecture, xxx, 187; rationalist compositional theory and, 26–27; urbanism and, 183

Lange, Torsten, 239n68

Latour, Bruno, 199, 204, 207

Law of Bone Remodeling (Wolff), 41

Lazursky, Alexander, 236n27

Lebedeva (Mavrina), Tatyana: work of, plate 20

Lebensphilosophie, xxviii

Le Corbusier, xii, 20, 63, 71, 76, 113, 127, 148, 223n36; on colors/space, 149

Lefebvre, Henri, 28, 29

Léger, Fernand, 141, 151; work of, 149, plate 13

leisure, 165–72, 194, 254n22

Lenin, Vladimir, xxv, xxvi, xxvii, 100, 134, 144, 214n12, 218n50; on Taylorism, 76

Leningrad Institute of Civil Engineers, 247n10

Leningrad Society of Architects, 242n13

Leonardo da Vinci, 228n12

Leontyev, Alexey N., 257n65; activity theory of, 160, 203; work in the Central Park of Culture and Leisure, Moscow, 188–93

Lessing, Gotthold Ephraim, 124, 244n55

Letatlin (Tatlin), 74

Levitov, Nikolay, 92, 103

Lewin, Kurt, xxiii, 188, 192, 258n66

Liberated Labor factory, Moscow, 257n47

life, concept of, xix–xxi, xxv–xxxii, 10–11, 24–25, 28, 42–44, 75–76, 110 (fig.), 111, 122–25, 129, 136–39, 148, 193, 197–99, 202, 205, 207, 214n12, 215n25, 219n57, 220n67

liglazomer, 92, 92 (fig.)

Lipps, Theodor, 20, 91

Lisagor, Solomon, xvi, 214n10

Lissitzky, El, xii, xxviii, xxix, xxx, 31–55, 57, 62–67, 70, 113, 123, 127, 131–34, 138, 146, 159, 183–86, 203, 227n5, 227n10, 228n16, 228n19, 230n54, 231n62, 231n63, 232n73, 233n76, 233n87, 246n79; "A. and Pangeometry" of, 36, 39 (fig.), 42–44, 48 (fig.); *Abstract Cabinet,* 54; "Americanism in European Architecture," 64; on anthropocentrism, 31–36, 38–42; ASNOVA and, 31, 227n1; Central Park of Culture and Leisure, Moscow, 172–79; *The Constructor,* of, 33–40; "demonstration spaces," 52; on *fotopis',* 159; furniture design, 131–38; kitchen-element (with Lissitzky-Küppers), 136; "Man Is the Measure of All Tailors," 32 (fig.), 53 (fig.);

Narokomvin building, furniture for, 134, 135 (fig.), 136 (fig.), 137 (fig.); Park of Culture and Leisure, Sverdlovsk (with Korobov), 185 (fig.); on perspective, 36, 38–39, 44–45; Pravda, complex for, 67, 69, 69 (fig.); Prouns of, 33, 44, 46, 47 (fig.), 65, 67; Spiral Side, 175, 177 (fig.); Stroykom and, 133–34; Tatlin at Work on the Monument to the Third International, 44, plate 3; on typification, xxx; *Wolkenbügels* of, xiii (fig.), 31, 33, 57, 63, 64, 65, 66, 66 (fig.), 67, 68 (fig.), 233n87; work of, xiii (fig.), xiv (fig.), 32 (fig.), 33, 34–35, 43 (fig.), 36, 37 (fig.), 38, 39 (fig.), 40, 40 (fig.), 42–43, 43 (fig.), 44, 47 (fig.), 53 (fig.), 54, 55 (fig.), 57, 63, 64 (fig.), 66 (fig.), 69, 69 (fig.), 70, 134 (fig.), 135 (fig.), 137 (fig.), 173–74, 175 (fig.), 177 (fig.), 178, 179 (fig.), plate 3, plate 4, plate 5, plate 6

Lissitzky-Küppers, Sophie, 34; kitchen-element (with Lissitzky), 136; work of, 137 (fig.)

Lobachevsky, Nikolay, 42, 44

Locke, John, 90

Lönberg-Holm, Knud, 54, 56, 57, 231n63; ASNOVA and, 233n76

London, Jack, xxviii

London Zoo, xv, 174

López-Durán, Fabiola, 163, 193

Lovelock, James, 204, 205, 261n29

Lubetkin, Berthold, xxv, 174

Lueder, Christoph, 123

Lunacharsky, Anatoly, xxvi, xxvii–xxviii, xxix, xxxi, 8, 10, 79, 80, 123, 165, 168, 169, 194, 201, 216nn30–31, 223n33, 254n7, 254n21, 255n25, 255n36; aesthetics of, xxvi–xxxviii, 10, 24–25, 28, 168–70; on anthropagogy, 188, 189; collectivism of, 2, 194; on education, 76; god-building and, 172–73; on individuality, 84; on mass spectacle, 226n77; Nietzscheanism and, 219n58; on rhythm, 24, 25

Luria, Alexander, 9, 38, 229n25

Lysenko, Trofim, xxviii, 220n69
Lyudvig, Genrikh, 214n10
Lyushin, Alexander, plate 19

Mach, Ernst, xiv, xx, 8, 17, 19, 96, 102, 124, 198, 201–3, 205, 216n32, 218n50, 249n29; empiriocriticism of, 204; epistemology of, 17–18, 19; illustration by, 18 (fig.)
McLeod, Mary, 74
Mácza, János, 158–60, 252n76, 253n86
Maertens, Hermann, 48
Maison Dom-Ino (Le Corbusier), 223n36
Malevich, Kazimir, 46, 206, 247n4
Malyarnoe delo, 145, 151, 154, 158, 247n2, plate 17
Malyarstroy. *See* State Trust for Wall-Painting Works
"Man Is the Measure of All Tailors" (Lissitzky), 32 (fig.), 53 (fig.); text of, 31
Mann, Thomas, and Heinrich, xxviii
Mapu, Georgy, 2, 227n11
Marbe, Karl, 124
Marin, Louis, 203–4
Martin, Rudolf, xxvi
Marx, Karl, xxvi, 9, 84, 167, 194, 198, 254n13, 255n23; on labor, xx–xxi, 166; on history, 200
Marxism, xx, xxi, xxvi, xxvii, 8, 193, 194, 197, 200, 205
materialism, xiv, 44, 132, 189, 198, 207; idealism and, 219n18
Materialism and Empirio-Criticism (Lenin), xxvii
Matorin, Sergey, 255n34
Matsa, Ivan. *See* Mácza, János
Matveeva, Sofia, 146, 146 (fig.)
Matyushin, Mikhail, 141, 146, 152, 155, 159, 160, 247n4, 253n86; on complementary color, 142–43; on expanded seeing, 142; work of, 143, plate 9, plate 10
May, Ernst, 245n68, 248n15, 249n25
Mayakovsky, Vladimir, xxv, 12, 223n38
Mazmonyan, Mikael, 173–75, 194, 214n10, 255n34; work of, 174 (fig.)

"Measure of All Things, The" (Arp), 40–41
mechanicism, xix, xx, 1, 28, 75, 76, 77, 79, 85, 103–4, 123, 133, 157, 160, 161, 215n24
Mechnikov, Ilya, 216n32
Meister, Anna-Maria, 242n21
Melnikov, Konstantin, xvii, 150, 172, 183, 184, 257n52; project for Central Park of Culture and Leisure, Moscow, 186; work of, 181 (fig.); zoning and, 180
Mendelsohn, Erich, 36, 48, 54, 55, 231n63
Mensch als Industriepalast, Der (Kahn), 85 (fig.)
Merz, 41, 62
Meyer, Hannes, 69, 73, 82, 122, 148, 222n23
Meyerhold, Vsevolod, 75, 80, 81, 173; theater of, 174, 175 (fig.)
Meynert, Theodor, xxvii, 219n59
Mies van der Rohe, Ludwig, xxviii, 46, 62, 63, 65, 69, 215n18; work of, 41 (fig.), 42, 65 (fig.)
Milinis, Ignaty, 127, 149; work of, 128 (fig.), plate 14. *See also* Government Building, Almaty; Narkomfin building, Moscow
Milyutin, Nikolay, 127, 150, 180, 182, 194, plate 16
Minnesota Spatial Relations Test, 230n55
Mochalov, Sergey, 2, 221n17; proclamation by, 3 (fig.)
moderne Zweckbau, Die (Behne). See *Modern Functional Building, The*
Modern Functional Building, The (Behne), xii, xiii (fig.), 17, 213n8
modernism, xi, xvi, xvii, xviii, xx, xxvi, xxvii, xxxii, 73, 103, 138, 148, 194, 202, 207, 213n3, 215n19, 217n45; functionalism and, 233n76; German, 161–62
modernity, xxv–xxvi, xxx, xxxii, 31, 33, 52, 54, 56, 71, 148, 215n19

modernization, xiv, xv–xxi, xxiii, 72, 194

Moede, Walther, 92; angle-measuring device of, 95 (fig.)

Moholy-Nagy, László, xxv, xxviii, 54, 175, 177, 222n23, 256n43; work of, 176 (fig.)

Molecular Red (Wark), 204

monism, xiv, xx, xxi, xxv–xxvi, xxx, xxxii, 197, 199, 214n18, 216n26; Russian Revolution and, xxvi–xxix

Monism of the Universe, The (Tsiolkovsky), xxviii

Monist, The, xiv

Monist League, xix, xxi, xxi, 147, 258n1

Montreal Industrial Painting Company, 154, 155 (fig.)

Moore, Bryan, 69–70

Morris, William, 168, 169

Moscow, 54, 80, 84, 86, 90–94, 122, 144, 150, 161, 163, 180, 184

Moscow Architectural Artel, 34, 84

Moscow Central Park of Culture and Leisure. *See* Central Park of Culture and Leisure, Moscow

Moscow Council of Workers' Deputies (Mossovet), 165, 214n10

Moscow Higher Technical College, 149

Moscow Institute of Artistic Culture (INKhUK), 2, 8, 35, 220n6

Moscow Institute of Statistics (Izostat), 148

Moscow Testological Association, 80

Moscow Union of Consumption Associations, 249n20

Mosso, Angelo, 153, 154

motion: perception of, 52–53, studies, 79

Mowris, Peter Michael, 226n69

Muller, H. J., 216n30

Muller, Johannes, 111

Münsterberg, Hugo, 79, 81, 86, 90, 124, 236n25; *Augenmaß* (visual estimation) and, 91; *Augenmassapparat* and, 92; psychotechnics and, 126; work of, 94 (fig.)

Muthesius, Hermann, 8, 157

Narkomfin. *See* Soviet Ministry of Finance

Narkomfin building, Moscow (Ginzburg and Milinis), 127, 128 (fig.), 131, 137, 147, 149, 150, 15, 152, 156, 161, 162, plate 12, plate 16; furniture for, 136 (fig.); kitchen-element for, 137 (fig.); social program of, 148

Narkompros. *See* People's Commissariat of Culture and Education

National Research Association for Efficiency in Construction and Housing (Germany), 147

Natural History (de Buffon), xxi

natural sciences, xix, 198, 200

nature, xxi, xxxi, 72, 165, 166, 199, 258n4; return to, 38, 40–44

Nauen, Germany, 231n62

Naval Correctional Facility, Seattle, 162

Nechaev, Alexander, 236n27

Neufert, Ernst, 12, 63, 109

Neurath, Otto, 148

New Economic Policy, xv

Newman, Oscar, 213n3

News from Nowhere (Morris), 168

New Work Regulation, 242n25

Nietzsche, Friedrich, 25, 38, 70, 116, 220n67

Nikolsky, Alexander, 143, 247n10

Nisbet, Peter, 43

Nishenko, N., 145

Noiré, Ludwig, xxvii, 241n11

Normalisierung, 114

normalization, 116, 118, 122, 129, 131

norming, 114, 115, 118–22

Normung. See standardization

NOT. *See* scientific organization of labor

object, subject and, 17–18

Objective Analysis, Working Group of (INKhUK), 2, 5, 220n7

Office of Design, Malyarstroy, 145, 146, 249n20

Office of Design and Planning, Central Park of Culture and Leisure, Moscow, 172, 181, 255n34

oglazomer, 92, 96 (fig.)

Okhitovich, Mikhail, xvi, 214n10

Olgyay, Aladar, xxv
Olgyay, Victor, xxv
Oppel, Vladimir, 85
organicism, xii, xxv, 207
organism, xii, xx, 18, 25, 84, 111, 123, 126, 131, 133; environment and, 90; human, 158
organizational work, 5, 103, 104, 111, 112
Organization of Contemporary Architecture (OSA), xii, xxx, 143, 257n52
orgdobavki, 120
orientation, 44, 52, 67, 124; spatial, 90
Orlyuk, Alexander, 178, 256n47; work of, 179 (fig.)
OSA. *See* Organization of Contemporary Architecture
Osman, Michael, xxiii, 72
Osmerkin, Alexander, 249n36
Ostwald, Wilhelm, 48, 147, 157, 216n31, 216n32, 218n53, plate 11; color theory of, 151, 159, 160, 249n29; color triangle by, plate 19; energeticism and, xx, 153
otium, 168
Ouspensky, P. D., 46, 142
Ovsyaniko-Kulikovsky, Dmitry, 10
Ovsyannikova, Elena: work of, plate 16
Ozenfant, Amédée, 149

Painters Magazine, The, image from, 155 (fig.)
Palace of the Soviets, 214n16, 249n36, 256n39
panarchitecture, 57
Pangeometry (Lobachevsky), 42
pangeometry and, 52, 54, 56, 58
Panideal (Holzapfel), 201
"Parallelepiped" (Petrov), 15 (fig.)
Parkhurst, Helen, 81
Park of Culture and Rest. *See* Central Park of Culture and Leisure, Moscow
Pasternak, Alexander, 126
Pearson, Karl, 8, 216n30, 223n42
pedagogy, xxv, xxx, 14, 16, 23, 71, 80, 84, 86, 123, 161, 188, 220n4

Peirce, Charles Sanders, xiv
Pelican Drawing Ink, 228n16
Pelz (Fur) exhibition (Lissitzky), xxiv (fig.)
People's Commissariat of Culture and Education (Narkompros), xxvii, 1–3, 8, 76, 82, 104, 161, 254n7
PEP. *See* Political and Economic Planning
personal development, 171, 189, 192
Peter the Great, 109, 114
Petrov, A., 12, 14, 223n38, 224n45, 225n59
Petrov, V. A., 16, 21; work of, 15 (fig.)
Petrović, Mihailo, 241n11
Petrov-Vodkin, Kuz'ma, 231n62
Peus, Heinrich, xxi
Pezo, Mauricio: work of, 138, plate 8
Philosophical Notebooks (Lenin), 214n12
Philosophy as Thinking about the World according to the Principle of the Smallest Measure of Force (Avenarius), 9–10
Philosophy of Architecture (Rozenberg), 112
Philosophy of the Unconscious (Hartmann), 9, 199
physiological, 81, 91, 102, 104, 156
Picasso, Pablo, 2
Pinheiro dos Santos, Lucio Alberto, 227n80
Piscator, Erwin, xxviii
planning, economic, xxv, 74, 126, 144, 197, 217n4
"plan of the center of Moscow with the skyscrapers along the A circle, The" (Lissitzky), 64 (fig.)
Platten, Fritz, xxvi
Plekhanov, Georgy, xxvi, 218n50
Plenge, Johann, 241n11
Pliny the Younger, 254n20
ploglazomer, 92, 93 (fig.), 94
Poetics of Space, The (Bachelard), 28
Poincaré, Henri, xx, 10, 198, 216n32, 222n29
Political and Economic Planning (PEP), xxiii, 122
political theory, 197, 202

politics, xxiii, 160, 199, 201, 202

Polykleitos, 107, 108, 108 (fig.), 109

Pomortsev, Nikolay, 159

Popova, Lyubov, 2, 5, 80

Popova, T.: work of, 75 (fig.)

positivism, xiv, xviii

post-Fordism, 105, 194

posthumanism, 69, 70

postmodernism, 70

Potebnya, Alexander, 10

"Practicum of Color Theory," plate 19

Pravda, 165, 214n13; complex for (Lissitzky), 67, 69, 69 (fig.)

Pressa exhibition, Cologne, 54

Price, Cedrik, 139

Primer of Higher Space (The Fourth Dimension), A (Bragdon), 49 (fig.)

Principles of Biology (Spencer), xix

Problem of Form in the Fine Arts (Ladovsky), 14

Production of Space, The (Lefebvre), 28

Production-Technical Sector, 145

productivism, xxv, 28, 72, 104, 161, 194

Prokhorova, Militsa I., 255n34, 257n52; project of, 184, 186–87, 186 (fig.)

Proletarian Culture (Proletkult) movement, xxvii, 75, 204, 219n62

Proletarskaya Kultura, 10

prostrometr. See space-meter

Protagoras, 133

"Proun on the theme of horizontal skyscraper" (Lissitzky), 47 (fig.)

Proun Room (Lissitzky), 65

Prouns (Lissitzky), 33, 44, 46, 47 (fig.), 65, 67

psychoanalysis, xiv, 8–9, 28, 222n19; consumer/political propaganda and, 226n74

"Psychoanalysis as a System of Monist Psychology" (Luria), 9

psychoanalytical method of architecture (Ladovsky). *See* analytical method in art and architecture

Psychoanalytical Psychotechnics (Giese), 9

Psychological Atlas (Katz), 39

Psychological Brigade of the All-Union

Institute of Experimental Medicine, 188

psychological profiles, 79, 88 (fig.)

psychological testing, 80, 91

psychology, xxv, 20, 23, 45, 90, 104, 123, 154, 159; applied, 9; architectural, 86; environmental, 162; experimental, 187; Gestalt, 38, 43; labor, 154; rhythmanalysis in, 28

psychophysiological, xxx, 124

Psychotechnical Laboratory of Architecture (VKhUTIEN), xxx, 11, 56, 71, 84, 156, 222n23

psychotechnics, xiv, xxv, 11, 71, 79, 80, 81, 84, 86, 87 (fig.), 91, 93–94, 97, 104, 222n23, 236n26

purism, 149

Purkinje, Jan Evangelista, 142

pyramid, perspective representation of, 39 (fig.)

Rabinbach, Anson, 153

Raphael, 34; work of, 35 (fig.)

Rasch, Bodo and Heinz, 57; work of, 59 (fig.)

rationalism, 44, 104, 221n17, 222n30, 230n42; Cartesian, 70; in Soviet architecture, xii, 1, 5, 8, 11–12, 16–18, 21–28

rationality, 11, 46, 118, 158; architectural, 5; spatial, 118; technical, 5, 11

rationalization, xxii, xxv, 29, 72, 74, 86, 114, 127, 131, 156, 193; organization of labor and, 11

Record (Lissitzky), 54, 55 (fig.)

Red Stadium, Moscow (project), 54

Regional Construction Plan for Petrograd region (Rozenberg), 242n13

Reinheimer, Hermann, xxi

relationships: spatial, 56, 99; visual proportional, 233n83

Renaissance, 38, 41, 42, 45

residential cell, 129

revealing, method of, 4 (fig.), 12, 14, 15 (fig.), 22, 23 (fig.)

rhythm, 23–25, 28–29; aesthetic, 24; spatial, 25

rhythmanalysis (Lefebvre), 28, 227n80
Rhythm in Architecture (Ginzburg), 24–25
Richter, Hans, xxviii
Riddle of the Universe, The (Haeckel), xix
Riemann, Bernhard, 44, 46
Riemann space, 44–46, 48, 50–52
Rietveld, Gerrit, 132
Rio de Janeiro Psychological and Philosophical Society, 227n80
Robespierre, 173
Robinson, Kim Stanley, 204, 261n32
Rochefort, Nicholas de, 242n24
Rodchenko, Alexander, 2, 5, 231n60
Roentgen technology, 36, 38, 102
Rolland, Romain, 201, 254n19
Rosenblum, A. N., 257n65
Rosengart, G. L., 257n65
Roshchin, L., 173
Rossolimo, Grigory, 230n55, 236n27, 238n49
Rot-Front (Rote Front) Brigade, 82
Rozenberg, Alexander V., 110, 112, 113, 118, 120, 126, 129, 136, 203, 205, 242n13, 242nn24–25, 243n27, 243n30; biographical information about, 241–42n13; Bogdanov and, 116; on documentation of factors, 120; on normalization, xxx, 118, 122, 138; work of, 110 (fig.), 119 (fig.); *Work Regulation* and, 118, 120
Rozenfel'd, N. B., 223n41
Rudik, Petr, 86, 88, 90, 98
Rukhlyadev, Aleksey, 221n17
Russell, Bertrand, xiv
Russell, Edward Stuart, xi
Russian Academy of Sciences, 216n31
Russian Psychoanalytical Society, 222n18
Russian Revolution, monism and, xxvi–xxix
Russian State Archive of Literature and the Arts, 213n8
Rybakov, Fedor, 238n49

scale, 62–65, 67, 69–70, 133, 233n83
Scharoun, Hans, xii

Schauss, Alexander, 162
Scheper, Hinnerk, xxxi, 127, 144, 147, 148, 149, 152, 153, 156, 203, 251n70, plate 18; color schemes of, 151, 245n67; work of, 145, 146, 146 (fig.), plate 12, plate 15, plate 17
Scheper, Lou, 145
Schlemmer, Oskar, 148
Schmarsow, August, 20, 97, 148
School of Athens, The (Raphael), 34, 35 (fig.)
Schopenhauer, Arthur, 124
Schroeder house, Utrecht (Rietveld), 132
Schultze-Naumburg, Paul, 249n25
Schulze, Rudolf, 79
Schütte-Lihotzky, Margarete, 246n75
Schwitters, Kurt, 41, 62, 229n30
Science of Life, The (Wells, Wells, and Huxley), xxiii, xxv, 163, 164, 170; cover of, plate 1
scientific management, xiv, xxv, 11, 28, 126
Scientific-Methodological Center, Central Park of Culture and Leisure, Moscow, 172
scientific organization of labor (NOT), 11, 218n48
Scientific-Research Cabinet, Leningrad Institute of Civil Engineers, 247n10
Scientific-Technical Society of Construction Workers, 257n52
Second Independent State Artistic Workshops (SGKhM), 1, 2–3
Section of the Socialist Settlement, 245n65
Section of Transportation Architecture (ASNOVA), 54
Section of Typification (Construction Commission), 126, 128, 147, 245n65
Sector of Architects of Socialist Construction (SASS), 257n52
seeing, 45, 90; expanded, 141–44
Self-Portrait with Wrapped Head and Compass (Lissitzky), 38, 40, 40 (fig.), 63
Sensation and Movement (Féré), 153–54
Sestroretsky, V., 145

Set of Norms, The (Rozenberg), 118, 120
set theory, 93
setup *(ustanovka, Einstellung),* 191–92, 203, 205, 235n14, 245n60; purposeful (Ginzburg), 124–26
SGKhM. *See* Second Independent State Artistic Workshops
Shaw, George Bernard, xxviii, 216n30
Shelton Hotel, New York, 50
Shklovsky, Viktor, 51, 151
Shueninova-Nikolskaya, Vera, 247n10
Siberian tiger, xxiv (fig.)
Signaletik, 148
Simmel, Georg, 62, 220n67, 233n77
Sinclair, Upton, xxviii
Six Stories with Easy Endings (Ehrenburg), illustration to, plate 3
Sixteenth Conference of the All-Union Communist Party of Bolsheviks, 214n9
Smith, Adam, 254n13
social condenser, 131, 134, 147, 246n77
social democracy, xxi, xxxi, 214n18
social transformation, biological evolution and, 193
"Socialist Alteration of Man, The" (Vygotsky), 193
socialist realism, xvi, 187, 202
Sociology of Art (Friche), 159
Sokolsky, Viktor, 114, 118, 127
Sorel, Jacques-Louis, 151
Soviet Academy of Architecture, xvi, 214n10
Soviet Ministry of Finance (Narkomfin), 127. *See also* Narkomfin building, Moscow
Sovremennaya arkhitektura, 123, 150, 151, 152; cover of, plate 13; diagram from, 117 (fig.)
space, 20, 45, 48, 54, 67, 97, 148, 149; binocular, 45; color and, 148; demonstration (Lissitzky), 52; irrational, 46, 48 (fig.); monocular, 45, 101; Riemann, 44–46, 48, 50–52; urban, 67
"Space" course, 4 (fig.), 5
space-meter *(prostrometr),* 71, 96–105,

97 (fig.); stereoscope and, 102 (fig.); *Tiefenwahrnehmungsapparat* and, 100
Spassky, Yury, 21, 225n59
spatial combination, 90, 93
spatiality, 23, 69, 90, 97, 103
spatial perception, 20, 71, 93, 96, 99
Spearman, Charles Edward, 90
Spencer, Herbert, xxvi, 111, 199; survival of the fittest and, 259n10; synthetic philosophy of, xix; works of, 216n27
Spencerianism, xx, xxi
Spengler, Oswald, 43, 44
Spielrein, Isaak, xxv, 80, 218n48
Spinoza, Baruch, xiv, xxvii, xxxi, 70, 194, 218n50; posthumanism and, 69
Spinozism, xxvi, 218n50
Spiral Slide (Lissitzky), 175, 177 (fig.)
Stalin, Josef, xv, xxviii
Stalinism, xvi
standardization, xxv, 51, 74, 129, 132, 136, 138, 141, 147, 156, 157–59, 161, 230n54, 242n18, 242n22; notion of, 115 (fig.); organization and, 109–15; Soviet, xxx, 107, 114
Stanislavsky, Konstantin, 80–81
State Institute of Art History, Leningrad, 142
State Institute of Artistic Culture (GINKhUK), 142
State Planning Committee (Gosplan), 245n65
State Trust for Wall-Painting Works (Malyarstroy), xv, 141, 144, 145, 146, 147, 150, 153, 161, 162, 248n18, 249n23; attack on, 157–58; work of, plate 11, plate 12, plate 15
State Trust of Design and Construction (Gosproektstroy), 74
Steiner, Hadas, 174
Steiner, Rudolf, 24
Stenberg, Georgy, 2, 221n11
Stenberg, Vladimir, 2, 221n11
Stepanova, Varvara, 2
stereography, 102, 103, 239n77
stereoscope, 100–102
stereoscopy, 71, 75, 90, 98, 103, 230n43

Stern, William, 79
Stierli, Martino, 234n96
Stokolov, Efim, 144, 145
St. Petersburg, 109, 110, 141, 143
St. Petersburg Academy of Sciences, 45
Stroitelstvo Moskvy, 81
Stroykom. *See* Construction Commission
Strumilin, Stanislav, xxv, 122
Student Profile Form, 89 (fig.)
Stumpf, Carl: theory of, 20
Style and Epoch, 124
subjectivity, xiv, xv, xvi, xviii, 25, 103, 141, 153, 197, 198, 205
Sullivan, Louis, xx
Sum-Shik, Grigory, 126
superconscious, 200
suprematism, 2, 44, 46
Supreme Council of the People's Economy of the USSR, 74, 144
"Surrationalisme, Le" (Bachelard), 226n79
"suspended houses" (Rasch brothers), 59 (fig.)
Suvorov, Sergey, xxvi, 199, 203
switching, principle of, 179–84, 186–87
switching zones, 184, 186 (fig.)
synthesis, xix, xx, xxi, 11, 20–25, 28–29, 103, 157

Tafuri, Manfredo, 217n42
Tarasov, V., 184; work of, 187 (fig.)
Tatlin, Vladimir, 44, 74
Tatlin at Work on the Monument to the Third International (Lissitzky), 44, plate 3
Taut, Bruno, xxviii, 76
Taylor, Frederick Winslow, 11, 72, 75, 79, 104
Taylorism, 1, 74, 76, 79, 80, 104, 120, 122, 129
Technical Everyday and Contemporary Art, The (Toporkov), xxviii–xxix, 107
Technical-Pedagogical Institute, Leningrad, 242n13
Technical Station, Central Park of Culture and Leisure, Moscow, 191 (fig.)

technology, 33, 36, 38, 42, 43, 44, 76, 80, 101, 144, 145; art and, 159
tectology, 111–12
Tectology (Bogdanov), 111
teleology, 199, 200, 202, 203, 204
Teplov, Boris: color typology and, 151
Theory of Creative Work (Engelmeyer), 124
thermodynamics, 153, 181
Thomas, Marion, 241n3
Thomas, William, 244n57
Thompson, D'Arcy, xii
Thomson, Arthur, xx
Tiefenwahrnehmungsapparat (Hering), 98, 100 (fig.), 101 (fig.)
Time League, xxv
Timiriazev, Kliment, 8
Timiriazev Biological Museum, Moscow, 170
Tolstoy, Leo, 200, 201, 204
topology, architecture and, 45–46
Toporkov, Alexander, xxviii–xxix, 64, 246n85; *Doryphoros* and, 107, 109, 123
totalitarianism, xvii, 197, 254n22
Troitsky, Vera, 253n92
Troitsky (Norman), Nikolay, 161, 253n92
Trotsky, Leon, 141, 193, 218n48
Tsiolkovsky, Konstantin, xxviii, 54, 232n73
tsvetopis' (Kostin), 158–59
Turkin, N. V., plate 11
Turkus, Mikhail, 21, 22
Typen-Streit, 157
typification, 114, 115, 126, 127, 138

Überbewusste. *See* superconscious
Udovički-Selb, Danilo, xvi, 214n13
Uexküll, Jacob von, xii
uglazomer, 92, 95, 95 (fig.)
uglomer, 92
Ukhanov, Konstantin, 165
unconscious, 9, 91, 199; social, 126
UNESCO, xix
Union of Cooperatives building (Le Corbusier), 71

Union of Soviet Architects, xvii, 161, 242n13

United Left Studios (Obmas), 3

urbanism, xxx, 12, 20, 31, 33, 36, 42, 62, 67, 180, 183, 246n79

urotoxic coefficient, 183

Uznadze, Dmitry, 124, 126, 191–92, 245n60

Valdner, S. S.: photo of, 189 (fig.)

Valsiner, Jaan, 193

Van der Veer, René, 193

Van der Velde, Henry, 157

Van Doesburg, Theo, xxviii

Vasari, Giorgio, 34

VASI. *See* Higher Institute of Architecture and Construction

Vasilyev, P. I., 242n25, 251n62

Venus de Milo, 41

Verein Ernst Mach (Ernst Mach Society), 148

Vereinheitlichung. See standardization

vertical development, 188–89, 191–95

Vertov, Dziga: cine-eye of, 50

Vesnin, Alexander, xii, xvii, 5, 80

Vesnin, Viktor, xvii

via media, 214–15n18

"Victory over the Sun" (Matyushin), 247n4

"View from Nikitsky Boulevard" (Lissitzky), plate 6

Village of Science and Technology, Central Park of Culture and Leisure, Moscow, 170

Vinogradov, P. I., 232n73, 242n25

Virchow, Rudolf, 111

Vischer, Robert, 20

vision: binocular model of, 33, 100, 101, 104; peripheral, 152; stereoscopic, 71, 90, 98, 103, 104

"Visual Deformation of a Dynamic Form, The" (Krutikov), 57, plate 4

visual estimation *(glazomer, Augenmaß)*, 91, 93, 96

vitalism, xxvi, 28

Vitruvian man, 38

VKhUTEIN. *See* Higher Art and Technical Institute

VKhUTEMAS. *See* Higher Art and Technical Studios

Vladimirov, Vladimir, 126

Vlasov, Alexander, 172

Vogotsky, Lev, 160

Vogt, Oskar, xxviii

Vöhringer, Margarete, 33, 227n5, 234n1

Vossoughan, Nader, 242n21

Vsekhimprom. *See* All-Union Association of the Chemical Industry

Vujošević, Tijana, 80

Vutke, Oleg, execution of, 214n10

Vygotsky, Lev, 193, 194, 252n87

wall-painting, 118, 141, 144, 145, 147, 149, 153–57, 160, 161

War and Peace (Tolstoy), 200

Wark, McKenzie, 204–5, 260n30

War of the Worlds (Wells), 166

Watt, Henry, 124

Wealth of Nations, The (Smith), 254n13

Weber-Fechner law, 249n29

Weeks, Kathy, 195

Weißenhofsiedlung, Stuttgart, 57

Wells, George Philip (G. P.), xxiii, xxv, xxviii, 163, 164 (fig.)

Wells, Herbert George (H. G.), xxii, 70, 163, 164 (fig.), 166, 253n5; PEP and, xxiii, 122

Werkbund, Deutscher, 157

Wheatstone, Charles, 96, 100, 103, 150–51

"Wheel, Propeller, and What Follows" (Lissitzky), 57

Whitehead, Alfred North, xix, xxiii, 104

Wlassak, Rudolf, xxvi

Wölfflin, Heinrich, 8, 90, 103

Wolkenbügels (Lissitzky), xiii (fig.), 31, 33, 57, 63, 64, 65, 66, 66 (fig.), 67, 68 (fig.), 233n87

Work and Rhythm (Bücher), 24

"Worker and the Machine" (Kuktyniksy), 78 (fig.)

Working Group of Architects (INKhUK), 8, 12, 18, 224n45
Working Group of Objective Analysis (Bauhaus), 2, 5
Work Regulation, 114–15, 118, 120, 243nn24–25
Workshop of Wall-Painting, 145, 147
Worringer, Wilhelm, 8, 12, 223n39
Worster, Donald, xxi
Wundt, Wilhelm, xix, 20, 91, 124, 151, 226n69

Yerkes, Robert, 239n62

Zalesskaya, Lyubov S., 255n34, 257n52
Zalkind, Aron, xxv, 218n48
Za proletarskoe iskusstvo, 158
Zeising, Adolf, 24, 228n23
Zhivskul'ptarkh, 2, 220n6
Zholtovsky, Ivan, 255n34
Zhuravlev, Vladimir, 146 (fig.)
Znaniecki, Florian, 244n57
zoē, xviii, xxii
zoning, 80, 136, 180, 181, 183, 184
Zorved, 142
Zurich Polytechnic Institute, 223n33

Alla Vronskaya is professor of architectural history at the University of Kassel, Germany.